Ace the LSAT Logic Games

Published by Get Prepped!, LLC

Published in the United States by:
Get Prepped! LLC
www.getprepped.com
P.O. Box 2163
Longmont, CO 80502

ISBN: 0-9748533-6-4

Get Prepped is the only national test-preparation firm to specialize exclusively in LSAT preparation classes, tutoring, and publications. Our targeted focus on the LSAT means that we provide the most current and comprehensive instruction to our students. Our mission is simple: We help students get great LSAT scores.

Bulk Sales
Get Prepped publications are available at special discounts for bulk purchases by universities, test-preparation firms, and similar groups. Contact the bulk sales representative for more information.

ACKNOWLEDGMENTS

A successful LSAT preparation book is the culmination of the efforts of many individuals. Without their efforts, this book would remain unwritten. The editors would like to use this opportunity to thank them. First and foremost, thank you to Patrick O'Malley for writing this book. Thanks to Scott Simons for contributing several tests. Thanks to John Richardson of Richardson Test Prep for his valuable feedback on many matters. Thanks to Jeff Kolby of Nova Press for his publishing guidance. Also, a thank you is owed to Alice McDaniel for her continuing efforts great and small. Most importantly, we would like to thank the many Get Prepped students who have taught us so much while we were teaching them to master the LSAT.

CONTENTS

Higher Score – Guaranteed!

We make two guarantees that no other LSAT prep company can make:

Get Prepped guarantees your score will improve.
Students who use this book increase their score on the logic games, every single time. This is a bold claim, but based on our experience, we know it is true. To prove it, we will refund 200% of your purchase price if your score on the games does not improve after you complete this book.

Get Prepped guarantees that you will like this book.
If you begin using this book and decide that it is not right for you for any reason, we will refund you 100% of your purchase price.

The fine print-
200% money back guarantee: Mail your sales receipt, the completed book, and your two LSAC score reports to the address below.

Satisfaction guarantee: Return the book to the place of purchase. If the retailer has a no-return policy, mail your sales receipt and the unused (or lightly used) book to the address below.

Get Prepped Publishing, P.O. Box 2163, Longmont, CO 80502
Maximum one refund per customer/entity. Terms subject to change without notice.

We make these guarantees because we know this book is the best.
There are many LSAT games books. Some are terrible and some are good, but none are as good as this book. This book is better than the books produced by every other prep company, and (dare we say it?) is better than the books written by the creators of the LSAT.

What makes this book better?

- **This book has more games.**
  Most prep books have 15 to 20 games (the equivalent of four or five LSAT tests). This book has 83 games (the equivalent of almost 21 LSAT tests). Ask any top scorer; they will tell you that 15 or 20 games is not nearly enough practice, but 83 is plenty.
- **This book has real games.**
  Some books do not use *any* real LSAT games. This book contains 12 real games from the most recent three LSATs, and 71 games that replicate authentic games. You get the best of both worlds. Real games *and* plenty of practice tests.
- **This book has better games.**
  Some books contain unrealistic games. The 71 simulated games in this book replicate the phrasing, formatting, style, and difficulty of authentic LSAT games.
- **This book has the most recent games.**
  Other books are out of date before they are printed because the LSAT continually changes. This book has the 12 most recent games from the three most recent LSATs. Because this book is updated every year, it teaches you how to do the games that will be on your LSAT, not the games were on the LSAT five or ten years ago. If a games book is more than two years old it is obsolete – don't use it!
- **This book has better techniques.**
  Some books teach techniques that are too complex, too confusing, or too time consuming. The techniques in this book are realistic and practical. They yield correct answers quickly, as proven by thousands of Get prepped students.
- **This book explains the games.**
  Most books by LSAC, the creators of the test, don't explain the answers. The popular "10 Actual LSATs" books contain no explanations; you are on your own to figure out how to answer the questions. LSAC publishes one small book that contains explanations, but it definitely does not give away any secrets or shortcuts.
- **This book guides you as you study.**
  For less then the price of 80 old LSAT games from LSAC, with no explanations and no guidance, you can buy this book. It has 83 games, all explained in detail, and it teaches you techniques to master the games. Although you should buy at least ten old LSATs to practice the reading comprehension and logical reasoning sections, this book should be your primary guide to the games section.

Getting Started

Is this the right book for you?

If you want to improve your score on the games section, this is the book for you. If you are new to the LSAT, this book will help you build a solid foundation of skills and provide all the practice tests you need to excel. If you have already begun studying for the LSAT, this book will fill in the gaps in your skills and move you to the next level.

This book prepares you for the logic games section of the LSAT. You will need other books to prepare for the logical reasoning and reading comprehension sections. To prepare for those sections, we suggest "The Next 10 Actual Official LSAT PrepTests" (ISBN-0-942639-89-8) and a companion book, "LSAT Explained: Unofficial Explanations for 'The Next 10 LSATs'" (ISBN-0-9748533-5-6).

How this book is organized

The first section of this book assumes that you have little or no prior knowledge of the games. It shows you the types of games and the answering techniques for each type. The second section contains 14 full games sections (a total of 56 games), each with detailed explanations. By practicing with these games you will master the skills taught in the first section. The third section contains the games sections from the three most recent LSATs (a total of 12 games), also with full explanations. After you complete the three most recent games sections, you will be confident that you will dominate the games section of your LSAT.

A brief overview of the LSAT

You probably have already done some research on the LSAT, but if you haven't, then all you need to know for now is that the LSAT has 101 questions. Of the 101 questions, 22-24 are games questions. Even though the games section represents less than a quarter of the points on the test, it is the section that students can dramatically improve their score in the shortest period of time. In terms of your preparation efforts, the games play a much bigger role than the small number of questions would seem to warrant.

How do you find the correct answer to any games question?

For most questions, the fastest way to find the correct answer is to use a diagram. Diagrams organize the information. After organizing the information, you make additional conclusions and add them to the diagram. These additional conclusions are what the questions are testing. Even though diagramming is the primary technique, it is not the only way to find the correct answer. This book will show you when and how to use shortcuts that allow you to skip the diagramming step.

How to use this book

The authors of this book know that students learn by doing games, not by reading about games. By practicing, and yes, making mistakes, you will learn how to use the techniques and how to avoid common pitfalls. You should plan to complete this entire book. Year after year, the highest-scoring students tell us that they completed the entire book. If you have already done a great deal of games work and simply want practice questions, you may choose to skip the introductory sections, although it never hurts to review the concepts.

Now it is time to get started

You will start by doing a game that provides context for the techniques and concepts that will be introduced later. You need 8 minutes and 45 seconds of uninterrupted test-taking time. As you work on this game, don't worry if you feel completely bewildered and get few, or even no, correct answers. Even students who do poorly on the first game go on to earn excellent scores. If this is your first game ever, you probably will not finish in the allotted time. Don't worry; you will have a chance later to try this game again. For now, just consider this game to be an introduction. Begin when you are ready.

Note – Use a pencil when taking the tests. You are required to use a pencil when taking the LSAT, so become accustomed to doing so now.

Note – The formatting of the games in this book may appear unusual at first. For example, the next page begins with question 7. To ensure that you get the most effective preparation, the games in the book are designed to be as realistic as possible. The games have authentic formatting and instructions. The pages with games are not numbered, nor do they have any formatting or text that does not appear on the LSAT.

Questions 7–13

Six airplanes—R, S, T, U, W, and X—must land at an airport that has one runway. The airplanes must land one at a time and all the planes must land at the airport. The order that the airplanes land must adhere to the following rules:

T lands earlier than R.
U lands earlier than R and later than X.
W lands immediately before or after T lands.

7. Which one of the following could be an accurate matching of airplanes to landing times?

(A) First: W; second: S; sixth: R
(B) Second: U; fourth: S; fifth: W
(C) Third: U; fourth: S; sixth: R
(D) Second: X; fourth: T; fifth: U
(E) First: W; third: U; fourth: R

8. If X lands second, then which one of the following must be true?

(A) U lands third.
(B) S lands third.
(C) T lands first.
(D) U lands fifth.
(E) R lands sixth.

9. If X lands third, then each of the following could be true EXCEPT:

(A) S lands fifth.
(B) U lands fourth.
(C) R lands fourth.
(D) T lands second.
(E) W lands second.

10. Which one of the following CANNOT be true?

(A) T lands fourth.
(B) R lands fourth.
(C) W lands fourth.
(D) S lands sixth.
(E) X lands fourth.

11. Which one of the following is a complete and accurate list of the times that U can land?

(A) first, second, third
(B) first, third, fourth, fifth
(C) second, third, fourth, fifth
(D) second, third, fourth, fifth, sixth
(E) third, fourth, fifth

12. If U lands later than T, then the latest W can land is:

(A) first
(B) second
(C) third
(D) fourth
(E) fifth

13. Suppose the rule that W lands immediately before or after T is replaced by the rule that the landings of W and T are separated by exactly one other landing. If the other rules remain unchanged, then the latest X can land is:

(A) first
(B) second
(C) third
(D) fourth
(E) fifth

GO ON TO THE NEXT PAGE.

Answer Key:

Answer Key

7. D
8. E
9. C
10. B
11. C
12. D
13. D

Moving Forward

How did you do?

Most students answer only one or two questions correctly on their first logic game; some get no correct answers. Does that mean they cannot do well on the LSAT? No, it does not. Students don't do well at first because games are complex and unfamiliar. You wouldn't expect to ride a bike on your first attempt, so don't expect to excel at something that is just as complex and requires just as much practice. But, once you learned to ride a bike, the skill became instinctual. The same is true of the games. It is difficult to get up and pedaling; but once you do, it becomes second nature.

Even someone who is a "natural" at the games must still practice to get a top score. Even after that person has practiced many games, they will occasionally miss a question because the time limits simply don't allow one to exhaustively work every question, so errors do happen. Take comfort in the fact that scoring well on the LSAT requires excellence, but not perfection.

Overview of a game

Now that you have seen a game it is time to review some basic information. Every game has three parts: the setup, the rules, and the questions.

The setup paragraph introduces the "story". In this game the setup begins, "Six airplanes…". The setup provides clues to determine what kind of diagram to use. The setup always contains the names of the members. Here the names are, "R, S, T, U, W, and X." Sometimes, like here, the names are single letters. Other times the names are full words, usually people's names. When the names are full words, you should abbreviate them. The names are always listed in alphabetical order, and each name has a different first letter. This is helpful because it eliminates the possibility you will confuse two members when abbreviating their names.

The rules are listed below the setup paragraph. The first rule of this game is, "T lands earlier than R." All games have three to six rules. The types of rules depend on the kind of diagram. In this game, a line game, the rules describe the sequential landing of the members (the airplanes). The information in the setup paragraph is different than the information in the rules. The setup provides the diagram and the members. The rules place the members on the diagram. Put another way, the setup describes the structure, and the rules place the members on this structure. Put in even simpler terms, the setup provides the blanks and the rules fill in the blanks.

Although correctly diagramming the rules is necessary in order to answer the questions, it is not sufficient to answer the questions. The important work begins after you diagram the rules. After diagramming the rules, you must make additional conclusions about **what can and cannot be true. In the airplane game there were several additional** conclusions that had to be made before you could answer the questions. For example, you should have concluded that R could not land first, second, third, or fourth. After you create the diagram, diagram the rules, and make the extra conclusions, then you are ready to move to the questions. If you can't make any conclusions after diagramming the rules, don't worry; sometimes it is not possible. If so, the questions will add more information that will allow you to draw conclusions. Each type of game has certain typical conclusions. As you become familiar with the different games, you will learn the typical conclusions associated with each game.

The final, and most important, part of a game is the questions. Questions take many forms. They may ask what must be true, what could be true, what must be false, what cannot be true, etc. No matter how questions are phrased, they are merely testing how well you make conclusions. Sometimes a question adds new rules; sometimes it does not. When a question adds new rules, incorporate the rules into the diagram and then make additional conclusions. When a question does not add new a new rule, the answer is found by consulting the conclusions you made after diagramming the initial rules.

What do diagrams look like?

There are two types of games, *ordering* and *grouping*. Within these two categories, there are many types of diagrams that could possibly be tested, but only a handful are regularly tested. The other diagrams are used once every few years, or even less often.

Ordering games – Most games focus on the linear *order* that the members can be placed into.

The airplane-landing-sequence game tests the linear order of the members. It is called a *simple line* game because it required just one set of dashes. A simple line game could also ask, for example, for the order that seven songs are played on a radio station.

Complex line games require two or three sets of dashes; these games are called *multiple line* games. A multiple line game could test the order that ten airplanes land on two runways. You will see examples of multiple line games later.

Although there are ordering games besides simple line games and multiple line games, they are very rare. You will see examples of these rare games later.

Grouping games – On your test there will be one game (sometimes two) that asks you to create an ending *group* or *groups* by selecting members from an initial group or groups. For example, the game may provide a list of nine people and ask you to select a group of five of them to serve on a committee. The rules restrict the selection of members. For example, two people will not be permitted to be on the committee at the same time. There are two types of grouping games.

Selection games ask you to create a group by selecting members from one, two, or three starting groups. The committee selection game discussed above is a selection game.

Assignment games ask you to assign all the members of the starting group to two or three ending groups. For example, six people must go to one of three movies. Certain people will not be permitted to go to a particular movie and certain people will be required or prohibited from attending the same movie together.

Other games – Some games do not neatly fit into the categories of ordering games or grouping games, but they are rarely tested. These rare games include matrix games, multiple rounds games, and games that are hybrids of two other game types. Don't worry about these games for now. We will study them later, once you have built a solid foundation for ordering and grouping games.

Budgeting time

There are four games in each games section. You have 35 minutes to complete the section. This is an average of 8 minutes and 45 seconds for each game. Budgeting your time is vital. Beginning students often spend too much time on the first two games, leaving themselves too little time to complete the third and fourth games. Since the games are not always presented in order of difficulty, these students often spend most of their time on what may be the most difficult games, leaving them little time to earn points on easier games.

How to approach a games section if you are running out of time

After finishing this book, most students can complete all four games in less than 35 minutes. But if you still struggle with the games after completing this book, you will need to decide if the best strategy is to select three of the games and spend more time doing them. Use this strategy if you get more correct answers by attempting fewer games but correctly answering a higher percentage of the questions you attempt. If you decide to do three of the games, make sure to pick the right ones. First, review all four games before doing any work. Try to determine what diagram is needed for each game. Then consider the number of questions each game has. Games can have as few as five questions or as many as eight. You want the games that have the most questions and are the easiest to diagram. Most students find the line games easiest, but the choice is yours to make once you learn your strengths and weaknesses.

How to approach a game

The best approach for a game is to read, to understand, to plan, to diagram, and to answer.
Read the setup and the rules. Don't read the questions yet.

Understand the setup and the rules. Don't rush. If you misread a rule or misinterpret it, it will cost you far more time than the few seconds you gained by rushing. Reflect on how the setup and the rules interact. Sometimes a rule contains a key property that dramatically modifies the diagram, instead of merely placing information on the diagram.
Plan the kind of diagram you will use and how it should be modified to best reflect the setup and the rules.
Diagram the information provided by the setup and the rules. Additional conclusions can be diagramed either as you diagram each rule, or after you have diagrammed all the rules. It is a matter of personal preference. Most students make some conclusions as they diagram each rule, more conclusions after they have added all the rules to the diagram and see new connections, and even more conclusions as they answer questions and see new connections.
Answer the questions. Some questions can be answered once you diagram the rules and make the initial conclusions. Most questions add new information. You must diagram the new information and make new conclusions before answering.

The next step

The next step is to learn the games. You will begin with the three most common types of games. For each of these games you will do one game as an introduction to the game type. The game is then explained in detail using step-by-step solutions and diagrams. This is followed by information on the rules and diagrams that are used for this type of game. Because there are commonly occurring rules, there are common conclusions that result from these rules. These common conclusions are revealed to you as well. After the overview of the game type, short exercises will reinforce the concepts. To test your new understanding of the game type, you will do additional practice games.

After you learn the common games, you will learn about the questions; both how they are phrased and how you should answer them. Exercises will sharpen your answering skills. For example, you will learn to distinguish between a "must be true" question and a "could be true" question, and how to efficiently solve each kind.

The section on the questions is followed by a discussion of the overall strategies and approaches that you should consider.

Next, you will be introduced to the hybrid games, the unusual games, and the unique games. There will be examples and pointers on how these games are designed and how you should answer them.

Finally, you will practice many games, 68 games to be exact. The skills required to solve these games are not quickly mastered. You must practice many games before you become comfortable using your new skills.

Simple Line Games

You will now do the "airplane landing order" game a second time. Spend as much time as you need to answer all the questions. After you finish, compare your work with the "tutor page", which demonstrates how to organize your work and where to draw the diagrams.

Using the landing-order game as a starting point, you will learn the different ways a simple line can be tested and how to complete a simple line game quickly and effectively. This is followed by a series of practice exercises. You will finish by doing two simple line games under timed conditions and reviewing your work.

Questions 7–13

Six airplanes—R, S, T, U, W, and X—must land at an airport that has one runway. The airplanes must land one at a time and all the planes must land at the airport. The order that the airplanes land must adhere to the following rules:

T lands earlier than R.
U lands earlier than R and later than X.
W lands immediately before or after T lands.

7. Which one of the following could be an accurate matching of airplanes to landing times?

(A) First: W; second: S; sixth: R
(B) Second: U; fourth: S; fifth: W
(C) Third: U; fourth: S; sixth: R
(D) Second: X; fourth: T; fifth: U
(E) First: W; third: U; fourth: R

8. If X lands second, then which one of the following must be true?

(A) U lands third.
(B) S lands third.
(C) T lands first.
(D) U lands fifth.
(E) R lands sixth.

9. If X lands third, then each of the following could be true EXCEPT:

(A) S lands fifth.
(B) U lands fourth.
(C) R lands fourth.
(D) T lands second.
(E) W lands second.

10. Which one of the following CANNOT be true?

(A) T lands fourth.
(B) R lands fourth.
(C) W lands fourth.
(D) S lands sixth.
(E) X lands fourth.

11. Which one of the following is a complete and accurate list of the times that U can land?

(A) first, second, third
(B) first, third, fourth, fifth
(C) second, third, fourth, fifth
(D) second, third, fourth, fifth, sixth
(E) third, fourth, fifth

12. If U lands later than T, then the latest W can land is:

(A) first
(B) second
(C) third
(D) fourth
(E) fifth

13. Suppose the rule that W lands immediately before or after T is replaced by the rule that the landings of W and T are separated by exactly one other landing. If the other rules remain unchanged, then the latest X can land is:

(A) first
(B) second
(C) third
(D) fourth
(E) fifth

GO ON TO THE NEXT PAGE.

Questions 7–13

Six airplanes—R, S, T, U, W, and X—must land at an airport that has one runway. The airplanes must land one at a time and all the planes must land at the airport. The order that the airplanes land must adhere to the following rules:

T lands earlier than R.
U lands earlier than R and later than X.
W lands immediately before or after T lands.

7. Which one of the following could be an accurate matching of airplanes to landing times?

(A) First: W; second: S; sixth: R
(B) Second: U; fourth: S; fifth: W
(C) Third: U; fourth: S; sixth: R
(D) Second: X; fourth: T; fifth: U
(E) First: W; third: U; fourth: R

8. If X lands second, then which one of the following must be true?

(A) U lands third.
(B) S lands third.
(C) T lands first.
(D) U lands fifth.
(E) R lands sixth.

9. If X lands third, then each of the following could be true EXCEPT:

(A) S lands fifth.
(B) U lands fourth.
(C) R lands fourth.
(D) T lands second.
(E) W lands second.

10. Which one of the following CANNOT be true?

(A) T lands fourth.
(B) R lands fourth.
(C) W lands fourth.
(D) S lands sixth.
(E) X lands fourth.

11. Which one of the following is a complete and accurate list of the times that U can land?

(A) first, second, third
(B) first, third, fourth, fifth
(C) second, third, fourth, fifth
(D) second, third, fourth, fifth, sixth
(E) third, fourth, fifth

12. If U lands later than T, then the latest W can land is:

(A) first
(B) second
(C) third
(D) fourth
(E) fifth

13. Suppose the rule that W lands immediately before or after T is replaced by the rule that the landings of W and T are separated by exactly one other landing. If the other rules remain unchanged, then the latest X can land is:

(A) first
(B) second
(C) third
(D) fourth
(E) fifth

GO ON TO THE NEXT PAGE.

How to use the tutor page

The facing page is a "tutor page." When a Get Prepped student works with a tutor, the tutor demonstrates how to efficiently and effectively diagram a game. The tutor page recreates the tutoring experience by showing you how and where to draw the diagrams.

A tutor page has two components. The first component is the initial diagram. Here, the initial diagram is at the bottom of the page and includes two features: the order of the members (W/T < R, etc.) and the six-dash line with the negative letters underneath. The second component of the tutor page is the diagram next to each question. These diagrams incorporate the information provided by the question.

Each game in the first half of this book has a tutor page. To get the most from the tutor pages, you should complete the game and then compare your work with the tutor page. You want to determine why you did not find the correct answer, or how you could have found the correct answer more quickly. Do not expect your work to look exactly like the tutor page. Instead, use the tutor page as a reality check to ensure you are not creating too many diagrams, overly complex diagrams, or doing other unnecessary work.

The setups for simple lines

The setup paragraph introduces a situation where there are six, seven, or eight different elements that must be organized in either a time sequence or a place sequence. You will use a horizontal set of dashes to serve as the six, seven, or eight places. Always make the left-most dash the lowest number, the earliest time slot, etc. The right-most dash will be the highest number, latest time slot, etc. Some examples are listed below:

"Six customers pay at the cash register of the grocery store."

___	___	___	___	___	___
1	2	3	4	5	6

This setup requires a series of dashes to keep track of the time sequence in which the customers will reach the cash register. Although numbering the spaces is useful when first learning the games, once you become more skilled you can save time by omitting the numbers.

"A bank has six teller windows along one wall."

___	___	___	___	___	___
1	2	3	4	5	6

This setup is similar to the previous one. The only difference is that the ordering is spatial (physical location) instead temporal (time order).

"Seven cars are parked on one side of the street."

___	___	___	___	___	___	___
1	2	3	4	5	6	7

This setup specified that the cars are on one side of the street. The setups are always very precise when detailing the scenario. For example, here it says that all cars are on one side of the street. If this were a multiple line diagram, the setup would specify that there are cars on both sides of the street. The setup will never be ambiguous, leaving it unclear whether the cars are on one side or two sides of the street.

"An office worker performs eight tasks during the work day."

___	___	___	___	___	___	___	___
1	2	3	4	5	6	7	8

Six is the most common number of spaces, seven is not uncommon, and eight spaces or five spaces are occasionally used. These is because six or seven spaces allows the test-maker sufficient flexibility to create an assortment of questions, while not creating so much flexibility that test-takers are bogged down with too many options. If there are eight spaces, the rules will be more restrictive. Restrictive rules limit the number of possible permutations to a more manageable number. If there are only five spaces, then a second dimension will be added to the diagram in order to increase the complexity, usually making the diagram a multiple line instead of a simple line.

Horizontal (side to side) lines are the best way to diagram a simple line game. Although it is possible to use a vertical (up and down) line to accomplish the same tasks, this is usually more difficult than using a horizontal line. Also, the language of a setup often specifically calls for a horizontal order, but never for one that is vertical.

The rules for the simple lines

Pay close attention to the following information. Most of what you are about to learn applies to all types of games, not just simple lines.

The following are common simple line rules. The language of the rule is provided, as well as an example of how the rule should be diagrammed.

1. "A is first or last."

   ___ ___ ___ ___ ___ ___
   (A) (A)

   Often a rule requires one member to be either first or last; it is a rule the test-makers like to include. By putting the (A) below the line, we show that it is only a fifty-fifty possibility for each of these two spaces. The parentheses clarify that A is only a fifty-fifty possibility for a particular space. We put the A above the line, without parentheses, when we want to show that A must be in that space.

   This may also be phrased as, "A must be the earliest or latest meeting."

   Negative variation: "A cannot be first or last." Depict as: ~~A~~, and place the ~~A~~ under the appropriate spaces. Because A is *not* in these spaces, you do not enclose it in parentheses.

2. "A is earlier than B."
   A<B
   This rule is a mainstay of both the simple line games and the multiple line games. The "<" symbol is used to show that a member is before (in time or place) another member. A mistake test-takers often make is assuming that A is immediately before B, instead of merely somewhere earlier than B. As you will see later, this rule can be combined with other rules to make very useful conclusions.
   This may also be phrased as, "A is on a lower-numbered shelf than B."
   Negative variation: Never used.

3. "A is immediately before B."
   A B
   Place the two members next to each other with dashes underneath them. This helps you visualize that A is before B, and that A is immediately before B.

   This rule should be treated carefully because it is often confused with rule 4.

   This may also be phrased as, "B is placed immediately to the right of A."
   Negative variation: "A is not immediately before B." Depict as: ~~A B~~

4. "A is next to B."
   A B A or A B / B A – Use the one you find easier to understand.
   This rule does not specify which one comes first. Many test-takers incorrectly graph this rule, making it appear that A *must* be before B, instead of before or after B.

   This may also be phrased as, "A is immediately before or immediately after B."
   Negative variation: "A is not next to B." Depict as: ~~A B A~~ or ~~A B~~ / ~~B A~~

5. "A is earlier than B and C."
   A < B/C or A < B & A < C – Use the one you find easier to understand.
   This is a variation on the common rule, "A is earlier than B." The mistake test-takers often make is to depict this rule as A < B < C, which yields a very different, and very wrong, result.

   This may also be phrased as, "Both B and C are heavier than A."
   Negative variation: Never used.

6. "If A is second, B is fifth."

   __ __ __ __ __ __
   (A) ——————→ (B)

   This is a conditional rule, so it applies only in the situation where A is second. As such, even if your diagram shows that B is fifth, this does not necessarily mean that A is second. Many test-takers make exactly this mistake. Also, if B is not fifth, then A cannot be second. You will see this situation come up in many line games, so get used to working with it.
   Negative variation: Never used.

7. "Either A or B is fourth."
   __ __ __ A/B __ __
   The slash between A and B shows that one of them must be in this space.
   Negative variation: "Neither A nor B is fourth." Depict this as: ~~A~~, ~~B~~, and place them under the fourth space.

8. "A and B are separated by one space."
   A/B __ B/A or A __ B / B __ A

This rule causes test-takers to make one of two mistakes. The first mistake is that they think there are either no spaces separating the two members, or that there are two spaces separating the two members. The second mistake is thinking that A must come before B.

This may also be phrased as, "Exactly one customer is after A but before B."

Negative variation: Never used.

Note: The rule may dictate two full spaces between A and B instead of just one space. Never has a rule placed three full spaces between two members.

You will see these rules in every simple line game. You will also see these rules in multiple line games and possibly in other games. If you are skilled at using these rules, it is easy to modify the diagram when the rule is phrased somewhat differently, as sometimes happens.

Once you have diagrammed a game's setup and the rules, the next step is to make additional conclusions that will add more information to your diagram.

Additional conclusions for simple line games

Just as there are common setups and common rules, there are common additional conclusions you must make. There are two occasions when you can make conclusions. First, you can sometimes make a conclusion based on a single rule. You can make and diagram these conclusions as soon as you diagram the rule. Second, you can sometimes make a conclusion based on the effect and overlap of two or three rules. You make and diagram these conclusions after you have diagrammed all the rules and have considered the interaction of the rules.

1. "A is earlier than B."

__	__	__	__	__	__
~~B~~					~~A~~

When A is earlier than B, it is not possible for B to be first and it is not possible for A to be last. When you are able to combine this rule with another rule, to learn, for example, $A < B < C$, then you can eliminate several more possibilities for A, B, and C, as shown below.

__	__	__	__	__	__
				~~A~~	~~A~~
~~B~~					~~B~~
~~C~~	~~C~~				

2. "A is immediately before B."

1	2	3	4	5	6
___	___	___	___	___	___
~~B~~					~~A~~

When A is before B, there is no way that B can be first, and no way that A can be last. This is diagrammed above. This rule becomes even more useful when one space is already filled by a different member, because this determines two more spaces where A and B cannot be. In the example below, C fills the third space. This prevents A from being in the second space, and B from being in the fourth space.

1	2	3	4	5	6
___	___	C	___	___	___
~~B~~	~~A~~		~~B~~		~~A~~

3. "A and B are separated by one other appointment."
By itself, you cannot use this rule to make a conclusion, but if you have other information, for example, that C is fourth, then you know that neither A nor B can be second or sixth.

1	2	3	4	5	6
___	___	___	C	___	___
	~~A~~				~~A~~
	~~B~~				~~B~~

Exercises

Now it is time to practice what you have learned. The following exercises are designed to reinforce the basic concepts for simple line games. There are exercises for diagramming the setup, followed by exercises for diagramming the rules, and finally, exercises that have you do both.

Exercises – setups

Compare your diagrams with the examples that follow this exercise.

1. A television series must be scheduled for broadcast once a week for an eight-week period. Each of the eight episodes—A, B, C, D, E, F, G, and H—must be scheduled exactly once.

2. James paints a mural using six cans of paint—amber, black, cayenne, ecru, green, and lime. Each can of paint is used exactly once and only one can of paint can be used at a time.

3. A college professor gives a series of seven lectures—D, F, G, H, I, K, and L—during the summer term. Exactly one lecture is given during each class.

4. A football coach is scheduling the upcoming season of eight games against seven opposing teams—J, K, L, M, N, O, and P. The coach schedules exactly one opposing team for each game.

5. A convention planner must schedule seven consecutive speeches to be given during the convention. The six speakers who give speeches are Arundel, Boyle, Canabra, Dalton, French, and Rial.

6. Customers at a spa schedule appointments for one of four treatments—kiwi, lime, mud, and nutrient—to be administered during each of six consecutive sessions, numbered one through six.

Answers – setups

Appropriate diagrams for the setups are as follows:

1. **A television series.**

There are eight episodes and eight spaces to fill. Each episode is used once. A simple eight-dash line will suffice. Numbering the dashes is optional. As you improve and your confidence increases, you will find that numbering the spaces slows you down, and that the numbers merely get in your way.

___ ___ ___ ___ ___ ___ ___ ___
1 2 3 4 5 6 7 8

2. **James paints a mural.**

There are six cans of paint. The setup specifies that only one can is used at a time, and that once a can is used, it will not be used again.

___ ___ ___ ___ ___ ___
1 2 3 4 5 6

3. **A college professor gives a series of seven lectures.**

There are seven lectures. One lecture is given during each class. A set of seven dashes will suffice.

___ ___ ___ ___ ___ ___ ___
1 2 3 4 5 6 7

4. **A football coach schedules games.**

This is a tricky one. There are eight games, but only seven opposing teams. This means that coach will schedule one of the opposing teams twice. Although important to know, this does not change the diagram. Eight dashes are needed, one for each game.

___ ___ ___ ___ ___ ___ ___ ___
1 2 3 4 5 6 7 8

5. **A convention planner schedules speeches.**

Once again, there are more spaces to fill than members to fill them, so one member will repeat.

___ ___ ___ ___ ___ ___ ___
1 2 3 4 5 6 7

6. **Spa customers schedule appointments.**

The important thing to focus on is that there are six consecutive sessions. There are only four members to fill the six spaces, so at least one of the members repeats.

___ ___ ___ ___ ___ ___
1 2 3 4 5 6

Exercises – rules

Practice diagramming the common rules for simple line games. Draw a six-space line for each rule. If you can make additional conclusions, diagram them as well.
Compare your diagrams with the examples that follow this exercise.

1. "A is the third play."

2. "B is not the second book."

3. "A is first or sixth."

4. "A is served immediately before B."

5. "A is younger than B."

6. "A is earlier than B and C."

7. "A and B have meetings on consecutive days."

8. "Either A or B is printed fourth."

Answers – rules

Appropriate diagrams for the rules are as follows:

1. "A is the third play."
When a rule provides a definite location for a member, place it above the line.

__ __ A __ __ __

2. "B is not the second book."
When a member cannot be in a space, note it below the line.

__ __ __ __ __ __
  ~~B~~

3. "A is first or sixth."
This is a common rule. Use parentheses to indicate the conditional nature of A.

__ __ __ __ __ __
(A)   (A)

4. "A is served immediately before B."
You can conclude that A cannot be in the last space and B cannot be in the first space.

A B: __ __ __ __ __ __
  ~~B~~   ~~A~~

5. "A is younger than B."
A is before B. A cannot be last and B cannot be first.

A<B: __ __ __ __ __ __
  ~~B~~   ~~A~~

6. "A is earlier than B and C."
Diagram this as: A < B/C or as A < B & A < C. Many test-takers diagram this rule incorrectly. Both B and C must come later than A, so A cannot be last, or second to last. Neither B nor C can be first, but one of them could be second.

A<B: __ __ __ __ __ __
  ~~B~~   ~~A~~ ~~A~~
A<C ~~C~~

7. "A and B have meetings on consecutive days."
Diagram this as: A B A or A B / B A. Remember, either A or B could be the earlier member.

__ __ __ __ __ __

A B / B A

8. "Either A or B is printed fourth."
Put them above the line, with the slash.

__ __ __ A/B __ __

Exercises – setups and rules

Diagram the setups and rules. Also, diagram any additional conclusions you are able to make.

1. Exactly six songs—N, O, P, Q, R, and S—will each be played once during a radio program. The order they will be played is determined by the following requirements:

   N is played before R is played.
   Q is not played first or third.
   P is played after R is played.
   At least one other song is played after N and before S.

2. An office worker begins a seven-hour workday at 8:00am and must perform six tasks during the work day—answering calls, boxing products, copying documents, delivering mail, e-mailing proposals, and eating lunch. The worker performs one task at a time for exactly one hour and, except for answering calls, performs each task exactly once. The order the worker accomplishes the tasks is subject to the following requirements:

   The worker cannot begin eating lunch before 11:00am or later than 1:00pm
   At least one other task must be performed between delivering mail and eating lunch.
   E-mailing proposals must be done immediately after boxing products.
   The worker performs exactly two other tasks between answering calls.
   Copying documents must be started at 12:00 noon.

3. During the course of a five-day workweek a supervisor has exactly seven meetings with employees. Each meeting is with exactly one of the following five employees: Chowdry, Dunn, Eflin, Ghoshn, and Hepplewhite. The following restrictions control the scheduling of meetings with employees.

The supervisor meets with Ghoshn exactly two times.

No employee meets with the supervisor twice in row.

All of Eflin's meetings take place earlier in the week than all of Hepplewhite's meetings.

At least two other employees must meet with the supervisor before Dunn meets with the supervisor.

4. A file cabinet has space for exactly six file folders from the front to the back of the cabinet. There are three categories of folders—research, marketing, and warranty—and there is one closed and one active folder for each category. The six folders must be filed in accordance with the following procedures:

The warranty folders are separated by exactly two other folders.

Three closed folders cannot be filed immediately next to each other.

The closed research folder is filed immediately before or after the active marketing folder.

The closed marketing folder is filed third from the front.

5. Exactly seven commercials—A, B, C, D, E, F, and G—will be broadcast during a radio show. Each commercial will be broadcast exactly once, in accordance with the following requirements:

If D or G is broadcast third, the other is broadcast seventh.

B is broadcast earlier than D and C.

E is broadcast later than C.

Either A or C must be broadcast second.

Answers – setups and rules

The appropriate diagrams are as follows:

1. Exactly six songs—N, O, P, Q, R, and S—will be played once during a radio program. The order they will be played is determined by the following requirements:

    N is played before R is played.
    Q is not played first or third.
    P is played after R is played.
    At least one other song is played after N and before S.

	__	__	__	__	__	__
Q:	~~Q~~		~~Q~~			
N<R<P:	~~R~~				~~N~~	~~N~~
	~~P~~	~~P~~				~~R~~
N _ ( ) S:	~~S~~	~~S~~		~~N~~		

There are six songs, each played once, so draw six dashes. Rules 2 and 3 should be combined to make a chain that allows us to eliminate several possibilities for N, P, and R. From the rule, "At least one other song is played after N and before S," the earliest S can be played is third and then only if N is first. N cannot be fourth. Why? If N were fourth, there would not be enough spaces left to fit R, P, and S. To diagram the fourth rule, we place a (_) between N and S to show that there may be a second space between N and S, or there may not. A third and fourth space could be between N and S, but it would be too confusing to graph these possibilities. The current diagram should be sufficient to remind you of the effect of the fourth rule.

2. An office worker begins a seven-hour workday at 8:00am and must perform six tasks during the workday—answering calls, boxing products, copying documents, delivering mail, e-mailing proposals, and eating lunch. The worker performs one task at a time for exactly one hour and, except for answering calls, performs each task exactly once. The order the worker accomplishes the tasks is subject to the following requirements:

    The worker cannot begin eating lunch before 11:00am or later than 1:00pm
    At least one other task must be performed between delivering mail and eating lunch.
    E-mailing proposals must be done immediately after boxing products.
    The worker performs two other tasks between answering calls.
    Copying documents must be started at 12:00 noon.

	__	__	__	__	C	__	__
	8	9	10	11	12	1	2
L:	~~L~~	~~L~~	~~L~~				~~L~~
B E:	~~E~~			~~B~~		~~E~~	~~B~~
A _ _ A:		~~A~~					
D _ ( ) L: or							
L _ ( ) D:							

There are seven time slots, and six tasks to fill them. Answering calls, A, will be used twice. Because C is at 12, the number of places B and E can occupy is reduced, but C has no effect on D or L since they are very flexible. A cannot be at 9, because C is at 12, which would prevent the second A from being at 12.

3. During the course of a workweek, a supervisor has exactly seven meetings with employees. Each meeting is with exactly one of the following five employees: Chowdry, Dunn, Eflin, Ghoshn, and Hepplewhite. The following restrictions control the scheduling of meetings with employees.

The supervisor meets with Ghoshn exactly two times.
No employee meets with the supervisor twice in row.
All of Eflin's meetings take place earlier in the week than all of Hepplewhite's meetings.
At least two other employees must meet with the supervisor before Dunn meets with the supervisor.

	__	__	__	__	__	__	__
E<H:	~~H~~						~~E~~
?<?<D:	~~D~~	~~D~~					
G=2, ~~GG~~							

Careful, the fact that it is a workweek is not relevant. There are seven meetings to schedule, and five employees to fill those seven meetings. Thus, either one employee has three meetings, or two employees have two meetings each. The key is in Rule 1. Since G meets exactly twice, that means that one of the other employees also meets exactly twice, and the other three meet once. Rule 2 is difficult to diagram effectively, just remember not to put the same employee twice in a row. Rule 3 is more complex then it initially appears. E is earlier than H, but if E is used twice, then both Es must be earlier than H. If there are two Hs, then they must be later than the E. The basic information is listed on the diagram, but this contingency when there are two Es or two Hs will have to be kept in mind. Finally, Rule 4 essentially says that D cannot be first or second.

4. A file cabinet has space for exactly six file folders from the front to the back of the cabinet. There are three categories of folders—research, marketing, and warranty—and there is one closed and one active folder for each category. The six folders must be filed in accordance with the following procedures:

The warranty folders are separated by exactly two other folders.
Three closed folders cannot be filed immediately next to each other.
The closed research folder is filed immediately before or after the active marketing folder.
The closed marketing folder is filed third from the front.

	?W	AR	CM	?W	__	__
W _ _ W:						
CR AM CR:	no	no	no	no	CR/AM	

Although this game is a little more difficult to visualize, there are six spaces, to be filled by six different folders. It's best to start with is Rule 4; CM is third. Using this as a starting point, we can deduce that the two Ws must be first and fourth. (If they were second and fifth, this would not allow two spaces for CR and AM.) Once the Ws have been fixed on first and fourth, AR is the only one remaining that will fit on space 2. CR and AM must be fifth and sixth, but we don't know their exact order.

5. Exactly seven commercials—A, B, C, D, E, F, and G—will be broadcast during a radio show. Each commercial will be broadcast exactly once, according to the following requirements:

If D or G is broadcast third, the other is broadcast seventh.
B is broadcast earlier than D and C.
E is broadcast later than C.
Either A or C must be broadcast second.

	__	A	D/G	__	__	__	G/D
B<C & D:	~~C~~						
C<E:				~~E~~			

	B	C	D/G	__	__	__	G/D
B<C & D:							
C<E:							

The setup is very typical, seven members to fill seven spaces. Usually, the anchor rule is listed last, so look there first. Here, Rule 4 states that either A or C is second. Usually we create one line, but sometimes, like here, it makes sense to use two. The first line shows A as the second broadcast, the other shows C as the second broadcast. Now, we can diagram Rule 1. Since either D or G must be third, and the other must be seventh, we can place this information above the line, instead of below it. Since B is broadcast earlier than C, C cannot be first. Since C is broadcast before E, E cannot be first.

Practice games

Spend 8 minutes and 45 seconds for each of the following games, answering as many questions as you can. Then review the explanations that follow the games.

Questions 7–12

A package delivery service must deliver seven boxes—A, B, C, D, E, F, G. The boxes must be delivered one at a time, and all seven boxes must be delivered. The order the boxes are delivered in must satisfy the following conditions:

Box A must be delivered earlier than box D.
Box B cannot be delivered immediately before or immediately after box C.
Exactly two boxes must be delivered after the delivery of box E and before the delivery of box D.
Box B is delivered first, third, or fifth.
Box F is delivered fourth.

7. Which of the following could be an accurate list of the boxes in order of delivery, from first to seventh?

(A) A, E, B, F, D, C, G
(B) B, E, G, F, D, C, A
(C) B, A, D, F, G, E, C
(D) C, B, E, F, A, D, G
(E) A, B, E, F, G, D, C

8. Each of the following boxes could be delivered fifth EXCEPT:

(A) A
(B) B
(C) D
(D) E
(E) G

9. If exactly two boxes are delivered between the delivery of boxes B and C, which of the following must be true?

(A) Box E is delivered second.
(B) Box B is delivered third.
(C) Box D is delivered sixth.
(D) Box G is delivered seventh.
(E) Box C is delivered second.

10. Which of the following is a complete and accurate list of the boxes that could be delivered second?

(A) A, D, G
(B) A, E, G
(C) A, C, E, G
(D) A, B, C, E, G
(E) A, B, C, D, E, G

11. Which of the following is a complete and accurate list of the times that box C can be delivered?

(A) First, fourth, fifth, seventh
(B) First, third, fifth, sixth
(C) Second, third, sixth, seventh
(D) First, second, sixth, seventh
(E) First, second, fifth, sixth, seventh

12. If box C is delivered before box B, which of the following must be true?

(A) Box C arrives first.
(B) Box E arrives third.
(C) Box A arrives second.
(D) Box B arrives third.
(E) Box C arrives second.

GO ON TO THE NEXT PAGE.

Questions 7–12

A package delivery service must deliver seven boxes—A, B, C, D, E, F, G. The boxes must be delivered one at a time, and all seven boxes must be delivered. The order the boxes are delivered in must satisfy the following conditions:

Box A must be delivered earlier than box D.
Box B cannot be delivered immediately before or immediately after box C.
Exactly two boxes must be delivered after the delivery of box E and before the delivery of box D.
Box B is delivered first, third, or fifth.
Box F is delivered fourth.

7. Which of the following could be an accurate list of the boxes in order of delivery, from first to seventh?

(A) A, E, B, F, D, C, G
(B) B, E, G, F, D, C, A -1
(C) B, A, D, F, G, E, C -3
(D) C, B, E, F, A, D, G -2
(E) A, B, E, F, G, D, C -4

8. Each of the following boxes could be delivered fifth EXCEPT:

(A) A
(B) B
(C) D
(D) E
(E) G

9. If exactly two boxes are delivered between the delivery of boxes B and C, which of the following must be true? 7A, 10C

B/C — — C/B

(A) Box E is delivered second.
(B) Box B is delivered third.
(C) Box D is delivered sixth. 7A
(D) Box G is delivered seventh.
(E) Box C is delivered second. 7A

10. Which of the following is a complete and accurate list of the boxes that could be delivered second? 7A + analysis + work

(A) A, D, G - no E
(B) A, E, G
(C) A, C, E, G   A C E G B D G
(D) A, B, C, E, G
(E) A, B, C, D, E, G

(no clues from diagram)

11. Which of the following is a complete and accurate list of the times that box C can be delivered?
7A, c is 6th, 10C, c is 2nd

(A) First, fourth, fifth, seventh
(B) First, third, fifth, sixth
(C) Second, third, sixth, seventh
(D) First, second, sixth, seventh   B A E F C D G
(E) First, second, fifth, sixth, seventh

12. If box C is delivered before box B, which of the following must be true?
A/C   A/C E F B D G

(A) Box C arrives first.
(B) Box E arrives third.
(C) Box A arrives second.
(D) Box B arrives third.
(E) Box C arrives second.

GO ON TO THE NEXT PAGE.

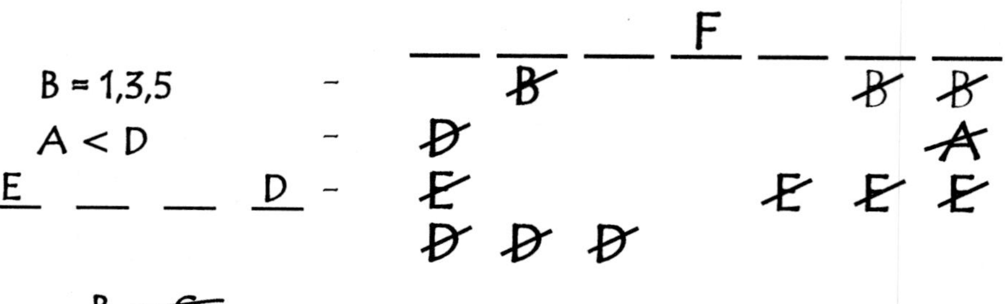

Delivery order

This game is a typical simple line with some common rules and some uncommon rules. There are seven boxes. Each must be delivered separately, and delivered exactly once. You should use a seven-dash simple line. Now, review the rules. The two easiest rules to diagram are Rule 4 and Rule 5. Rule 5 puts F in the fourth space. Rule 4 says that B is first, third, or fifth. This is difficult to graph, so instead, consider where B cannot be. B cannot be second, sixth, or seventh, so diagram this. (Figure 1a) Once those rules are diagrammed, consider Rule 1, A is before D. This means that A is not seventh and D is not first. (Figure 1b) Now, Rule 4 says that E is before D, and that two boxes are delivered between them. This allows us to conclude that E cannot be fifth or later, and that D cannot be earlier than fifth. Additionally, because F is fourth, this prevents E from being first, because D cannot be fourth. It also prevents D from being seventh, because E cannot be fourth. (Figure 1c) There are no conclusions we can make yet using Rule 2, B and C are not next to each other, so just note it on the left side of the diagram.

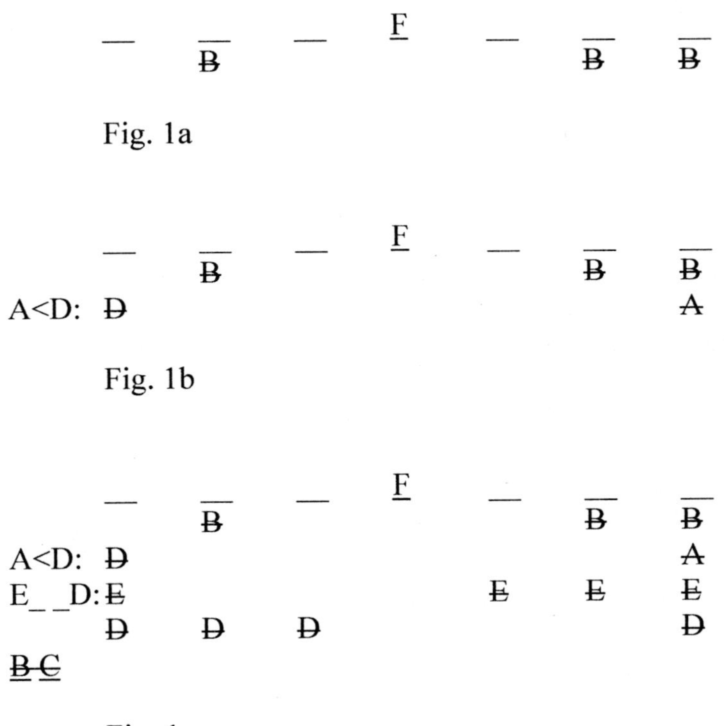

7. (A) – For the first question in the set, you can normally use each rule to eliminate one answer choice. Start with the first rule and determine if any answer choices violate the rule. Then do the same for each subsequent rule.
(A) * This does not violate any rules.
(B) This violates Rule 1 because it shows D before A.
(C) This violates Rule 3 because it shows D before E.
(D) This violates Rule 2 because it shows C and B next to each other.

(E) This violates Rule 4 because it shows B on the second space.

8. (D) – The work done in the initial analysis shows that E is the only member that cannot be fifth.
(A) See the initial diagram.
(B) See the initial diagram.
(C) See the initial diagram.
(D) * See the initial diagram, E cannot be fifth.
(E) See the initial diagram.

9. (D) – This question is more complex then the previous two. You may want to skip it until you finish the easier questions, and then come back to it and use the correct answers from previous questions to answer it. If you do, you could use the correct answers from Question 7 and Question 10 to eliminate four of the answer choices, thus saving yourself a great deal of work. If you went the route of doing all the work, you would simply try to disprove each answer choice.
(A) The work done for Question 10 shows that when B and C are separated by two spaces, it is not necessary that E is delivered second, or that B be delivered third. If you did the work for this one, you would have placed E on space 3. D would have to be sixth. C would be second and B would be fifth. A would be first and G would be seventh.
(B) See (A). The work we did in (A) proved that B can be fifth.
(C) In Question 7(A), we saw that when B and C are separated by two deliveries, it is not necessary that D be sixth.
(D) * Correct, G must be seventh when B and C are separated by two deliveries.
(E) In Question 7(A), we saw that when B and C are separated by two deliveries, it is not necessary that C be second.

10. (C) – The most effective way to answer this question is to use a combination of techniques. First, use the correct answer from Question 7. Question 7(A) lists E as being second, so clearly, E can be second. This eliminates answer choice (A). Next, look at the initial diagram. Neither B nor D can be second. This eliminates three answer choices, (A), (D), and (E). Only answer choices (B) and (C) remain. The only difference between these two is the presence of box C. Draw a quick diagram to determine if box C can be delivered second. (Figure 2) The diagram shows that it can, so we have the correct answer.
(A) In Question 7 we saw that box E can be second, so we can eliminate this answer choice because it does not contain E.
(B) See the analysis.
(C) * C can be delivered second.
(D) B cannot be delivered second.

(E) Neither B nor D can be delivered second.

	A	C	E	F	B	D	G
		~~B~~				~~B~~	~~B~~
A<D:	~~D~~						~~A~~
E_ _D:	~~E~~				~~E~~	~~E~~	~~E~~
	~~D~~	~~D~~	~~D~~	~~D~~			~~D~~

Fig. 2

11. (E) – There are two ways to approach this question. First, you can review the initial diagram and see that it does not show any places where C cannot be. Second, you can use previous correct answers. Question 7(A) shows that C can be sixth. Question 10(C) shows that C can be second. This allows us to eliminate answer choices (A) and (B). Now consider the three remaining answer choices. The only difference between them is whether box C can be first and/or fifth. A quick diagram shows that C can be fifth. (Figure 3) Now it is no longer necessary to confirm that C can be first.
(A) C can be second or sixth.
(B) C can be second or sixth.
(C) C can be fifth.
(D) C can be fifth.
(E) * C can be in any of these five spaces.

	B	A	E	F	C	D	G
		~~B~~				~~B~~	~~B~~
A<D:	~~D~~						~~A~~
E_ _D:	~~E~~				~~E~~	~~E~~	~~E~~
	~~D~~	~~D~~	~~D~~				~~D~~

Fig. 3

12. (B) – Once again, you can use a combination of previous correct answers and a simple diagram to solve this question. If C is before B, then B can only be third or fifth. Diagram both of these possibilities. (Figure 4) It does not work to have B third, because there is no way to diagram this without violating the rule that A must be earlier than D. It is possible to have B fifth. This determines the order of all the other packages except A and C.
(A) A or C can be first.
(B) * E must be third.
(C) See (A).
(D) B must be fifth.
(E) See (A).

C E B F D __ __

A/C C/A E F B D G

Fig. 4

Conclusion of simple lines

Points to remember:

The first or second game of the four games is always a simple line game.

There is always one simple line game in a section, and often there are two.

There are usually six or seven spaces to be filled.

There are usually as many members as there are spaces to fill.

There are sometimes fewer members than spaces to fill. If so, one or two members will be used more than once.

There may be more members than spaces to fill, though this is very unusual. If so, one or more members will not be used.

There are only a few simple line rules. Memorize these rules and the conclusions that result from them.

Some conclusions can only be made after considering the overlap and interactions of two or more rules.

You have now finished a comprehensive introduction to the simple line games. You have learned what the setups look like, what the rules look like, and what the questions look like. You have learned how to draw the diagrams, how to depict the rules, and how to make additional conclusions.

Much of what you have learned will be useful for the other types of games. Some of what you have learned will not sink in until you do practice tests, so plan to review this section as you practice the simple lines in the tests found later in this book.

Multiple Line Games

Give yourself 8 minutes and 45 seconds to solve as many questions as you can in the following game. When time is up, review the explanations. Using this game as a starting point, you will learn the different ways multiple lines are tested and how to complete a multiple line game quickly and effectively. This will be followed by a series of exercises so you can practice what you learned. You will finish by doing three more multiple line games under timed conditions and reviewing your work.

SECTION I

Time—35 minutes

22 Questions

Directions: Each group of questions in this section is based on a set of conditions. In answering some of the questions, it may be useful to draw a rough diagram. Choose the response that most accurately and completely answers each question and blacken the corresponding space on your answer sheet.

Questions 1–5

At a summer camp, six campers—George, Henry, Molly, Xeno, Yvonne, and Zachary—will sit in two canoes numbered 1 and 2. Each canoe has a front seat, a middle seat, and a back seat. Each camper sits in one seat, and no campers share a seat. The following conditions determine where the campers will sit:

Molly always sits in the front seat.
Henry never sits in the middle seat.
George always sits in the front seat.
Xeno and Yvonne sit in different canoes.

1. Which one of the following could be a complete and accurate list of the campers seated in a canoe 1, from front to back?

(A) George, Xeno, Henry
(B) Molly, Henry, Xeno
(C) Yvonne, George, Henry
(D) George, Zachary, Henry
(E) Xeno, Molly, Henry

2. If Zachary is in canoe 2, then which one of the following must be true?

(A) Henry is in canoe 1.
(B) Xeno is in canoe 1.
(C) Yvonne is in canoe 1.
(D) George is in canoe 2.
(E) Molly is in canoe 2.

3. Each of the following pairs can be seated in the same canoe EXCEPT:

(A) Molly and Xeno
(B) Zachary and Henry
(C) Yvonne and Zachary
(D) George and Yvonne
(E) Henry and Xeno

4. Which of the following pairs could be seated in the middle seats of canoe 1 and canoe 2, in that order?

(A) Henry and Yvonne
(B) George and Xeno
(C) Xeno and Molly
(D) Zachary and Henry
(E) Yvonne and Zachary

5. If Xeno is not in the same canoe as Zachary, which of the following must be true?

(A) Xeno is in canoe 1.
(B) Zachary is in canoe 2.
(C) Yvonne is in the back of canoe 1.
(D) Xeno sits in the middle of the canoe that Henry sits in.
(E) Zachary sits in the middle of the canoe that Yvonne sits in.

GO ON TO THE NEXT PAGE.

SECTION I

Time—35 minutes

22 Questions

Directions: Each group of questions in this section is based on a set of conditions. In answering some of the questions, it may be useful to draw a rough diagram. Choose the response that most accurately and completely answers each question and blacken the corresponding space on your answer sheet.

Questions 1–5

At a summer camp, six campers—George, Henry, Molly, Xeno, Yvonne, and Zachary—will sit in two canoes numbered 1 and 2. Each canoe has a front seat, a middle seat, and a back seat. Each camper sits in one seat, and no campers share a seat. The following conditions determine where the campers will sit:

Molly always sits in the front seat.
Henry never sits in the middle seat.
George always sits in the front seat.
Xeno and Yvonne sit in different canoes.

1. Which one of the following could be a complete and accurate list of the campers seated in a canoe 1, from front to back?

(A) George, Xeno, Henry
(B) Molly, Henry, Xeno - 2
(C) Yvonne, George, Henry - 3
(D) George, Zachary, Henry - 4
(E) Xeno, Molly, Henry - 1

2. If Zachary is in canoe 2, then which one of the following must be true?

(A) Henry is in canoe 1.
(B) Xeno is in canoe 1.
(C) Yvonne is in canoe 1.
(D) George is in canoe 2.
(E) Molly is in canoe 2.

Interchangeable

M/G Y/X H
M/G Z X/Y

3. Each of the following pairs can be seated in the same canoe EXCEPT:

(A) Molly and Xeno
(B) Zachary and Henry
(C) Yvonne and Zachary
(D) George and Yvonne
(E) Henry and Xeno

M & G are totally interchangeable
X & Y are totally interchangeable

4. Which of the following pairs could be seated in the middle seats of canoe 1 and canoe 2, in that order?

(A) Henry and Yvonne
(B) George and Xeno
(C) Xeno and Molly
(D) Zachary and Henry
(E) Yvonne and Zachary

5. If Xeno is not in the same canoe as Zachary, which of the following must be true?

(A) Xeno is in canoe 1.
(B) Zachary is in canoe 2.
(C) Yvonne is in the back of canoe 1.
(D) Xeno sits in the middle of the canoe that Henry sits in.
(E) Zachary sits in the middle of the canoe that Yvonne sits in.

G/M X H   G/M Y Z
M/G Z Y   M/G X H

GO ON TO THE NEXT PAGE.

F M B
1 G/M ___ ___ X/Y
2 M/G ___ ___ Y/X
H̶
G
M

M/G ___ ___
G/M ___ ___

Canoe seats order

This game is as easy a multiple line game as you could hope for. There are two canoes; each canoe has three seats, one each in the front, middle, and back. Six campers will fill these six seats. There will be one camper per seat, and all the campers will be used once. The first step is to create a diagram. (Figure 1a) Two sets of three dashes will do the job nicely. Now consider the rules. Rule 1 states that M is always in a front seat. Place an M under the "front" column, and place a negative M under the other two columns. Skipping to Rule 3, G also sits in a front seat. This means that G and M will occupy the two front seats. Since G occupies one front seat and M occupies the other, no other camper may sit in the front seats. This is a very useful conclusion. Place a G/M on both of the front seats to make this clear. (Figure 1b)

Rule 2 states that H never sits in the middle seat. Since the front seats are no longer open to H, this means that H must sit in a back seat. Note this below the appropriate columns. Finally, Rule 4 specifies that X and Y be in different canoes. This means that X and Y are like G and M. X will be in one canoe; Y will be in the other. We don't know whether X and Y will be in the middle or back of their canoes, or one of each. Place an X/Y to the side of the two rows. We now have a useful diagram.

	Front	middle	back
1	____	____	____
2	____	____	____

Fig. 1a

	Front	middle	back	
1	G/M	____	____	X/Y
2	G/M	____	____	X/Y
	M	~~M~~	~~M~~	
	G	~~G~~	~~G~~	
		~~H~~	H	

Fig. 1b

1. (A) – In the first question, you can usually use each rule to eliminate one answer choice.

   (A) * This is a valid seating order. These campers sitting in canoe 1 do not violate any rules, and it is possible to seat the three remaining campers in canoe 2 without violating any rules.

   (B) This violates Rule 2 by placing H in a middle seat.

(C) This violates Rule 3 by placing G in a middle seat.
(D) This violates Rule 4 because it requires that both X and Y be in canoe 2.
(E) This violates Rule 1 because it places M in a middle seat.

2. (A) – If Z is in canoe 2, what must be true? Draw a quick diagram with Z in the middle seat of canoe 2. (We could just as easily put Z in the back seat, sometimes you just have to pick a permutation and run with it.) Either X or Y must be in the back of canoe 2. In canoe 1, H must be in the back. Either X or Y must be in the middle of canoe 1.
(A) * Yes, H must be in canoe 1.
(B) X and Y are interchangeable.
(C) See (B).
(D) G and M are interchangeable.
(E) See (D).

	Front	middle	back	
1	G/M	X/Y	H	X/Y
2	G/M	Z	X/Y	X/Y

Fig. 2

3. (B) – Since this question does not add new information, it should be answerable without doing new work. Consider that X and Y are interchangeable. So, if X is in a canoe, it is just as possible that Y could switch places with X. The same is true for M and G. Thus, any answer choice that has any of these members is always a possible seating arrangement.
(A) M and X are both flexible.
(B) * Z and H cannot be in the same canoe. Because X or Y and G or M take up two of the three seats in each canoe, it is not possible to ever have both Z and H in the same canoe.
(C) Y is interchangeable with X.
(D) G and Y are both flexible.
(E) X and Y are interchangeable.

4. (E) – Consider the rules. Neither H nor M can be in the middle seat. Neither G nor M can be in the middle seat. X, Y, or Z can be in the middle seat.
(A) H cannot be in the middle seat.
(B) G cannot be in the middle seat.
(C) M cannot be in the middle seat.
(D) H cannot be in the middle seat.

(E) * Both Y and Z can be in the middle seats.

5. (D) – If X is not in the same canoe as Z, then X must be in the canoe with H. Since H must sit in the back, X must sit in the middle.
(A) We do not know which canoe X is in.
(B) We do not know which canoe Z is in.
(C) We do not know which canoe Y is in and don't know where Y sits.
(D) * Yes. X is not with Z, so X is with H. H can't sit in the middle, so X does.
(E) Although we know that Z and Y must sit in the same canoe, we don't know where they sit in that canoe.

The setups for multiple lines

Simple line games are, in a word, simple. They have an easy-to-see, easy-to-understand design. They have a series of dashes on which you place one member per dash. For example, there are six landing spots and six planes that must land. The structure is obvious, a line of six dashes. It is also clear what needs to be placed on the dashes, one member name per dash.

A multiple line game also has a structure and things to place on the structure, but sometimes it is difficult to determine which items are part of the structure and which are the things to be placed on the structure. This makes multiple line games more difficult than simple line games. Sometimes the structure and the items to be placed on the dashes are obvious, like when the setup tells you there are five days, and that two members must be present each day. You simply create five dashes with space for two members on each dash, like this:

__|__ __|__ __|__ __|__ __|__

Or the setup may describe five warehouses, each of which contains one type of perishable food and one type of nonperishable food. In the example below, the top set of dashes is for the perishable foods, and the bottom set is for the nonperishable foods.

____ ____ ____ ____ ____
____ ____ ____ ____ ____

Fortunately, this five-column, two-element multiple line is the most common multiple line setup. But sometimes the structure is not obvious. If so, you must decide what structure will organize the information in the most useable format. Some examples are as follows:

The following is a simple scenario that requires a deceptively simple setup.

"Students in a History class are required to meet with the teaching assistant once per semester. The teaching assistant offers meeting times on one day: one in the morning, one in the afternoon, and one in the evening. The students in the History class this semester are Frank, Gina, Harry, Jon, Kaspar, Leon, Marc, and Nino."

____	____	____
morn	noon	eve

This setup merely requires one space for each of the three meeting times. Since there are eight students and only three meetings, at least one meeting will have more than one student.

The following is a more common setup: there are two elements for each column.

"In each of six consecutive classrooms numbered, 1–6, students will demonstrate exactly one of three science projects—astronomy, biology, and chemistry—and exactly one of three art projects—dance, etching, and folk music."

1	2	3	4	5	6	
__	__	__	__	__	__	Science
__	__	__	__	__	__	Art

There are six slots or columns (the classrooms) and each of the six slots must have one science project and one art project. It is common in multiple line games for each column to have two elements, so be on the lookout for this type of structure.

The following is another typical setup.

"Nine volunteers—G, H, I, J, K, L, M, N, and O—are available to staff a telephone help line during a four day pledge drive that is held on Monday, Tuesday, Wednesday, and Thursday. There is a morning and afternoon shift on each day. Exactly one volunteer staffs the help line during each shift, and a volunteer can work only one shift during the pledge drive."

Mon	Tue	Wed	Thu	
__	__	__	__	AM
__	__	__	__	PM

The four days of the week and the AM/PM shifts provide a natural structure. Nine members are available to fill the eight spaces. One member will not be used. The most difficult games are those that have more members than spaces to fill.

Because there are more members than there are spaces in which to put them, this puzzle is more difficult than if there were the same number of members as spaces, or if there were fewer members than spaces.

The following setup is more difficult.

"A theater troupe will perform seven skits during an evening performance. The performers include five experienced actors–Ariana, Bronte, Carlow, Dabia, and Eric–and five novice performers–Nabiel, Sam, Thomas, Jackie, and Kyrasaki. Each performer will perform in exactly one skit according to the following requirements:"

__ __ __ __ __ __ __

Since there are seven skits and 10 actors who each do one skit, some of the skits will have more than one actor. Because some of the skits will have more than one member, this is a multiple line, not a simple line (even though the diagram above is a single set of dashes). If this setup had said that there is one experienced actor and one inexperienced actor for each skit, then we would have drawn two parallel lines of seven dashes each. One line would be for the experienced actors, the other for the inexperienced actors.

The rules for the multiple lines

All of the simple lines rules can be used in the multiple lines. But because the multiple lines are more complex, the rules can be used in more complex ways. Additionally, there are rules that are used in multiple line games that are not used in simple line games.

The following are examples of rules that appear frequently in multiple line games, but never appear in simple line games. These rules have many variations, so you always need to be creative and flexible when diagramming them. The language of the rule is provided below, along with a depiction of how the rule should be diagrammed.

1. Rule: "At most, two employees attend a training session."
   Paraphrase: Max. 2 per session.

   This rule creates three possibilities: no employees attend a session (i.e., no employee fills a dash), one employee attends, or two employees attend. By establishing an upper occupancy limit for each dash, this rule reduces the diagram's complexity. For example, in the theater troupe example above, if a rule had specified that no more than two actors performed each skit, then you would modify the diagram to look like this:

   __|__ __|__ __|__ __|__ __|__ __|__ __|__

2. Rule: "Each employee attends exactly two training sessions."
   Paraphrase: Each is used 2x.

   In simple line games, the number of spaces to be filled is usually equal to the number of members available to fill them. Multiple line games often have more spaces to fill than members to fill them, so rules will limit how often members repeat, and in what ways they are permitted to repeat.

3. Rule: "If Sam plays the kazoo, then Roland plays the lyre."
   Paraphrase: if S | k → R | l

In this game, the people each play one of several instruments. In the situation where Sam plays kazoo, then R plays the lyre. This is somewhat similar to the simple line rule that says, "If A is second, B is fifth."
This rule says nothing about the *order* of their appearance, so make sure your diagram does not create the impression that R must be after S.

Note- You can make this diagram clearer by writing all the initials of one group (the people's names) in upper case letters, and all of the initials of the other group (the musical instruments) in lower case letters.

4. Rule: "The musician playing the kazoo performs immediately after James and immediately before Sam."
Paraphrase: R|__ __|k S|__.

This rule is very useful because it specifies the order of three elements. If a game has this kind of rule, it will be the starting point for your entire diagram.

5. Rule: "The second orange is placed in the same basket as the first pear."
Paraphrase: O2 in same as P1 or O2=P1

In this game, you asked to fill five baskets with fruit. There may be several pieces of each fruit in each basket. When a game tests sequential order (first basket, second basket, etc.), you need to keep track of *when* a member (the pieces of fruit) is used, as well as how often it is used.
This may also be phrased as, "The second pineapple is put in the third basket."

6. Rule: "If a building is gray, then it is Victorian."
Paraphrase: If g → V

This is another conditional rule, so it applies only when the building is gray, but not when the building is Victorian. So, even when your diagram shows that a building is Victorian, this does not necessarily mean that the building is gray. Many test-takers make this mistake. Also, if the building is not Victorian, then it will not be gray.

7. Rule: "A is used more often then B."
Paraphrase: #A > #B

Since a member is sometimes used more than once, some rules dictate the frequency that a member appears. Using the "#" symbol clarifies that it is the number of As that is greater than the number of Bs, not that A is later than B (which would be indicated B<A, since all lines you create should go from least to

greatest). When the game has this kind of rule you will be able to determine exactly how many times A and B are used, greatly simplifying the diagram. Always do the math when you have this kind of rule.

8. Rule: "Professional team B plays later than any amateur team."
   Paraphrase: Amateur < B

   Team B is later than all of the amateur teams. Another way to diagram this is to list the amateur teams, for example, x, y, z < B.

Every multiple line game will have at least one of these rules. Multiple line games also use simple line rules. To become skilled at using the multiple line rules you must first become skilled with the simple line rules. Then you must be creative, adapting those rules to work for the multiple line games.

After you have read the setup and rules of a game, and diagramed the rules, the next step is to make the vital conclusions that add more information to your diagram.

Additional Conclusions for multiple line games

In the simple line games, there are certain conclusions that flow naturally from the common rules. For example, a simple line rule that says A is earlier than B automatically means that A cannot be last, and B cannot be first. You can make this conclusion based on this single rule. When a multiple line game uses these same rules, you get the same conclusions. But multiple lines also have more complex diagrams and more complex rules. As a result, there is no standard set of multiple line conclusions. Instead, you must focus on the interplay of two or three rules with each other and with the diagram. Only by doing this can you make additional conclusions. You make these conclusions after you diagram all the rules and consider the interaction of the rules. The exercises that follow will develop your skill at making conclusions.

Exercises

Now it is time to practice what you have learned. The following exercises are designed to reinforce the basic concepts for multiple line games. There are exercises for diagramming the setup, followed by exercises for diagramming the rules, and finally, exercises that have you do both.

Exercises – setups

Compare your diagrams with the examples that follow this exercise.

1. Six dart players—A, B, C, D, E, and G—will play four consecutive games. Exactly two players will play against each other in each game.

2. A construction crew will build five houses on one side of a street. Each building will have exactly one style—contemporary, prairie, or ranch—and will be 1500 square feet, 2000 square feet, or 2500 square feet.

3. From Monday to Thursday a company makes exactly three styles of aquariums—cylindrical, octagonal, and rectangular. During the week, each style is made in exactly three sizes—50 gallon, 75 gallon, and 100 gallon.

4. Three companies—A, B, C—each manufacture exactly three of the following six products—balls, bottles, caps, clocks, diodes, and dresses.

5. A zoo has exactly four habitats—K, L, M, and O—that each must be occupied by exactly two species. The species housed in the habitats include birds—A, B, and C—and mammals—E, F, G, and H.

Answers – setups

The following are sample diagrams for the setups:

1. **Six dart players.**

There are four dart games in a row, and two people in each game. This is depicted with two parallel sets of dashes. In this game, it does not matter which player goes on the top line and which goes on the bottom line. There are eight spaces, and six people. Thus, either one player will play in three games, or two players will play two games each.

__ __ __ __
__ __ __ __

2. **Five houses.**

Each house has two elements, the style and the size. This is a common setup. Use five columns. The top dash is the style and a bottom dash is the size.

__ __ __ __ __
__ __ __ __ __

3. **Aquariums.**

This setup is tricky. It does not work to use four columns with two dashes underneath. Each of the three styles has three sizes. That makes a total of nine aquariums. Since nine aquariums are being made in four days, and there is no indication of a maximum or minimum number on each day, make columns for the four days and then add however many dashes you end up needing. In this situation, the rules will contain clues indicating how many are made each day, thereby simplifying the diagram.

Mon Tue Wed Thu

4. **Three companies.**

It is best to organize this setup using three columns, titled A, B, and C. Under each column, draw three dashes, since each company makes exactly three items.

A B C
__ __ __
__ __ __
__ __ __

5. **Zoo habitats.**

The key feature of this setup is that there are exactly two species per habitat. Based on the information in the setup it makes sense to list K, L, M, and O in the order they appear, although later information may necessitate using a different order.

K L M O
__|__ __|__ __|__ __|__

Exercises – rules

Practice diagramming the common rules for multiple line games. If you can make additional conclusions, diagram them as well. Compare your diagrams with the examples that follow this exercise.

1. Six dart players—A, B, D, E, G, and S—will play four consecutive games. Exactly two players will play against each other in each game.

   A plays exactly two times, and does not play against D.

   E plays immediately before S plays and sometime later than S plays.

2. From Monday to Thursday a company makes exactly three styles of aquariums—cylindrical, octagonal, and rectangular. During the week, each style is made in exactly three sizes—50 gallon, 75 gallon, and 100 gallon.

   No more than one size for an aquarium style is made on a single day.

   The second octagonal aquarium is made the day after the second rectangular aquarium is made.

3. A zoo has exactly four habitats—K, L, M, and O—that each must be occupied by exactly two species. The species include birds—A, B, and C—and mammals—E, F, G, and H.

   Habitat K is not next to habitat L or habitat M.

   Species E is in habitat O with one other mammal.

   Species A is in a habitat that contains a mammal species and is immediately next to a habitat that contains exactly one bird species.

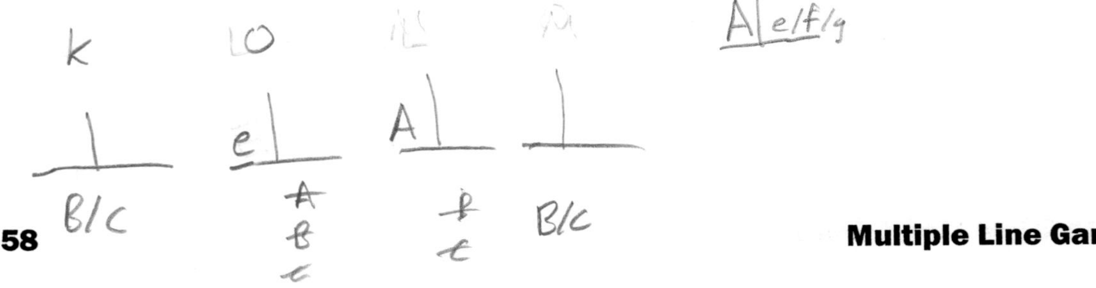

Answers – rules

The appropriate diagrams for the rules are as follows:

1. **Six dart players.**

The first rule has two parts: A plays twice, and A never plays D. Break this into two parts and list them under the diagram. The next rule says that E is immediately before S, and also sometime after S, as depicted under the diagram. The (_) between S and E shows that this space may be between them, or it may not. After giving the rules some thought, you may realize something helpful. We determined earlier that two of the members play twice, while the others all play one game. We now know that A plays twice and E plays twice. This is a big help. For example, since we know that S plays once, S must be second or third; S cannot be first or fourth, since that would violate the rule, "E plays immediately before S."

"A plays exactly two times, and does not play against D."

"E plays immediately before S plays and sometime later than S plays."

	__	__	__	__
	__	__	__	__
A=2x:				
~~AD~~:				
E S (_) E:	~~S~~			~~S~~

2. **Aquariums.**

We know there are three styles and three sizes, so there are nine aquariums to be made. The first rule is that the most that can be made in a day is one size of each style. So, if all three styles were made each day, it would still require three days to make all nine aquariums. The next rule is difficult. It states that the second octagonal is made the day after the second rectangular. This limits the possibilities for both styles. The second octagonal must be on Wednesday; otherwise, there is no other way to fit in the first two rectangular and the third octagonal. The third octagonal must be Thursday. The first rectangular must be Monday and the second rectangular must be Tuesday.

"No more than one size for an aquarium style is made on a single day."

"The second octagonal aquarium is made the day after the second rectangular aquarium is made."

	Mon	Tue	Wed	Thu
R2nd O2nd:			O2|__	O3|__
	R1|__	R2|__		

3. **Zoo habitats.**

Start with the first rule, K is not next to L or M. This means that K must be on one of the ends, and must be next to O. It doesn't appear to matter whether K is at the left end or right end of the diagram, so just choose one side. The second rule places E, a mammal, in habitat O, along with another mammal. This means that no birds are in habitat O, as noted below. Finally, species A, a bird, is in a habitat with a mammal, and A's habitat is next to a habitat that has exactly one bird. This information allows us to conclude that A must be in the habitat next to O. Why? The only place where two bird species can be in adjoining habitats is the two habitats to the right of O. Once again, it is not important if you put A in the habitat next to O, or the final habitat in the row, as long as you diagram the information correctly. The B/C under both K and the unnamed habitat indicate that either B or C must be in these habitats.

"Habitat K is not next to habitat L or habitat M."
"Species E is in habitat O with one other mammal."
"Species A is in a habitat that contains a mammal species and is immediately next to a habitat that contains exactly one bird species."

K	O		
__|__	E|__	A|__	__|__
	~~A~~		
B/C	~~B~~	~~B~~	B/C
	~~C~~	~~C~~	

Exercises – setups and rules

Diagram the setups and rules, and diagram any additional conclusions you can make.

1. During a five-day work schedule, three employees—Dontale, Ebbert, and Fowler—must each perform exactly three tasks—interviewing, researching, and training. An employee performs each task once during the week. Each task requires exactly one day to complete and each task is finished the same day it is started. The order the employees complete the tasks is determined by the following requirements:

    No more than two employees perform tasks during one day.
    All interviews are finished before any day that training is performed.
    Dontale interviews the day after Ebbert interviews.

2. Five singers—Gannymead, Martin, Nick, Pat, and Quinn—are assigned solo performances for the holiday festival. Each singer sings exactly once and in exactly one of three singing voices—alto, bass, or contralto.

    Gannymead sings earlier than Nick and Quinn.
    There is one more alto than contralto.
    A bass does not perform immediately before or after another bass.
    Nick is a bass.

3. Three students—Berger, Cohen, and Dorn—will select exactly two of the following courses—Religion, Science, Theater, Western Literature, and Zoology.

    Berger and Cohen select exactly one of the same courses.
    Dorn does not select any course that Berger or Cohen selects.
    No student selects both Religion and Science.
    No student selects both Western Literature and Zoology.

Answers – setups and rules

The appropriate diagrams for the rules are as follows:

1. During a five-day work schedule, three employees—Dontale, Ebbert, and Fowler—must each perform exactly three tasks—interviewing, researching, and training. An employee performs each task once during the week. Each task requires exactly one day to complete and each task is finished the same day it is started. The order the employees complete the tasks is determined by the following requirements:

No more than two employees perform tasks during one day.
All interviews are finished before the first day that training is performed.
Dontale interviews the day after Ebbert interviews.

	1	2	3	4	5
	—	—	—	—	—
	—	—	—	—	—
Ei Di:	~~Di~~		~~Ei~~		~~Ei~~
i < t:	~~Dt~~	~~Dt~~		~~Di~~	~~Di~~
	~~Et~~	~~Et~~		~~Ei~~	~~Ei~~
	~~Ft~~	~~Ft~~		~~Fi~~	~~Fi~~

That there are five days is the first clue as to the proper diagram. The second clue is Rule 1, which says that there are no more than two tasks or employees each day. Since the three employees each do three tasks, there are nine tasks to be placed in ten possible spaces. Draw five columns and place two spaces below each column (one of the ten spaces will not be filled). Rule 3 is an easy rule to start with; D interviews the day after E interviews. This is the same kind of rule as you see in simple lines. Using this rule, we can conclude that E does not interview on the fifth day and D does not interview on the first day. Rule 2 is very useful. It states that all the interviews are finished before the first day that training is done. This means that training cannot start earlier than the third day, because, at a minimum, the interviews would occupy three of the four spaces in the first two days. Similarly, no interviews can be done later than the third day, in order to allow sufficient space for the three trainings. Combining Rules 2 and 3, we also realize that since D cannot interview on the fourth day, it is impossible for E to interview on the third day.

2. Five singers—Gannymead, Martin, Nick, Pat, and Quinn—are assigned solo performances for the holiday festival. Each singer sings exactly once and in exactly one of three singing voices—alto, bass, or contralto.

Gannymead sings earlier than Nick and Quinn.
There is one more alto than contralto.
A bass does not perform immediately before or after another bass.

Nick is a bass.

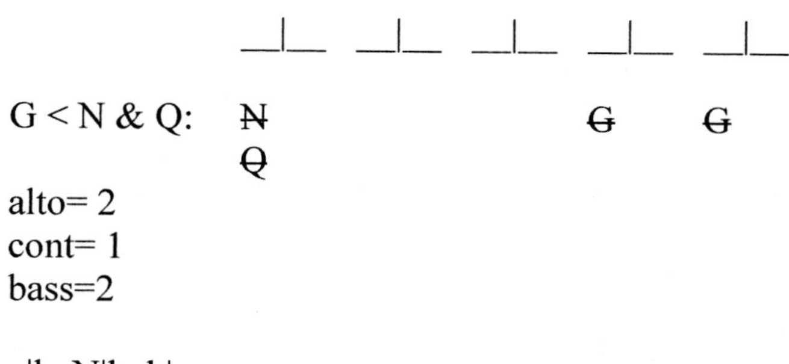

_|b N|b b|_

Again, it is a five-day setup. Since each singer performs once, the diagram is pretty basic. The first rule is one we often see in simple line games, and it is easy to diagram. Using Rule 1, we can conclude that G cannot be either of the last two performers, and neither N nor Q can be first performer. Rule 4 specifies that Nick sings bass, and Rule 3 specifies that a bass singer does not have a bass singer on either side. Rule 2 states that there is one more alto than contralto. This is a common rule. Always do the math when you have this kind of rule. If there were zero contraltos, there would be one alto and thus four bass. That will not work, since the bass performers cannot be next to each other. On the other hand, if there were one contralto, there would be two altos and thus two bass. That doesn't seem to violate any rules. But, if there were two contraltos, there would be three altos and thus no bass. We know that doesn't work: Nick is a bass, so there is at least one bass. This means there are one contralto, two altos, and two bass. Always do the math because it helps you to narrow the possibilities.

3. Three students—Berger, Cohen, and Dorn—will select exactly two of the following courses—Religion, Science, Theater, Western Literature, and Zoology.

Berger and Cohen select exactly one of the same courses.
Dorn does not select any course that Berger or Cohen selects.
No student selects both Religion and Science.
No student selects both Western Literature and Zoology.

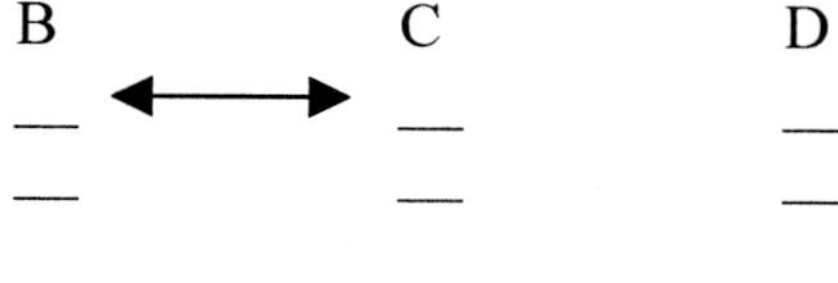

RS
WZ

The three students form three columns, each with two dashes underneath. Rules 3 and 4 are limiting, reducing the flexibility in selecting the classes. After considering the possibilities, it can be concluded that each of the classes will be selected once and one class will be selected twice (by students B and C), making a total of six classes. This link between B and C is denoted using a two-way arrow.

Practice games

In each of the following games, spend 8 minutes and 45 seconds answering as many questions as you can. Then review the explanations that follow the game.

Questions 7–11

A museum curator is planning two exhibits of an artist's paintings to take place simultaneously in Chicago and Denver. Exactly three of the seven paintings will be exhibited in each city. The paintings are from the artist's early period—Bichelli, Chaos, Finlet, Gord—as well as from the artist's late period—Jelisse, Lorac, and Oxram. The exhibition of the paintings is subject to the following conditions:

The exhibit in each city must include at least one painting from the artist's late period.
Bichelli is not exhibited in Chicago.
Finlet and Gord are not exhibited in the same city.
Chaos and Jelisse are not both exhibited.

7. Which one of the following could be an accurate list of paintings on exhibit?

(A) Chicago: Jelisse, Lorac, Oxram
Denver: Finlet, Bichelli, Gord
(B) Chicago: Oxram, Finlet, Gord
Denver: Lorac, Bichelli, Chaos
(C) Chicago: Oxram, Finlet, Gord
Denver: Lorac, Bichelli, Chaos
(D) Chicago: Finlet, Bichelli, Lorac
Denver: Chaos, Gord, Oxram
(E) Chicago: Finlet, Lorac, Oxram
Denver: Gord, Jelisse, Bichelli

8. If Jelisse is exhibited in Chicago, which one of the following must be true?

(A) Bichelli is exhibited in Denver.
(B) Finlet is exhibited in Denver.
(C) Chaos is exhibited in Chicago.
(D) Lorac is exhibited in Chicago.
(E) Oxram is exhibited in Chicago.

9. Which one of the following is a pair of paintings, both of which must be exhibited?

(A) Jelisse and Oxram
(B) Lorac and Finlet
(C) Bichelli and Jelisse
(D) Chaos and Bichelli
(E) Gord and Chaos

10. If Finlet is on exhibit in Chicago, what is the maximum number of combinations of paintings on exhibit?

(A) two
(B) three
(C) four
(D) five
(E) six

11. Which one of the following is a complete and accurate list of paintings, any one of which could be exhibited with Bichelli?

(A) Gord, Jelisse, Lorac
(B) Chaos, Finlet, Gord, Jelisse, Oxram
(C) Finlet, Gord, Jelisse, Lorac, Oxram
(D) Chaos, Finlet, Jelisse, Lorac, Oxram
(E) Jelisse, Lorac, Oxram

GO ON TO THE NEXT PAGE.

Questions 7–11

A museum curator is planning two exhibits of an artist's paintings to take place simultaneously in Chicago and Denver. Exactly three of the seven paintings will be exhibited in each city. The paintings are from the artist's early period—Bichelli, Chaos, Finlet, Gord—as well as from the artist's late period—Jelisse, Lorac, and Oxram. The exhibition of the paintings is subject to the following conditions:

The exhibit in each city must include at least one painting from the artist's late period.
Bichelli is not exhibited in Chicago.
Finlet and Gord are not exhibited in the same city.
Chaos and Jelisse are not both exhibited.

7. Which one of the following could be an accurate list of paintings on exhibit?

(A) Chicago: Jelisse, Lorac, Oxram – 1
Denver: Finlet, Bichelli, Gord
(B) Chicago: Oxram, Finlet, Gord – 3
Denver: Lorac, Bichelli, Chaos
(C) Chicago: Oxram, Finlet, Gord – 3
Denver: Lorac, Bichelli, Chaos
(D) Chicago: Finlet, Bichelli, Lorac – 2
Denver: Chaos, Gord, Oxram
(E) Chicago: Finlet, Lorac, Oxram
Denver: Gord, Jelisse, Bichelli

8. If Jelisse is exhibited in Chicago, which one of the following must be true? – no C

(A) Bichelli is exhibited in Denver.
(B) Finlet is exhibited in Denver.
(C) Chaos is exhibited in Chicago.
(D) Lorac is exhibited in Chicago.
(E) Oxram is exhibited in Chicago.

F/G L/O J
F/G B L/O

9. Which one of the following is a pair of paintings, both of which must be exhibited? Not C or J

(A) Jelisse and Oxram
(B) Lorac and Finlet
(C) Bichelli and Jelisse
(D) Chaos and Bichelli
(E) Gord and Chaos

10. If Finlet is on exhibit in Chicago, what is the maximum number of combinations of paintings on exhibit? work it out

(A) two
(B) three
(C) four
(D) five
(E) six

F C ~~LJ~~ ~~OLOO~~L — 1, 2, 3, 4, 5
G B ~~JOLLO~~ J/L/O

11. Which one of the following is a complete and accurate list of paintings, any one of which could be exhibited with Bichelli? not C, see rule #1

G/F ___ ___
F/G B ___

(A) Gord, Jelisse, Lorac
(B) Chaos, Finlet, Gord, Jelisse, Oxram
see #10 (C) Finlet, Gord, Jelisse, Lorac, Oxram
see #10 (D) Chaos, Finlet, Jelisse, Lorac, Oxram
(E) Jelisse, Lorac, Oxram

GO ON TO THE NEXT PAGE.

Chi G/F ___ ___ ~~B~~
Den F/G B J/L/O B
Late

~~F G~~
– C or J, so all the others must be exhibited

Exhibits

This is a multiple line game of average difficulty. Consider the setup. There are two exhibits, and each exhibit has three paintings. This means that six paintings will be exhibited, out of seven possible paintings. A basic diagram will suffice. (Figure 1a) The rules clear up some questions that you may have had after reading the setup. A quick scan of the rules reveals Rule 4; C and J are not both exhibited. This is a valuable rule. Because they are not both exhibited, either C or J is exhibited. Thus, the other five paintings are always exhibited. With that in mind, graph the other rules. Rule 1 states that each exhibit must include at least one painting from the late period (paintings J, L, and O). The best way to diagram this is to reserve one column for J, L, and O. (Figure 1b) Rule 2 is easy to diagram, simply place a negative B in Chicago and a B in Denver. (Figure 1c) Rule 3 specifies that F and G are not in the same city. We have seen this kind of rule before, and it is easy to diagram. Either F or G must be in Chicago, and the other one must be in Denver. Reserve one column for F and G. We now have a good diagram, so move on to the questions.

Chi	___	___	___
Dnv	___	___	___

Fig. 1a

Chi	___	___	___ J/L/O
Dnv	___	___	___ J/L/O

Fig. 1b

Chi	F/G	___	___ J/L/O	~~B~~
Dnv	F/G	B	___ J/L/O	B
C or J				

Fig. 1c

7. (E) – This list question should be answered by working with each rule to eliminate answer choices.
   (A) This answer choice violates Rule 3 (F and G are not in the same city) and Rule 1 (Each exhibit has at least J, L, or O).
   (B) This answer choice violates Rule 3.

(C) This answer choice violates Rule 3.
(D) This answer choice violates Rule 2.
(E) * This is a valid answer choice.

8. (A) – J is in Chicago. Thus, C will not be used, so we can eliminate answer choice (C).
   (A) * Yes, B must be in Denver. Because all six of the paintings besides C must be used, B must be used. B can only be used in Denver.
   (B) F and G are interchangeable.
   (C) C is not used if J is used.
   (D) L could be in Chicago, or in Denver, and O will be in the other city.
   (E) See (D).

Chi	F/G	___	J J/L/O	~~B~~
Dnv	F/G	B	___ J/L/O	B
C or J				

Fig. 2

9. (B) – All of the paintings must be exhibited, except for C or J. So, any answer choice pair that has either C or J is not an accurate pair of paintings that must be exhibited.
   (A) See the analysis.
   (B) * Both L and F must be exhibited.
   (C) See the analysis.
   (D) See the analysis.
   (E) See the analysis.

10. (D) – If F is in Chicago, then G is in Denver. Now we need to do as many permutations as we can. If C is used, then J is not. C would be in Chicago. Either L or O would be in Chicago, and the other in Denver. This makes two permutations. Now, if J is used and C is not, then L and O must fill the remaining spaces. If J is in Denver, then L and O are in Chicago. That makes a third permutation. If J is in Chicago, then either L or O is in Chicago, and the other is in Denver. That makes a fourth and fifth permutation.
   (A) See the analysis. When the question asks for a maximum number, the correct answer will not be the lowest number.
   (B) See the analysis.
   (C) See the analysis.
   (D) * See the analysis.
   (E) See the analysis.

Chi	F/G	___	___ J/L/O	~~B~~
Dnv	F/G	B	___ J/L/O	B
C or J				

Fig. 2

11. (C) – B can only be in Denver. J, L, and O can all be with B. C can never be in Denver. This means we can eliminate two answer choices. Both F and G are permitted to be exhibited with B.
(A) This choice lists G, but not F, yet F is just as likely as G to be with B.
(B) C can never be in Denver.
(C) * This is an accurate list of all the paintings that can be exhibited with B, every painting except C.
(D) C can never be in Denver.
(E) This choice lists neither F nor G.

SECTION I

Time—35 minutes

22 Questions

Directions: Each group of questions in this section is based on a set of conditions. In answering some of the questions, it may be useful to draw a rough diagram. Choose the response that most accurately and completely answers each question and blacken the corresponding space on your answer sheet.

Questions 1–5

For the annual school fundraising event, four student clubs will each prepare a different food. The clubs are the archery club, the chess club, the dance club, and the French club. Each of the four foods—lemon pie, melon balls, nachos, and omelettes—can only be prepared once by one club, and each food must be completed before the next food can be prepared. The following conditions apply:

If the archery club prepares the first food, the chess club prepares melon balls.

The nachos are prepared immediately before the melon balls are prepared.

Exactly one club prepares food between the archery club and the dance club.

Exactly one club prepares food between the French club and the chess club.

Neither the dance club nor the chess club prepares the first food.

1. Which one of the following is an acceptable pairing of the clubs and the food they prepare, in the order they are prepared, from first to last?

(A) French club: nachos; dance club: melon balls; chess club: omelettes; archery club: lemon pie
(B) Dance club: lemon pie; chess club: nachos; archery club: melon balls; French club: omelettes
(C) French club: lemon pie; archery club: omelettes; dance club: nachos; chess club: melon balls
(D) French club: omelettes; archery club: melon balls; chess club: nachos: dance club: lemon pie
(E) Archery club: omelettes; chess club: nachos; dance club: melon balls; French club: lemon pie

2. Which one of the following could be true?

(A) The archery club prepares nachos immediately before the dance club prepares a food.
(B) The French club prepares omelettes immediately after the nachos are prepared.
(C) The dance club prepares nachos immediately after the lemon pie is prepared.
(D) The chess club prepares lemon pie immediately after the omelettes are prepared.
(E) The chess club prepares nachos immediately before the French club prepares a food.

3. Which of the following CANNOT be true of the omelettes?

(A) They are prepared by the French club immediately after the archery club prepares lemon pie.
(B) They are prepared by the archery club immediately after the dance club prepares nachos.
(C) They are prepared by the chess club immediately after the archery club prepares melon balls.
(D) They are prepared by the chess club immediately before the dance club prepares lemon pie.
(E) They are prepared by the dance club immediately after the chess club prepares melon balls.

4. If the dance club prepares the second food, then which one of the following could be true?

(A) The French club prepares melon balls.
(B) The chess club prepares nachos.
(C) The archery club prepares nachos.
(D) The dance club prepares a food immediately after the archery club prepares a food.
(E) The archery club prepares the first food.

5. If the chess club does not prepare the third food, then each of the following could be true EXCEPT:

(A) The archery club prepares nachos.
(B) The French club prepares lemon pie.
(C) The archery club prepares omelettes.
(D) The dance club prepares omelettes.
(E) The dance club prepares melon balls.

GO ON TO THE NEXT PAGE.

SECTION I
Time—35 minutes
22 Questions

Directions: Each group of questions in this section is based on a set of conditions. In answering some of the questions, it may be useful to draw a rough diagram. Choose the response that most accurately and completely answers each question and blacken the corresponding space on your answer sheet.

Questions 1–5

For the annual school fundraising event, four student clubs will each prepare a different food. The clubs are the archery club, the chess club, the dance club, and the French club. Each of the four foods—lemon pie, melon balls, nachos, and omelettes—can only be prepared once by one club, and each food must be completed before the next food can be prepared. The following conditions apply:

If the archery club prepares the first food, the chess club prepares melon balls.
The nachos are prepared immediately before the melon balls are prepared.
Exactly one club prepares food between the archery club and the dance club.
Exactly one club prepares food between the French club and the chess club.
Neither the dance club nor the chess club prepares the first food.

1. Which one of the following is an acceptable pairing of the clubs and the food they prepare, in the order they are prepared, from first to last?

(A) French club: nachos; dance club: melon balls; chess club: omelettes; archery club: lemon pie
(B) Dance club: lemon pie; chess club: nachos; archery club: melon balls; French club: omelettes
(C) French club: lemon pie; archery club: omelettes; dance club: nachos; chess club: melon balls
(D) French club: omelettes; archery club: melon balls; chess club: nachos: dance club: lemon pie
(E) Archery club: omelettes; chess club: nachos; dance club: melon balls; French club: lemon pie

2. Which one of the following could be true?

(A) The archery club prepares nachos immediately before the dance club prepares a food.
(B) The French club prepares omelettes immediately after the nachos are prepared.
(C) The dance club prepares nachos immediately after the lemon pie is prepared.
(D) The chess club prepares lemon pie immediately after the omelettes are prepared.
(E) The chess club prepares nachos immediately before the French club prepares a food.

3. Which of the following CANNOT be true of the omelettes?

(A) They are prepared by the French club immediately after the archery club prepares lemon pie.
(B) They are prepared by the archery club immediately after the dance club prepares nachos.
(C) They are prepared by the chess club immediately after the archery club prepares melon balls.
(D) They are prepared by the chess club immediately before the dance club prepares lemon pie.
(E) They are prepared by the dance club immediately after the chess club prepares melon balls.

4. If the dance club prepares the second food, then which one of the following could be true?

(A) The French club prepares melon balls.
(B) The chess club prepares nachos.
(C) The archery club prepares nachos.
(D) The dance club prepares a food immediately after the archery club prepares a food.
(E) The archery club prepares the first food.

5. If the chess club does not prepare the third food, then each of the following could be true EXCEPT:

(A) The archery club prepares nachos.
(B) The French club prepares lemon pie.
(C) The archery club prepares omelettes.
(D) The dance club prepares omelettes.
(E) The dance club prepares melon balls.

GO ON TO THE NEXT PAGE

Clubs and foods

This game may have been confusing at first, but a well-organized diagram will simplify it. The diagram requires two sets of four dashes each. The club name will be on the top line, while the food name will be on the bottom line. Scan the rules. Rules 3 and 4 are important because they simplify the diagram. A and D are separated by one other club, and F and C are separated by one other club. Although we don't know much yet, this information will prove useful once we read Rule 5, neither D nor C is first. This allows us to conclude that either F is first or A is first, and either D or C is third. Turning to Rule 2, N is immediately before M, so N cannot be fourth and M cannot be first. (Figure 1) Rule 1 is a conditional rule. Refer to Rule 1 whenever A is the first club.

F/A	__	C/D	__
__	__	__	__
~~M~~			~~N~~

Fig. 1

1. (A) – This question asks for a valid and permissible order. Work through each rule to eliminate one answer choice.
   (A) * This is a valid order. It does not violate any rules.
   (B) Rule 5 specifies that D cannot be first.
   (C) Rule 3 specifies that A and D are separated by one other club.
   (D) Rule 2 specifies that the melon balls be prepared after the nachos.
   (E) Rule 1 specifies that if A is first, then C prepares melon balls, not nachos.

2. (C) – Absent new information, the answer choices should be easy to eliminate using the initial analysis and the rules.
   (A) A and D must be separated by one other club.
   (B) This choice violates Rule 2.
   (C) * This is permissible, see figure 2.
   (D) When you try to create a diagram where C prepares lemon pie after the omelettes are prepared, you find that it is not possible.
   (E) One other club must separate C and F.

F	D	C	A
L	N	M	O
~~M~~			~~N~~

Fig. 2

3. (B) – It may be necessary to create new diagrams to answer this question.
(A) Can F be immediately after A? Yes, if A is first. When A is first, then Rule 1 requires that C prepare melon balls. This is a valid permutation. The omelettes and lemon pie have no special restrictions.
(B) * Can A be immediately after D? Never.
(C) C can be immediately after A. A would have to be second, so as to allow F to make nachos.
(D) C can be third, and D could be fourth. F would be first and A would be second. F makes nachos, and A makes melon balls.
(E) This is a permissible order. C would be third, D would be fourth, F would be first and F would prepare lemon pie.

4. (B) – When D is second, A is fourth, F is first, and C is third. The only other thing we know is that nachos must be immediately before melon balls.
(A) Melon balls cannot ever be first.
(B) * C could prepare nachos. D would then prepare melon balls.
(C) Since A is last, A cannot prepare nachos.
(D) D is second and A is fourth.
(E) A is fourth, not first.

5. (E) – If C is not third, then C must be second or fourth. D must be third. A must be first. Since A is first, then C must prepare melon balls. See the diagrams below for more information. If C is second, then we have figure 3a. If C is fourth, then we have figure 3b.
(A) A can prepare nachos.
(B) F can prepare lemon pie.
(C) A can prepare omelettes, in figure 3b.
(D) D can prepare omelettes, in figure 3a.
(E) * D cannot prepare melon balls in either scenario.

A	C	D	F
N	M	__	__
~~M~~			~~N~~

Fig. 3a

A	F	D	C
__	__	N	M
~~M~~			~~N~~

Fig. 3b

Questions 7–11

A travel agent is assigning seats for clients to sit in during a charter flight. There are three rows of available seats numbered 1, 2, and 3, and each row has a window seat, a center seat, and an aisle seat. Each of the eight clients—J, K, L, M, N, O P, and Q—are assigned exactly one seat and two clients are not assigned to sit in the same seat.

J sits in the row immediately in front of the row K sits in.
M sits in the same row as K.
If N sits in an aisle seat, L sits in a window seat and if L sits in an aisle seat, N sits in a window seat.
P sits next to the empty seat and next to N.
Q sits in the aisle seat of the third row.

7. Which one of the following could be a complete and accurate list of clients assigned to sit in the aisle seats, listed in order from row 1 to row 3?

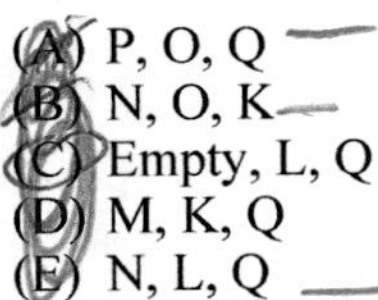

(A) P, O, Q
(B) N, O, K
(C) Empty, L, Q
(D) M, K, Q
(E) N, L, Q

8. If J is assigned to sit in an aisle seat, then each one of the following could be true EXCEPT:

(A) N sits in an aisle seat.
(B) P sits in a center seat.
(C) N sits in an aisle seat and L sits in a center seat.
(D) One aisle seat is empty.
(E) M sits in a center seat and L sits in a center seat.

9. If J is not assigned to sit immediately next to O, which one of the following must be true?

(A) J sits in an aisle seat.
(B) N sits in a window seat.
(C) O sits in a window seat.
(D) M sits immediately behind J.
(E) K sits immediately behind O.

10. If O is assigned to sit in the seat immediately behind P, then each of the following could be true EXCEPT:

(A) L sits immediately behind N.
(B) J sits immediately behind the empty seat.
(C) L sits immediately beside J.
(D) J sits immediately beside O.
(E) N sits in a window seat.

11. If K sits in the seat immediately behind the seat that J sits in, which one of the following statements cannot be true?

(A) J sits immediately behind the empty seat.
(B) L sits immediately behind the empty seat.
(C) M sits immediately behind the seat O sits in.
(D) J sits immediately behind the seat P sits in.
(E) Q sits immediately behind the seat O sits in.

GO ON TO THE NEXT PAGE.

Questions 7–11

A travel agent is assigning seats for clients to sit in during a charter flight. There are three rows of available seats numbered 1, 2, and 3, and each row has a window seat, a center seat, and an aisle seat. Each of the eight clients—J, K, L, M, N, O P, and Q—are assigned exactly one seat and two clients are not assigned to sit in the same seat.

J sits in the row immediately in front of the row K sits in.
M sits in the same row as K.
If N sits in an aisle seat, L sits in a window seat and if L sits in an aisle seat, N sits in a window seat.
P sits next to the empty seat and next to N.
Q sits in the aisle seat of the third row.

7. Which one of the following could be a complete and accurate list of clients assigned to sit in the aisle seats, listed in order from row 1 to row 3?

(A) P, O, Q
(B) N, O, K
(C) Empty, L, Q
(D) M, K, Q
(E) N, L, Q

8. If J is assigned to sit in an aisle seat, then each one of the following could be true EXCEPT:

(A) N sits in an aisle seat.
(B) P sits in a center seat.
(C) N sits in an aisle seat and L sits in a center seat.
(D) One aisle seat is empty.
(E) M sits in a center seat and L sits in a center seat.

9. If J is not assigned to sit immediately next to O, which one of the following must be true?

(A) J sits in an aisle seat.
(B) N sits in a window seat.
(C) O sits in a window seat.
(D) M sits immediately behind J.
(E) K sits immediately behind O.

10. If O is assigned to sit in the seat immediately behind P, then each of the following could be true EXCEPT:

(A) L sits immediately behind N.
(B) J sits immediately behind the empty seat.
(C) L sits immediately beside J.
(D) J sits immediately beside O.
(E) N sits in a window seat.

11. If K sits in the seat immediately behind the seat that J sits in, which one of the following statements cannot be true?

(A) J sits immediately behind the empty seat.
(B) L sits immediately behind the empty seat.
(C) M sits immediately behind the seat O sits in.
(D) J sits immediately behind the seat P sits in.
(E) Q sits immediately behind the seat O sits in.

GO ON TO THE NEXT PAGE

Airplane seats

It may have taken you a few moments to get your bearings with this game. There are three rows, and each row has a window seat, a center seat, and an aisle seat. There are nine seats, but only eight people to fill them, so the empty seat will make things a little more difficult. Diagram the three rows of three seats. (Figure 1a) There are quite a few rules to work with. Start with the anchor rule, Q is in the aisle of the third row. This means that the group comprised of N, P, and the empty seat cannot fill the third row. Can they be in the second row? No. J is in the row immediately in front of K. The only way to accommodate J and K as well as N, P, and the empty seat, is for J to be in the second row, with K and M in the third row with Q. The first row is the only one with three seats available for N, P, and the empty seat. (Figure 1b) This makes the diagram fairly complete. The major difficulty now will be keeping track of tricky Rule 3, which influences the location of N and L.

Win	Cent	Aisle	
___	___	___	~~K~~ ~~M~~
___	___	___	
___	___	Q	~~J~~

Fig. 1a

Win	Cent	Aisle	
N/x	P	x/N	
___	___	___	J & O & L
___	___	Q	K & M

Fig. 1b

7. (C) – Use each rule to eliminate one answer choice. Although the question asks about the aisle seats, make sure with each answer choice that you also consider what is going on with the window seats.
   (A) Rule 4 forces P to always be in the middle seat.
   (B) Q must sit in the aisle seat of row three. This choice violates Rule 5.
   (C) * This is a valid ordering. Because L sits in the aisle seat, N must sit in the window seat, which means the empty seat in the first row must be on the aisle.
   (D) This choice violates Rule 2.
   (E) This choice violates Rule 3.

8. (C) – J is in the second row. Although J is in the aisle seat, this will not trigger Rule 3 and thereby influence the locations of N and L. The options are still wide open. Because L can no longer sit in the aisle seat, N may sit in either the aisle seat or the window seat.
(A) N may sit in the aisle seat.
(B) P must always sit in the center seat.
(C) * N may sit in the aisle seat; but if he does, then L is must sit in a window seat, per Rule 3.
(D) It is possible for the aisle seat in row 1 to be empty.
(E) It is possible for L and M to both be in center seats.

9. (B) – In order for J to not sit next to O, they must be separated by L, who will sit in the center seat. Since L is now in the center seat, N cannot sit in the aisle seat (Rule 3), so N will sit in the window seat.
(A) J may sit in an aisle seat, but this is not required.
(B) * N must sit in the window seat.
(C) O is like J; O may or may not sit in the aisle seat.
(D) Since the location of J and O are not fixed and the location of K and M are not fixed, this is only a possibility, not a requirement.
(E) See (D).

10. (C) – If O is immediately behind P, then O is in the center seat of row 2. Hence, L and J are to either side of O.
(A) If N and L are both in the window seats, then L can sit behind N.
(B) If N and L are both in the window seats, J can sit behind the empty seat.
(C) * Since O is in the center seat of row 2, L and J cannot be next to each other.
(D) J must sit next to O.
(E) N may sit in a window seat.

11. (A) – There are two places K can be, the window seat or the aisle seat. If K is in the center seat, then J is also in the window seat. By having J in the window seat, L is not able to be in the window seat, which means that N must not be in the aisle seat. So, N is in the window seat. Alternatively, if K is in the center seat and J is in the center seat, this allows N and L to be wherever they like.
(A) * J sits behind either N or P, but never the empty seat.
(B) L can sit behind the empty seat.
(C) M can sit behind the seat O sits in.
(D) J sits behind P in all but one of the permutations.
(E) Q can sit behind O.

Conclusion of multiple lines

Points to remember:

There is always at least one multiple line game in each section.

The most common multiple line diagram has five columns with two spaces under each column.

Often there are fewer members then there are spaces to fill. If so, one or more members will be used more than once.

There may be more members than there are spaces to fill. This is very unusual.

The simple line rules are also used in the multiple lines.

The important conclusions in a multiple line diagram can only be made after considering the overlap and interactions of two or more rules, unlike the simple lines, where a conclusion might sometimes be based on the effect of a single rule.

You have now finished a comprehensive introduction for the multiple line games. You have learned what the setups look like, what the rules look like, and what the questions look like. You have learned how to draw the diagrams, how to depict the rules, and how to make additional conclusions.

Some of the information you have learned will not sink in until you do practice games, so plan to review this section as you practice the multiple lines in the tests found later in the book.

Grouping Games

Give yourself 8 minutes and 45 seconds to solve as many questions as you can in the following game. When time is up, review the explanations that follow. Using this game as a starting point, you will learn the different ways grouping games are tested and how to complete a grouping game quickly and effectively. This will be followed by a series of exercises so you can practice what you learned. You will finish by doing two more grouping games under timed conditions and reviewing your work.

SECTION I

Time—35 minutes

22 Questions

Directions: Each group of questions in this section is based on a set of conditions. In answering some of the questions, it may be useful to draw a rough diagram. Choose the response that most accurately and completely answers each question and blacken the corresponding space on your answer sheet.

Questions 1–5

A textbook publisher will print five of the textbooks in its catalog. The books to be printed will be selected from among four physics books—C, D, F, and G—and three history books—N, P, and Q. The final selection of books to be printed is determined in accordance with the following policies:

At least two textbooks from each of the two subjects must be printed.
If C is printed, then D is printed.
If G is printed, then Q is not printed.
If F is printed, then P is printed.

1. Which one of the following could be an accurate list of the books that are printed?

(A) C, F, G, N, P
(B) C, D, F, N, Q
(C) D, F, G, N, Q
(D) C, D, G, N, P
(E) C, D, F, G, N

2. Which one of the following must be printed?

(A) D
(B) F
(C) G
(D) C
(E) Q

3. If C is printed, then which one of the following must also be printed?

(A) F
(B) G
(C) N
(D) P
(E) Q

4. If exactly two physics books are printed, which one of the following must be false?

(A) C is printed.
(B) D is printed.
(C) G is printed.
(D) N is printed.
(E) Q is printed.

5. If N is printed, then how many possible printing selections can be made?

(A) two
(B) three
(C) four
(D) five
(E) six

GO ON TO THE NEXT PAGE.

SECTION I
Time—35 minutes
22 Questions

Directions: Each group of questions in this section is based on a set of conditions. In answering some of the questions, it may be useful to draw a rough diagram. Choose the response that most accurately and completely answers each question and blacken the corresponding space on your answer sheet.

Questions 1–5

A textbook publisher will print five of the textbooks in its catalog. The books to be printed will be selected from among four physics books—C, D, F, and G—and three history books—N, P, and Q. The final selection of books to be printed is determined in accordance with the following policies:

At least two textbooks from each of the two subjects must be printed.
If C is printed, then D is printed.
If G is printed, then Q is not printed.
If F is printed, then P is printed.

1. Which one of the following could be an accurate list of the books that are printed?

(A) C, F, G, N, P
(B) C, D, F, N, Q
(C) D, F, G, N, Q
(D) C, D, G, N, P
(E) C, D, F, G, N

2. Which one of the following must be printed?

(A) D
(B) F
(C) G
(D) C
(E) Q

3. If C is printed, then which one of the following must also be printed?

(A) F
(B) G
(C) N
(D) P
(E) Q

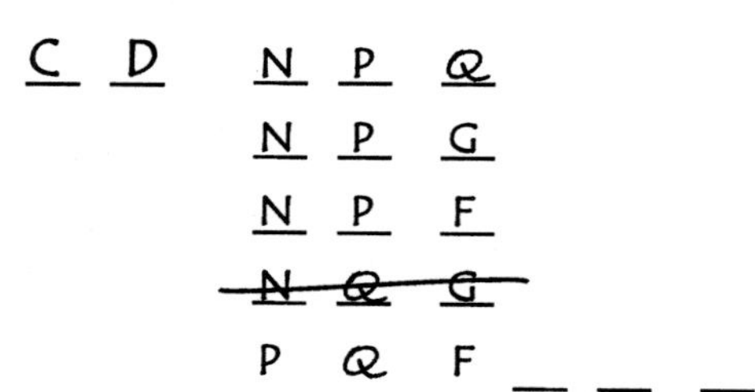

4. If exactly two physics books are printed, which one of the following must be false?

(A) C is printed.
(B) D is printed.
(C) G is printed.
(D) N is printed.
(E) Q is printed.

5. If N is printed, then how many possible printing selections can be made?

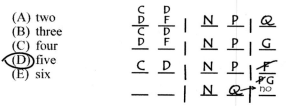

(A) two
(B) three
(C) four
(D) five
(E) six

GO ON TO THE NEXT PAGE.

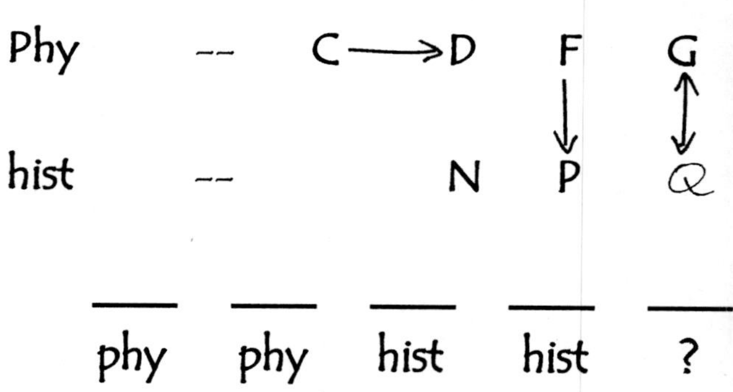

Textbook selection

This game is a standard grouping game. The setup dictates that five books will be printed. There are seven books to choose from. Grouping games in which you select a small final group from a large starting group(s) are called *selection* grouping games. Later, you will see a grouping game where you assign all the members of the large starting group to three or four ending groups. That kind of game is an *assignment* grouping game. Now, back to the game at hand. Draw five dashes for the final group of five books. Then make a line with the names of the physics books and one for the history books. (Figure 1a) Review the rules. Rule 1 dictates that at least two books from each category will be printed. This is reflected in figure 1a by writing "physics" and "history" under the dashes and reserving two dashes for each of them by drawing the vertical lines. The question mark under the fifth dash indicates that we don't know which category the fifth book will be from. Rule 2 requires a one-way arrow from C to D, if C is printed, then D is printed. Rule 3 requires a negative arrow connecting G and Q because if G is printed Q is not printed (and if Q is printed G is not printed.) The "x" on the arrow between G and Q shows that this is a negative arrow. Rule 4 requires a one-way arrow from F to P. The hallmark of grouping games is these arrows that connect members. There are three types of arrows: one-way arrows, like the one from C to D and from F to P; two-way arrows, of which there are none in this game; and negative two-way arrows, like the one connecting G and Q.

You should pause after diagramming the rules and decide if there are any obvious conclusions to be made. You could have concluded that D must always be selected. You could also have concluded that P must always be selected. (Figure 1b) Do not worry if you failed to make these conclusions; the questions are still answerable–but they are much easier if you first make these conclusions.

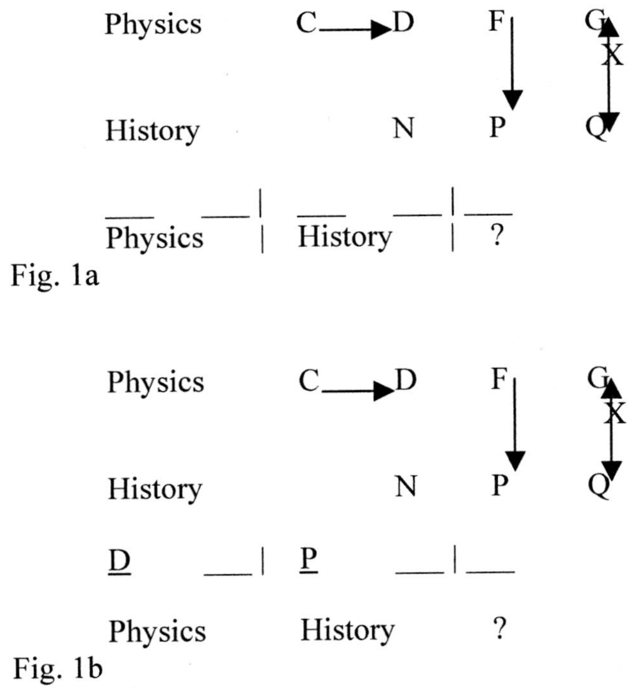

Fig. 1a

Fig. 1b

1. (D) – For this question, you can use each rule to eliminate one answer choice.
   (A) This violates Rule 2 by selecting C but not D.
   (B) This violates Rule 4 by selecting F but not P.
   (C) This violates Rule 3 by selecting G and Q.
   (D) * This is a valid selection.
   (E) This violates Rule 1 because it only has one history book. It also violates Rule 4 by selecting F but not P.

2. (A) – If you did the initial analysis correctly, you already knew that D must be printed. If not, you could figure it out now by trying to do a permutation that excludes the member named in each answer choice.
   (A) * It is impossible to make a permutation without using D: If D is not printed, then C is not printed (Rule 1). Since at least two physics books are printed, both F and G must be printed. Now, if G is printed, then Q is not (Rule 3). Thus, we have excluded three of the seven books: C, D, and Q. Since five books must be printed, this is impossible.
   (B) It is possible to avoid using F, for example: C, D, G, N, P.
   (C) It is possible to avoid using G, for example, C, D, F, N, P.
   (D) It is possible to avoid using C, for example, D, F, G, N, P.
   (E) It is possible to avoid using Q, see all three examples listed above.

3. (D) – Although this question adds new information, it is actually answerable using the initial analysis. If you did not initially conclude that P must always be printed, you must do all four permutations in which C is used.
   (A) F is not necessary. C, D, G, N, P.
   (B) G is not necessary. C, D, N, P, Q.
   (C) N is not necessary. C, D, F, P, Q.
   (D) * P is necessary.
   (E) Q is not necessary. C, D, G, N, P.

4. (C) – If exactly two physics books are printed, then all three history books– N, P, and Q–are printed. When Q is printed, G cannot be printed. That leaves C, D, and F, from which we must select two. We can either select C and D, or D and F.
   (A) C may or may not be printed.
   (B) D may or may not be printed.
   (C) * G cannot be printed, because Q is printed.
   (D) N must be printed.
   (E) Q must be printed.

5. (D) – If N is printed, then how may permutations can be made? The fastest way to solve this is simply to do the permutations and then count them. Start with N, P, and Q. Either C and D or D and F can be with them. That makes two permutations. Now try N and P, without Q. Either C, D, and G, or D, F, and G can be with both N and P. That makes a total of four permutations. Also, N and P can be with C, D, and F. That makes five permutations. Finally, try N and Q without P. This doesn't work, since we can't get three physics books because we cannot use F or G.
   (A) See the analysis.
   (B) See the analysis.
   (C) See the analysis.
   (D) * See the analysis. For a "maximum number" question, the correct answer is normally the second-highest or third-highest number. Since the answers are always listed from least to greatest, the correct answer choice will normally be (C) or (D).
   (E) See the analysis.

The setups for grouping games

Simple line games and multiple line games have so much in common that once you become skilled at simple line games it doesn't take much effort to become skilled at multiple line games. Test takers find the line games to be intuitive, since it is usually easy to visualize and diagram the scenario described by the setup. Grouping games present a challenge because they do not have an obvious diagram. Their setups do not describe a physical order. Because of this, you must be creative when diagramming them. You must also be careful to differentiate between the information that determines the structure and the information about what should be placed on the structure.

There are three types of grouping games, and thus three types of grouping diagrams. *Selection* games require you to select a small group from a large group or groups. There are two varieties of selection games. The first is called a *mono-group selection game*. These games begin with a single group of six or seven members. You must select a group of members, but there is no specific number that must be selected. The second variety of selection game is the *multi-group selection game*. Like the textbook printing game you just did, these begin with two or three groups (the two types of textbooks) that have three or four members each. You must select a specific number of members, usually five, to be the final group of members. *Assignment* games, the third type of grouping game, require you to assign all the members from the one large group to three or four groups.

A typical *mono-group selection game* involves a starting group of six or seven members. The members must be either selected or not selected (chosen for the team/not chosen for the team, etc.). If certain members are selected, certain other members cannot be selected. If certain members are selected, certain others must be selected. There is no definite final number of members that must be selected. Although the questions will ask about the group of members that are chosen, you must pay just as much attention to the members that are not chosen, since you do not want the group of non-chosen members to have any conflicts either. This game is the most common type of grouping game. In the last few years, this type of grouping game has been tested more often then the other two types combined. A typical diagram looks like this:

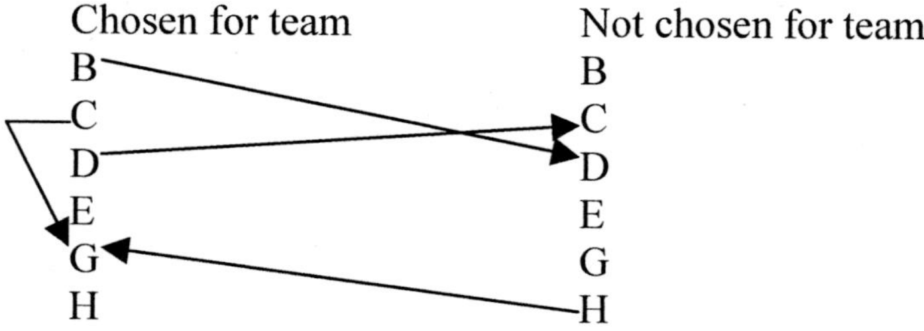

A typical *multi-group selection game* has two or three starting groups, each with three to five members. The textbook game we just studied is a multi-group selection game. The rules will specify the number of members that can be selected from each group and the total number of members that must be selected. A typical diagram looks like this:

Group A: R → P Q S

Group B: W X Y Z

Final group: __ __ __ __ __

A typical *assignment grouping game* also has two groups. The first group of members (usually people) normally has six or seven members. These members should be listed at the top of the diagram. The other group (usually some kind of activity the people will do, or locations they will go) normally has three or four members. These members should be listed on the line below. Although the setup will not state how many people are assigned to each of the activities, it is important that you work with the rules to determine how many people are assigned to each activity. For example, you may be able to conclude that exactly one person is assigned to activity W, or that either two or three people are assigned to activity X. Always do the math to determine the occupancy requirement for each of the activities. Occupancy limits are critical for answering the questions.

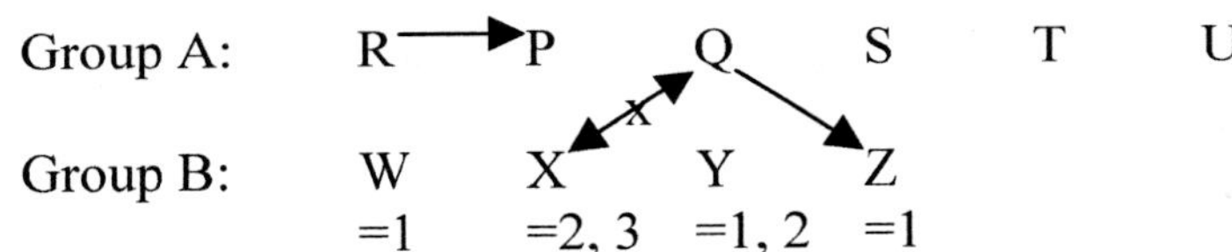

Selection games are more common than assignment games. Occasionally, a grouping game takes a slightly different form or is used in a hybrid game. But for now, you should focus on these three common formats. Review the following examples of typical grouping games:

The following is a basic multi-group selection game.
"A coach must select five players to play in the co-ed basketball game. The players will be selected from among four boys—R, P, Q, and S—and four girls—W, X, Y, and Z. Selection of the players is governed by the following requirements:"

Group A: R P Q S

Group B: W X Y Z

Final group: __ __ __ __ __

The setup tells you how many members must be in the final group. Make a series of dashes below the two groups so that you remember how many members must be selected.

The following setup is a typical mono-group selection game.
"A chamber music orchestra contains six instruments—cello, flute, guitar, harp, oboe, and piccolo. One or more instruments will play pieces of music during the concert. The following conditions determine which instruments will play a piece of music:

Playing	Not playing
C	C
F	F
G	G
H	H
O	O
P	P

The language of the setup leaves open the possibility that some pieces of music require just one instrument while other pieces require several instruments. The rules will tell you which instruments cannot play the same piece of music; this will establish the maximum and minimum number of instruments that must play any given piece of music.

The following is a typical assignment grouping game.
"Seven diners—R, P, Q, S, T, U, and V—will each have exactly one of the following four entrees—W, X, Y, and Z. The following conditions determine the entrée ordered by each person:"

Group A: R P Q S T U

Group B: W X Y Z

The assignment setup does not indicate how many people order which meal, but the rules will contain hints that help you determine this.

Sometimes a multi-group selection game has three starting groups.
"A panel of five judges will be appointed. Judges must be drawn from among three lawyers—A, B, and C—three citizens—D, E, and F—and three staffers—H, J, and K. The selection of the judges must satisfy the following criteria:"

A B C

D E F

H J K

— — — — —

Create three lines for the three starting groups. The rules will usually limit how many may be selected from each group. If not, you will be able to make conclusions that limit how many may come from each group.

The rules for grouping games

There are three rules that are unique to grouping games. The following are examples of those rules, but there are always variations, so be flexible and creative. The language of the rule is provided, along with a depiction of how the rule should be diagrammed.

1. "If Adam or Brenda is on the team, the other is also on the team."
   A ⟷ B or A+B

   This rule is very straightforward. In any situation where either A or B is in the final group, then the other one must also be in the group.

   This may also be phrased as, "Adam and Brenda are on the same team."

2. "Adam is on the team if Brenda is on the team."
   B ⟶ A

   This is a one-way arrow. If B is on the team, then A must be on the team. The common mistake students make is thinking that since A happens to be on the team, then B must also be on the team. Those students confuse this one-way arrow rule with the two-way arrow rule. Also, remember the corollary; if A is not on the team, then it is not possible for B to be on the team.

3. "If Adam is on the team, Brenda is not on the team."
   A ◀—x—▶ B

   Although this rule says that if A is on the team then B is not on the team, it is equally true that if B is on the team then A cannot be on the team. Think about it in simple terms. If A is on the team, then B is not on the team. If B happens to be on the team, then this means that A must not be on the team.

   This may also be phrased as, "A and B are not both selected for the team."
   For mono-group selection games that use the two-column format, this rule is graphed as a one-way arrow from the A in the first column ("selected for the team") to the B in the second column ("not selected for the team"). Also,

remember to graph an arrow from B in the first column to A in the second column.

Once you read the setup and rules, and have diagrammed the rules, the next step is to make the vital conclusions that will add more information to your diagram.

Additional conclusions for multiple line games

As you learned in the simple line games chapter, there are specific conclusions that flow naturally from each type of rule in a simple line game. For the multiple line games, there is no standard set of conclusions. Instead, you must consider the interplay of two or three rules with each other and with the diagram. Similarly, in grouping games the conclusions also result from the interplay of the rules. The exercises that follow will develop your skill at making these conclusions.

Exercises

Now it is time to practice what you have learned. The following exercises are designed to reinforce the basic concepts for grouping games. There are exercises for diagramming the setup, followed by exercises for diagramming the rules, and finally, exercises that have you do both.

Exercises – setups

Compare your diagrams with the examples that follow this exercise.

1. A scientist is attempting to find a cure for a disease by combining exactly five chemical compounds selected from among three types of containers: test tubes—A, B, and C—beakers—D, E, and G—and pipettes—X, Y, and Z.

2. A dispatcher scheduling taxi routes for the day must assign six taxi drivers—Ari, Boone, Crawford, Dupre, Eagleberger, and Fienes—to at least one of the following taxi stands—the museum, the stadium, and the theater.

3. Each parent on the school board also serves on at least one of three advisory panels. Parents in the first group—R, S, and T—have children who are students in middle school only. Parents in the second group—V, X, and Y—have children who are students in both middle school and high school. There are either two or three parents on each advisory panel.

4. A new model of automobile has at least one additional feature added by the customer at the time the car is purchased. The available additional features include: air horn, black trim, chrome accents, navigation system, racing package, standard transmission, and theft protection.

Answers – setups

The appropriate diagrams for the setups are as follows:

1. **Scientist.** There are three starting groups of three members each. The ending group has five members. This is a typical setup, so it should be familiar to you by now.

tt A B C

b D E G

p X Y Z

__ __ __ __ __

2. **Taxi dispatcher.** Each of the six drivers is assigned to at least one of the three ending groups. Until you read the rules and make additional conclusions, you do not know how many drivers go to each location or how many taxi stands each driver goes to.

A B C D E F

M S T

3. **Parents.** This setup is challenging. The parents are listed in two starting groups. Until you read the rules, you will not know why the distinction between the two types of parents is important. The setup is uncharacteristically vague, saying that there are either two or three parents in each ending group. Also unusual for a grouping game, some of the members can be used more than once (i.e., they serve on more than one panel).

R S T

V X Y

__ __(__)   __ __(__)   __ __(__)

4. **Automobile features.** Since the number of features theoretically ranges from one to seven, do not draw any dashes. Use the two-column format.

Selected	Not selected
A	A
B	B
C	C
N	N
R	R
S	S
T	T

Exercises – rules

Practice diagramming the common rules for grouping games. If you can make additional conclusions, diagram them as well. Compare your diagrams with the examples that follow this exercise.

1. A scientist is attempting to find a cure for a disease by combining exactly five chemical compounds selected from among three types of containers: test tubes—A, B, and C—beakers—D, E, and G—and pipettes—X, Y, and Z.

   At least one compound from each type of container is used.
   If B is used, then neither A nor C is used.
   If E is used, then Z is used.
   If X is used, then Y is not used.

2. A dispatcher scheduling taxi routes for the day must assign six taxi drivers—Ari, Boone, Crawford, Dupre, Eagleberger, and Fienes—to at least one of the following taxi stands— the museum, the stadium, and the theater.

   Ari and Boone are each assigned fewer stands than Crawford.
   Dupre is not assigned to any stand that Eagleberger or Fienes is assigned to.
   If Dupre is assigned to a stand, then Crawford must be assigned to the stand.
   Boone is assigned to the stadium or the theater.

3. Each parent on the school board also serves on at least one of three advisory panels. Parents in the first group—R, S, and T—have children who are in middle school only. Parents in the second group—V, X, and Y—have children who are students in both middle school and high school. There are either two or three parents on each advisory panel.

   At least one parent from each group serves on each panel.
   If R serves on a panel, S serves on the panel.
   X and T do not serve on the same panel.

4. A new model of automobile has at least one additional feature added by the customer at the time the car is purchased. The available additional features include: air horn, black trim, chrome accents, navigation system, racing package, standard transmission, and theft protection.

   Neither black trim nor a navigation system can be added if chrome accents are added.
   If a navigation system is not added, then theft protection must be added.
   If a racing package is added, then standard transmission must be added.

Answers – rules

Appropriate diagrams for the rules are as follows:

1. **Scientist combines compounds.**

The first rule provides a minimum number—at least one compound from each type of container must be used. Note this under the dashes by reserving one dash for each of the three types of container. The second rule is easy, draw a negative arrow from B to A and from B to C. The next rule says that if E is used, then so is Z. This requires a one-way arrow. Finally, if X is used then Y is not used. Draw a two-way negative arrow. There are no obvious conclusions to make yet, so you would proceed to the questions.

At least one compound from each container is used.
If B is used, then neither A nor C is used.
If E is used, then Z is used.
If X is used, then Y is not used.

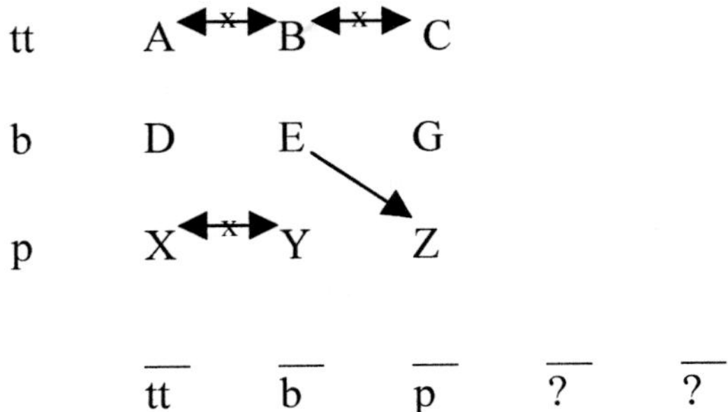

2. **Taxi dispatcher assigns taxis.**

Each taxi driver is assigned to at least one stand, and it seems likely that some will be assigned to more than one. Drivers A and B get fewer stands than C. So, if C has two stands, A and B would each get one stand. But, if C has three stands, then A and B can each have one or two stands. D is not assigned to the same stands as E or F. So, if E and F are both assigned to (the same) two stands, then D is assigned to one (the third) stand. If E and F are both assigned to the same single stand, then D is assigned to either one or two stands. For Rule 4, show where B cannot be assigned, instead of where it could be.

Ari and Boone are each assigned fewer stands than Crawford.
Dupre is not assigned to any stand that Eagleberger or Fienes is assigned to.
If Dupre is assigned to a stand, then Crawford must be assigned to the stand.
Boone is assigned to the stadium or the theater.

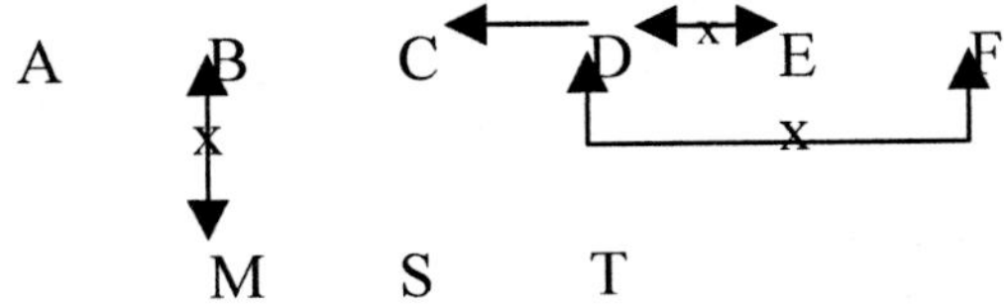

3. **Parents serve on panels.**
Rule 1 is important. It tells you that at least one parent from each of the two groups is on each panel. Diagram this by making three columns of dashes. Reserve the first column for the group of parents with middle school students and the second column for the group of parents with both kinds of students. The third column may or may not be filled for any or all of the panels. The other two rules are easy to diagram. Rule 2 allows us to make two conclusions. The first conclusion is that R and S must serve together on one panel. The second conclusion is that either S alone, or R and S together, must serve on a second panel. We can't easily diagram this, but it is definitely worth remembering. As a final step, you can arbitrarily assign R, S, and T each to one of the three panels, since the spatial location of the panels is irrelevant and we know that every parent must serve on a panel.

At least one parent from each group serves on each panel.
If R serves on a panel, S serves on the panel.
X and T do not serve on any of the same panels.

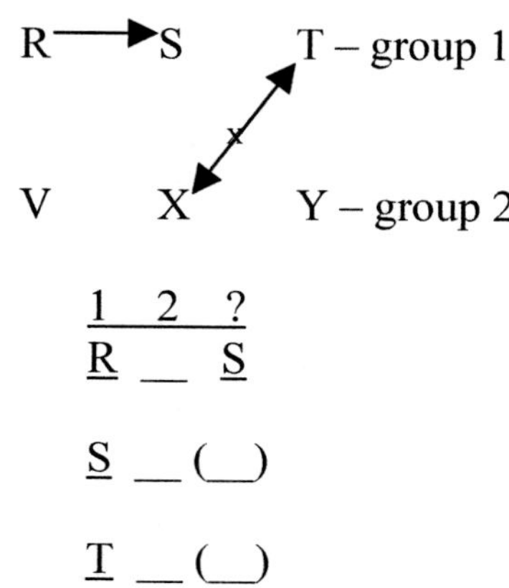

4. Automobile features on a car.

Rule 2 is interesting. It tells you that if N is not added, then T must be added. But N and T could both be added. We can conclude that, at a minimum, either N or T must be added. The other two rules are easy to diagram. In this kind of game it is usually worth the time and effort to figure-out the maximum and minimum number that must be selected, since there is normally a question that will ask this. Here, the maximum is six, when we add all the features except C. The minimum is one, T. The best diagram for this game is a two-column diagram (Figure 1b). Experienced test takers may opt for the diagram in figure 1a, since a single row of members is sometimes quicker to diagram, although it can be more difficult to use.

Neither black trim nor a navigation system is added if chrome accents are added.
If a navigation system is not added, then theft protection must be added.
If a racing package is added, then standard transmission must be added.

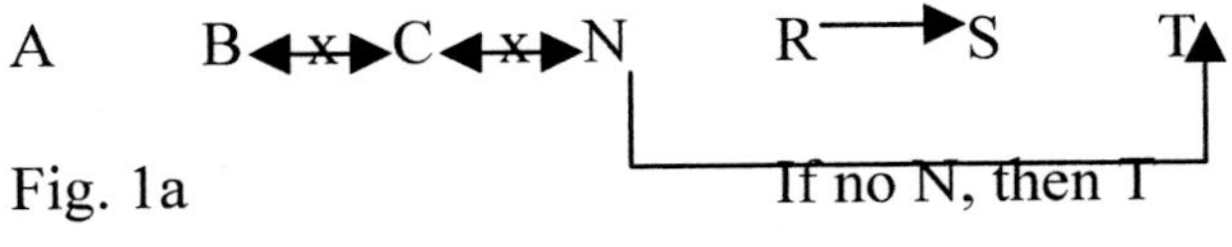

Fig. 1a

Or

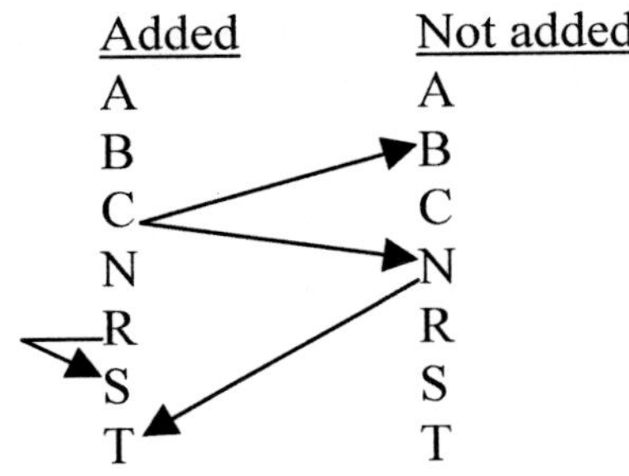

Fig. 1b

Exercises – setups and rules

Diagram the setups and rules. Diagram any additional conclusions you are able to make.

1. During the morning rush hour, five shuttle buses—A, B, C, D, and E—must stop at one, two, or three of the following locations—X, Y, and Z—and stop at no other locations. The following conditions determine where the buses stop:

   A and exactly two other buses stop at X.
   C makes exactly two stops.
   B and C do not stop at the same locations.
   More buses stop at X than stop at Y or stop at Z.

2. Five performers will be selected to play in a band. The band members will be chosen from among three singers—F, G, and H—three guitarists—J, K, and L—and three percussionists—P, Q, and R. The selection of band members must be in accordance with the following requirements:

   No more than two band members may be selected from any of the three types of performers.
   If two guitarists are selected, then one percussionist is selected.
   K and J cannot both be selected.
   If K and L are both selected, then H is selected.
   If either F or P is selected, then the other is also selected.

3. Seven factory workers—A, B, C, D, E, F, and G—serve on exactly one of two committees—the safety committee or the benefits committee. The committee a worker serves on is determined by the following requirements:

   If A serves on the safety committee, then C serves on the benefits committee.
   If B serves on the safety committee, then D serves on the safety committee.
   D serves on a different committee than C serves.
   If E serves on the benefits committee, then F serves on the benefits committee.

Answers – setups and rules

Appropriate diagrams are as follows:

1. During the morning rush hour, five shuttle buses—A, B, C, D, and E—must stop at one, two, or three of the following locations—X, Y, and Z—and stop at no other locations. The following conditions determine where the buses stop:

A and exactly two other buses stop at X.
C makes exactly two stops.
B and C do not stop at the same locations.
More buses stop at X than stop at Y or stop at Z.

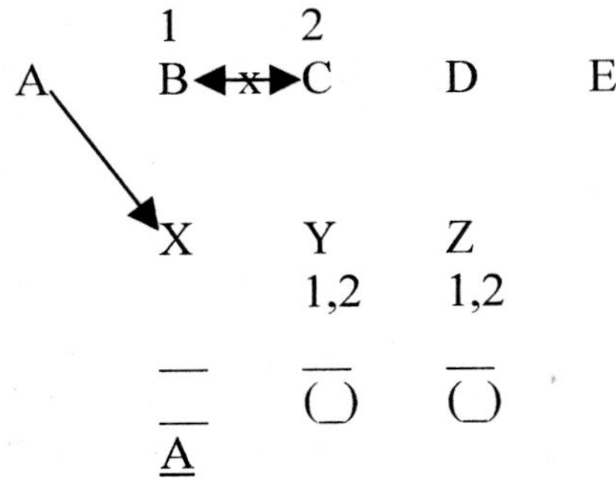

Rule 1 states that bus A must stop at location X and that X has a total of three buses. Draw three dashes under X and put an A on one of them. Rule 2 states that bus C makes exactly two stops. Rule 3 states that B and C do not stop at the same locations. Since C makes two stops, you can conclude that B makes one stop. Note this information above B and C. Finally, in Rule 4, Y and Z get fewer buses than X, thus Y and Z get one or two buses each. Quickly checking the possibilities, we learn that it is not possible for Y and Z to both have just one bus. Thus, one of them has one bus and the other has two, or else they both have two buses.

2. Five performers will be selected to play in a band. The band members will be chosen from among three singers—F, G, and H—three guitarists—J, K, and L—and three percussionists—P, Q, and R. The selection of band members must be in accordance with the following requirements:

No more than two band members may be selected from any of the three types of performers.
If two guitarists are selected, then one percussionist is selected.
K and J cannot both be selected.
If K and L are both selected, then H is selected.
If either F or P is selected, then the other is also selected.

___	___	___	___	___
sing	guit	perc	?	?

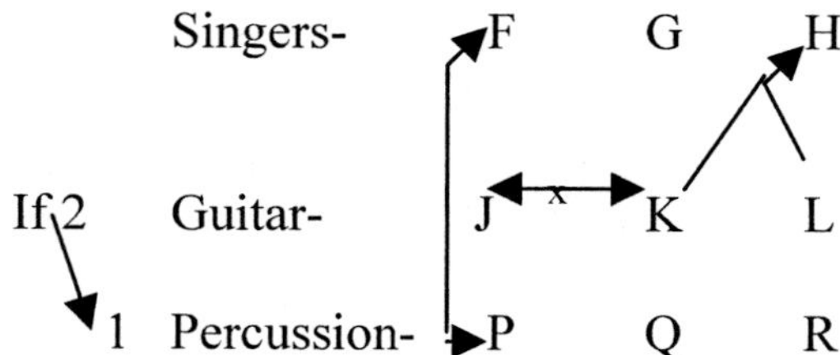

This game has some interesting rules. Rule 1 states that no more than two band members may come from one group. So, for example, if there were two singers and two guitarists, then there is one percussionist. The effect of this rule is that there must be at least one band member from each of the three groups. This is noted under the three dashes. The fourth and fifth spaces are up for grabs. Rule 2 (if there are two guitarists, then is one percussionist) is a bit tricky to diagram. Make a note of it to the side of the guitar group and return to this rule as you work through the questions. Rule 3 requires a negative two-way arrow. Rule 4 is complex and is often graphed incorrectly by students. The diagram shows that both K and L must be selected before it is necessary to select H. The lines from K and L meet, and then point to H. Rule 5 requires a two-way arrow.

3. Seven factory workers—A, B, C, D, E, F, and G—serve on exactly one of two committees—the safety committee or the benefits committee. The committee that a worker serves on is determined by the following requirements:

If A serves on the safety committee, then C serves on the benefits committee.
If B serves on the safety committee, then D serves on the safety committee.
D serves on a different committee then C serves.
If E serves on the benefits committee, then F serves on the benefits committee.

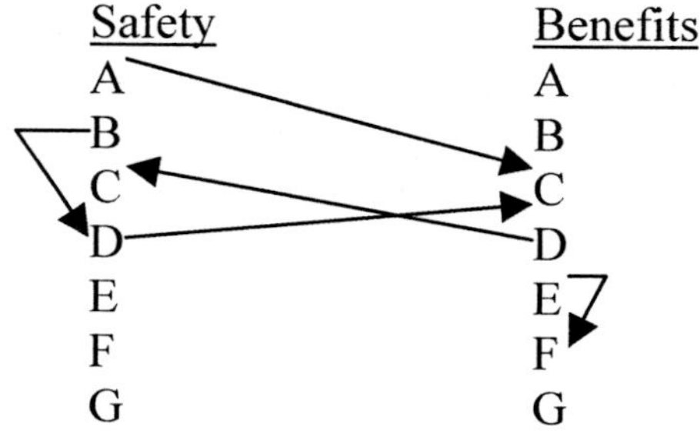

Make one column for the safety committee and one for the benefits committee. For Rule 1, draw a one-way arrow from A in the safety column to C in the benefits column. For Rule 2, draw an arrow from B to D in the safety column. Rule 3 requires D and C to be in opposite columns. Draw arrows from D to C to remind you that either D or C must be in each column. You could draw the arrows from C to D; it makes no difference. For Rule 4, an arrow from E to F in benefits shows the relationship.

Practice games

Spend 8 minutes and 45 seconds answering as many questions as you can in each of the following games. Then review the explanations that follow each game. Compare your answers with the explanations.

SECTION I

Time—35 minutes

22 Questions

Directions: Each group of questions in this section is based on a set of conditions. In answering some of the questions, it may be useful to draw a rough diagram. Choose the response that most accurately and completely answers each question and blacken the corresponding space on your answer sheet.

Questions 1–5

Five students—R, S, T, V, and Y—will register for up to three elective arts courses—composition, dance, and exhibits. Each student will register for at least one course, and each course has at least one student. The three elective courses have a total of exactly nine students. The registration of students for courses is subject to the following limitations:

Dance has exactly one more student then composition.
R registers for composition and for no other course.
T registers for more courses than R.

1. Which one of the following could be an accurate list of the students registered for the three courses?

(A) Composition: S, T
Dance: V, Y, T
Exhibits: R, Y, V, T
(B) Composition: R, S, V
Dance: V, Y, T
Exhibits: T, S, Y
(C) Composition: R, S
Dance: S, Y, V
Exhibits: Y, V, T
(D) Composition: R, S, Y
Dance: S, Y, V, T
Exhibits: S, T
(E) Composition: R, S, V
Dance: S, Y, V, T
Exhibits: S, Y, T

2. If V and Y register for the same courses, which one of the following must be false?

(A) T registers for three courses.
(B) S registers for one course.
(C) V and Y register for composition.
(D) V and Y register for composition and exhibits.
(E) S and T register for composition, dance, and exhibits.

3. If S registers for three courses, each of the following could be true, EXCEPT:

(A) T registers for composition.
(B) V and Y register for composition.
(C) S and T register for the same courses.
(D) V and Y register for exhibits.
(E) T registers for three classes.

4. If S registers for exactly one course, then which one of the following must be true?

(A) S registers for composition.
(B) S registers for dance.
(C) T registers for dance.
(D) V registers for exhibits.
(E) Y registers for composition.

5. If V and Y each register for exactly one course, then which one of the following must be false?

(A) S and T register for composition.
(B) S and T register for exhibits.
(C) T registers for dance.
(D) V registers for dance.
(E) Y registers for exhibits

GO ON TO THE NEXT PAGE.

SECTION I

Time—35 minutes

22 Questions

Directions: Each group of questions in this section is based on a set of conditions. In answering some of the questions, it may be useful to draw a rough diagram. Choose the response that most accurately and completely answers each question and blacken the corresponding space on your answer sheet.

Questions 1–5

Five students—R, S, T, V, and Y—will register for up to three elective arts courses—composition, dance, and exhibits. Each student will register for at least one course, and each course has at least one student. The three elective courses have a total of exactly nine students. The registration of students for courses is subject to the following limitations:

Dance has exactly one more student then composition.
R registers for composition and for no other course.
T registers for more courses than R.

1. Which one of the following could be an accurate list of the students registered for the three courses?

#2 (A) Composition: S, T
Dance: V, Y, T
Exhibits: R, Y, V, T

2/3/4 or 3/4/2

(B) Composition: R, S, V
Dance: V, Y, T
Exhibits: T, S, Y
} 3/3/3

#3 (C) Composition: R, S
Dance: S, Y, V
Exhibits: Y, V, T

(D) Composition: R, S, Y
Dance: S, Y, V, T
Exhibits: S, T

(E) Composition: R, S, V
Dance: S, Y, V, T
Exhibits: S, Y, T
} 10 total

2. If V and Y register for the same courses, which one of the following must be false?

(A) T registers for three courses. see →
(B) S registers for one course. see →
(C) V and Y register for composition.
(D) V and Y register for composition and exhibits.
(E) S and T register for composition, dance, and exhibits.

if V + Y once	if V + Y twice
V + Y	V + Y, V + Y
R	R
S S S	S S (or S)
T T T	T T (or T T T)
9 total	9 total

R = 1   T = 2 or 3

R S T V

C D E   D = C + 1   9 tot.

C	D	E
1	2	6 – no
2	3	4 – ok
3	4	2 – ok
4	5	0 – no

	Comp.			Dance				Exhibit			
no–	__	R		O	S	T		V	Y	S	T
ok–	S	T	R	V	Y	S	T	S	T		
ok–	T S	R		S T	V	Y		V	Y	S	T
ok–	V	Y	R	S	T	V	Y	S	T		

3. If S registers for three courses, each of the following could be true, EXCEPT: see work for Q2

Q2 (A) T registers for composition.
(B) V and Y register for composition.
Q2 (C) S and T register for the same courses.
Q2 (D) V and Y register for exhibits. S R | S T Y V | V Y S
Q2 (E) T registers for three classes.

4. If S registers for exactly one course, then which one of the following must be true? see work for Q2

(A) S registers for composition.
(B) S registers for dance.
(C) T registers for dance.
(D) V registers for exhibits.
(E) Y registers for composition.

C. D. Ex.
T/V/Y R | T V Y | V Y S T
T/V/Y/R V Y S T T/V

5. If V and Y each register for exactly one course, then which one of the following must be false? is dance

Q2 (A) S and T register for composition.
Q2 (B) S and T register for exhibits.
Q2 (C) T registers for dance.
Q2 (D) V registers for dance.
(E) Y registers for exhibits

no – __ R | S S T | S T V Y
yes – S T R | S T V Y | S T

GO ON TO THE NEXT PAGE

Student registrations

This game employs a typical scenario where five members (students) are assigned to three groups (courses). Each student has at least one course, and each course has at least one student. This is very typical, so far. But then things get difficult. There are a total of nine students in the three classes. It is up to us to figure-out the possible arrangements. With that in mind, diagram the three easy rules. Rule 1 states that dance has exactly one more student than composition. This will turn out to be a very important rule. Rule 2 states that R registers for only one class, composition. (Figure 1a) Rule 3 states that T registers for more classes than R. This means T registers for either two or three classes. That is it for the rules, yet the diagram is still sparse. The paucity of rules alerts you to the fact that you must make conclusions in order to answer the questions. So what might those conclusions be? You know that there are nine students in the three classes. Do the math to determine the possible combinations. Start low and work your way up. For example, if composition has one student, then dance must have two students. (Figure 1b) This would mean that exhibits must have six students; but that is impossible, since there are only five students. What if composition had two students? Then dance would have three students and exhibits would have four students. That adds up to nine, so that is a permissible permutation. What if composition had three students? Dance would have four and exhibits would have two. That adds up to nine, so that is fine. Continuing on, we determine that composition cannot have four students. By working through the possibilities in this way, we can determine the occupancy limits, which is always vital for assignment games.

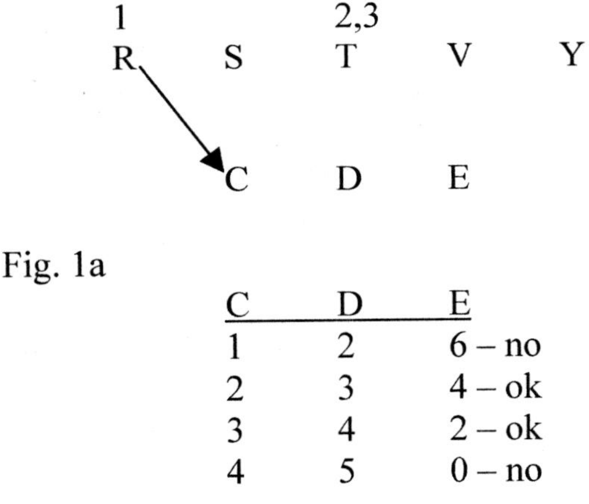

Fig. 1a

C	D	E
1	2	6 – no
2	3	4 – ok
3	4	2 – ok
4	5	0 – no

Fig. 1b

1. (D) – Use each rule to eliminate one answer choice.
   (A) Rule 2 specifies that R must register for composition.
   (B) Rule 1 states that dance has exactly one more student than composition.
   (C) Rule 3 states that T has more courses than R.
   (D) * This is a permissible permutation.
   (E) This choice violates the setup paragraph. This choice has the students enrolled in ten classes, but the enrollment is exactly nine.

2. (D) – Consider the possibilities. Can V and Y each register for one course? Yes, this would be fine. Can V and Y register for two courses? Yes. Can V and Y register for three courses? No. Graph these possibilities. (Figure 2)
(A) T can register for three courses; see the second permutation.
(B) S can register for one course if T registers for two classes and V and Y register for two courses each.
(C) V can register for composition. See the third permutation.
(D) * V and Y cannot register for both composition and exhibits in the same permutation. Doing so would run afoul of the permissible occupancy limits.
(E) S and T can both register for all three courses.

Cmp Dance Exhibits
__ R | __ S T | S T V Y – no

Cmp Dance Exhibits
S T R | S T V Y | S T – ok

Cmp Dance Exhibits
V Y R | S T V Y | S T – ok

Cmp Dance Exhibits
S/T R | S/T V Y | S T V Y – ok (T must be used two or three times, and S used one or two times.)

Fig. 2

3. (B) – It is unnecessary to do new work for this question. Instead, refer to the work you did for question 2. This is why you should do neat work and save it.
(A) The second permutation in figure 2 shows that T can register for composition when S registers for three courses.
(B) * Correct. V and Y cannot both register for composition if S registers for three courses, because S and R will take two of the three available spaces in composition.
(C) The second permutation in figure 2 shows that S and T can be in all three courses together.
(D) V and Y can register for exhibits even if S is in three courses. It is possible if three students are in dance. One will be S, the other will be T, and the third will be either V or Y.
(E) T can be in the same three courses as S, see the second permutation in figure 2.

4. (C) – You could consult figure 2 for guidance for when S is used once. You would soon realize that when S is used once, S must be in the class that has four students. So there are two possibilities, both of which are diagrammed in figure 3.

(A) S cannot register for composition.
(B) S may register for dance.
(C) * T must register for dance.
(D) V may register for exhibits.
(E) Y may register for composition.

Cmp Dance Exhibits
? R | T V Y | S T V Y – ok (? Stands for T, V, or Y.)

Cmp Dance Exhibits
? ? R | S T V Y | ? ? – ok (? Stands for T, V, or Y.) Must be two or three T.

Fig. 3

5. (E) – In question 2 we did the permutations for when V and Y register for exactly one course, so you can use that work to answer this question. You could also do all the work again, if you didn't realize this shortcut was available. We know that if V and Y are used exactly once, they must be used together in the course that has four students. After doing the work, we see that they must both be in dance. (Figure 4)

(A) S and T must both register for composition.
(B) S and T must both register for exhibits.
(C) T must register for dance.
(D) V must register for dance.
(E) * Y cannot register for exhibits.

Cmp Dance Exhibits
S/T R | S T __ | S T V Y – no, nothing can fill the empty space in dance.

Cmp Dance Exhibits
S T R | S T V Y | S T – ok

Fig. 4

Questions 19–23

Seven students—Chandra, Dow, Fowler, Goldfarb, Hylton, Jones, and Kalinski—are visiting a dance club. The students are either inside or outside the club. The exact location of the students must be in accordance with the following conditions:

If Chandra is in the club, then Goldfarb is outside the club.
If Fowler is in the club, then Hylton is in the club.
If Jones is outside the club, Dow is in the club.
If Dow is outside the club, Hylton is in the club.

19. Which one of the following could be a complete and accurate list of those students who are outside the club at the same time?

(A) Chandra, Goldfarb, Jones, Kalinski
(B) Goldfarb, Hylton, Jones
(C) Chandra, Dow, Jones
(D) Dow, Fowler, Goldfarb, Hylton
(E) Dow, Fowler, Kalinski

20. If Dow and Hylton are together, which one of the following must be true?

(A) Chandra is outside the club.
(B) Hylton is inside the club.
(C) Jones is outside the club.
(D) Fowler is inside the club.
(E) Kalinski is outside the club.

21. What is the maximum number of students that can be outside the club at the same time?

(A) three
(B) four
(C) five
(D) six
(E) seven

22. If Goldfarb and Hylton are outside the club, then each of the following pairs of students could also be outside the club EXCEPT:

(A) Fowler and Jones
(B) Dow and Jones
(C) Chandra and Fowler
(D) Jones and Kalinski
(E) Fowler and Kalinski

23. Assume that the original condition that if Fowler is in the club then Hylton is in the club is replaced by the condition that Fowler and Hylton are never together. If all the other initial conditions remain unchanged, what is the maximum number of students that can be outside the club at the same time?

(A) three
(B) four
(C) five
(D) six
(E) seven

GO ON TO THE NEXT PAGE.

S T O P

IF YOU FINISH BEFORE TIME IS CALLED, YOU MAY CHECK YOUR WORK ON THIS SECTION ONLY.
DO NOT WORK ON ANY OTHER SECTION IN THE TEST.

Questions 19–23

Seven students—Chandra, Dow, Fowler, Goldfarb, Hylton, Jones, and Kalinski—are visiting a dance club. The students are either inside or outside the club. The exact location of the students must be in accordance with the following conditions:

If Chandra is in the club, then Goldfarb is outside the club.
If Fowler is in the club, then Hylton is in the club.
If Jones is outside the club, Dow is in the club.
If Dow is outside the club, Hylton is in the club.

19. Which one of the following could be a complete and accurate list of those students who are outside the club at the same time?

(A) Chandra, Goldfarb, Jones, Kalinski
(B) Goldfarb, Hylton, Jones 2
(C) Chandra, Dow, Jones 3
(D) Dow, Fowler, Goldfarb, Hylton 4
(E) Dow, Fowler, Kalinski 1, no G or C

20. If Dow and Hylton are together, which one of the following must be true? - Inside club

(A) Chandra is outside the club.
(B) Hylton is inside the club.
(C) Jones is outside the club.
(D) Fowler is inside the club.
(E) Kalinski is outside the club.

21. What is the maximum number of students that can be outside the club at the same time?

(A) three
(B) four
(C) five
(D) six
(E) seven

six, all except D

22. If Goldfarb and Hylton are outside the club, then each of the following pairs of students could also be outside the club EXCEPT:

(A) Fowler and Jones
(B) Dow and Jones
(C) Chandra and Fowler
(D) Jones and Kalinski
(E) Fowler and Kalinski

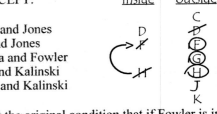

23. Assume that the original condition that if Fowler is in the club then Hylton is in the club is replaced by the condition that Fowler and Hylton are never together. If all the other initial conditions remain unchanged, what is the maximum number of students that can be outside the club at the same time?

(A) three
(B) four
(C) five
(D) six
(E) seven

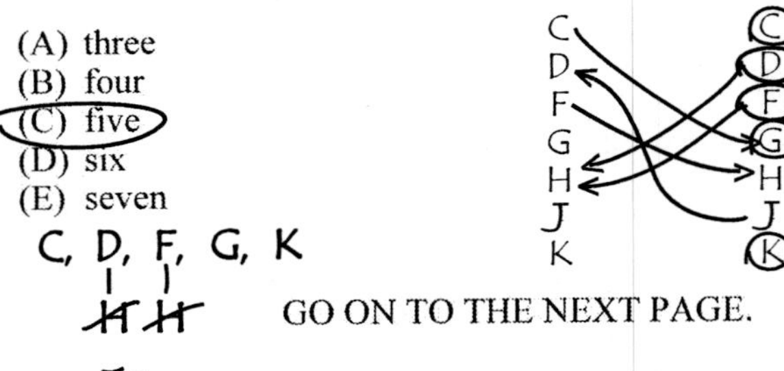

GO ON TO THE NEXT PAGE.

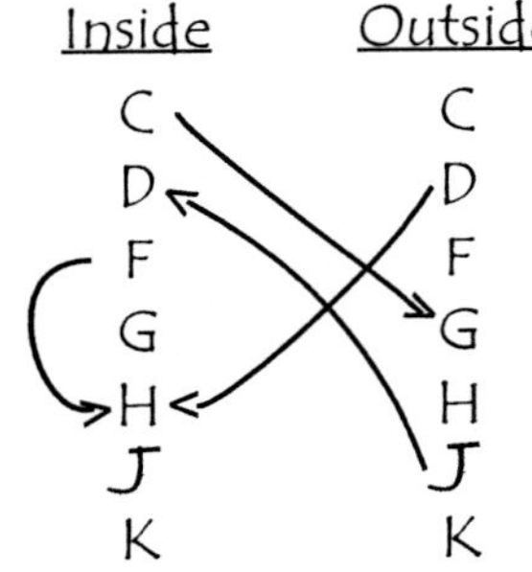

free agent - K

S T O P

IF YOU FINISH BEFORE TIME IS CALLED, YOU MAY CHECK YOUR WORK ON THIS SECTION ONLY.
DO NOT WORK ON ANY OTHER SECTION IN THE TEST.

Dance club students

This is a mono-group selection game. The setup describes seven students that are either inside or outside the dance club. Create a two-column diagram and diagram the rules. (Figure 1) Rule 1 states that if C is in the club, G is outside the club; use a one-way arrow. Rule 2 states that if F is in the club then H is in the club. Another one-way arrow will suffice. Rule 3 states that if J is outside the club then D is in the club. A one-way arrow from J in the outside column will show this. Finally, Rule 4 states that if D is outside the club, then H is inside the club. Notice that K is a free agent and so can be anywhere. Although you could now do some permutations, no useful conclusions emerge. Carefully review the rules when answering each question. Always keep in mind that even if a member is not specifically mentioned in the answer choice, it is just as important as those that are.

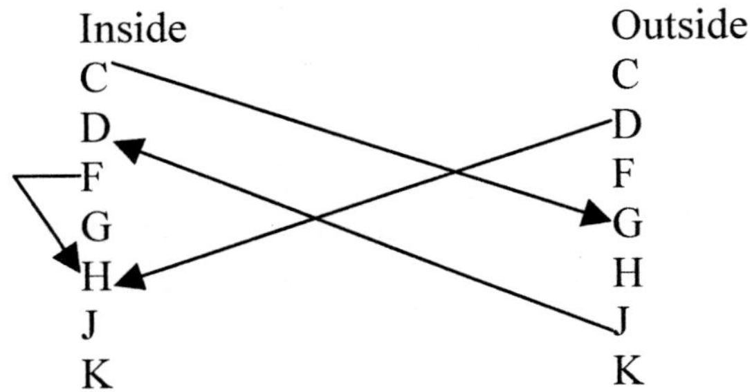

Fig. 1

19. (A) – For the first question in the set, you can normally use each rule to eliminate one answer choice.
    (A)* This group can be outside the club, while all the unnamed members can be inside the club.
    (B) This violates Rule 2 because it has H outside the club, but F inside the club.
    (C) This violates Rule 3 because it has D and J both outside the club.
    (D) This violates Rule 4 because it has D and H both outside the club.
    (E) This violates Rule 1 because it has both C and G inside the club.

20. (B) – Look at the diagram for guidance. If D and H are together, are they outside the club? No, because when D is outside the club, H is supposed to be inside. So, D and H must both be inside the club. Check the answers now, before investing more time, since this minimal analysis may be sufficient.
    (A) C can be either inside or outside.
    (B) * Yes, H must be inside the club with D.
    (C) J can be either inside or outside the club.
    (D) F can be either inside or outside the club.
    (E) K is a free agent and so can always be in either location.

21. (D) – With a maximum number question, start by looking at the "outside the club" column and eliminating any member that cannot be with other members. We see two conflicts. First, D and H cannot both be outside. Second, J and D cannot both be outside. So, by placing D inside the club, H and J can now be outside the club. All the other members can be outside the club. Six members can be outside.

(A) See the analysis. The correct answer to a "maximum" question is never the lowest number.
(B) See the analysis.
(C) See the analysis.
(D) * See the analysis. The correct answer to a "maximum" question is always one of the three highest numbers, and is usually the second or third highest.
(E) See the analysis.

22. (B) – Consulting the "outside the club" column, we don't see any arrows going from G or H to other members. Consulting the "inside the club" column, we see that if H is not inside the club, then F cannot be inside the club, and D cannot be outside the club. As for C, J, and K, they can either be inside or outside.

(A) F must be outside and J can be outside.
(B) * D must be inside the club.
(C) C can be outside and F must be outside.
(D) J and K can both be outside.
(E) F must be outside and K can be outside.

23. (C) – The easiest way to handle this rule change is to create a new diagram from scratch using the old rules and this new rule. To show that F and H are never together, draw a one-way arrow from F in the inside column to H in the outside column and a one-way arrow from F in the outside column to H in the inside column. Now work down the column to find members that conflict. C can be outside; there is no conflict. If D is outside, H cannot be. If F is outside, H cannot be. G can be outside. J cannot be outside if D is outside. K can be outside. So, C, D, F, G, and K can be outside.

(A) See the analysis. The correct answer to a "maximum" question is never the lowest number.
(B) See the analysis.
(C) * See the analysis.
(D) See the analysis.
(E) See the analysis.

Conclusion of grouping games

Points to remember:

Most LSATs have at least one grouping game, and, when a test has one grouping game, it often has two grouping games.

There are thee types of grouping games: games where you assign all the members to three or four ending groups, games where an unspecified number of members of the group must be selected, and games where you must select one group of five or six members from two or three starting groups.

Unlike simple line games, additional conclusions for a grouping game can only be made after considering the overlap and interactions of the rules.

Always be aware of the number of spaces that have to be filled and the number of members available to fill those spaces.

You have now finished a comprehensive introduction to the grouping games. You have learned what the setups look like, what the rules look like, and what the questions look like. You have learned how to draw the diagrams, how to depict the rules, and how to make additional conclusions.

Some of the information you have learned will not sink in until you do practice games, so plan to review this section as you practice the games you will find later in the book.

Review Exercises

You were introduced to many rules in the previous three sections. Test your diagramming skills and identify areas where you need more practice.

Rules review exercise

Compare your diagrams with the examples that follow this exercise.

"A is first or last."

__ __ __ __ __ __

"A is earlier than B."

__ __ __ __ __ __

"A is immediately before B."

__ __ __ __ __ __

"A is next to B."

__ C __ __ __ __

"A is earlier than B and C."

__ __ __ __ __ __

"If A is second, B is fifth."

__ __ __ __ __ __

"Either A or B is fourth."

__ __ __ __ __ __

"A and B are separated by one space."

__ __ __ C __ __ __

"If Sam plays the kazoo, then Roland plays the lyre."

_|_ _|_ _|_ _|_

"The musician playing the kazoo performs immediately after James and immediately before Sam."

_|_ _|_ _|_ _|_

"If a building is gray, then it is Victorian."

— — — — – color

— — — Tudor – type

"If Adam or Brenda is on the team, the other is also on the team."

A B C

R T X Y

— — — —

"Adam is on the team if Brenda is on the team."

A B C

R T X Y

— — — —

"If Adam is on the team, Brenda is not on the team."

A B C

R T X Y

— — — —

Answers to rules review exercise

"A is first or last."

— — — — — —
(A) (A)

Putting the (A) below the line shows that A is a fifty-fifty possibility for either of these two spaces.

"A is earlier than B."

— — — — — —
A<B: ~~B~~ ~~A~~

This is a common rule for simple line games and multiple line games. Test-takers often mistakenly assume that A is immediately before B, instead of just somewhere before B.

"A is immediately before B."

— — — — — —
A B: ~~B~~ ~~A~~

Place the two members next to each other with dashes underneath them. The dashes indicate that A is immediately before B.

"A is next to B."

C
— — — — — —
A B A: ~~A~~
~~B~~

A B A or A B / B A – Use the one you find easier to understand.
This rule does not specify which comes first. Many test-takers mistakenly graph this rule so that it appears that A must be before B, instead of before or after B.
Even though C is second, A or B can be third, as long as the other is fourth.

"A is earlier than B and C."

— — — — — —
~~B~~ ~~A~~ ~~A~~
~~C~~

A < B/C or A < B & A < C – Use the one you find easier to understand.
Test-takers sometimes incorrectly depict this rule as A < B < C.
A cannot be fifth or sixth, because B and C must be to the right of A.

"If A is second, B is fifth."

— — — — — —
(A)————————→(B)

This conditional rule applies only in situations where A is second. As such, even when your diagram shows that B is fifth, it does not necessarily mean A is second. Many test-takers make exactly this mistake. But, if B is not fifth, then A cannot be second.

"Either A or B is fourth."

__ __ __ A/B __ __

Putting them above the line reserves the space, preventing you from putting another member in the space.

"A and B are separated by one space."

__ __ __ C __ __ __

(second space: ~~A~~ ~~B~~; sixth space: ~~A~~ ~~B~~)

A/B __ B/A or A __ B / B __ A

This rule causes test-takers to make one of two mistakes. First, they miscount, thinking there are either no spaces separating the two members (yielding A B) or that there are two spaces separating the two members (yielding A _ _ B). Second, they assume that A must come before B. The presence of C in the fourth space prevents A and B from being second and sixth.

"If Sam plays the kazoo, then Roland plays the lyre."

S | k → R | l

In the circumstance where Sam plays kazoo, then R plays the lyre. This rule says nothing about the order of their appearance, so make sure your diagram does not create the impression that R must be after S.

"The musician playing the kazoo performs immediately after James and immediately before Sam."

R|__ __|k S|__

A long chain of members like this helps anchor your diagram.

"If a building is gray, then it is Victorian."

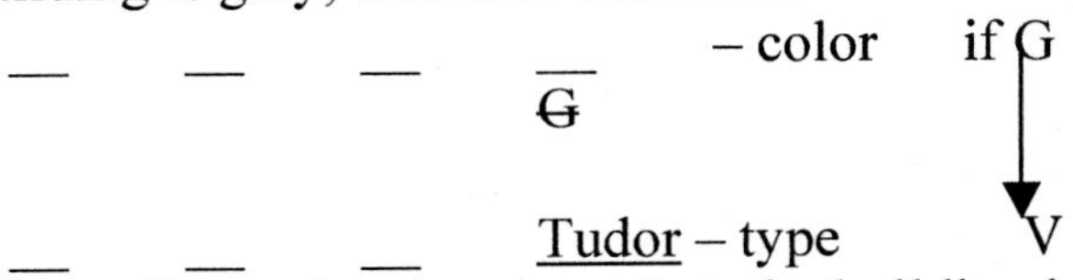

__ __ __ __ – color if G
G̶

__ __ __ Tudor – type V

This rule applies to the situation when the building is gray, not to the situation when the building is Victorian. Even if your diagram shows that a building is Victorian, this does not necessarily mean that it is gray. But if the building is not Victorian, then the color cannot be gray.

"If Adam or Brenda is on the team, the other is also on the team."

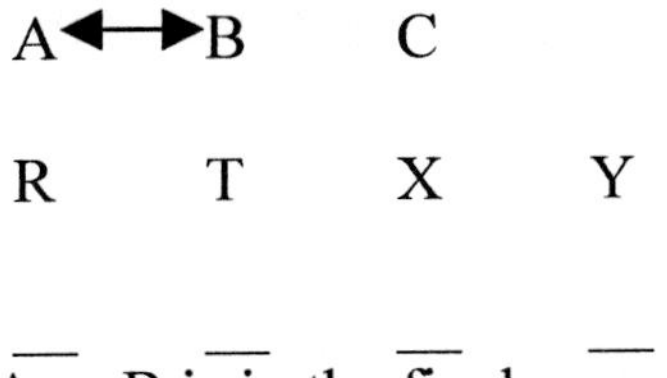

A↔B C

R T X Y

__ __ __ __

When A or B is in the final group, then the other one must also be in the group.

"Adam is on the team if Brenda is on the team."

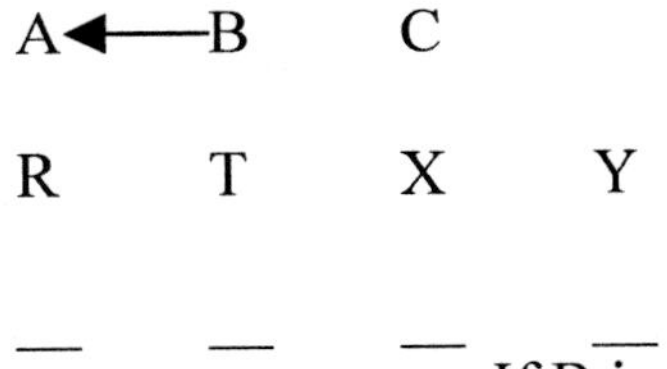

A←B C

R T X Y

__ __ __ __

This is a one-way arrow. If B is on the team, then A must be on the team. A common mistake students make with this rule is thinking that since A happens to be on the team, then B must also be on the team. Also, if A is not on the team, then B cannot be on the team.

"If Adam is on the team, Brenda is not on the team."

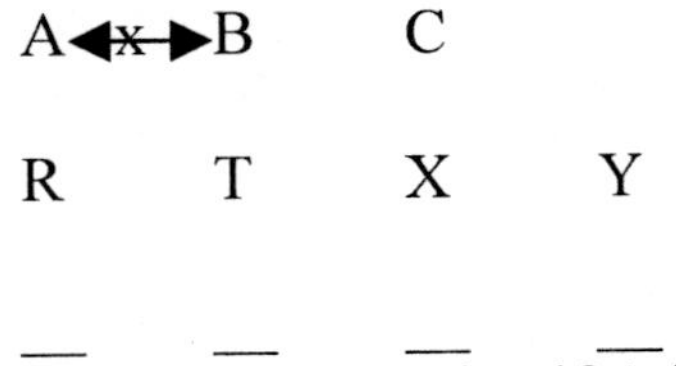

A←x→B C

R T X Y

__ __ __ __

Although this rule says that if A is on the team then B is not on the team, it is equally true that if B is on the team then A is not on the team. Think about it in simple terms. If A happens to be on the team, then B cannot be on the team. If B happens to be on the team, then A cannot be on the team.

Games review exercise

You have learned how to diagram simple lines, multiple lines, and grouping games. The following exercise presents six games, in no particular order. Diagram the setup and rules and make warranted conclusions when possible. Compare your diagrams with the samples following the exercise.

The six employees of a small company—Cal, Dave, Fred, Greg, Harrison, and Jake—may or may not eat lunch during a workday. Employees may eat lunch by themselves, or as part of a group, but only one group, consisting of one or more employees, will eat lunch during the workday. The following conditions must apply:

> If Dave eats lunch, then Fred eats lunch with him.
> Cal and Greg do not eat lunch together.
> If Harrison eats lunch, then he does not eat alone.
> Jake will not eat lunch unless exactly two people join him.
> If only two people eat lunch, then Greg does not eat lunch.

On a single day, a supervisor must schedule one-hour performance reviews with six different employees—D, F, G, H, J, and X. Meyers meets with each employee once, exactly one employee at a time, and each meeting requires exactly one hour. The times available for scheduling the meetings are 9:00 AM, 10:00 AM, 11:00 AM, 12:00 noon, 1:00 PM, and 2:00 PM. The following conditions apply:

> The meeting for X must be scheduled at some time before the meeting for F.
> The meeting for J cannot be scheduled for 12:00 noon or later.
> The meeting for H must be scheduled at some time before the meeting for X.
> There must be exactly one meeting scheduled between the meetings of D and F.

Whenever a company takes delivery of a new computer, the software technician must load at least one program from each of the following three categories: word processing programs—F, G, H; database programs—O, P, R; internet browsers—T, U, W. When the software technician loads the programs, the following requirements must be satisfied:

An equal number of programs from each category must be loaded on the computer.
T and P are not both loaded on the same computer.
If R is loaded on a computer, U must also be loaded.
O must be loaded on a computer if F is loaded on the computer.
R is not loaded if P is loaded on the computer.

Four students—Williams, Xi, Ybarra, and Zoë—cooperate by each typing the lecture notes for the two classes they have in common—Anthropology and Biology. Each student types the notes for exactly two classes a week. Each class meets once per day on Monday, Tuesday, Wednesday, and Thursday. The typing of the notes conforms to the following conditions:

A student may type notes for only one class a day.
Xi and Ybarra do not type notes for classes that meet the same day.
Zoë does not type notes for Anthropology classes.
Williams does not type notes for classes that meet on Thursday.

Seven machine parts—A, B, C, D, E, F, and G—must be added to four machines, numbered 1, 2, 3, and 4. Each machine must each receive at least one part, and each part must be used exactly once, in one machine. The following standards regulate the adding of machine parts to the machines:

Part B is used in machine 1.
Machine 2 receives exactly twice as many parts as machine 1.
Part G is added to the same machine that part F is added to.
Part C is not added to the same machine that part D is added to.
Part F is not added to machine 2 or machine 4.

At an award ceremony, awards will be presented to one student from the freshman, sophomore, junior, and senior classes, as well as to one faculty member. Three of the awards will consist of a scholarship and a plaque, and two awards will consist of a scholarship alone. The following conventions will determine the presentation of the awards:

The freshman receives an award either first or second.
The sophomore receives an award at some time after the junior receives an award.
The faculty award consists of a scholarship and a plaque and is presented immediately prior to the senior award.
No more than two consecutive awards can consist of a scholarship and a plaque.
The first award consists of a scholarship.

Answers to games review exercise

Employee lunch groups.
The standard mono-group selection diagram works fine. List all the members in each column and use arrows to show the relationships created by rules 1 and 2. In rules 3, 4, and 5, G, H, and J are burdened with certain restrictions. H cannot eat alone. So H eats with one or more others. J eats with exactly two others. G either eats alone, with two others, or with more than two others. G does not eat with exactly one other employee. All of this is noted under the main diagram.

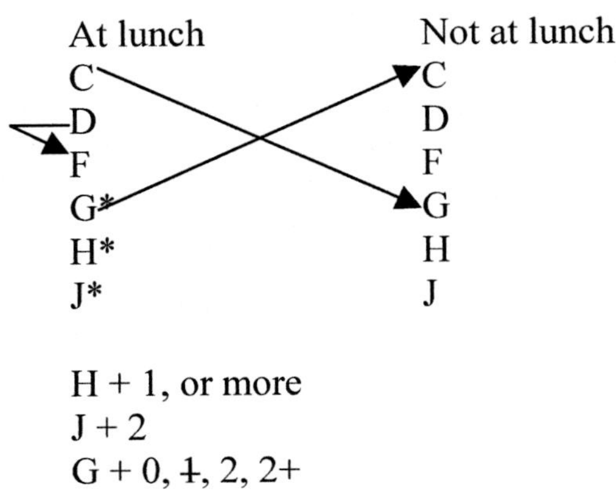

Performance reviews.
This easy simple line has six slots, each to be filled by one member. Further simplifying your task, each member is used exactly once. A line puzzle does not get any easier than this. Combine rules 1 and 3 to create the chain H < X < F. Rule 2 is self-explanatory: J cannot be on 12:00, 1:00, or 2:00. (Figure 1) Rule 4 is slightly more complex. Remember, it could be F __ D or it could be D __ F. All that remains is to make warranted conclusions and diagram the results. To make conclusions, start with the chain of H < X < F. F must come later than H and X, thus F cannot be in 9 or 10. Similarly, because H must come before F and X, H cannot be in 1 or 2. H must also come before D, because only one other student separates D and F. So, H cannot be in 12. What about X? X must, at a minimum, be later than H and earlier than F, so X cannot be in 9 or 2. If you still have difficulty seeing this, use your fingers to measure out the length of the block of the three letters, and place your fingers on the diagram to help you visualize how this happens. Although you may have made additional conclusions, these conclusions are more than adequate to begin answering the questions.

9	10	11	12	1	2
__	__	__	__	__	__
			~~J~~	~~J~~	~~J~~
~~F~~	~~F~~		~~D~~	~~D~~	~~D~~
			~~H~~	~~H~~	~~H~~
~~X~~					~~X~~

Software groups.

This game requires a classic selection-grouping diagram. There are three groups from which you must choose certain members. This puzzle has a small twist on the classic diagram. Usually, there is a fixed number of members that must be selected; five or six is typical. In this puzzle, there is a minimum number of three—at least one member must be taken from each of the three categories. A second factor also influences the size of the ending group. Rule 1 requires that an equal number of programs must be selected from each category. You can make the warranted conclusion that if one program is selected from each category then there is a total of three programs. Furthermore, if two programs are selected from each category, there is a total of six programs. Can three programs be selected from each category? No. Rules 2 and 5 prevent you from selecting three from each category to get a total of nine members, because these two rules establish a practical maximum of eight members, since all the software can be selected at the same time, except P. Returning to Rule 1, there are either three or six members in the final group. The basic diagram requires positive one-way arrows and negative two-way arrows.

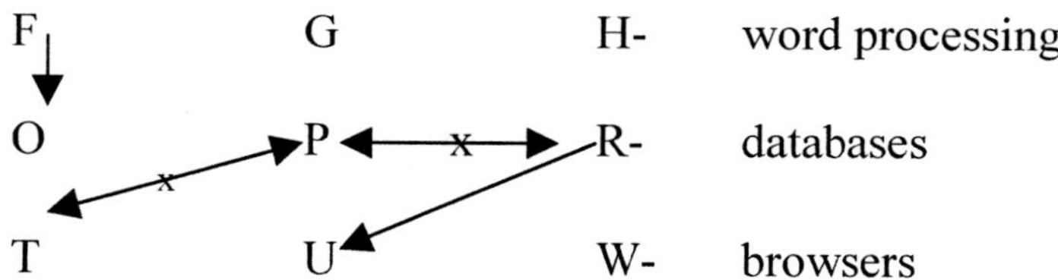

Class order.

This game uses a common multiple-line diagram. It is not a simple line because each day (with two classes each) has a special relationship that governs what can be in the two slots for that day. Once you get your bearings it is not difficult to create the diagram. The rule regarding Z is easy to depict, as is the rule regarding W. It should be easy to remember not to put X and Y on the same day. The best way to make warranted conclusions is to check the spaces with the most activity underneath them. For Thursday Anthropology, neither Z nor W fits. Thus, either X or Y must do that class. Since the other one now cannot be on Thursday, the only member now available for Thursday Biology is Z.

Mon			Tue			Wed			Thur	
__	__	||	__	__	||	__	__	||	X/Y	Z
Ant	Bio		Ant	Bio		Ant	Bio		Ant	Bio
~~Z~~			~~Z~~			~~Z~~			~~Z~~	
									~~W~~	~~W~~

~~XY~~

Machine parts.

This is an assignment grouping game. The seven members from the starting group must be assigned to four ending groups. As is always the case with assignment games, you must focus on the occupancy limits to solve the game. Scan the rules for the one that helps determine the occupancy limits. Rule 2 states that machine 2 has twice as many members as machine 1. We know that machine 1 has at least one member. This means that machine 2 has at least two members. What if machine 1 had two members? Then machine 2 would have four members. That would use up six of the seven members, not leaving enough for machine 3 and machine 4 to each have at least one member. Thus, machine 1 has one member. The three possible occupancy limits are listed below. Now, diagram the rules. Rule 1 assigns B to machine 1. Rule 3 places F and G in the same machine. Combine this with Rule 5, that F is not added to machine 2 or 4. Since we concluded that machine 1 is fully occupied by B, the only place F and G can be is in machine 3. Now we are making real progress. Because F and G cannot be in machine 4, machine 4 cannot have three parts. At most, two parts can be in machine 4. This allows us to eliminate one of the three possibilities for the occupancy limits. This is a pretty good diagram and the occupancy limits will be helpful.

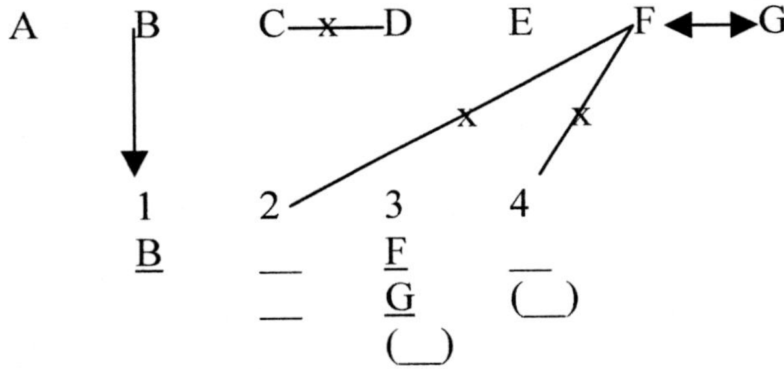

Put the 7 members into the 4 groups

Machine 1	Machine 2	Machine 3	Machine 4
1	2	2	2
1	2	3	1
~~1~~	~~2~~	~~1~~	~~3~~
~~2~~	~~4~~	~~0~~	~~1~~

Class awards.

This game had some challenging features. First, it was not immediately obvious that this is a multiple line game. Second, the four classes and the one faculty member make it harder to see that this was, in fact, a single set of members. Third, it is easy to get confused by the "scholarship" and "scholarship and a plaque" phrasing. After considering the setup and rules, it became clear that two sets of five dashes are sufficient. Moving through the rules, Rule 1 specifies that Fr is first or second. Thus, Fr is not third, fourth, or fifth. Rule 2 says that Sph is later than Jnr. Thus, Sph cannot be first, and Jnr cannot be fifth. Rule 3 says Fac is awarded a plaque (and a scholarship), and Fac is immediately before Snr. Thus, Fac is not last, and Snr is not first. For Rule 4, no more than two plaques (with scholarships) can be awarded in a row. Leave this rule alone for a moment. Finally, Rule 5, the first award is a scholarship (with no plaque). Since the first award is a scholarship, how will you accommodate the fact that three plaques remain, yet only two of them can be immediately next to each other? Consider the possibilities; it turns out that there are two. One, the plaques must be second, third, and fifth. Two, the plaques must be second, fourth, and fifth. In both situations, there are plaques second and fifth. This is a very valuable conclusion. The remaining plaque must be third or fourth. One final conclusion: since Fac gets a scholarship, Fac is not second. This diagram has more information and warranted conclusions than a typical multiple line game

___	___	___	___	___	- class
		~~Fr~~	~~Fr~~	~~Fr~~	
~~Sph~~				~~Jnr~~	
~~Snr~~	~~Fac~~			~~Fac~~	
Sc	Pl	___	___	Pl	- award

The Unstated Impact of Rules

The only reason the LSAT has the logic games is to test your ability to use rules to make conclusions. (They are certainly not interested in your ability to draw diagrams.) To make the best conclusions you must carefully consider both the direct and indirect impacts of each rule. When you create diagrams and answer questions, the indirect impacts are much more important than the direct impacts. The following exercises help reinforce your understanding of direct and indirect impacts.

A typical rule might be as follows:
If Bob is blue, then Fred is green.

There are several results from this rule
The direct impact of this rule is that in the single situation where Bob is blue, then Fred must be green. This impact is direct, and obvious. But, Fred *can* be green even when Bob is some color besides blue. Just because Fred happens to be green today does not mean that Bob is blue today. But, if Bob happens to be blue today, then Fred has no choice; Fred must be green today.
The indirect impact of this rule is that if Fred is not green today (maybe he is red), then Bob cannot be blue. This indirect impact of the rule is not obvious, but you must get used to doing this analysis for every single rule. If you do not get in the habit of identifying the indirect impact of rules, you will never succeed on the logic games.

To recap, this rule kicks in only when Bob is blue or when Fred is not green:
Situation #1 – Bob is blue; therefore Fred is green.
Situation #2 – Fred is not green; therefore Bob cannot be blue

That's all there is to it. Although this concept is easy, it takes practice before you will be comfortable using it and recognizing the different ways it might be phrased. Use the following examples to develop your skills.

Examples-

Rule – When Jeff plays soccer, he cannot play football on the same day.
In this rule, the two sports are mutually exclusive.
Results-
Situation #1 – If Jeff plays soccer today, he cannot play football today. – Direct impact.

Situation #2 – If Jeff plays football today, he cannot play soccer. – Indirect impact.

Rule – John does not play any instrument that Adam plays.
Results-
Situation #1 – If John plays a tuba, then Adam does not play a tuba.
Situation #2 – If Adam plays a trumpet, then John does not play a trumpet.

Rule – Gerald plays immediately after Jane.
Results-
Situation #1 – If Gerald plays fourth, then Jane plays third.
Situation #2 – If Jane plays fifth, then Gerald plays sixth.

Rule – R must play sometime before X.
Results-
Situation #1 – If X plays third, R plays first or second.
Situation #2 – If R plays fourth, X plays fifth, sixth or seventh.

Rule – If James is on the team, neither Adam nor Bob are on the team.
Results-
Situation #1 – If James is on the team, neither Adam nor Bob is on the team.
Situation #2 – If Adam (and/or Bob) is on the team, James is not on the team.

A good test taker does not take the rules at face value. A good test taker looks for the indirect impacts of the rules. Actively looking for indirect impacts is the key to success.

The contrapositive. Test takers become unnecessarily worried when discussion turns to the concept of the contrapositive. Contrapositive is a term used in the study of formal logic. Since you do not need formal logic for the LSAT, it is not necessary to waste your time with a confusing definition. Once you understand the indirect impacts of the rules, as was discussed above, then you know everything about the contrapositive that you need.

Are you still nervous about the contrapositive? If you understand the following explanation, you will be fine. To find the contrapositive of any if-then rule, *reverse* and *negate* the two elements. The resulting rule will also be true. For example, the original rule is: "If Paula orders an entrée, then she does not order a dessert." After you reverse and negate the two elements you get: "If Paula orders a dessert, then she does not order an entrée." It really is this simple; so don't worry about it. Contrapositive simply means that every rule has a direct effect and an indirect effect.

The Question Types

As you have learned, the LSAT uses just a handful of diagram types. Similarly, it uses just a few types of questions. You saw these questions as you worked through the preceding sections. This section reviews the question types; both what they look like and how best to answer them.

To begin with, there are two general types of questions, those that add new information and those that do not.

Adds no new information
Questions that do not add new information are slightly more common than those that add new information. When a question in a simple line game does not add new information, you can answer it simply by looking at the diagram, if you made the initial conclusions. For more complex games, you usually need to do additional analysis to answer a question that does not add new information.

Examples of questions that do not add new information:

> "Which of the following students could be seated in the fifth seat?"
>
> "Which of the following could be true?"
>
> "Which of the following could be an accurate list of the boxes in order of delivery, from first to seventh?"
>
> "Which of the following is a complete and accurate list of the times that box C can be delivered?"
>
> "Which one of the following is a pair of paintings, both of which must be exhibited?"

Adds new information
Questions that add new information require more work. When the question stem adds new information, you must plug the new information into your partially complete diagram and make additional conclusions. It is your skill at finding these additional conclusions that the question is testing.

Examples of questions that add new information:

"If Xeno is not in the same canoe as Zachary, which of the following must be true?"

"If York has the second session, which of the following must be true?"

"If Doyle does not have a session earlier than fifth, which of the following could be true?"

"If U lands later than T, then the latest W can land is:"

"If X lands third, then each of the following could be true EXCEPT:"

All questions, whether or not they add new information, will ask you to select the answer choice that "could be true" or the answer choice that "must be true".

"Could be true" questions

For a "could be true" question, you want to circle the answer choice that is a possible valid permutation. So, if you can find a valid permutation that incorporates that answer choice, then that answer choice could be true and you should select it. If you cannot find any valid permutations that contain that answer choice, then it is not the one you want. Cross it off and move on. Four of the answer choices will not have a valid permutation. So, four choices will be false, and one will be a possible permutation.

Examples of "could be true" questions:

"If the dance club prepares the second food, then which one of the following could be true?"

"Which of the following could be true?"

"If Doyle does not have a session earlier than fifth, which of the following could be true?"

"Which of the following is a complete and accurate list of the boxes that could be delivered second?"

"Which of the following is a complete and accurate list of the times that box C can be delivered?"

"Must be true" questions
To satisfy the requirements for a "must be true" question, you need to eliminate four of the answer choices by finding valid permutations that disproves each of them. If the answer choice is not true 100% of the time, in every single permutation, then it is not the answer choice you want.

Examples of "must be true" questions:

"If Zachary is in canoe 2, then which one of the following must be true?"

"If York has the second session, which of the following must be true?"

"If exactly two boxes are delivered between the delivery of boxes B and C, which of the following must be true?"

"If X lands second, then which one of the following must be true?"

"If Finlet is on exhibit in Chicago, what is the maximum number of combinations of paintings on exhibit?"

Some questions mix things up by phrasing the question differently. "Could be true EXCEPT" questions and "CANNOT be true" questions are two question types that are used to keep test-takers on their toes.

"Could be true EXCEPT" questions
In this question type, four answer choices could be true and one choice cannot be true. Since four of the answer choices are valid permutations, don't waste time laboriously confirming their validity. Instead, skim the five answer choices looking for an answer choice that seems out of place. Often, the answer choice you want will be an obviously impossible permutation. If it isn't obvious at first glance, only then should you check each answer choice. If an answer choice seems like a valid permutation, go on to the next one. A frustrating mistake test-takers often make with this type of question is that they actually do identify the answer choice that cannot be true, but then they forget to circle it. Because a student's natural tendency is to select an answer choice that could be true, they select one of the other four choices, all of which are very attractive, since they all could be true. When answering an EXCEPT question, remind yourself that you are, in fact, looking for the "wrong" (i.e., invalid permutation) answer choice.

Examples of "could be true EXCEPT" questions:

"If X lands third, then each of the following could be true EXCEPT:"

"Each of the following boxes could be delivered fifth EXCEPT:"

"Each of the following pairs can be seated in the same canoe EXCEPT:"

"CANNOT be true" questions
This question type is basically the same as the "could be true EXCEPT" questions. These questions have four answer choices that either *must* be true or *could be* true. The other answer choice, the one you want, is the one that is never true. Again, do not spend time working out the permutations for each answer choice, since four of them either could be true or must be true. Instead, look for the answer choice that doesn't work when you try to make a permutation using it.

Examples "CANNOT be true" questions:

> "Which one of the following CANNOT be true?"
>
> "Which of the following students CANNOT be scheduled for the fifth session?"

Taken together, "CANNOT be true" questions and "could be true EXCEPT" questions are about half as common as "could be true" questions. This means they are fairly common. Since they are an important part of your score, you must become comfortable answering them. We are all predisposed to select the valid or "right" permutations, instead of the invalid or "wrong" permutation. You must overcome your natural tendency and select the invalid permutation when answering this kind of question. This is a case where the "wrong" permutation is the correct answer, and the four "right" permutations are the incorrect answers. You have to love the LSAT.

Specific types of questions

To recap, every question asks either what must be true or what could be true. Also, every question either adds or does not add new information. In addition to these two features seen in every question, there are some very specific types of questions that are used regularly. These include questions that ask what the maximum number of members is, or what the minimum number of members is. Other questions ask you to select the list of members in correct order. Some questions even alter the rules, forcing you to redo all your work. As you take practice tests, you will see examples of the following types of questions:

Lists of members questions
A "list of members" question is usually the first question in a simple line or multiple line game. These questions are easy. Simply start with Rule 1 and compare it to each of the five answer choices. One of the answer choices will violate Rule 1. Then do the same with Rule 2, Rule 3, and so on, until you have eliminated four of the five answer choices. The remaining answer choice is the one you want to select. This technique is called rule violator answer elimination and was discussed earlier.

"Which one of the following could be a complete and accurate list of the campers seated in canoe 1, from front to back?"
(A) George, Xeno, Henry
(B) Molly, Henry, Xeno
(C) Yvonne, George, Henry
(D) George, Zachary, Henry
(E) Xeno, Molly, Henry

Maximum number questions
Occasionally, a question asks for the maximum number of members that can be used. This type of question is found mostly in mono-group selection games. In the history of the LSAT, the correct answer has never been the smallest number or the second smallest number. So, when answering these questions, start with the largest number, which will be answer choice (E). Determine if this number can be selected and still make a valid permutation. If not, go to answer choice (D) and examine it. The credited answer choice will always be (C), (D), or (E); usually it will be (D) or (C).

"What is the maximum number of students that can be outside the club at the same time?"
(A) three
(B) four
(C) five
(D) six
(E) seven

Minimum number questions
Questions that ask for the minimum number of members that can be selected are less common than questions that ask for the maximum number. The correct answer is never the largest number or the second largest number. When answering these questions, start with answer choice (A), which is the smallest number. Determine if this number can be selected and still make a valid permutation. If not, go to answer choice (B) and examine it. The credited answer choice will always be (A), (B), or (C); usually it will be (B) or (C).

"What is the minimum number of airplanes that can land on Tuesday?"
(A) zero
(B) one
(C) two
(D) three
(E) four

Complete and accurate list of members question

Occasionally, a question will ask you "which of the following is a complete and accurate list of members that can be used/selected." Answer choice (A) will often list just one member, and the list of members will grow longer as you move through the five answer choices. There is a specific technique for answering this question type: First, scan each of the five answer choices. Is there any member that is listed in all five choices? In the example below, Jelisse is. You now know that this member, Jelisse, must be included, so you don't need to check it. Next, in the five answer choices, is there any member that is listed in four of them, but not all five? Here, Lorac is. You can eliminate the single answer choice that does not have Lorac. You can be confident that Lorac will be in the credited answer choice, so there is no need to check it. Scan the four remaining answer choices to determine any common members. In this example, Gord is in two choices, and Oxram is in three. The most efficient technique is to now check whether Gord is valid. If it is, then you have narrowed the possibilities down to choice (A) and choice (C). Then you would check for Finlet. If Finlet is valid, then you know that choice (C) is correct. By comparing the answer choices to each other we can quickly narrow the list and only needed to check the validity of two members. This is much quicker then checking the validity of all the members.

> "Which one of the following is a complete and accurate list of paintings, any one of which could be exhibited with Bichelli?"
> (A) Gord, Jelisse, Lorac
> (B) Chaos, Finlet, Gord, Jelisse, Oxram
> (C) Finlet, Gord, Jelisse, Lorac, Oxram
> (D) Chaos, Finlet, Jelisse, Lorac, Oxram
> (E) Jelisse, Lorac, Oxram

Possible pairs questions

Questions in which the answer choices list possible pairs are similar to questions in which the answer choices contain complete and accurate lists. As such, possible pair questions require a similar approach. Each of the five answer choices will contain two members. The most efficient approach is to scan the five answer choices, looking for a member that is used in three (or more) of the answer choices. In the example below, J is in three answer choices. Check to see if J is a valid member. If J is a valid member, then eliminate choices (B) and (D), since they don't contain J. If J is not valid, eliminate (A), (C), and (E), because they contain J. By taking a moment to determine that J has the most impact, you are able to check the validity of this member and quickly eliminate two or three answer choices.

> "Which of the following could be a pair of members that both sit next to A?"
> (A) C and J.
> (B) D and E.
> (C) D and J.
> (D) C and E.
> (E) H and J.

Count the possible permutations questions

Once in a while, a question provides a new piece of information and then asks how many permutations are possible. Simply do all the permutations, count them, and then you know the correct answer. The correct answer will be one of the three smallest numbers, similar to minimum number questions. The correct answer choice will be (A), (B), or (C).

> "If Finlet is on exhibit in Chicago, what is the maximum number of combinations of paintings on exhibit?"
> (A) two
> (B) three
> (C) four
> (D) five
> (E) six

Questions that alter the original rules

This is another rare question type. If it appears, it will be the final question of a game. The question will state that one of the initial rules is modified or suspended. You will need to re-create your diagram to incorporate the new information. This kind of question can be very difficult because by the time you reach it you have internalized an understanding of the diagram, which you then must then disregard in order to answer the question.

> "Suppose the rule that W lands immediately before or after T is replaced by the rule that the landings of W and T are separated by exactly one other landing. If the other rules remain unchanged, then the latest X can land is"
> (A) first
> (B) second
> (C) third
> (D) fourth
> (E) fifth

Answer choices that add new information

The most time-consuming questions are those that add new information in each of the five answer choices. It may be necessary to rework the diagram five times to find the credited answer choice. To avoid getting mired in one of these questions, you should attempt it only after you have answered the other questions. You should use correct answers and work from other questions to eliminate some of the answer choices. This will save some work. Mercifully, these questions are rare.

> "Which one of the following must be true?"
> (A) If J works on Monday, R works on Wednesday.
> (B) If T works on Tuesday, S works on Wednesday.

(C) If T or W works on Wednesday, then R works earlier in the week than Q.
(D) If R does not work, then S works exactly two days.
(E) If S works on Friday, at least one worker works on two consecutive days.

Two answer choices that share the same analysis

This is such a common occurrence that you should always be on the lookout for it. You will discover, either during the initial analysis or while working on a question, that two members are interchangeable. For example, a rule may state that A and B are always together. This means that each of them is equally likely to fill a certain space. What you will see in the answer choices is that one answer choice will contain A, and another answer choice will contain B. You will be able to eliminate both of these answer choices.

"If C is selected for the team, which of the following must be true?"
(A) A is selected for the team.
(B) B is selected for the team. – See choice (A).
(C) D is selected for the team.
(D) E is selected for the team.
(E) F is selected for the team.

If we know that A is not necessarily selected for the team and that B is used every time A is used, then we know that B is not necessarily selected for the team. So neither A nor B must be selected for the team. Because the two members share the same analysis, once we can eliminate answer choice (A), we can also eliminate (B).

Strategies

You need a strategy for how to approach the games. The best strategy is the one that yields the most correct answers. As such, you should experiment with the strategies outlined below to find the mix of strategies that yields the best results for you.

Making conclusions.
There are three stages when you may be able to make the all-important additional conclusions. First, you can sometimes make conclusions after you diagram a single rule. This often happens in simple lines, less often in other games. Second, you can make conclusions after you have diagrammed two or more rules and realize there is an overlap. For multiple lines games and grouping games, you will make most conclusions at this point. Sometimes you are not able to make conclusions after diagramming the rules. Don't worry; this is common. When this happens, consult the questions. Do all of the questions add new information? If so, then don't try to draw any conclusions before going to the questions, since there are none to be made. But, if at least some of the questions do not add new information, this means you failed to make a conclusion. With that in mind, reconsider the diagram and rules, looking for conclusions you can make. If you still do not see any conclusions, don't worry, go to the first question that adds new information and answer that question. Often, after answering a few questions, you gain new insights into the diagram. You can then incorporate these insights into your diagram.

Save work and refer to it later.
You will find that you can sometimes use a correct answer, or a diagram, from one question to eliminate an answer choice in a different question. This is called "bootstrapping" your way to a correct answer. Recycling previous work in this way saves a lot of time. It takes experience and confidence to use this technique, and your work must be neat. The bootstrapping technique works best for simple lines. It works reasonably well for small multiple line games. It is difficult to use for grouping games or other diagram-intensive games. Sometimes the diagram is so big and complex that you must erase your work from the diagram so that you can reuse it for the next question, making it difficult to use this technique.

Doing three of the four games.
You will probably do all four games. If so, you can do them in order, or you can skip around, doing the easier games first, if that makes you more comfortable. The drawback to skipping around is that sometimes a game looks easy at first, but turns out to be difficult once you start working on it, or vice versa. If you decide to do only three out of four games, then you must skip around. Since it can be difficult to determine which games are easiest at first glance, have a plan for which games to do and which to skip. Always do the question-rich games before the question-poor games. (You will be interested to know that games with many questions are often easier than games with few questions because question-rich games usually have simpler diagrams.) Another consideration when skipping around is that you may prefer games where the questions add new information, instead of games where the questions do not add new information.

The order in which you do questions in a game.
If timing isn't a problem, you should do the questions within a single game in the order they appear. If keeping to the time limits is a problem, you may want to experiment with different approaches. For example, if you have trouble making the initial warranted conclusions, you may have more success by first doing the questions that add new information, and then doing the no-new information questions.

Transferring answers from your test book to the answer sheet.
Jumping back and forth from your test book to the answer sheet after every question is inefficient and can lead to transfer mistakes. Instead, finish all the questions in a game, and then transfer all of the answers to the answer sheet. Make sure that you start and finish on the correct numbers. If you did not answer a question, make sure that you still fill in a bubble for that question. That way, if you don't get back to that question later you still have a chance of getting credit for it.

Doing all the permutations right away.
Some prep books recommend doing all the permutations for a game. This is very bad advice. For nearly every game in the last ten years, it would have been a complete waste of time to do all the permutations first. Doing this makes sense only once in a rare while, when there are a half-dozen permutations. But, if the game is that easy, it makes just as much sense to solve for those permutations when you reach the questions. The best plan is to do the initial analysis and make conclusions about what must be true or must not be true. Doing this will answer about half of the questions. It will also provide the solid foundation you will need to answer the questions that supply new information.

Hybrid Games

Nearly all LSAT games are either line games or grouping games. Once every few years a game blurs this distinction by combining elements of both types of games. This doesn't happen often. Even when it does happen, it poses no special challenges. If you are proficient at diagramming line games and grouping games, then hybrids are easy…well, at least reasonably easy. Occasionally, we hear a test taker complain that there was a hybrid on their test, but it almost always turns out that it was a common game type that was more difficult than average or just looked a little different. The moral of this story is that you should not go into every difficult game thinking it is a potential hybrid. Instead, approach every game as though it is a line game or grouping game. If, after a great deal of effort, you can't diagram the game using the normal line and grouping techniques, only then consider the possibility that is a hybrid game, an unusual game, or a unique game.

Hybrid simple line/grouping game

A hybrid simple line/grouping game will have six or seven starting members. For example: A, B, C, D, E, F, and G. You will be asked to select five of the members. So far, this is a typical selection grouping game. But then you will be asked to take those five members you picked and rank them in a linear order. A typical rule might say something like: "A is played before C if both A and C are played." The way to diagram this rule is: "If A & C, then A < C." Then, when you run into a permutation where both A and C are played, you will know that A is played before C.

Hybrid multiple line/grouping game

A hybrid multiple line/grouping game will have six or seven starting members. You will be asked to assign all of the starting members to two or three ending groups. So far, this is a typical assignment grouping game. But then the game will have a definite number of members in each ending group, unlike most assignment grouping games, where the number of members in each group varies. There are no special rules or diagramming techniques for this kind of hybrid game. Simply work through the rules as carefully as you would for any other game.

Unusual Games

Most (and probably all) of the games on your LSAT will be simple lines, multiple lines, and grouping games. But once every three or four years an LSAT has a game that is not a line game or a grouping game. Although these games do not appear often, it is prudent to acquaint yourself with them in case one shows up on your LSAT. These unusual games share many features with the common games, but they are different enough to require special diagrams. These games include the matrix, the circle, the network map, the divisible line, and the multiple rounds games. This chapter provides background information about each game type, and an example of each with explanations.

If this book is your first exposure to the LSAT games, you may want to skip this section and go directly to the practice tests. After you have mastered the common types of games, you can return to this section to learn more about these unusual games.

Matrix games

Until a few years ago, the LSAT loved to test matrix games. Out of date prep books still emphasize matrix games. The typical matrix game employed a scheduling scenario. There would be five days, with a morning and afternoon time slot for each day. This was diagrammed using a grid with five horizontal columns and two vertical rows, creating ten boxes. You then had to figure out which members could be in the boxes. The other kind of matrix had a grid with four horizontal columns and four vertical rows, yielding 16 boxes. The setup would describe, for example, four people who each buy one to four items. Instead of putting the names of the members in the boxes, as is done for the scheduling matrix, you put a checkmark or "X" or something similar in the box to show that it is true or not true. In recent years, matrix games have tended to be this second type. A pitfall of both types of matrix games is that, at first glance, they look like grouping games. Only after trying to diagram the rules will you find that a grouping diagram does not work because it cannot capture the large amount of information that comes with a matrix game.

The following is an example of a typical matrix game.

Five students—A, B, C, D, and E—each play on as many as four of the following school sports teams—football, basketball, soccer, and hockey. Each student plays on at least one team. No student plays on any other kind of sports team. The following regulations determine the teams the students play on:

No more than three students play basketball.
A plays basketball and exactly one other sport.
C plays on at least one of the teams that B plays on.
E plays on more teams than any other student.
D plays on all the teams that A plays on and all the teams B plays on.

Make a grid with the students on the horizontal axis and the teams on the vertical axis, as shown below. Start with Rule 1: one, two, or three students play basketball. For Rule 2, note that A plays basketball, and plays exactly two sports. Rule 3 is difficult to diagram, so use an arrow to remind you of this rule and come back to it when necessary. Rule 4 requires that you make a conclusion. E plays on more teams than anyone else. Student A plays on two teams, so E cannot play on one team or two teams, and so must play on either three or four teams. Rule 5 is difficult to depict, so an asterisk next to D will have to suffice. We now know that since A plays basketball, D must play basketball. We can conclude that at least two students play basketball. We can also conclude that since A is on two teams, and if B happened to be on the same team(s) as A, then D must be on at least two teams. D could also be on three teams. D cannot be on four teams (Rule 4).

Football					
B-ball ~~1~~,2,3	Yes			Yes	
Soccer					
Hockey					
	A=2	B ◄────	───►C	D*=2, 3	E=3, 4

Questions 7–11

A caterer must make four holiday fruit baskets, numbered 1 through 4. There are sixteen apples, eight kiwis, eight pineapples, and sixteen oranges. All of the fruit must be used. The following conditions must be satisfied:

If kiwis are in a basket, an equal number of pineapples must be in the basket, and if pineapples are in the basket, an equal number of kiwis must be in the basket.

A basket cannot contain both oranges and kiwis.

There are exactly four kiwis in basket 1 and exactly four oranges in basket 3.

Each basket contains exactly eight, twelve, or sixteen pieces of fruit.

If a type of fruit is in a basket, then there are exactly four, eight, or twelve pieces of that fruit in the basket.

7. If the caterer places four pineapples in basket 2, then which one of the following must be true?

(A) There are four oranges in basket 2.
(B) There are four oranges in basket 4.
(C) There are apples in basket 1.
(D) There are apples in basket 2.
(E) There are apples in basket 3.

8. If there are oranges in basket 2, which one of the following could be true?

(A) There are eight apples in basket 2.
(B) There are four apples in basket 3.
(C) There are four kiwis in basket 2.
(D) There are twelve apples in basket 1.
(E) There are four oranges in basket 4

9. Which one of the following CANNOT be true?

(A) There are as many apples in basket 3 as oranges in basket 4.
(B) There are twice as many apples in basket 3 as there are oranges in basket 2.
(C) There are twice as many apples in basket 3 as kiwis in basket 2.
(D) There are four pineapples and eight apples in basket 2.
(E) There are as many oranges in basket 4 as apples in basket 3.

10. If there are the same number of apples in basket 3 as there are oranges in basket 4, then which one of the following must be true?

(A) There are eight apples in basket 3.
(B) There are four apples in basket 1.
(C) There are twelve apples in basket 3.
(D) There are four apples in basket 4.
(E) There are twelve oranges in basket 2

11. Suppose that instead of eight, twelve or sixteen pieces of fruit in each basket, there is now either only eight or twelve. If the other conditions remain in effect, which one of the following must be true?

(A) There are four apples in basket 1.
(B) There are four apples in basket 2.
(C) There are four apples in basket 3.
(D) There are four apples in basket 4.
(E) There are eight apples in basket 4.

GO ON TO THE NEXT PAGE.

Questions 7–11

A caterer must make four holiday fruit baskets, numbered 1 through 4. There are sixteen apples, eight kiwis, eight pineapples, and sixteen oranges. All of the fruit must be used. The following conditions must be satisfied:

If kiwis are in a basket, an equal number of pineapples must be in the basket, and if pineapples are in the basket, an equal number of kiwis must be in the basket.

A basket cannot contain both oranges and kiwis.

There are exactly four kiwis in basket 1 and exactly four oranges in basket 3.

Each basket contains exactly eight, twelve, or sixteen pieces of fruit.

If a type of fruit is in a basket, then there are exactly four, eight, or twelve pieces of that fruit in the basket.

7. If the caterer places four pineapples in basket 2, then which one of the following must be true?

(A) There are four oranges in basket 2.
(B) There are four oranges in basket 4.
(C) There are apples in basket 1.
(D) There are apples in basket 2.
(E) There are apples in basket 3.

8. If there are oranges in basket 2, which one of the following could be true?

(A) There are eight apples in basket 2.
(B) There are four apples in basket 3.
(C) There are four kiwis in basket 2.
(D) There are twelve apples in basket 1.
(E) There are four oranges in basket 4

9. Which one of the following CANNOT be true?

(A) There are as many apples in basket 3 as oranges in basket 4.
(B) There are twice as many apples in basket 3 as there are oranges in basket 2.
(C) There are twice as many apples in basket 3 as kiwis in basket 2.
(D) There are four pineapples and eight apples in basket 2.
(E) There are as many oranges in basket 4 as apples in basket 3.

10. If there are the same number of apples in basket 3 as there are oranges in basket 4, then which one of the following must be true? 0 or 12

(A) There are eight apples in basket 3.
(B) There are four apples in basket 1.
(C) There are twelve apples in basket 3.
(D) There are four apples in basket 4.
(E) There are twelve oranges in basket 2

11. Suppose that instead of eight, twelve or sixteen pieces of fruit in each basket, there is now either only eight or twelve. If the other conditions remain in effect, which one of the following must be true?

(A) There are four apples in basket 1.
(B) There are four apples in basket 2.
(C) There are four apples in basket 3.
(D) There are four apples in basket 4.
(E) There are eight apples in basket 4.

GO ON TO THE NEXT PAGE

4/8/12

	1	2	3	4
16 = Orng	0	12	4	0
8 = K	4	0	0	4
8 = P	4	0	0	4
16 = A			4+	

8/12/16

	1	2	3	4
16 Orng	0	0	4	12
8 K	4	4	0	0
8 D	4	4	0	0
16 A			4+	

Fruit baskets

This matrix game tests your ability to keep track of occupancy limits. The diagram is a standard four by four grid. Since occupancy limits are important, make sure the numbers are easy to read. (Figure 1) Rule 1 forces K and P into the same baskets. By combining rules 1 and 2, we know that O cannot be in the same basket as K and P. Rule 3 provides quantities and baskets for K and O. Using these numbers, we can conclude that O is not in basket 1 and that K and P are not in basket 3. Rules 4 and 5 establish occupancy limits for the number of pieces of fruit in each basket and how the types of fruit are divvied up. Looking at figure 1, you might notice that all of the remaining K and P must be in either basket 2 or 4. The remaining twelve O must be in the opposite basket. At this point you could have created two grids. The first grid would have the remaining K and P in basket 2 and the remaining O in basket 4. The second grid would be the reverse, having K and P in basket 4 and O in basket 2. Don't worry if you didn't do this, the questions are still very solvable using one grid. The only remaining uncertainty is how to divvy up the sixteen A. At least four A must be in basket 3 in order to get that basket up to the minimum of eight pieces of fruit.

4/8/12 of each kind

K = 8	4		-	
P = 8	4		-	
O = 16	-		4	
A = 16				
	1	2	3	4

8/12/16 in each basket

Fig. 1

7. (E) – Use the diagram to answer this question. If there are four P in basket 2, then there are four K in basket 2 and no O in basket 2. Thus, the twelve O are in basket 4. The sixteen A are divvied up, with at least four going to basket 3.
   (A) There are no O in basket 2.
   (B) There are twelve O in basket 4.
   (C) There may be some A in basket 1, but it is not definite.
   (D) There may be some A in basket 2, but it is not definite.
   (E) * There are at least four A in basket 3.

8. (B) – If there are any O in basket 2, there must be twelve O in that basket. The four K and four P are in basket 4.
   (A) If there were eight A and twelve O in basket 2, there would be twenty pieces of fruit, but the maximum is sixteen.
   (B) * There must be at least four A in basket 3, so there could be four A in basket 3.
   (C) Because O is in basket 2, there are no K in basket 2.
   (D) Twelve A added to the eight other pieces of fruit would make twenty pieces of fruit, which is too many.
   (E) There cannot be any O in basket 4 because K and P are there.

9. (B) – As you consider each answer choice, you may need to do some work to determine if they can be true.

(A) If there are zero O in basket 4, there cannot be zero A in basket 3. But, if there are twelve O in basket 4, there can be twelve A in basket 3. This can be true.

(B) * Correct. If there are zero O in basket 2, there cannot be zero A in basket 3. If there are twelve O in basket 2, there cannot be twenty-four A in basket 3. This answer choice cannot be true.

(C) If there are four K in basket 2, there can be eight A in basket 3.

(D) There can be four P and eight A in basket 2.

(E) If there are twelve O in basket 4, there can be twelve A in basket 3.

10. (C) – For O in basket 4, there are two possibilities, zero or twelve. There cannot be zero A in basket 3. There can be twelve A in basket 3, so place twelve O in basket 4. The K and P will be in basket 2. There are four remaining A to be placed in either basket 1, 2, or 4.

(A) There are twelve A in basket 3.

(B) There need not be four A in basket 1.

(C) * Yes, there must be twelve A in basket 3.

(D) There need not be any A in basket 4.

(E) The twelve O must be in basket 2.

11. (A) – This question lowers the maximum number of pieces of fruit in a basket from sixteen to twelve. The effect of this is that the sixteen A will be distributed more widely than before. If, for example, there are twelve O in basket 4, then the sixteen A will need to be distributed among the first three baskets. The only way to make this work would be to put four A in basket 1, four A in basket 2, and eight A in basket 3.

(A) * Yes, there must be four A in basket 1. This is true whether the twelve O are in basket 4 or in basket 2.

(B) There may be four A in basket 2, if the K and P are in basket 2. But if the twelve O are in basket 2, then no A can be in basket 2.

(C) There must be eight A in basket 3.

(D) There may be four A in basket 4, but not if there are twelve O in basket 4.

(E) There cannot be eight A in basket 4.

Circle games

The circle game (also called the table game) is a very old game. It used to be tested occasionally, but then disappeared for many years. It seemed that the circle game had been permanently retired until it made a surprise reappearance in October 2003. It is unlikely the circle game will appear again, but if it does, you will be ready for it. The typical circle game has people sitting around a circular table. They sit in seats that are evenly spaced around the table. The rules dictate that certain people must sit next to each other, or must not sit next to each other, or must sit directly across from each other. All in all, circle games aren't difficult, because it is easy to visualize the scenario and the relationships of the members. They usually employ a circular table, but it is possible the shape will be a square or rectangle, and it might not be an actual table.

The following is an example of a difficult circle game.

A square city block has four sides of equal length. On the block there are three retail buildings—A, B, and C—and five office buildings—T, W, X, Y, and Z. Each building must be located on exactly one corner of the block, or at exactly one of the points located halfway between two corners. The following restrictions apply to the location of the buildings:

X must be on a corner.
No retail building may be immediately next to another retail building.
Z is located between W and Y and no other buildings.
Three buildings are located between T and W.

This game is a variation of the circle game, and it is a bit more difficult. Seeing game variations is good for you; it keeps you flexible. In this case the diagram is a square, not a circle. Each corner and each midpoint between corners has one building. (Figure 1a) How do you diagram the rules? The most useful block of members is WZY (or YZW). These three office buildings take up a nice big block of space. Combine this with Rule 4—T is separated by three buildings from W—and you have the beginnings of a diagram. Arbitrarily place W at the top (Figure 1b) and see what happens. It turns out that this will not work because X can't be on a corner while also keeping A, B, and C separated. But, if you place W on a corner instead of a middle space, it is possible to accommodate all the members. (Figure 1c)

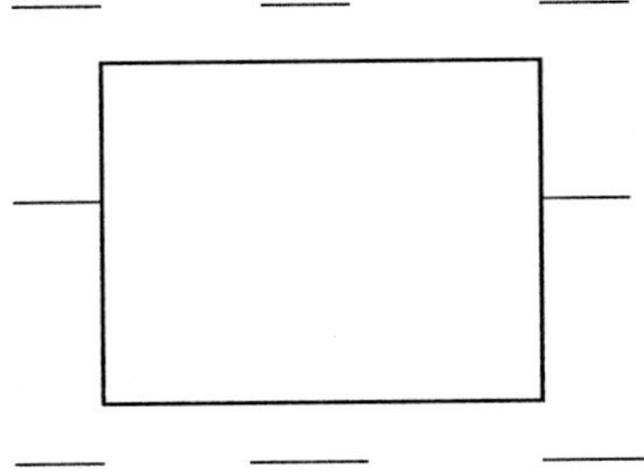

Fig. 1a

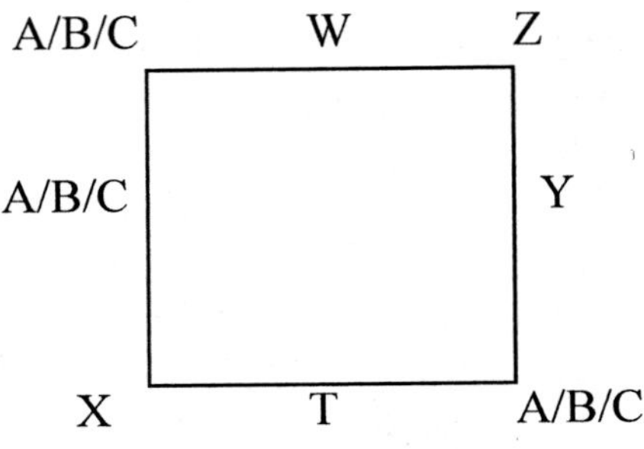

Fig. 1b

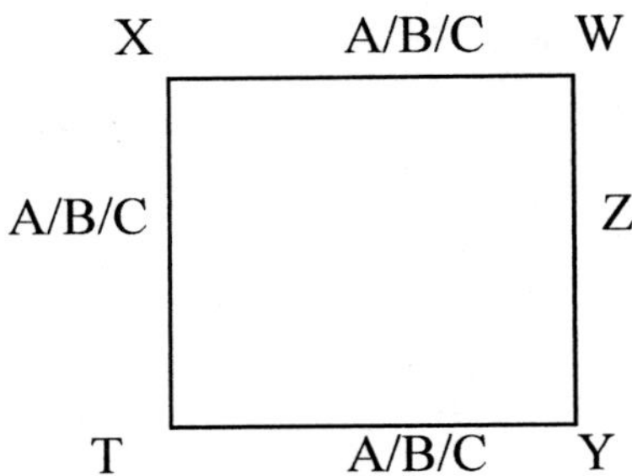

Fig. 1c

Questions 12-16

Company board members A, B, C, D, E, H, and J are sitting around a circular conference table that has eight chairs that are evenly spaced around the table. A board member is considered to be sitting across from another member if there are exactly three chairs between them. The seating of the board members must satisfy the following requirements:

A and B sit directly across from each other.
An empty chair and one other chair separate C and B.
D and E do not sit immediately next to each other.
C sits immediately next to H.

12. Which of the following could be an accurate seating list of the board members?

(A) A, H, C, B, E, J, D
(B) C, H, B, D, J, E, A
(C) B, H, A, E, J, C, D
(D) J, D, B, C, H, A, E
(E) E, J, A, C, H, B, D

13. If D sits immediately next to B, what is the minimum and maximum number respectively, of board members that must sit between C and E?

(A) 2, 2
(B) 2, 3
(C) 1, 4
(D) 1, 5
(E) 1, 6

14. Which one of the following is a complete and accurate list of members that can sit next to B?

(A) C
(B) D
(C) D, E
(D) H, D, E
(E) D, E, J

15. Which of the following could be a pair of members that both sit next to A?

(A) C and J.
(B) D and E.
(C) D and J.
(D) C and E.
(E) H and J.

16. Assume that the original condition that an empty chair and one other chair separate C and B is replaced by the condition that exactly two chairs separate C and B. If all other conditions remain unchanged, which one of the following must be false?

(A) H sits next to B.
(B) E sits next to H.
(C) C sits next to A.
(D) J sits next to B.
(E) J sits next to H.

GO ON TO THE NEXT PAGE.

Questions 12-16

Company board members A, B, C, D, E, H, and J are sitting around a circular conference table that has eight chairs that are evenly spaced around the table. A board member is considered to be sitting across from another member if there are exactly three chairs between them. The seating of the board members must satisfy the following requirements:

A and B sit directly across from each other.
An empty chair and one other chair separate C and B.
D and E do not sit immediately next to each other.
C sits immediately next to H.

12. Which of the following could be an accurate seating list of the board members?

(A) A, H, C, B, E, J, D - #2
(B) C, H, B, D, J, E, A
(C) B, H, A, E, J, C, D - #1
(D) J, D, B, C, H, A, E - #2
(E) E, J, A, C, H, B, D - #3

13. If D sits immediately next to B, what is the minimum and maximum number respectively, of board members that must sit between C and E?

(A) 2, 2
(B) 2, 3
(C) 1, 4
(D) 1, 5
(E) 1, 6

14. Which one of the following is a complete and accurate list of members that can sit next to B?

(A) C
(B) D
(C) D, E
(D) H, D, E
(E) D, E, J

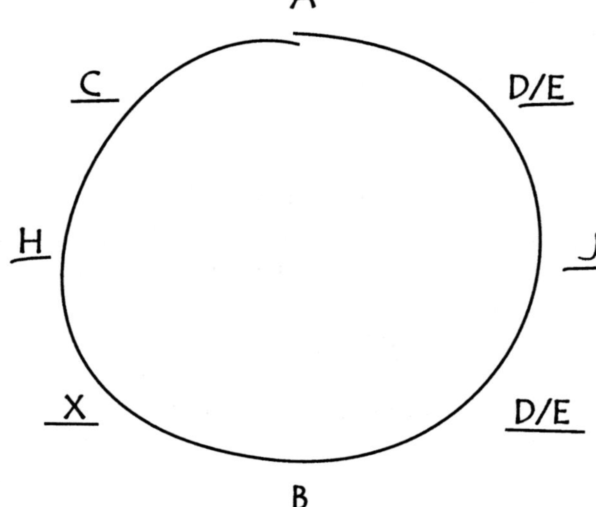

15. Which of the following could be a pair of members that both sit next to A?

(A) C and J.
(B) D and E.
(C) D and J.
(D) C and E.
(E) H and J.

16. Assume that the original condition that an empty chair and one other chair separate C and B is replaced by the condition that exactly two chairs separate C and B. If all other conditions remain unchanged, which one of the following must be false?

(A) H sits next to B.
(B) E sits next to H.
(C) C sits next to A.
(D) J sits next to B.
(E) J sits next to H.

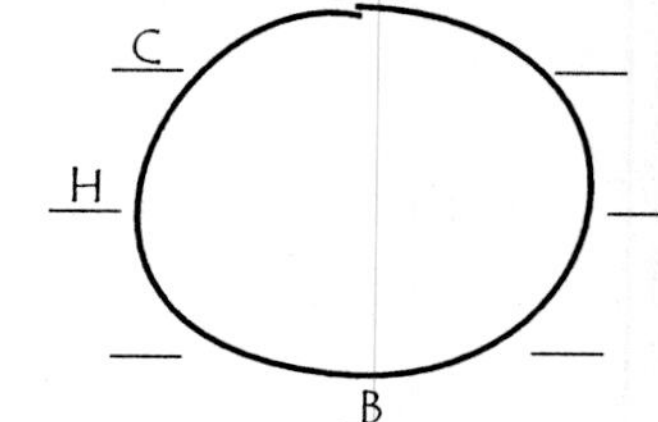

GO ON TO THE NEXT PAGE

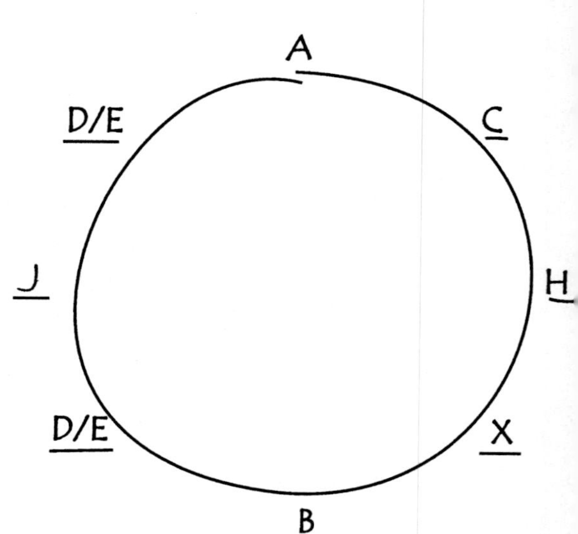

Conference table

In circle games, there is no specific starting point, so an answer choice can start the list of members anywhere in the continuum and still be correct. For example, a proper order for this circle game could be A, D, J, E, B, empty seat, H, and C. (Figure 1) But it is just as correct to start the list from a different member, or go counterclockwise instead of clockwise. For example, D, J, E, B, empty seat, H, C, and A. These members are in the same order in relation to one another as the first example; the only difference is that the order started with D instead of A. A distinctive feature of this particular game is the empty seat. Watch out for empty seats, they won't be named in an answer choice, but an empty seat prevents a member from occupying that space.

For this game, draw a circle. Place eight dashes around the circle. (Figure 1) Pick an arbitrary point on the circle and begin diagramming the rules. In this example, we have placed A at the top of the circle. Diagram Rule 1: A and B are separated by three seats. This puts B at the bottom of the circle. Rule 2 builds off the location of B; make sure to leave two spaces, one empty seat and one other seat, and then have C. Working from C, Rule 4 places C and H next to each other. This means that the order is now B, empty seat, H, C, and A. We still need to place D, E, and J. Rule 3 requires that E and D not be next to each other, so J must separate them. The two circles in figure 1 show the possible orders going clockwise and counterclockwise.

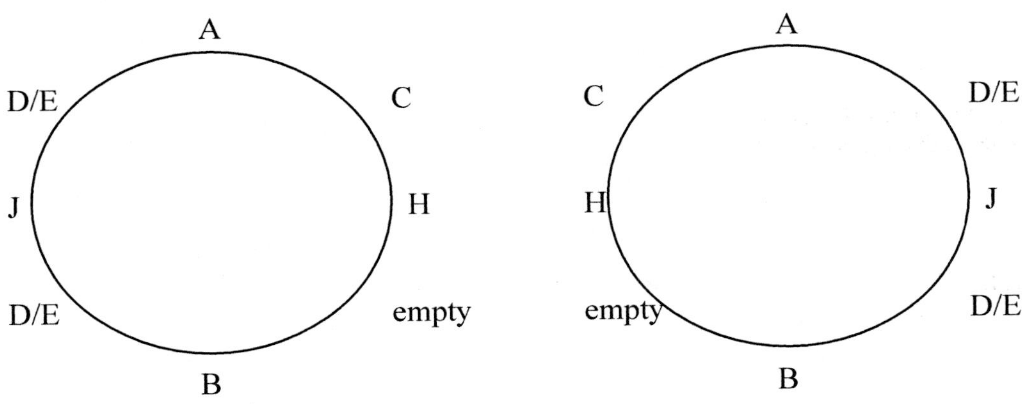

Fig. 1

1. (B) – Use the rules to eliminate the answer choices. Remember, it doesn't matter what member is listed first, focus on the relative order of the members.
   (A) This choice violates Rule 2 because it has C and B next to each other, but two seats are supposed to separate C and B.
   (B) * This is a valid order. Start at C, and then go on to H and the rest of the members.
   (C) This choice violates Rule 1, because three seats are supposed to be between A and B.

(D) This choice violates Rule 2 because it has C and B next to each other, but two seats are supposed to separate C and B.
(E) This choice violates Rule 3 because it has D and E sitting next to each other. This was hard to see because E was listed first and D was listed last.

2. (C) – If D sits immediately next to B, then E sits next to A. (Figure 2) C sits on the other side of A. So at least one board member, A, separates C and E. This eliminates choices (A) and (B). Going the other direction around the table, H, B, D, and J sit between C and E. So, at most, four members sit between C and E. Do not count the empty seat, since this question asked about the number of board members, not the number of chairs.
(A) See the analysis.
(B) See the analysis.
(C) * See the analysis.
(D) See the analysis.
(E) See the analysis. It is impossible for six board members to sit between C and E, because there are only seven board members.

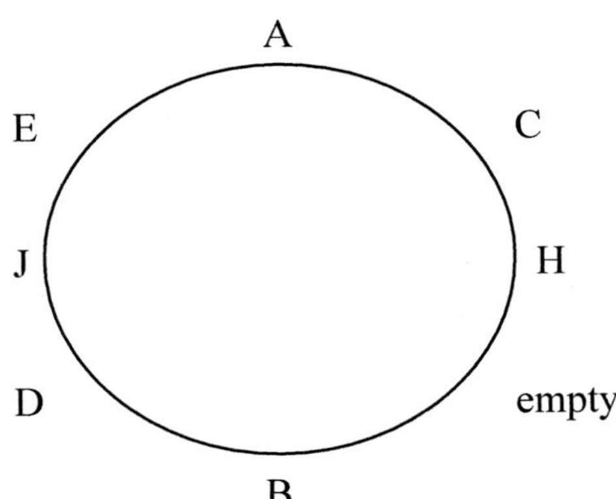

Fig. 2

3. (C) – Since this question does not add new information, consult the initial diagram. (Figure 1) D and E are the only ones that can sit next to B. To the other side of B is always the empty seat.
(A) See the diagram.
(B) See the diagram.
(C) * See the diagram.
(D) See the diagram.
(E) See the diagram.

4. (D) – Because this question asks for the pair of members who can sit next to A, both members must be able to sit next to A at the same time. What pair can sit next to A at the same time? C and E can. C and D can.
(A) See the analysis.
(B) See the analysis.
(C) See the analysis.
(D) * See the analysis.
(E) See the analysis.

5. (A) – When a game is easy the final question will sometimes change one of the rules, forcing you to go back and rework the entire diagram. This rule change means that two seats must be between C and B, but it doesn't specify that one of those seats has to be empty. C must still sit next to H, but the seat that was formerly empty can now be filled by J, E, or D.
(A) * Correct. This must be false. H cannot sit next to B, because H sits next to C, and C is separated from B by two seats.
(B) E can sit next to H, now that the rules have changed.
(C) C always sits next to A.
(D) Now that the rules have changed, J can sit next to B.
(E) Now that the rules have changed, J can sit next to H.

Network map

Another very old type of game is the network map. It was tested several times in the early and mid 1990s and then disappeared until it was used in June 2003. Whether it will reappear again is for LSAC to decide, but you can familiarize yourself with it to eliminate any surprises. The network map involves drawing connecting lines between subway stations, islands, etc. Each line represents a subway line, a bridge, etc., that connects two members. Keep close count of the number of lines coming and going from each member; occupancy limits are important in network maps. Apart from that, there is nothing particularly difficult about the network maps.

The following is an example of a network map.

Train tracks connect six cities: Arborville, Benson, Cherryville, Dawson, Eagle, and Frederick. Two cities are connected by one track that runs between the two cities and does not pass through any other cities. Tracks do not intersect. Every city is connected to at least one other city. The following regulations govern the placement of tracks:

Frederick is connected to Arborville and Cherryville, and no other cities.
Arborville is connected to exactly one more city than Eagle is.
Dawson is connected to Eagle and to exactly one other city.
Cherryville is connected to exactly one city.

This network map is pretty typical. There is no special order you must list the members, just allow enough space to draw the connecting lines. (Figure 1) Although the setup says that tracks do not intersect, if you can simply remember this, there is no need to draw awkward loops and curved lines in order to avoid intersecting two tracks. Draw the lines from F to A and C, and from D to E. Then consider the limits. F cannot be connected to any more cities, nor can C. D can be connected to one other city. B has no specified limit. A has to connect to one more city than E does. How many cities can A possibly connect to? A could connect to B, D, F, and E, for a total of four cities. This would require E to connect to a total of three cities, A, B, and D. If E connects to two cities, A would have to connect to three cities. If E connects to one city, A would have to connect to two cities. This A/E occupancy feature is the important part of this game.

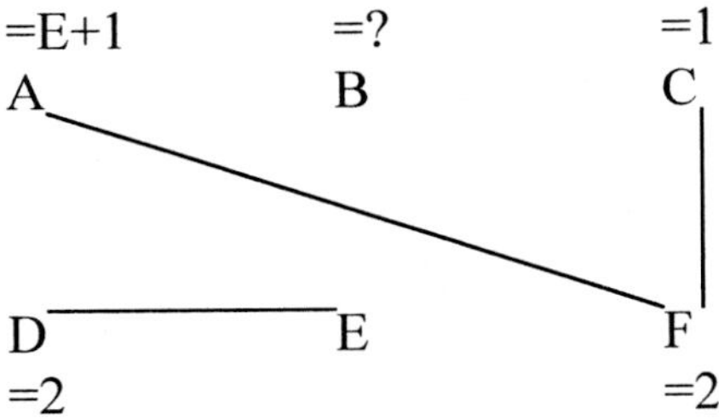

Fig. 1

Questions 7–11

Six cities—X, Y, Z, Q, R, and S—are to be connected by a new highway system. Each city has at least one new highway connecting it to another city. Each new highway connects two cities, and no other cities. No highways intersect. The following regulations determine the placement of the new highways:

X, Y, and Z are each connected to exactly two other cities.

Q, R, and S are each connected to no more than three other cities.

X is connected to Z and to Y.

Y and Z each must connect to at least one of Q, R, and S.

7. Which one of the following is a complete and accurate list of the cities, any one of which could be directly connected to Q?

(A) X
(B) Y
(C) Y, Z, R
(D) Y, Z, R, S
(E) Y, Z, R, X, S

8. If a highway connects R with Z, and a highway connects Y and S, which of the following could R connect with?

(A) X
(B) Y
(C) X and Y
(D) S and Q
(E) Y, Q, and S

9. If S has only one highway and it connects to Q, and Q has exactly two highways, one of which connects to R, then what is the minimum number of cities that a traveler leaving S must pass through to reach X?

(A) 1
(B) 2
(C) 3
(D) 4
(E) 5

10. Each of the following could be a possible listing of two cities connected by one highway EXCEPT:

(A) X and Z.
(B) Q and R.
(C) Y and Z.
(D) Y and Q.
(E) R and S.

11. Suppose that the condition that requires X to be connected to Z and Y is replaced with the condition that X is connected to Q. Which one of the following CANNOT be true?

(A) Y is connected to X and Z.
(B) Q is connected to Y, and Y is connected to Z.
(C) R is connected to Z and to no other city.
(D) S is connected to Q and no other city.
(E) Q is connected to Y and Z, and Y is connected to Z.

GO ON TO THE NEXT PAGE.

Questions 7–11

Six cities—X, Y, Z, Q, R, and S—are to be connected by a new highway system. Each city has at least one new highway connecting it to another city. Each new highway connects two cities, and no other cities. No highways intersect. The following regulations determine the placement of the new highways:

X, Y, and Z are each connected to exactly two other cities.

Q, R, and S are each connected to no more than three other cities.

X is connected to Z and to Y.

Y and Z each must connect to at least one of Q, R, and S.

7. Which one of the following is a complete and accurate list of the cities, any one of which could be directly connected to Q?

(A) X
(B) Y
(C) Y, Z, R
(D) Y, Z, R, S
(E) Y, Z, R, X, S

8. If a highway connects R with Z, and a highway connects Y and S, which of the following could R connect with?

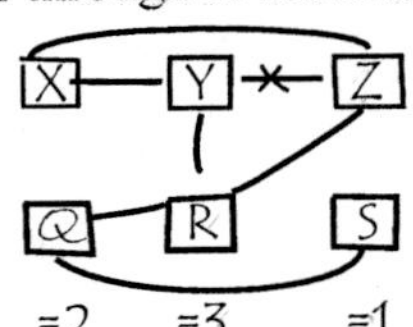

(A) X
(B) Y
(C) X and Y
(D) S and Q
(E) Y, Q, and S

9. If S has only one highway and it connects to Q, and Q has exactly two highways, one of which connects to R, then what is the minimum number of cities that a traveler leaving S must pass through to reach X?

(A) 1
(B) 2
(C) 3
(D) 4
(E) 5

10. Each of the following could be a possible listing of two cities connected by one highway EXCEPT:

initial analysis

(A) X and Z.
(B) Q and R.
(C) Y and Z.
(D) Y and Q.
(E) R and S.

11. Suppose that the condition that requires X to be connected to Z and Y is replaced with the condition that X is connected to Q. Which one of the following CANNOT be true?

(A) Y is connected to X and Z.
(B) Q is connected to Y, and Y is connected to Z.
(C) R is connected to Z and to no other city.
(D) S is connected to Q and no other city.
(E) Q is connected to Y and Z, and Y is connected to Z.

GO ON TO THE NEXT PAGE

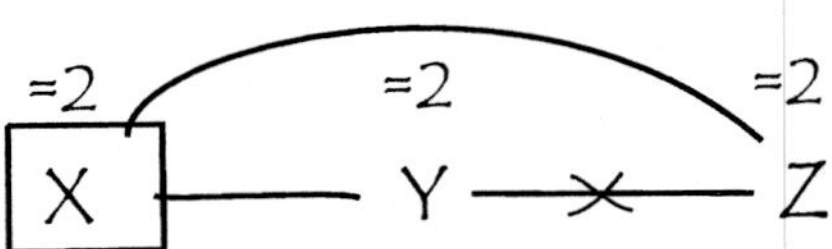

New highways

When the members are physical locations with something physically connecting them, you should automatically think of a network map. The first step is to decide how to draw the map. Allow enough space for the lines and the occupancy limits. (Figure 1) Rule 1 specifies that X, Y, and Z each have exactly two highways. Note this above them. Rule 2 specifies that Q, R, and S have three or fewer highways. Note this below them. Rule 3 is simple to diagram. Rule 4 is more difficult to diagram, so keep it in the back of your mind. The two things you will need to keep track of are the occupancy limits for each city and the requirement that Y and Z connect to at least one of Q, R, and S. Now, what conclusions can be made? You know that X cannot have any more highways. You can conclude that Y and Z cannot be connected by a highway, since doing so would prevent both of them from connecting to at least one of Q, R, and S. You can also conclude that of Q, R, and S, at least one of them will not be connected to Y or Z.

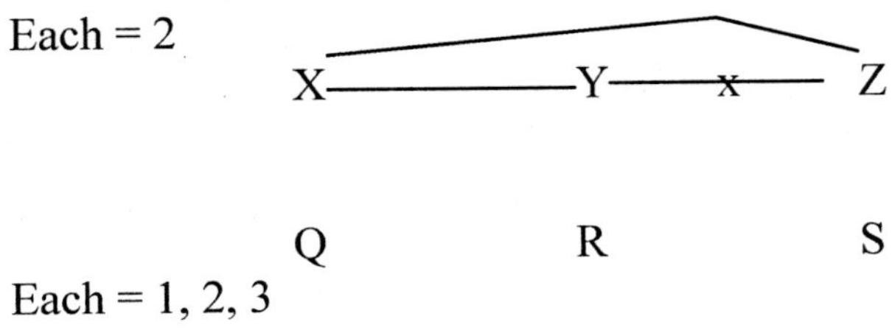

Fig. 1

7. (D) – Answer elimination will not work for this question, but you can still use a timesaving trick. Since Y is featured in four of the five answers, you don't need to check for Y; you can assume it is true. Checking for X, you see that X has reached its limit of two highways, and so cannot connect to Q. This eliminates two answer choices. Then you must determine that Z, R, S, and Y can potentially connect to Q.
   (A) See the analysis.
   (B) See the analysis.
   (C) See the analysis.
   (D)* See the analysis.
   (E) See the analysis.

8. (D) – After graphing this new information, you see that X, Y and Z have all reached their limit of two highways, so R cannot connect to X or Y.
   (A) See the analysis.
   (B) See the analysis.
   (C) See the analysis.
   (D)* See the analysis.
   (E) See the analysis.

9. (C) – Graphing this new information allows us to reach the maximum number of highways for each city. Then count the number of cities between X and S. The route must be S to Q, to R, to Z, to X, or it must be S to Q, to R, to Y, to X. So there are three cities to pass through.
(A) See the analysis.
(B) See the analysis.
(C) * See the analysis.
(D) See the analysis.
(E) See the analysis. There are not even five cities that could be passed through.

10. (C) – When a question does not add new information, the answer can usually be found in the initial analysis. The initial analysis showed that Y and Z could not be connected.
(A) See the analysis. Also, Rule 3 connects X and Z.
(B) See the analysis.
(C) * See the analysis.
(D) See the analysis.
(E) See the analysis.

11. (A) – Because this question alters the initial rules, you must go back and recreate the diagram from scratch. After doing so, consider the answer choices.
(A) * If Y were connected to X and Z, then Y would not be able to connect to Q, R, or S because Y must connect to exactly two other cities. This would violate Rule 4.
(B) There is no reason Q cannot be connected to Y and Y be connected to Z.
(C) R can be connected only to Z.
(D) S can be connected only to Q. Y and Z would not be able to connect to S, but that is fine.
(E) Y and Z can still fulfill their requirements if they are connected to Q. They would both be connected to exactly two cities. Q would be connected to exactly three cities. X would have to connect to one other city, and R and S would also have to connect to at least on other city.

Two final unusual games

The divisible line game and the multiple rounds game are the two remaining unusual games. The divisible line game has much in common with both simple line games and circle games. The multiple rounds game bears some similarity to multiple line games. That said, these two types of games are different enough to warrant special mention and a practice game with explanations for each. The divisible line game will be examined first, followed by the multiple rounds game.

Questions 6-10

A group of scientists is attempting to contact alien life forms by broadcasting into space a series of five symbols—Q, R, S, V, and W. After the scientists select an order for the five symbols, the order will be broadcast three times. The selection of symbols must satisfy the following requirements:

R must be broadcast before S.
V must be broadcast before Q.
W must be broadcast immediately before or after V is broadcast.

6. Which of the following could be an accurate list of the first eight symbols that are broadcast, beginning with the first symbol?

(A) S, W, V, R, Q, S, W, V
(B) R, W, S, V, Q, R, W, S
(C) V, W, R, Q, S, V, W, R
(D) R, Q, S, V, W, R, Q, S
(E) V, W, Q, R, S, W, Q, R

7. If V is the third symbol broadcast, which of the following must be the sixth symbol broadcast?

(A) Q
(B) R
(C) S
(D) V
(E) W

8. Which of the following is a complete and accurate list of symbols that cannot be broadcast seventh?

(A) R
(B) S
(C) Q, V
(D) R, Q
(E) R, S, V

9. The broadcast is fully determined if which of the following is true?

(A) W is fourth.
(B) R is third.
(C) V is third.
(D) Q is fifth.
(E) S is fourth.

10. Which of the following is a possible broadcast order of ten symbols that ends with the second symbol of the third broadcast?

(A) R, S, V, W, Q, R, S, V, W, Q
(B) W, Q, S, R, V, W, Q, S, R, V
(C) V, R, S, Q, W, V, R, S, Q, W
(D) R, Q, S, V, W, R, Q, S, W, V
(E) V, W, S, Q, R, V, W, S, Q, R

GO ON TO THE NEXT PAGE.

Questions 6-10

A group of scientists is attempting to contact alien life forms by broadcasting into space a series of five symbols—Q, R, S, V, and W. After the scientists select an order for the five symbols, the order will be broadcast three times. The selection of symbols must satisfy the following requirements:

R must be broadcast before S.
V must be broadcast before Q.
W must be broadcast immediately before or after V is broadcast.

6. Which of the following could be an accurate list of the first eight symbols that are broadcast, beginning with the first symbol?

(A) S, W, V, R, Q, S, W, V
(B) R, W, S, V, Q, R, W, S
(C) V, W, R, Q, S, V, W, R
(D) R, Q, S, V, W, R, Q, S
(E) V, W, Q, R, S, W, Q, R

7. If V is the third symbol broadcast, which of the following must be the sixth symbol broadcast?

(A) Q
(B) R
(C) S
(D) V
(E) W

8. Which of the following is a complete and accurate list of symbols that cannot be broadcast seventh?

(A) R
(B) S
(C) Q, V
(D) R, Q
(E) R, S, V

9. The broadcast is fully determined if which of the following is true?

(A) W is fourth.
(B) R is third.
(C) V is third.
(D) Q is fifth.
(E) S is fourth.

10. Which of the following is a possible broadcast order of ten symbols that ends with the second symbol of the third broadcast?

(A) R, S, V, W, Q, R, S, V, W, Q
(B) W, Q, S, R, V, W, Q, S, R, V
(C) V, R, S, Q, W, V, R, S, Q, W
(D) R, Q, S, V, W, R, Q, S, W, V
(E) V, W, S, Q, R, V, W, S, Q, R

GO ON TO THE NEXT PAGE

Scientist broadcast

We are told that five symbols will be broadcast. Five members are not enough to make a workable line game, so you knew that something more was involved. Once the order of the five symbols is chosen, the symbols are then broadcast three times in a row. For example, if the order RSWVQ is chosen, then the broadcast will be RSWVQ|RSWVQ|RSWVQ. The questions will try to trick you by having answer choices that start somewhere in the middle of an order. This is like the circle games, where the answer choice can start anywhere in the order. You must focus on the relationship of the members to one another, not on which one is first or last. Figure 1 shows the three rules. The only conclusion we can make so far is that Q comes after W.

R < S
V < Q
W V W

W V W < Q

Fig. 1

1. (C) – This question specifies that the answer choices begin with the first symbol. Draw a vertical line between the fifth and sixth symbols so that you know when the first round of five ends and the second round of five begins. Then look at the first five symbols and use rule violation answer elimination.
(A) This choice violates Rule 1 because it has S before R.
(B) This choice violates Rule 3 because it has W and V separated by one other symbol.
(C) * This is a valid permutation.
(D) This violates Rule 2 because it has Q before V.
(E) This choice violates the rules in the setup paragraph because the sixth, seventh, and eight symbols do not match the first, second, and third symbols.

2. (B) – If V is third, the next symbol to determine is W. Do two permutations: one with W second, and one with W fourth. In both permutations, R must be first and therefore sixth as well.
(A) See the analysis.
(B) * See the analysis.
(C) See the analysis.
(D) See the analysis.
(E) See the analysis.

3. (D) – To determine what symbol cannot be broadcast seventh, we first need to determine what symbol cannot be broadcast second. From the work in Question 2, we know that S can be second and seventh, which eliminates two

answer choices. Can R be second and seventh? No, because this doesn't allow the other symbols to be placed. Can Q be second and seventh? No, because V (and W) must be before Q.

(A) See (D).
(B) S can be second and seventh, see Question 2.
(C) R cannot be second and seventh, so this answer choice is wrong.
(D) * Neither R nor Q can be second and seventh.
(E) S can be second and seventh, see Question 2.

4. (A) – The best way to solve this problem is to simply plug in the new information and see what permutations emerge.

(A) * Yes, if W is fourth, then Q is fifth and V is third. R is first and S is second.
(B) If R is third, then either V or W can be second and the other first.
(C) If V is third, then W can be second or fourth, Q can be sixth, and R and S can be fit in wherever there is space.
(D) If Q is fifth, then S must be sixth. But W and V can be anywhere on first, second, or third.
(E) If S is fourth, then Q is fifth, but W and V are flexible.

5. (B) – Read the question very carefully. This series of ten symbols ends with the second symbol of the third broadcast. Draw a vertical line between the eighth and ninth symbols. Then count back five symbols to the left and draw another vertical line between the fourth and fifth symbols. Now that the series are clear, focus on the order of the five symbols that fall between the two lines (starting with the fourth symbol from the left.)

(A) Here, the fourth symbol, W, is separated from V, which is third. The problem is that W is in second series and V is in the first series, so although this initially looks like it does not violate Rule 3, it does.
(B) * This is a valid permutation.
(C) This choice has Q (fourth) before V (sixth), violating Rule 2.
(D) This choice has VW in the second broadcast, but WV in the third broadcast, violating the rule in the setup.
(E) This choice has Q (fourth) before V (sixth), violating Rule 2.

Questions 7–11

Three students—Ann, Bob, and Charles—are each assigned to be individually tutored by three tutors—Robert, Tamra, and Quentin. The initial order of tutors to students is Robert with Ann, Tamra with Bob, and Quentin with Charles. Each tutoring session lasts for one hour. After the tutoring session is over, a change will be made. Each of the following changes will be used exactly once:

Change 1: The students working with Robert and Tamra switch tutors.
Change 2: Ann and Bob switch tutors.
Change 3: Bob and Charles switch tutors.

7. If Quentin tutors Charles after the second change, then which one of the following must be true?

(A) Quentin tutors Charles after the third change.
(B) Quentin tutors Bob after the third change.
(C) Tamra tutors Ann after the second change.
(D) Robert tutors Bob after the second change.
(E) Robert tutors Charles after the third change.

8. Which one of the following cannot be true after the third change?

(A) Charles is tutored by Quentin.
(B) Charles is tutored by Robert.
(C) Ann is tutored by Robert.
(D) Bob is tutored by Tamra.
(E) Bob is tutored by Quentin.

9. If, after the second change, Bob is tutored by Tamra, which one of the following must be true?

(A) Bob was tutored by Tamra after the first change.
(B) Bob was tutored by Quentin after the first change.
(C) Charles was tutored by Quentin after the first change.
(D) Ann will be tutored by Quentin after the third change.
(E) Charles will be tutored by Robert after the third change.

10. Each of the following could be a possible listing of tutors and students after the second change EXCEPT:

(A) Robert: Charles; Tamra: Ann; Quentin: Bob
(B) Robert: Charles; Tamra: Bob; Quentin: Ann
(C) Robert: Bob; Tamra: Charles; Quentin: Ann
(D) Robert: Ann; Tamra: Bob; Quentin: Charles
(E) Robert: Charles; Tamra: Ann; Quentin: Bob

11. Suppose that the condition that requires each change to be used exactly once is replaced with the condition that one of the changes may be used exactly twice. Which one of the following CANNOT be a possible listing of tutors and students after the fourth change?

(A) Robert: Charles; Tamra: Ann; Quentin: Bob
(B) Robert: Bob; Tamra: Charles; Quentin: Ann
(C) Robert: Ann; Tamra: Bob; Quentin: Charles
(D) Robert: Charles; Tamra: Ann; Quentin: Bob
(E) Robert: Ann; Tamra: Charles; Quentin: Bob

GO ON TO THE NEXT PAGE.

Questions 7–11

Three students—Ann, Bob, and Charles—are each assigned to be individually tutored by three tutors—Robert, Tamra, and Quentin. The initial order of tutors to students is Robert with Ann, Tamra with Bob, and Quentin with Charles. Each tutoring session lasts for one hour. After the tutoring session is over, a change will be made. Each of the following changes will be used exactly once:

Change 1: The students working with Robert and Tamra switch tutors.
Change 2: Ann and Bob switch tutors.
Change 3: Bob and Charles switch tutors.

7. If Quentin tutors Charles after the second change, then which one of the following must be true?

(A) Quentin tutors Charles after the third change.
(B) Quentin tutors Bob after the third change.
(C) Tamra tutors Ann after the second change.
(D) Robert tutors Bob after the second change.
(E) Robert tutors Charles after the third change.

R	T	Q
A	B	C
B	A	C
A	B	C
A	C	B

8. Which one of the following cannot be true after the third change? Refer to later

(A) Charles is tutored by Quentin.
(B) Charles is tutored by Robert.
(C) Ann is tutored by Robert. - see 7
(D) Bob is tutored by Tamra.
(E) Bob is tutored by Quentin. - see 7

9. If, after the second change, Bob is tutored by Tamra, which one of the following must be true?

(A) Bob was tutored by Tamra after the first change.
(B) Bob was tutored by Quentin after the first change.
(C) Charles was tutored by Quentin after the first change.
(D) Ann will be tutored by Quentin after the third change.
(E) Charles will be tutored by Robert after the third change.

10. Each of the following could be a possible listing of tutors and students after the second change EXCEPT: (see 7 for work)

(A) Robert: Charles; Tamra: Ann; Quentin: Bob
(B) Robert: Charles; Tamra: Bob; Quentin: Ann
(C) Robert: Bob; Tamra: Charles; Quentin: Ann
(D) Robert: Ann; Tamra: Bob; Quentin: Charles
(E) Robert: Charles; Tamra: Ann; Quentin: Bob

11. Suppose that the condition that requires each change to be used exactly once is replaced with the condition that one of the changes may be used exactly twice. Which one of the following CANNOT be a possible listing of tutors and students after the fourth change? (use 10 work)

(A) Robert: Charles; Tamra: Ann; Quentin: Bob
(B) Robert: Bob; Tamra: Charles; Quentin: Ann
(C) Robert: Ann; Tamra: Bob; Quentin: Charles
(D) Robert: Charles; Tamra: Ann; Quentin: Bob
(E) Robert: Ann; Tamra: Charles; Quentin: Bob

GO ON TO THE NEXT PAGE

		R	T	Q
		A	B	C
1	#1	B	A	C
	#2	A	B	C
	#3	A	C	B
2	#1	B	A	C
	#3	C	A	B
	#2	A	B	A
3	#2	B	A	C
	#1	A	B	C
	#3	A	C	B
4	#2	B	A	C
	#3	C	A	B
	#1	A	C	B
5	#3	A	C	B
	#1	C	A	B
	#2	C	B	A
6	#3	A	C	B
	#2	B	C	A
	#1	C	B	A

Tutoring assignments
In this multiple rounds game, the initial order of the tutors is R, T, and Q. They will tutor students A, B, C, respectively. Each of the three rules is used once to shuffle the assignment of students to tutors. This kind of game can be very difficult because the questions will tell you what is true after the third shuffle and ask you what must have been true after the first shuffle. Working backwards like this is very difficult for test-takers. Instead of working backwards, another option is to simply do all the permutations at the outset. This requires you to swallow your pride in your LSAT prowess, but it gets the job done. As you can see in the previous page, there are six possible series of permutations. Once you start doing the permutations, it doesn't take as long as you might have thought. For this game, doing the permutations was more efficient than working backwards because you now have all the information at your fingertips when answering a question. However, for the vast majority of games, it is less efficient to do the permutations. In the highly unlikely event that you get a multiple rounds game, when should you do the permutations, and when should you work backwards? When there are three members being shuffled (like here) and three rules, each used once (like here), then do the six series of permutations. If there are more members or more rules, or if each rule may be used more than once, then it is better to work backwards for each question. To prevent confusion when doing all six series, do them in order: changes 1, 2, 3 then 1, 3, 2, then 2, 1,3, then 2, 3, 1, then 3, 1, 2, then 3, 2, 1.

7. (B) – Consult the permutations to find those where Q tutors C after the second change. There are two permutations, the first series and the third series. Using those two series, check the answer choices.
(A) Neither in series 1 or 3 does Q tutor C after the third change.
(B) * In both series 1 and 3, Q tutors B after the third change.
(C) T does not tutor A in either of these two series.
(D) R does not tutor B in either series.
(E) R does not tutor C at any time during these three series.

8. (A) – Check each series and see what is true after the third change.
(A) * In none of the six series does Q tutor C after the third change.
(B) C is tutored by R in series 2, 5, and 6.
(C) A is tutored by R in series 1, 3, and 4.
(D) B is tutored by T in series 2, 5, and 6.
(E) B is tutored by Q in series 1, 3, and 4.

9. (C) – Find the series where B is tutored by T after the second change. We find this in series 1 and 3. Check these series against the answer choices.
(A) B was not tutored by T after the first change in either series.
(B) B was not tutored by Q after the first change in either series.
(C) * In both series 1 and 3, C was tutored by Q after the first change.
(D) A is not tutored by Q after the third change in either series.

(E) C is not tutored by R in either series after the third change.

10. (B) – Check all six of the series to see what is not true after the second change.
(A) Check series 2 and you see this is possible.
(B) * In none of the six series is this true after the second change.
(C) In series 6 we see that this is possible.
(D) Check series 1 and you see this is possible.
(E) Check series 2 and you see this is possible.

11. (E) – Ouch, at first glance, this looks like it was going to be really painful. Fortunately, this rule change does not require you to go back and rework all of the permutations. Instead, look at each answer choice. Find a series where you can make a fourth change and reach the result in the answer choice.
(A) This result can be reached if you take series 1 and use change 1 for the fourth change.
(B) This result can be reached if you take series 2 and use change 1 for the fourth change.
(C) This result can be reached if you take series 3 and use change 3 for the fourth change.
(D) This result can be reached if you take series 1 and use change 1 for the fourth change.
(E) * There is no way to reach this result using the three rules and making four changes.

Conclusion of unusual games

Points to remember:

You can be virtually certain that you will only see line games and grouping games on your LSAT.

If you do get an unusual game, you will get only one.

If you do get an unusual game, consider doing it last, after you score all the points you can on games that you are familiar with.

You have seen the common variants of these unusual games. Never underestimate the creativity of the test-makers. Be ready to modify these diagrams and techniques when necessary.

Once you become skilled at executing line games and grouping games, you will have no trouble adapting the reasoning skills to other kinds of games.

You have now finished a comprehensive overview of the unusual LSAT games. You have learned what the setups look like, what the rules look like, and what the questions look like. You have learned how to draw the diagrams, how to depict the rules, and how to make additional conclusions.

This knowledge is the starting point. The next step is to become adept at using this knowledge. The practice tests in this book provide ample opportunity for you to sharpen your skills. At some point in your preparation, you should review the unique games discussion in the next section for insight on just how quirky the LSAT puzzles have been in the past.

Unique Games

Since 1991, there has been a few times when an LSAT contained a game that was completely unlike any game ever seen. Thankfully, this is extremely rare. If we discount the period from October 1993 to June 1995 as being anomalous, we could say that unique games don't exist. Unique games have not appeared for more than ten years. Since unique games are so exceedingly unlikely to be on your LSAT, it makes no sense to predict if they will appear, and if they appear, to predict what form they will take. The following discussion is meant to put your mind at ease, not to instruct you on how to do these unique puzzles (since, remember, you won't see one on your test). After studying the other sections of this book, you have everything you need to excel. If, by some odd chance, you get a unique game, the skills you have developed for the normal games will carry you through with flying colors.

The spelling game – Feb 1994

This game wins the award for being the all-time quirkiest game. It confounded test-takers because it doesn't have a diagram. The game consisted of a series of five nonsense "words" of four or more letters each. For example, erox, eroz, feroz, fzroz, zroz. Each string of five words had to be in alphabetical order from left to right. For example, bbrag, abrag would not be allowed. Each new "word" was derived by changing the word to its left, either by deleting, adding, or changing one letter. Other rules stated that a change could not be used twice in a row (so, aaaz, aabz, babz, which twice changes one letter, would not be permitted) and a rule that three words in a row couldn't start with the same letter (so, argha, argh, argg, all starting with the letter "a", would not be permitted). The questions gave partial information and asked about the possibilities. For example, one question asked, if the first word was "blender" and the third word was "slender," what could the second word be? (It was "lender," which was derived by deleting the "b" in "blender" and then adding an "s" to "lender" to make "slender.") Even after figuring-out the game and learning how to work with the rules, this game proved to be difficult to execute.

The radar map – June 1995

The radar map game was very odd, and very difficult. There were four circular radar zones. One of the radar zones (zone U) fell inside the area where two of the other zones (R and T) overlap. The fourth zone (zone S) overlapped with T, but not R, and therefore not U. Everything about the language of the setup was designed to encourage test-takers to use a Venn diagram of overlapping circles. The members (four airplanes) could or could not be in certain zones, and could or could not be in the same zones as other members. Although this was not a grouping game, skill at using grouping rules was necessary to get through the questions in a reasonable time.

The six-city map – October 1993

The test-makers took pity and provided a diagram for this game. On the diagram there were two columns of three boxes each, for a total of six boxes. The members (four hospitals, two jails, and two universities) were to be placed in the six boxes. The rules specified, for example, that if a city had a jail, then it had to have a hospital, or that any cities that bordered each other could not both have universities. This game was actually quite easy, despite being unusual.

The six-paintings on the wall – June 1997

Four years later, the six-city map was reincarnated, standardized, and improved. In this game there were two rows of three columns each, for a total of six boxes. Each of the six boxes represented one painting. Each painting had two characteristics: its medium, either oil or watercolor, and its age, either nineteenth century or twentieth century. All the watercolor paintings had to share common borders with each other (either above, below, or to the side of). All the oil paintings had to share common borders with each other. This common border requirement was also true of the age of the paintings. The effect of the common border rule was that if, for example, exactly two of the six paintings were watercolors, then they had to share a common border. There could not be an oil painting separating them. Once you figured-out that the paintings were clustered by their features, the game became easy. Because the setup provided a visual aid, virtually every test-taker used a six-box diagram, and if they did so, they had no difficulty solving the questions. But, as it turns out, this game could have been graphed using a multiple line, with two sets of three dashes, and each dash has the two features, as shown below. Arguably this game was not a unique game, but a multiple line game presented in a very unusual way.

```
__|__  __|__  __|__

__|__  __|__  __|__
```

The beaker mixing game – October 1994

This game frustrated every test-taker. There were four flasks: red, blue, green, and orange. The rules dictated that when any two of the flasks were mixed together, a new color would result. This game was difficult because there were so many rules and so many possible combinations. A modified "flow chart" diagram worked to keep track of the many rules, see below. Working through the answer choices required great attention to detail, since there were so many possible combinations. For example, a question would state that the three ending flasks were green, orange, and red. The test-taker had to identify that the green and the orange were the starting flasks, and then determine that the red and blue starting flasks had been mixed to create the red ending flask.

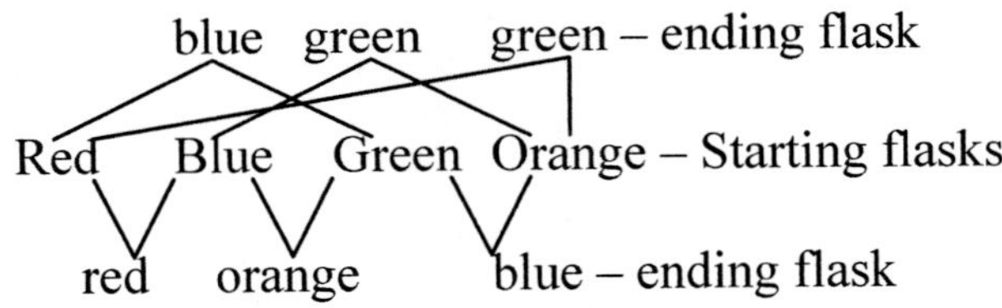

Practice Tests & Explanations

Now that you have learned everything you need to know about the games, you must learn how to use this knowledge in a test environment. Each of the following 14 practice tests is followed by detailed explanations. Spend 35 minutes doing each practice test. Grade yourself, then turn to the explanations to help you determine why you missed the questions you missed. Your diligent practice will begin to yield an improved score after just a few tests.

Practice Test 1

Spend 35 minutes doing this practice test. When time is up, review the explanations to help understand the questions that you did not answer correctly.

SECTION I

Time—35 minutes

25 Questions

Directions: Each group of questions in this section is based on a set of conditions. In answering some of the questions, it may be useful to draw a rough diagram. Choose the response that most accurately and completely answers each question and blacken the corresponding space on your answer sheet.

Questions 1–6

The manager of a clothing store must fill two display windows with the following seven articles of clothing: hat, gloves, scarf, purse, earmuffs, shorts, and sweater. At least three, and at most, four items are displayed together according to the following conditions:

The hat and gloves must be displayed together.
The shorts must not be displayed with the sweater.
If the purse is displayed with exactly three other items, one of those items must be the scarf.

1. Which one of the following is an acceptable arrangement of items that can be displayed together?

(A) Shorts, earmuffs, scarf, hat
(B) Shorts, sweater, purse, scarf
(C) Sweater, scarf, earmuffs, purse
(D) Shorts, sweater, earmuffs, scarf
(E) Sweater, earmuffs, hat, purse

2. Which one of the following could be a complete and accurate list of items displayed in the same window as the hat?

(A) Shorts
(B) Sweater, scarf
(C) Gloves, shorts, purse, scarf
(D) Gloves, sweater, shorts
(E) Gloves, sweater, scarf

3. If the gloves and scarf are displayed in different windows, then which one of the following must be true?

(A) The gloves are displayed with the sweater.
(B) The purse is not displayed with the hat.
(C) The hat is displayed with the scarf.
(D) The purse is displayed with the earmuffs.
(E) The hat is displayed with the earmuffs.

4. If the scarf is displayed with exactly two additional items, then which one of the following could be displayed with the scarf?

(A) The earmuffs and the purse.
(B) The earmuffs and the hat.
(C) The sweater and the purse.
(D) The hat and the gloves.
(E) The gloves and the earmuffs.

5. If the hat is displayed with three additional items, how many different items can be displayed at any given time with the hat?

(A) 2
(B) 3
(C) 4
(D) 5
(E) 6

6. Which one of the following must be true?

(A) If the purse is displayed with exactly three items, one item is the shorts.
(B) If the earmuffs are displayed with exactly two items, one item is a scarf.
(C) If the hat is displayed, it is displayed with exactly three other items.
(D) If the gloves are displayed, they are displayed with the purse.
(E) Either the sweater or the shorts are displayed with the earmuffs.

GO ON TO THE NEXT PAGE

Questions 7–12

Two students at a performing arts camp must each create a schedule with three or four classes. The students select, at most, one class from each of the following subjects: dance, brass band, orchestra, and theater. Each subject has three possible skill levels: intermediate, advanced, and expert. The students select their classes subject to the following conditions:

The students have no classes in common.
Neither student has classes at all three skill levels.
Each student has a different skill level for their brass band and orchestra classes.
Student 1 has advanced dance class.
Student 2 has exactly four classes.
Student 1 does not have a theater class.

7. Which one of the following could be a complete schedule for both of the students?

(A) Student 1: advanced dance, intermediate brass band, advanced orchestra
Student 2: intermediate dance, advanced brass band, expert orchestra, intermediate theater
(B) Student 1: advanced dance, expert brass band, advanced orchestra, advanced theater
Student 2: intermediate dance, intermediate brass band, expert orchestra, expert theater
(C) Student 1: advanced dance, advanced brass band, expert orchestra
Student 2: expert dance, intermediate brass band, intermediate orchestra, expert theater
(D) Student 1: advanced dance, advanced brass band, expert orchestra
Student 2: intermediate dance, expert brass band, intermediate orchestra, intermediate theater
(E) Student 1: advanced dance, advanced brass band, expert orchestra
Student 2: intermediate dance, advanced brass band, intermediate orchestra, advanced theater

8. If student 2 has advanced brass band, then which one of the following could be true?

(A) Student 1 has advanced brass band.
(B) Student 1 has expert orchestra.
(C) Student 2 has intermediate brass band.
(D) Student 2 has advanced orchestra.
(E) Student 2 has expert dance.

9. Which one of the following could be true?

(A) Student 1 has advanced brass band, and student 2 has advanced dance.
(B) Student 2 has intermediate theater, intermediate orchestra, and intermediate brass band.
(C) Student 1 has three advanced classes.
(D) The students have two classes in common.
(E) Student 2 has advanced brass band and advanced theater.

10. If at least four of the students' classes are intermediate skill level classes, then which one of the following must be true?

(A) Student 2 has advanced brass band.
(B) Student 2 has intermediate theater.
(C) Student 1 has at least two intermediate classes.
(D) Student 1 has at most two intermediate classes.
(E) Student 2 has at most two intermediate classes.

11. If there is only one intermediate level class, then which one of the following must be false?

(A) Student 2 has advanced orchestra.
(B) Student 1 has expert orchestra.
(C) Student 2 has intermediate theater.
(D) Student 1 has expert brass band.
(E) Student 2 has advanced brass band.

12. If Student 1 has advanced brass band, then which one of the following could be true?

(A) Student 2 has intermediate dance and advanced brass band.
(B) Student 1 has advanced orchestra, and student 2 has intermediate orchestra.
(C) Student 2 has intermediate brass band and expert orchestra.
(D) Student 2 has advanced theater and advanced dance.
(E) Student 2 has advanced brass band and advanced orchestra.

GO ON TO THE NEXT PAGE.

Questions 13–18

A convention planner must schedule seven consecutive speeches to be given during the convention. The six speakers who give speeches are: Arundel, Boyle, Canabra, Dalton, French, and Rial. The speeches must be scheduled subject to the following conditions:

Boyle must speak earlier than Dalton.
Rial must speak later than Arundel.
Arundel must speak immediately before or immediately after Boyle.
There must be exactly two speeches given between the speeches given by Canabra and Dalton.
French must speak first and must speak twice during the convention.

13. Which one of the following could be a complete list of the speeches to be given, from first to last?

(A) French, Canabra, Arundel, Boyle, Rial, Dalton, French
(B) French, Canabra, Boyle, Arundel, Dalton, French, Rial
(C) French, Rial, Canabra, Arundel, Boyle, Dalton, Eric
(D) French, Arundel, Rial, Canabra, French, Boyle, Dalton
(E) French, Dalton, Boyle, Arundel, Canabra, Rial, French

14. If Canabra is scheduled seventh, then which one of the following must be true?

(A) Boyle speaks after Rial.
(B) Arundel speaks before Boyle.
(C) Dalton speaks before Rial.
(D) French speaks first and second.
(E) Rial speaks before Dalton.

15. Which one of the following must be true?

(A) French never speaks third or fifth.
(B) Arundel or Boyle speaks third or fourth.
(C) Dalton always speaks after Canabra.
(D) Dalton never speaks before Rial.
(E) Canabra either speaks second or third.

16. The earliest Rial can speak is

(A) second
(B) third
(C) fourth
(D) fifth
(E) sixth

17. If Canabra speaks before Rial speaks, each of the following could be true EXCEPT:

(A) French speaks seventh.
(B) French speaks fourth.
(C) Arundel speaks fourth.
(D) Boyle speaks third.
(E) Canabra speaks second or third.

18. The order of the speeches is completely determined if which one of the following is true?

(A) Arundel is third, and Boyle is fourth.
(B) Arundel is fourth, and Boyle is fifth.
(C) Arundel is fourth, and Boyle is third.
(D) Canabra is third, and Rial is seventh.
(E) French is first and seventh.

GO ON TO THE NEXT PAGE.

Questions 19–24

A theater troupe will perform seven skits during an evening performance. The performers include five experienced actors—Ariana, Bronte, Carlow, Dabia, and Eric—and five novice performers—Nabiel, Sam, Thomas, Jackie, and Kyrasaki. Each performer will perform in exactly one skit according to the following requirements:

Bronte and Nabiel and no one else perform one skit.
Eric and Dabia and one novice perform one skit.
The first performance features no novices.
Carlow must perform after Bronte and Dabia.
The final performance features one novice.

19. Which one of the following could be a complete and accurate list of the skits, from first to last?

(A) Ariana, Bronte and Nabiel, Carlow, Jackie, Thomas, Eric and Dabia and Sam, Kyrasaki
(B) Thomas, Ariana, Bronte and Nabiel, Eric and Dabia and Thomas, Carlow, Jackie, Sam
(C) Ariana, Jackie, Bronte, Eric and Dabia and Nabiel, Carlow and Thomas, Kyrasaki, Sam
(D) Ariana, Sam, Kyrasaki, Jackie, Eric and Dabia and Thomas, Bronte and Nabiel, Carlow
(E) Ariana, Bronte and Nabiel, Eric and Dabia and Thomas, Kyrasaki, Carlow, Jackie, Sam

20. Which one of the following is a complete and accurate list of the skits that Bronte could participate in?

(A) fourth and sixth
(B) third, fourth, and fifth
(C) second, third, fourth, and fifth
(D) second, third, fourth, and sixth
(E) second, third, fourth, fifth, and sixth

21. If Sam and Jackie perform later than all the experienced actors, then which one of the following must be true?

(A) Thomas performs after Carlow.
(B) Thomas performs before Eric.
(C) Kyrasaki performs before Carlow.
(D) Nabiel performs before Jackie.
(E) Carlow performs fifth.

22. Which one of the following performers could perform in the final skit?

(A) Thomas
(B) Nabiel
(C) Carlow
(D) Bronte
(E) Ariana

23. What is the maximum number of skits that can be performed between the performances that include Kyrasaki and Carlow?

(A) one
(B) two
(C) three
(D) four
(E) five

24. Suppose that the condition that the first skit includes no novices is replaced with the condition that the first two skits include only novices. If all the other conditions remain unchanged, then which one of the following CANNOT be true?

(A) Thomas performs third.
(B) Ariana performs seventh.
(C) Bronte performs fifth.
(D) Thomas performs seventh.
(E) Carlow performs fifth.

S T O P

IF YOU FINISH BEFORE TIME IS CALLED, YOU MAY CHECK YOUR WORK ON THIS SECTION ONLY.
DO NOT WORK ON ANY OTHER SECTION IN THE TEST.

Answer key and explanations for Test 1

Answer Key

1. C
2. E
3. B
4. C
5. D
6. E
7. D
8. E
9. E
10. B
11. C
12. C
13. B
14. C
15. B
16. D
17. B
18. B
19. E
20. C
21. D
22. A
23. C
24. B

Clothing display

This game requires a typical multiple-line diagram. Line diagrams (which include simple lines and multiple lines) are the most frequently tested games. Of the line diagrams, simple lines are most common. An important condition in this setup is that at least three items are displayed together, and a maximum of four can be displayed together. This makes things much easier. You will assign seven items to two groups: a group of three and a group of four. One of the groups will be displayed in Window 1, while the other will be in Window 2. (The windows are labeled to keep things organized and make explanations easier. These labels are arbitrary, since the setup and questions never specify a window by name.) The three rules are easy to understand and diagram. The diagram should reflect this simplicity. The only rule you can place directly on the diagram is that the sweater and shorts must always be kept apart. Use a 50/50 slash or a "≠" to note Rule 2. (Figure 1) The other two rules cannot be placed on the diagram until the questions supply more information. Since there is not much to work with yet, you cannot make any easy warranted conclusions, so it is best to go to the questions instead of doing permutations.

[HG]
Sw ≠ Sh or Sw/Sh
If P + 3 → 1 is Sc

Window 1 Window 2

__ __ Sw/Sh || __ __ __ Sh/Sw

OR

__ __ __ Sw/Sh || __ __ Sh/Sw

Fig. 1

1. (C) – Typically the first question in the set requires you to use each rule to eliminate one answer choice. Start with the first rule and see if it is violated in any of the answer choices. Then do the same for each of the other rules.
   (A) The hat and the gloves must be displayed together, so this violates Rule 1.
   (B) The sweater and shorts must be displayed separately, so this violates Rule 2.
   (C) * Displaying the sweater, scarf, earmuffs, and purse together does not violate any rules.
   (D) See (B).
   (E) When the purse is displayed with three items, it must be displayed with the scarf, so this violates Rule 3. It also violates Rule 1.

2. (E) – Since the question directs your attention to the hat, review the rule that affects the hat. The hat must be displayed with the gloves. Knowing this allows us to eliminate choices (A) and (B) right away. Now review the rest of the answer choices.
(A) See the analysis.
(B) See the analysis.
(C) This choice has five items in the same display, which violates the initial condition that a maximum of four items are displayed together.
(D) This choice pairs the sweater and shorts, violating Rule 2.
(E) * This choice is a possible list of items displayed with the hat.

3. (B) – For "must be true" questions, the answer choice must always be correct. The other four choices will list things that are false, or things that may be true but are not required to be true. When you fill in the diagram of what is on display in Window 1, remember to diagram both for three items on display and four items on display. Now fill in the diagram. First, when the gloves are displayed, so is the hat. (Figure 2) This fills the three-item display, requiring the purse and earmuffs to be in Window 2. What about the four-item display? Can the earmuffs be displayed with the hat and gloves? Yes, the earmuffs are the free agent. Can the purse be displayed with the hat and gloves? No, because when the purse is displayed with three other items, one of them must be the scarf.
(A) There is a fifty percent chance that the sweater is displayed with the gloves.
(B) * Since the purse can never be displayed with the gloves in Window 1, it also cannot be displayed with the hat.
(C) In this scenario, the hat is never with the scarf.
(D) The purse can be with the earmuffs, but is not always with them.
(E) The hat is with the earmuffs in one of the two scenarios.

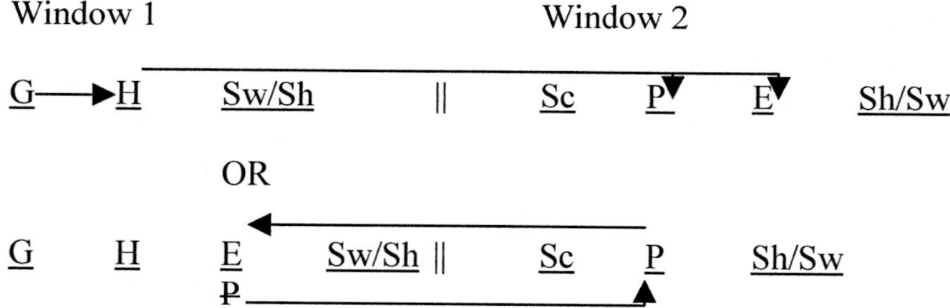

Fig. 2

4. (C) – Use the diagram. The scarf is displayed with exactly two additional items, one of which must be either the sweater or the shorts. The third item cannot be the hat or the gloves, because those two must always be together.

(Figure 3) Now consider Rule 3, which says that if the purse is with three other items, one must be the scarf. This prevents the purse from being with the hat and gloves, so the purse must be with the scarf in Window 1.

(A) Both the earmuffs and the purse cannot be with the scarf. The purse must be with the scarf. The earmuffs cannot be with the scarf.

(B) The hat cannot be with the scarf.

(C) * It is possible to have the purse with the sweater. Review Rule 3. The purse must be displayed with the scarf in this scenario, and the sweater may be displayed with them.

(D) Neither the hat nor the gloves can be with the scarf.

(E) The gloves cannot be with the scarf.

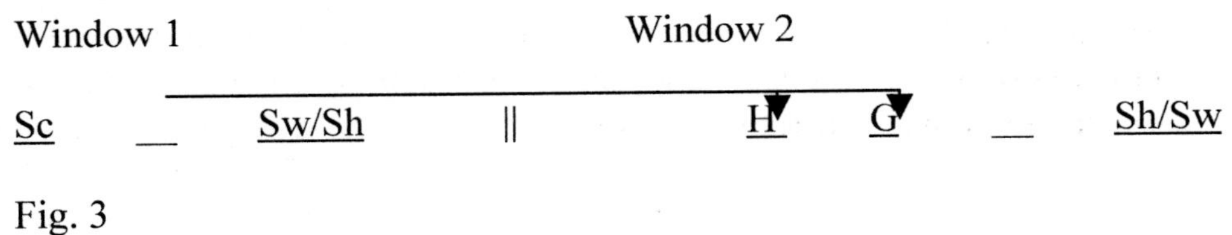

Fig. 3

5. (D) – This question resembles the previous question, but does not have the same analysis. Diagram for the hat using a four-dash line. Since the hat and gloves "travel" together, they fill two of the four dashes. You should fill one of the two remaining dashes with the mutually exclusive sweater/shorts. This leaves one dash to fill. The earmuffs are the free agent, so they could fill the spot. Can the scarf fill the spot? Yes, Rule 3 does not prevent this. Finally, can the purse be displayed with the hat? No, Rule 3 does prevent this. Counting the items that can be with the hat, we see that the purse is the only item that cannot be displayed with the hat. Thus, when displayed with three other items, the hat can appear with any of five of the six items. (Figure 4)

(A) See the analysis.

(B) See the analysis.

(C) See the analysis.

(D) * See the analysis.

(E) See the analysis.

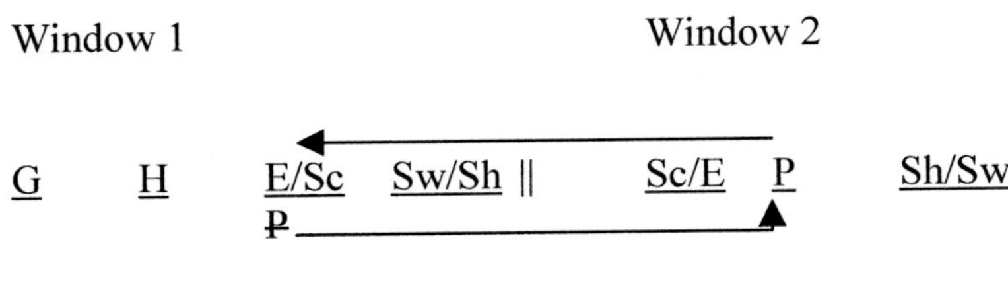

Fig. 4

6. (E) – Since this is a "must be true" question, you should be able to use previous work to narrow the choices. It may be necessary to do a little work with the answer choices.

(A) If you remembered that the sweater and shorts are interchangeable, you should have realized that neither of them *must* be with the purse.

(B) If the earmuffs are displayed with two other items, one of them must be the shorts or the sweater. The third item cannot be the hat or gloves. The third item must be the purse, not the scarf. Why? Because if the purse was in the second window, this would push the scarf to the first window, and this would violate Rule 3.

(C) It is possible to display the hat with exactly two other items, for example, the gloves and shorts.

(D) Consult the diagrams you did earlier; the gloves and purse need not be displayed together. Often, they are not displayed together.

(E) * This is clearly true. Either the shorts or the sweater must always be in the same window as the earmuffs.

Camp classes

This game uses a common multiple-line diagram. Each student has either three or four classes. Rule 5 says that student 2 has exactly four classes. Student 1 has exactly three classes because Rule 6 says that he does not have a theater class. Depict this information by drawing two parallel lines of three and four dashes each. Student 1 has advanced dance. Rule 1 specifies they can never have the same class, so we can conclude that student 2 cannot have advanced dance. You can mark this below or next to the appropriate space. Since there is no way to easily graph Rule 1, you must remember not to put them both into the same skill level for the same class. Rule 3 says each student has different skill levels for their brass band and orchestra classes. This condition is depicted in figure 1. Finally, Rule 2 requires that the students each have a maximum of two skill levels. When we combine the effect of this rule with the effect of Rule 3, we realize that each of the students must have exactly two skill levels; they cannot have just one skill level. There are no other obvious warranted conclusions to be made, so quickly move to the questions.

	Students #1	#2
Dance	A	___ ~~A~~
Brass	___	___
↕ x		
Orchestra	___	___
Theater	x	___
	A/?	?/? – each student has two skill levels

Fig. 1

7. (D) – Use each of the rules to eliminate the answer choices that violate them. The answer choice that remains is the correct answer.
   (A) This violates Rule 2, because neither student can have a schedule that includes three skill levels.
   (B) This violates Rule 6, because student 1 never has a theater class.
   (C) This violates Rule 3, because a student cannot have both intermediate brass and orchestra classes.
   (D) * This is a permissible schedule.
   (E) This violates Rule 1, because both students cannot have advanced brass band class.

8. (E) – Start by graphing the new information. (Figure 2) Student 1 cannot have the same brass band class as student 2; therefore, student 1 cannot have advanced brass. Also, student 1 must now have advanced orchestra, as a result of Rule 3. This means student 1 must have intermediate or expert brass. Since student 2 cannot have advanced dance or advanced orchestra, he has

either intermediate or expert classes for these subjects. That should be enough information to answer the question.

(A) Student 1 cannot have advanced brass band class.

(B) Student 1 cannot have expert orchestra because of Rule 2.

(C) Student 2 cannot have intermediate brass; this violates the given information.

(D) Student 2 cannot have advanced orchestra, because he has advanced brass.

(E) * Student 2 can have expert dance (or intermediate dance).

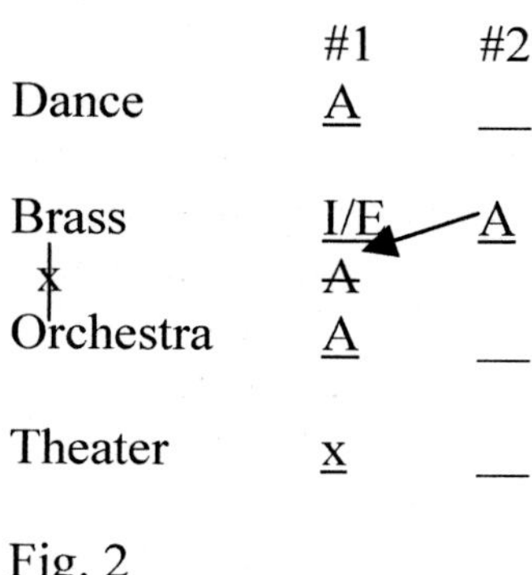

Fig. 2

9. (E) – This question can be answered using the information we already have, though it will be necessary to graph some of the permutations.

(A) Student 2 can never have advanced dance. (Figure 1)

(B) A student cannot have the same skill level for brass and orchestra, Rule 3.

(C) See (B).

(D) Rule 1 requires that the students never have classes in common.

(E) * It is okay for student 2 to have advanced brass, and just about any skill level is okay for the theater class, as long as Rule 2 is observed.

10. (B) – This question requires a different approach. Think about the impact of having four intermediate classes. We know student 2 could schedule three intermediate classes, but not four, because of the effect of Rule 3. The fourth intermediate class would have to be in student 1's schedule. Could student 2 have two intermediate classes? No, because student 1 cannot accommodate two intermediate classes. As you see in figure 3, the only uncertainty is about the brass and orchestra classes. This is enough information to answer the question.

(A) Student 2 may have intermediate (or advanced or expert) brass.

(B) * Student 2 must have intermediate theater.

(C) Student 1 only has one intermediate class.

(D) See (C).

(E) Student 2 must have exactly three intermediate classes.

#1 #2

Dance	A	I
Brass	I/A	?/I
Orchestra	A/I	I/?
Theater	x	I

Fig. 3

11. (C) – This question tests your creative scheduling skill in much the same way the previous question did. When there is only one intermediate class, the question becomes which student has the intermediate class, i.e., where should you put the single intermediate class? If you put it with student 2, then it would have to be for either the brass or orchestra class. Student 1 would then have advanced dance (a given), and advanced or expert brass band and orchestra. (Figure 4) Using figure 4, we can eliminate answer choices (B) and (D). Now try giving the intermediate class to student 1. The intermediate class would have to either be brass band or orchestra and the leftover class would be advanced. (Figure 5) In this case, student 2 would have expert dance for two reasons: first, because he can never have advanced dance, and second, because the single intermediate was already used. The rest of his classes would have to be advanced or expert. This means that student 2 could never have an intermediate theater class.
(A) Figure 5 shows that student 2 can have advanced orchestra.
(B) In figure 4, student 1 has expert orchestra.
(C) * Student 2 cannot have intermediate theater. If he did, this would cause problems, since this would leave only advanced and expert classes available for student 1 and only advanced or expert classes available for student 2. No matter how you try to schedule around this limitation, there would always be one subject where they would have the same skill level.
(D) Figure 4 shows that it is possible for student 1 to have expert brass band.
(E) Figure 5 shows that student 2 can have advanced brass band.

	#1	#2
Dance	A	E
Brass	A/E	E/I
Orchestra	E/A	I/E
Theater	x	E

Fig. 4

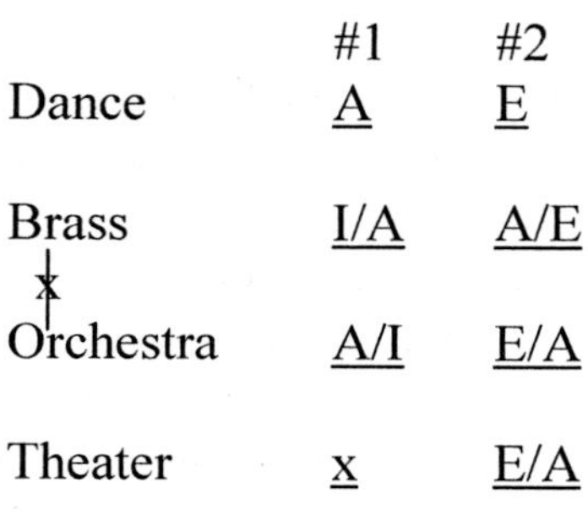

#1 #2
Dance A E
Brass I/A A/E
x
Orchestra A/I E/A
Theater x E/A

Fig. 5

12. (C) – Simply plug in the new information. You can now conclude that student 1 has either intermediate or expert orchestra, as a result of Rule 3. You know that student 2 cannot have the same skill levels as student 1, but that does not make things much clearer. Figure 6 shows the conclusions you can make. Since there are no more obvious conclusions to be made, turn your attention to the answer choices and do additional work if necessary.

(A) A quick check of the diagram shows that student 2 cannot have advanced brass band.

(B) Student 1 cannot have advanced orchestra.

(C) * Since the diagram is ambiguous, it requires a little work to confirm that this choice is correct.

(D) Student 2 cannot have advanced dance, because student 1 has advanced dance.

(E) Student 2 cannot have advanced brass band.

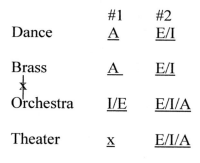

	#1	#2
Dance	A	E/I
Brass	A	E/I
x		
Orchestra	I/E	E/I/A
Theater	x	E/I/A

Fig. 6

Convention speeches

For this puzzle you will use a simple line diagram and greater-than/less-than notation. The basic setup is pretty clear—seven dashes. The only quirk, and it ends up being a minor one, is that there are six speakers, so French must speak twice. Whenever possible, you should combine two or more rules into a single compound rule. Since Boyle is earlier than Dalton, and Arundel is immediately before or after Boyle, Arundel must also be earlier than Dalton. Also, since Arundel and Boyle are earlier than Dalton and Rial, neither Arundel nor Boyle can be sixth or seventh. Always be looking for this kind of warranted conclusion. Since the Canabra and Dalton rule covers so much geography in the diagram, use it as the starting point. The graph in figure 1 shows all the rules and the combination rules. Rather than attempt to draw warranted conclusions (beyond combining the rules), it is more efficient to go directly to the questions. With a complicated compound rule like this one, you could waste a lot of time looking for warranted conclusions that may not be there.

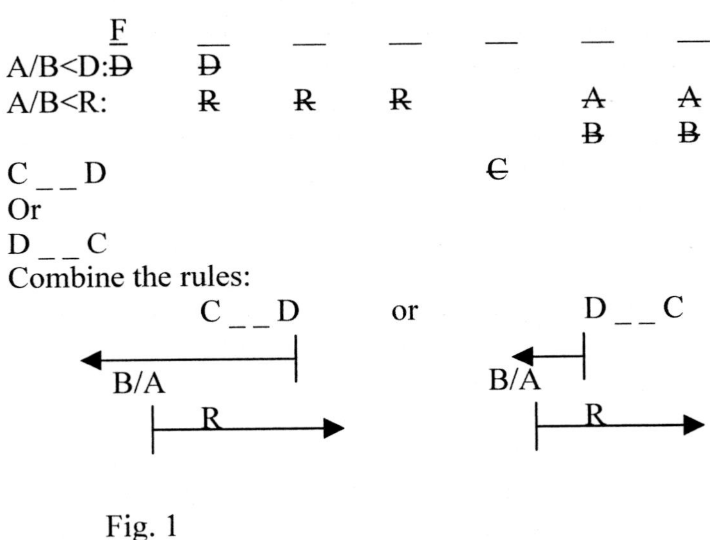

Fig. 1

13. (B) – Starting with the first rule, eliminate as many answer choices as possible, and then work your way down the list of rules.
(A) Canabra cannot be separated by three spaces from Dalton, Rule 4.
(B) * This is possible. Make note of this order since this correct answer may come in handy when answering later questions.
(C) This violates Rule 2 by putting Rial before Arundel
(D) This violates Rule 3 by separating Arundel and Boyle.
(E) This violates Rule 1 by putting Boyle after Dalton.

14. (C) – It is a simple matter to put Canabra seventh. Building from there, Dalton must be fourth. Boyle (and Arundel) must therefore be second or

third, you cannot know exactly where. This leaves spaces five and six open for Rial and the second French speech. (Figure 2)
(A) Rial must speak after Dalton, and Boyle must speak before Dalton.
(B) Arundel may or may not speak before Boyle; they are interchangeable.
(C) * Dalton definitely speaks before Rial.
(D) French must speak either sixth or seventh.
(E) Rial speaks after Dalton.

F A/B A/B D R/F F/R C

Fig. 2

15. (B) – There is a right way and a wrong way to find the correct answer for this question. The wrong way is to try all the permutations for each answer choice. That is a waste of time. The right way is to review the correct answers and diagrams from the previous two questions and eliminate answer choices that contradict those previous correct answers.
(A) In question 14, you saw that French can speak fifth.
(B) * By process of elimination, you would discover that this is the correct answer. Although you could do the permutations necessary to prove this, it would be a terrible use of your limited time.
(C) In question 14, you saw that Dalton can speak before Canabra.
(D) In question 14, you saw that Dalton can speak before Rial.
(E) In question 14, you saw that Canabra can speak seventh.

16. (D) – Before doing the work, review the previous questions. In question 14, we learned that Rial can be fifth, so we can eliminate answer choice (E). Now start with the lowest number and work up. Can Rial be second? No, because, at a minimum, French, Boyle, and Arundel must precede Rial. Does that mean that Rial can be fourth? Probably not, but do the diagram to make sure. If Rial were fourth, there would not be enough space left to accommodate two spaces between Canabra and Dalton. So can Rial be fifth? Yes, this would allow French, Arundel, Boyle, and Dalton/Canabra to fill the first four spaces.
(A) Since Rial must be preceded by French, Arundel, and Boyle, Rial cannot be second.
(B) Since Rial must be preceded by French, Arundel, and Boyle, Rial cannot be third.
(C) Since putting Rial fourth would prevent Canabra and Dalton from being properly placed, Rial cannot be fourth. If you did not make this conclusion during the initial analysis, mark this on your diagram now.
(D) * The earliest Rial can be placed is fifth.
(E) Rial can be placed fifth. You did not need to check this answer choice.

17. (B) – Since four of these answer choices will be valid and only one will be invalid, the most efficient approach is to graph each answer choice. The one that is not graphable is the correct answer.

(A) This could be graphed as FCABDRF.

(B) * This cannot be graphed. When French is fourth, there is not sufficient room to accommodate Canabra and Dalton and the two spaces between them, because Arundel and Boyle must occupy spaces two and three.

(C) This can be graphed as FCBADRF.

(D) See (C).

(E) See (C). Also, this can be graphed as FFCABDR.

18. (B) – The only way to do this question will be to graph the choices. But before graphing the answer choices, think about the two-speech block of Arundel and Boyle. Unless their positions are fixed by an answer choice, they will always be interchangeable, since they have no fixed order relative to each other. So, focus on the answer choices that fix Arundel or Boyle.

(A) If Arundel and Boyle are third and fourth, respectively, Rial and the second French are still interchangeable in the sixth and seventh positions: FCABD??.

(B) * If Arundel and Boyle are fourth and fifth, respectively, then Canabra and Doyle are forced into positions, which forces French and Rial into positions. The order of all the speakers is fixed as: FFCABDR.

(C) This is the same result and same analysis as choice (A). Remember, Arundel and Boyle are interchangeable.

(D) If Canabra is third, then Dalton is sixth. This would leave Arundel and Boyle in fourth and fifth, but we don't know which one is where: FFC??DR.

(E) When French is first and seventh, the positions of Canabra, Doyle, and Rial are fixed, but not Arundel or Boyle: FC??DRF.

Performing skits

The final game is yet another line problem. There is one quirky feature in this simple line. There are a total of ten people in two groups who must be assigned to seven open slots. This will lead to multiple people on some slots, and just one person in other slots. In order to make any progress, you must combine the rules. Both B and D feature in two rules. Combine these rules to show that B (plus N) and D (plus E and one novice) are earlier than C. Now, count heads. Four of the five experienced actors (B, C, D, and E) have been partially accounted for. Now, it is necessary to have the important insight—the "eureka" moment. The first performance has no novices, so it must be an expert. That expert cannot be B, D, or E because they all have novices with them. That expert also cannot be C because C cannot be earlier than B, D, or E. The only expert that remains is A. Therefore, A is first and is alone. (Figure 1) The second vital insight is that all four of the remaining novices can be anywhere, as long as one of them does the seventh skit. The third and final necessary insight is that the two skits with multiple performers have absorbed the three extra actors, so each of the other five actors will perform alone. This means that C is alone and cannot be seventh with one of the novices, because this would leave one skit unmanned.

[ED+novice]

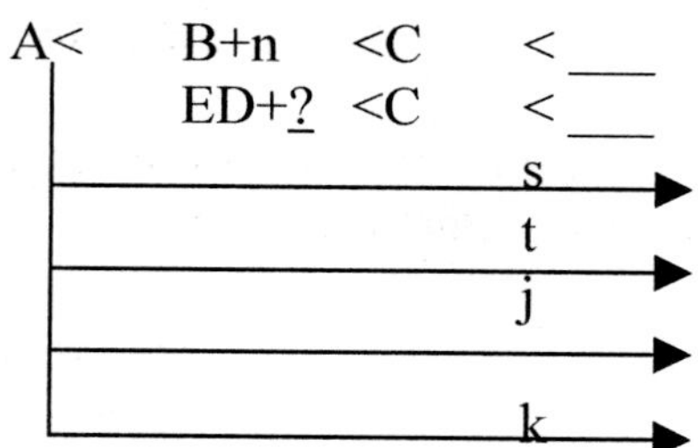

Fig. 1

19. (E) – Using the rules allows you to find the answer choice in just a few seconds.

(A) Dabia must be before Carlow, see Rule 4.

(B) The first performance must be Ariana alone; it cannot be a novice, see Rule 3.

(C) Bronte and Nabiel must perform together, see Rule 1.

(D) Carlow is an experienced actor, and only novice actors are permitted to be seventh, see Rule 5. Also, the warranted conclusion is that a single actor does the final performance.

(E) * This is a valid order.

20. (C) – Notice that choices (C), (D), and (E) are pretty similar. It is likely that one of them is the correct answer and that (A) and (B) are wrong. It is unnecessary to check whether Bronte can be second, third, or fourth, since these are listed in most of the answer choices. The easiest way to answer this question is to work from the right end of the line to figure out the latest skit that Bronte can feature in. Since at least one novice must come after Carlow and Carlow must come after Bronte, the latest Bronte could appear is fifth. Since answer choice (C) is the only one left that does not contain "sixth," it is likely the correct answer. If you were short on time you could stop here and move on to the next question, highly confident that (A) and (B) are not correct. As you can see, having a strategy helps you avoid doing time-consuming analysis.
(A) There is no reason Bronte cannot be second, for example. The correct answer for question 19 has Bronte second.
(B) See (A).
(C) * Since we know that Bronte cannot be sixth, this is the best choice.
(D) Bronte cannot be sixth.
(E) Bronte cannot be sixth.

21. (D) – Sam and Jackie are novices. If they perform after all the experienced actors finish, they must perform after Carlow. This leaves either Thomas or Kyrasaki to perform with Eric and Dabia. Then either Thomas or Kyrasaki (whichever one did not perform with Eric and Dabia) is a free agent who can perform anytime after Ariana.
(A) It is just as likely that Thomas performs before Carlow as after him.
(B) Thomas could perform before Eric, after Eric, or with Eric.
(C) Kyrasaki has the same analysis as Thomas in (A).
(D) * This is true. If Jackie is after the last experienced actor (Carlow) and Nabiel must always be with Bronte (who must be before Carlow), then Nabiel must always be before Carlow and thus be before Jackie.
(E) It is possible that Carlow performs fifth, as long as either Thomas or Kyrasaki is before Carlow. However, this is not a "must be true" answer.

22. (A) – This simple question tests how well you did the initial diagram.
(A) * Thomas is a free agent and a novice. Thus, Thomas can be the final performer.
(B) Nabiel is a novice but is also linked with Bronte who must perform before Carlow. So Nabiel cannot be the final performer.
(C) Carlow is an experienced actor, so he cannot be the final performer.
(D) See (C).
(E) See (C). Ariana must be first.

23. (C) – This question requires creativity. We know that the final performance is a novice, and that Carlow could be sixth. What is the earliest that Kyrasaki can appear? Since Kyrasaki is a free agent, there is no reason he cannot be second, with Eric and Dabia. Counting the spaces, the third, fourth, and fifth performances can separate Kyrasaki and Carlow.
(A) See the analysis.
(B) See the analysis.
(C) * See the analysis.
(D) See the analysis.
(E) See the analysis.

24. (B) – Once in awhile, the final question will suspend or replace one of the initial conditions. This can get ugly, as this question did. When faced with this situation, you need to make a gut decision whether to attempt to solve it, or just guess and move on. The problem with this kind of question is that it is confusing to change a condition you are accustomed to using. You may need to go back to square one and rework all the conditions in order to accommodate the change. Doing this potentially destroys all the warranted conclusions you made. To solve this question, consult figure 2 and follow along. Starting from scratch on this problem, the first two performances are easy to graph. Is Ariana now the third performance? Not necessarily. Ariana was first only because an experienced actor was required to be first, and Ariana was the only experienced actor that could fill the role (pardon the pun). Ariana can be anywhere between the second and the seventh performances. Ariana cannot be seventh, because that skit is still reserved for a novice.
(A) Thomas may perform in any of the seven slots.
(B) * Ariana cannot perform seventh.
(C) Bronte can perform third, fourth, or fifth.
(D) See (A).
(E) Carlow can perform fifth or sixth.

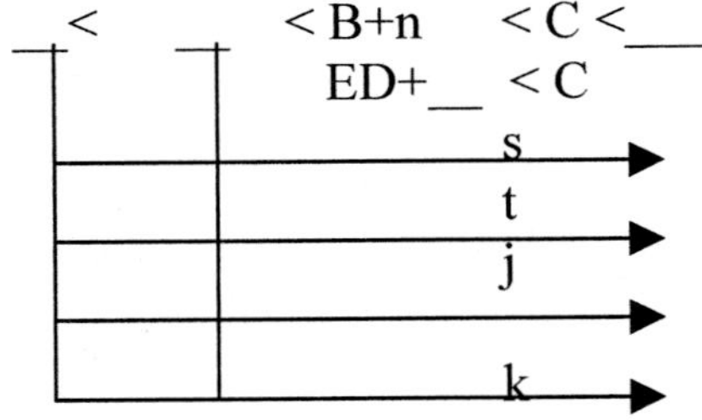

Fig. 2

Practice Test 2

Spend 35 minutes doing this practice test. When time is up, review the explanations to help you understand the questions that you did not answer correctly.

SECTION I
Time—35 minutes
23 Questions

Directions: Each group of questions in this section is based on a set of conditions. In answering some of the questions, it may be useful to draw a rough diagram. Choose the response that most accurately and completely answers each question and blacken the corresponding space on your answer sheet.

Questions 1–5

The manager of a package delivery service must schedule the delivery of packages for the following day. There are three types of containers that can be delivered: envelopes, tubes, and boxes. Each package is either a standard rate package or an express rate package. Exactly five packages will be delivered in accordance with the following requirements:

There is no standard tube package.
No more than two express boxes are delivered.
Exactly two container types are delivered daily.
At most, there are three standard packages delivered daily.
No more than three packages of the same container type and delivery rate are delivered daily.

1. Which one of the following could be a complete and accurate list of the packages delivered in a day?

(A) Standard envelope, express envelope, three standard boxes
(B) Three express envelopes, two express boxes
(C) Two standard envelopes, three express boxes
(D) Two standard envelopes, one express tube, two express boxes
(E) Two standard envelopes, two express tubes, one standard tube

2. Each of the following could be a complete and accurate list of the express rate packages delivered EXCEPT?

(A) Three express envelopes, two express boxes
(B) Three express envelopes, two express tubes
(C) One express tube
(D) One express tube, two express boxes
(E) One express envelope, one express tube

3. If there is exactly one standard rate package and it is a box, which one of the following must be true?

(A) Exactly one package is an express box.
(B) No more than two of the packages are express tubes.
(C) At least one package is an express envelope.
(D) There are exactly two fewer standard rate packages than express rate packages.
(E) There is at least one express box.

4. If there is exactly one more express rate package than there are standard rate packages, then which one of the following CANNOT be true?

(A) There are at least two express tubes and one express box.
(B) There are exactly three express envelopes and two standard boxes.
(C) There are exactly two express envelopes, one standard envelope, one express box, and one standard box.
(D) There are no express tubes.
(E) There are an equal number of express boxes and express tubes.

5. If the delivery manager schedules exactly one express tube and exactly one standard rate package, then which one of the following must be true?

(A) There are two fewer standard rate packages than express rate packages.
(B) Two express boxes are delivered.
(C) One standard box is delivered.
(D) Three express envelopes are delivered.
(E) No standard envelopes are delivered.

GO ON TO THE NEXT PAGE

Questions 6–10

A school's table tennis team will compete in a seven-game tournament. All games include exactly one member from the school's team. The team members—K, L, M, N, O, and P—will be assigned to play in games according to following conditions:

At most, two team members each play two games in the tournament.
If M plays in a tournament, then L plays, with at least one of L's games preceding at least one of M's games.
P and O never play games in the same tournament.
If K plays first, then L plays seventh.
If P plays in a tournament, both N and M play, all of N's games preceding any of M's games.
M always plays the fourth game and one additional game.

6. Which one of the following could be a complete and accurate list of the games played, from first to last?

(A) K, P, L, M, N, O, L
(B) K, P, L, M, M, N, L
(C) K, M, L, M, O, N, L
(D) M, L, M, L, O, K, N
(E) K, K, N, M, O, L, M

7. The first and seventh games could be played by all of the following players EXCEPT:

(A) L
(B) M
(C) N
(D) O
(E) P

8. If N plays in the sixth game, which one of the following players CANNOT play fifth?

(A) K
(B) L
(C) M
(D) O
(E) P

9. Which one of the following must be true?

(A) P plays before M plays.
(B) L plays twice.
(C) O plays in the tournament.
(D) Exactly five players play in the tournament.
(E) No more than four players play in the tournament.

10. If P plays third and seventh, then which one of the following could be true?

(A) N plays fifth.
(B) N plays sixth.
(C) O plays sixth.
(D) L plays fifth.
(E) K plays first.

GO ON TO THE NEXT PAGE.

Questions 11–16

Five singers—Gannymead, Martin, Nick, Pat, and Quinn—are assigned solo performances for the holiday festival. Each singer sings exactly once and in exactly one of three singing voices—alto, bass, or contralto. The solos are assigned according to the following rules:

Gannymead performs neither first nor last.
Martin performs immediately before or immediately after Nick.
Only one choir member is an alto.
Quinn performs before Nick performs.
Martin is a bass.
The first and last performers sing in different voices.

11. Which one of the following could be an accurate list of singers and the voices they sing, in the order they sing, from first to last?

(A) Pat: contralto, Gannymead: alto, Quinn: bass, Martin: bass, Nick: bass
(B) Pat: contralto, Quinn: alto, Gannymead: bass, Martin: bass, Nick: contralto
(C) Quinn: bass, Gannymead: alto, Pat: bass, Martin: bass, Nick: alto
(D) Quinn: bass, Martin: bass, Gannymead: contralto, Nick: alto, Pat: contralto
(E) Nick: bass, Martin: bass, Quinn: alto, Gannymead: contralto, Pat: contralto

12. If Pat sings third, which one of the following must be true?

(A) Pat is an alto.
(B) Quinn sings second.
(C) Either the fourth or fifth singer is a bass.
(D) Either the third or fourth singer is an alto.
(E) Either the first or fifth singer is a bass.

13. If Nick performs before Gannymead and Pat is the only contralto, which one of the following could be true?

(A) Nick is a bass and sings fourth.
(B) Quinn is a contralto and sings first.
(C) Quinn is an alto and sings first.
(D) Gannymead is an alto and sings first.
(E) Nick is an alto and sings fourth.

14. Which one of the following must be true?

(A) Quinn does not sing fourth.
(B) Quinn does not sing third.
(C) Martin sings third.
(D) Nick sings first.
(E) Gannymead sings third.

15. If Martin is the only bass and sings third, each of the following pairs could sing contralto at the festival EXCEPT:

(A) Nick and Gannymead
(B) Nick and Pat
(C) Pat and Gannymead
(D) Quinn and Gannymead
(E) Quinn and Pat

16. Suppose that in addition to the original five singers a sixth singer, Y, is added and performs immediately before Quinn. If all the other conditions remain unchanged, which one of the following CANNOT be true?

(A) Gannymead is second.
(B) Y is second.
(C) Quinn is fourth.
(D) Martin is third.
(E) Pat is fifth.

GO ON TO THE NEXT PAGE

Questions 17–23

A college professor gives a series of seven lectures—D, F, G, H, I, K, and L—during the summer term. One lecture is given during each class and each lecture is given exactly once. The following information is known about the order of the lectures:

D is given in an earlier class than I.
Exactly two lectures are given between lectures G and F.
L is given in a later class than F.
K is given in the fourth class.

17. Which one of the following could be the order of the lectures?

(A) H, F, I, K, G, L, D
(B) D, H, G, K, I, F, L
(C) H, D, G, K, F, L, I
(D) L, H, G, K, D, F, I
(E) D, H, F, L, I G, K

18. It must be true that the latest class that the professor can give the

(A) D lecture is fifth.
(B) F lecture is seventh.
(C) H lecture is seventh.
(D) G lecture is seventh.
(E) I lecture is fifth.

19. If L is the fifth lecture, which one of the following lectures could be given consecutively?

(A) G and D
(B) F and L
(C) K and G
(D) D and H
(E) L and I

20. What is the maximum number of lectures that can separate H and I?

(A) one
(B) two
(C) three
(D) four
(E) five

21. If K is given immediately before or after I, then which one of the following must be true?

(A) L is given after G.
(B) K is given before F.
(C) D is given before H.
(D) D is given first.
(E) G is given third.

22. If H is given later than K, then which one of the following must be true?

(A) G is given second.
(B) D is given first.
(C) I is given third.
(D) L is given seventh.
(E) H is given fifth.

23. If F is given later than G, all of the following could be true EXCEPT:

(A) D is given sixth.
(B) L is given sixth.
(C) G is given third.
(D) H is given first.
(E) I is given third.

S T O P

IF YOU FINISH BEFORE TIME IS CALLED, YOU MAY CHECK YOUR WORK ON THIS SECTION ONLY.
DO NOT WORK ON ANY OTHER SECTION IN THE TEST.

Answer key and explanations for Test 2

Answer Key

1. B
2. C
3. E
4. E
5. D
6. C
7. B
8. E
9. D
10. D
11. A
12. C
13. C
14. A
15. E
16. E
17. B
18. C
19. D
20. E
21. A
22. B
23. A

Delivery schedule

This game was designed to confuse you as to which diagram to use. At first, it appears to require a simple-line or a multiple-line diagram, but neither do a good job of organizing the rules. The best diagram for this puzzle is a matrix, but even a matrix will have limited utility for this game. The three types of packages are on the x-axis, and the two delivery rates are on the y-axis. (Figure 1) To depict Rule 2, write "0, 1, 2" in the appropriate box. Use a similar method to depict Rule 4, using "0–3." We can now draw an easy warranted conclusion that there are at least two express rate packages. Moving to Rule 3, you can try to depict that two package types are used, or you can just keep that rule in your head. This brings you to Rule 5—no more than three packages of the same container type and delivery rate can be delivered on one day. This is also a difficult rule to depict. It may also be easier to keep this one in your head. Although you should always try to make additional warranted conclusions, none are apparent at this stage, so go to the questions for more guidance.

Std. 0-3		None	
Ex. 2-5			(0,1,2)
	Env.	Tube	Box

(Use two types)

Fig. 1

1. (B) – For the first question in the set, you can normally use each rule to eliminate one answer choice. Start with the first rule and determine if any answer choices violate it. Then do the same for each subsequent rule.
(A) This choice violates Rule 4 because it has four standard rate packages.
(B) * This choice is correct because it does not violate any rules.
(C) This choice violates Rule 2 because it has three express boxes.
(D) This choice violates Rule 3 because it has all three package types.
(E) This choice violates Rule 1 because there is no standard tube package.

2. (C) – This question is a variation of the previous question. The only rule that directly impacts express rate packages is the rule that there be no more than two express rate boxes. Since no answer choice runs afoul of this rule, you will need to be more creative. Notice that this question asks only that you list the express rate packages. But to know the express rate packages, you also must know the standard rate packages. Keep this in mind as you consider each of the answer choices.
(A) Three express envelopes and two express boxes are permissible. There is no rule that requires a standard rate package. Rule 4 gives the maximum number of standard rate packages; it does not establish a minimum.
(B) See (A).

(C) * If there is only one express tube, then the four other packages delivered must all be standard rate packages. The problem is that Rule 4 establishes a maximum of three standard rate packages.
(D) This scenario is possible if you also have two standard rate boxes.
(E) This scenario is possible if you have three standard rate envelopes.

3. (E) – If there is only one standard rate package and it is a box, then the other package type (remember, Rule 3 requires two package types) can be a tube or an envelope, and it must be express rate. Consider how Rule 5 will affect this diagram.
(A) Actually, there can be one or two express boxes.
(B) Tubes and envelopes are interchangeable in this scenario.
(C) There is no reason that one of the packages must be an envelope, see (D).
(D) No, this is not required. A possible combination is one standard box, two express boxes, and two express tubes. This makes for three fewer standard rate packages than express rate packages.
(E) * Yes. Start with the single standard rate box. You are only allowed one other type of package, either express tubes or express envelopes. At the most, we can have three of them, because of Rule 5. This leaves one package slot to fill. The only possibility is an express box.

4. (E) – The only way to have one more express rate package than standard rate packages is to have three express rate packages and two standard rate packages. Keep that in mind as you work through the choices. It would be inefficient to try to determine what cannot be true without using the answer choices to guide you.
(A) This can be true. If there were two express tubes and one express box, then this would allow for two standard boxes, which would satisfy the requirements of this question.
(B) This is a possible order that satisfies the rules.
(C) This is a possible order that has three express rate packages and two standard rate packages.
(D) It is fine if there are no express tubes, as long as there are three express rate envelopes or boxes and two standard rate packages.
(E) * This cannot be true. If there were an equal number of express boxes and express tubes, there would be either one of each or two of each. Either way, it is impossible to the condition in the question that there be one more express package than standard packages.

5. (D) – The graph will help with this question. When there is one express tube, then the other package type must be either an envelope or a box. If it were a box, then the remaining three express packages would have to be boxes. But this violates Rule 2, which limits you to two express boxes. Therefore, the

other package type must be envelopes after all, not boxes. So, there must be one standard rate envelope and three express envelopes.

(A) This is false. There must be exactly one standard rate package and four express rate packages.
(B) No boxes are delivered, of either express or standard rate.
(C) No boxes are delivered, of either express or standard rate.
(D) * This is correct.
(E) As discussed above, three express envelopes are delivered.

Std. 0-3	**1**	None	
Ex.	**3**	**1**	(0,1,2)
	Env.	Tube	Box

(Use two types)

Fig. 2

Table tennis tournament groups

This is a tough game. It uses a hybrid of a simple line and some grouping rules, but does not require a grouping diagram. The simple line is used to keep track of the players and the order of the players, while grouping rules help us visualize the relationships. Start with the rules that are easiest to diagram. M plays fourth and one other time. Rule 1 tells you that at most two players play two games. This is a very confusing rule. What does it mean? If you weren't sure, reading the later rules would help clarify this complex rule. Rule 2 implies that it is not required to use every team member—one of them can be "benched". Counting the number of spaces to be filled (seven) and the number of players (six), we see that M plays twice. Is it required that a second player play twice? Not explicitly, but implicitly it is. Why? Because O and P never play in the same tournament (Rule 3). O and P are mutually exclusive. So you have only four players—K, L, N, and either O or P—available to fill the five open spaces. You can now make a warranted conclusion that in addition to M playing twice, exactly one other player must play twice.

That took some clever thinking. It is much easier to graph Rule 4 (the linear rule about K and L). It is trickier to graph Rule 5 (about P and N and M). The diagram and the rules that cannot be effectively graphed are contained in figure 1.

M plays twice. One other plays twice.
If M plays, L plays, & at least 1 L < at least 1 M
P/O
If K #1, then L #7
If P then N and M, & all N before any M

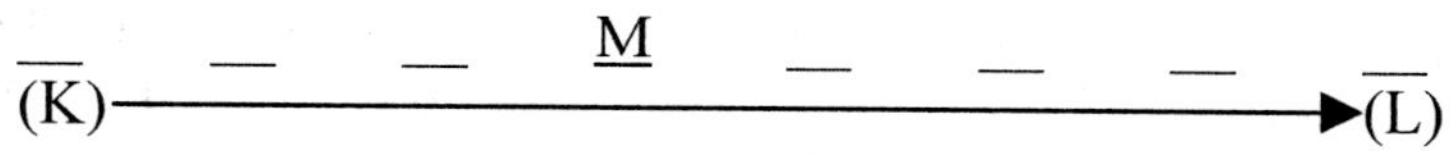

__ __ __ M __ __ __ __
(K)————————————►(L)

Fig. 1

6. (C) – Use each rule to eliminate the answer choice that violates it until only one choice remains.
   (A) This choice violates Rule 3, because P and O cannot play in the same tournament.
   (B) This choice violates Rule 5, because when P plays, N must precede M.
   (C) * This choice is a valid schedule.
   (D) This choice violates Rule 6, because M always plays the fourth game.
   (E) This choice violates Rule 4.

7. (B) – Start by looking at the rules that affect the first and seventh games. If K is first, L is seventh. So K cannot be the correct answer. Unfortunately, the test maker did not offer this answer choice. What other player cannot be first and last? Since M is always fourth, it cannot also be both first and last (each person plays at most two games).

(A) L can be first and last. For example: L, K, N, M, M, O, L
(B) * This was easy. M cannot be first and seventh, since there is only one spare M left after the first M is placed in game four.
(C) N can be first and last. N, K, L, M, M, O, N
(D) O can be first and last. O, N, L, M, M, K, O
(E) P can be first and last. P, N, L, M, M, K, P

8. (E) – When the question specifies the position of a specific member (like N), always focus on the rules that contain that member. If N plays sixth, then Rule 5 causes a problem. If P plays, then all of N's games must be before M's. That is impossible to do now, since N is already later than M. So, to avoid this problem, P cannot play in the tournament.
(A) K can be fifth. O, K, L, M, K, N, M
(B) L can be fifth. O, K, L, M, L, N, M
(C) M can be fifth. O, K, L, M, M, N, N
(D) O can be fifth. L, K, L, M, O, N, M
(E) * P cannot be fifth.

9. (D) – Since this is a "must be true" question, the answer should be pretty apparent based on the analysis we have done up to this point. Feel free to consult the correct answers and diagrams from earlier questions.
(A) Must P play before M? No—K, N, N, M, M, P, L.
(B) Must L play twice? No, see (A) and question 8 (C).
(C) Must O play in the tournament? No, see (A). Also, consider question 10 and Rule 5, which imply that P does play sometimes. This choice was easy to eliminate without doing any work.
(D) * Exactly five players play in the tournament. This is true. The initial warranted conclusion was that three players play once and two players play twice.
(E) See (D); this choice contradicts (D).

10. (D) – If P plays, then O cannot play. This leaves P and the other four to fill the five slots. Also, since P plays, Rule 5 is now relevant, all Ns must precede all Ms. Graph the given information and pay special attention to where N and M are placed. We can see from figure 2 that K now cannot play the first game. We must put the single N in game #1 or #2 in order to keep N before all Ms. Also, keep in mind that the single L must be before at least one of the Ms. Thus, L is either in #1, #2, or #5. Why can't the single L be in #6? Because this would mean that one of the Ms would not be later than L, as is required by Rule 2. This should be enough analysis to answer the questions.
(A) From the analysis, we learned that N must be in game #1 or #2.
(B) See (A).
(C) O cannot play at all in this tournament, because P is playing.

(D) * L can play fifth, so long as M plays sixth and K plays second.

(E) If P plays seventh, then K cannot play first, because if K plays first, L must play seventh, per Rule 4.

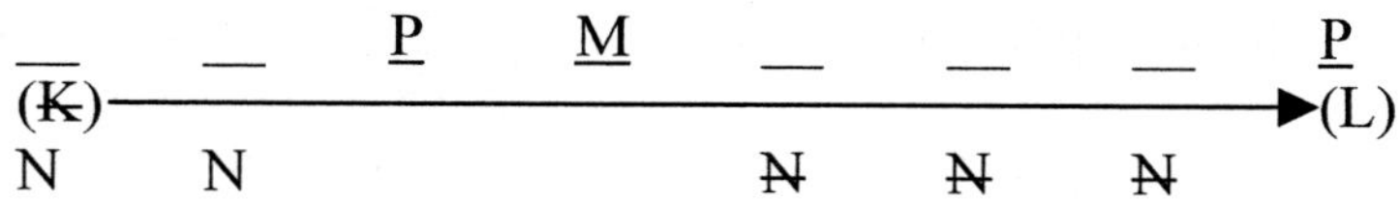

Fig. 2

Solo singers

This puzzle is a modified greater-than/less-than line. Use two lines to keep track of the two features—the singers and their singing voices. It is clearly a greater-than/less-than line, because most of the rules require one member to be earlier or later than another member. Occasionally, the issue of who sings in what voice is relevant, but this did not play as big a role as it initially appeared that it would. Rule 1 is easy to graph, as is Rule 6. Combine Rules 2 and 4 to make a three-member block of Q< M/N. This block will play a major role in several questions. Even with this work finished, the graph is skeletal. (Figure 1)

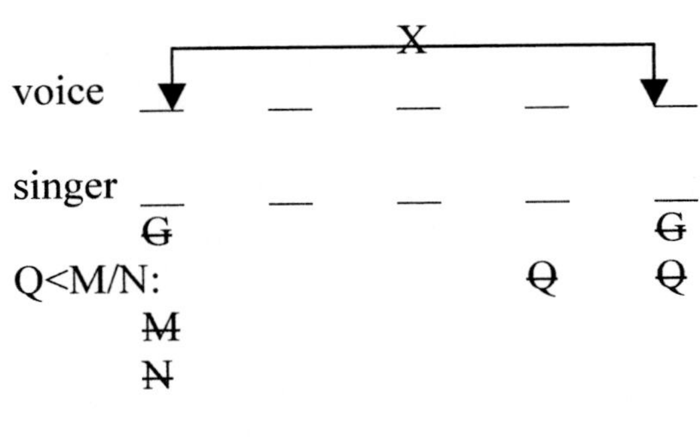

Fig. 1

11. (A) – As with all possible-order questions, start with the first rule and work your way down the list.
(A) * This is correct.
(B) This violates Rule 6, because the first and last singers must sing in different voices.
(C) This violates Rule 3, because there can be only one alto.
(D) This violates Rule 2, because M and N must be next to each other.
(E) This violates Rule 4, because Q must perform before N does.

12. (C) – Always check the rules that affect a member when that member is mentioned in the question. What do the rules say about P? Nothing, P is a free agent. That means this question is testing the effect that filling the third space has on the rest of the spaces. Thinking creatively, you might have realized that Q and G now must be first or second, but since G cannot be first, Q must be first. We see that M and N must be to the right of P, since Q must come before M and N. (Figure 2) This should be enough work to answer the question.
(A) There is no indication what voice P sings in.
(B) G must sing second.

(C) * Yes. Either the fourth or fifth singer is M, and M is a bass.
(D) We don't know who the fourth singer will be; it is either M or N. We have no idea who the alto is in this question.
(E) M, a bass, could be fourth and N could be a contralto and be fifth. The first singer is Q, who could be an alto.

Q G P M/N N/M

Fig. 2

13. (C) – Don't be paralyzed by information overload when the question stem provides two new items of information. Simply break it into manageable pieces. Deal with the first piece of information by graphing it and making the warranted conclusions. Then turn your attention to the second piece of information. First, If N is before G, there is now a four-member block, Q < M/N < G. (Figure 3) Since there are only five spaces to fill, a four-member block helpfully limits the possibilities. Since G cannot be on space five, G must be on space four. This means that P is the only one that can be on space five. Q is the only one that can be on space one. We don't know exactly where M and N are. Since P is fifth and is the only contralto, what voice must Q in space one sing in? Not contralto, because of P, so Q must sing in alto or bass. We now have plenty of information for answering the question. So there are three bass and one alto, and we don't know who is which.
(A) N can be a bass, but N cannot sing fourth.
(B) Q cannot be a contralto, although Q does sing first.
(C) * Q can be an alto and does sing first.
(D) G can be an alto, but G must sing fourth.
(E) N can be an alto, but N cannot sing fourth.

Q M/N N/M G P
a/b c
voice———X———voice

Fig. 3

14. (A) – Since this question stem does not add any new information, it should be answerable based on the initial analysis, consult figure 1. Also make use of work you did for previous questions.
(A) * As we learned from the initial analysis, Q does not sing fourth, because of the effect of Rule 2 and Rule 4, which create the three-member block of Q < M/N.
(B) The only spaces Q cannot occupy are spaces four and five.
(C) M can sing anywhere except first. The work you did for question 13 shows M as second or third.

(D) N has the same analysis as M does in choice (C).
(E) G can be anywhere except first and fifth, see question 13 for an example.

15. (E) – Just like in question 13, don't be intimidated when there are two new pieces of information. Deal with them one at a time. There is only one alto, so if M is the only bass, then the remaining three are contraltos. Put that information to the side for now. If M is third, then N is either second or fourth. Create two diagrams to reflect this. (Figure 4). Q must be earlier than N, so Q cannot be third, fourth, or fifth. But G can never be first. These permutations are shown in figure 4. What voices can Q and P sing? Neither of them can sing bass. Because of Rule 6, they can't both be contraltos, so one is an alto and the other a contralto. See if this is enough information to answer the question.
(A) N and G must both be contraltos in both permutations.
(B) N must be a contralto, and there is a 50% chance that P is as well.
(C) There is a 50% chance P is a contralto. G must be a contralto.
(D) There is a 50% chance Q is a contralto. G must be a contralto.
(E) * Thanks to Rule 6, Q and P cannot both be contraltos in the same permutation, since one of them must be an alto.

Qa/c Nc Mb Gc Pc/a

Qa/c Gc Mb Nc Pc/a

Fig. 4

16. (E) – Adding Y immediately before Q creates the four-member block of YQ<M/N. You will need to create a new diagram from scratch and make new warranted conclusions. A few of the permutations are listed in figure 5, but rather than waste time doing unnecessary permutations, turn to the answer choices. The important thing to realize is that either Y or P must be first. The singing voices have no impact on this question.
(A) G can be second, so long as P is first.
(B) Y can be second if the order is, for example: P Y Q G M N.
(C) Q can be fourth if the order is, for example: P G Y Q M N.
(D) M can be third, as shown in figure 5.
(E) * P cannot be fifth. If P is fifth, then Y is first and Q is second. M and N must be third and fourth. This would force G into sixth, which violates Rule 6.

Y Q M/N N/M G P – okay
Y Q M/N M/N P G – not possible

Fig. 5

Lecture order

This simple-line diagram had seven questions, in contrast to the five or six questions that each of the other puzzle sets had. Not only was this set worth more points, **but it was also significantly easier than the other sets. That is why you always budget** your time, so that you don't run out of time while doing an easy puzzle set. If your strategy is to do three out of four sets, then this should have been the first set you did. The rules and the diagram are about as simple as one could hope for. (Figure 1) Note that because K is placed in space four, the options for G and F become drastically limited. G and F are graphed as lower-case letters to make it easier to see that each of them is a 50/50 possibility. Now, consider the first space. You have learned that I, L, F, G, and K are all ineligible for the first space. Thus, either D or H must occupy it. Since the graph is pretty clear, go directly to the questions without spending time drawing any more warranted conclusions.

	1	2	3	4	5	6	7
	D/H	__	__	K	__	__	__
D<I	~~I~~						~~D~~
g/f _ _ g/f	~~g/f~~			~~g/f~~			~~g/f~~
F<L	~~L~~						~~F~~

Fig. 1

17. (B) – As is usually the case, the first question of the set is best answered using condition violation elimination.
(A) This choice violates Rule 1: D must be before I.
(B) *This choice is correct because it does not violate any rules.
(C) This choice violates Rule 2: G and F must have two lectures separating them.
(D) This choice violates Rule 3: F must be earlier than L.
(E) This choice violates Rule 4: K is lecture four.

18. (C) – This question requires more work than normal. Each answer choice potentially requires that you work a permutation. Try to find one counter-example to each answer choice. Consult the initial graph before doing the permutations.
(A) It is possible to have D as late as sixth: H, F, L, K, G, D, I.
(B) The initial analysis proved that neither F nor G could be seventh.
(C) * H, a free agent, can fill any space, and there is no later class than seventh, so this is correct.
(D) See (B).
(E) It is possible to have I in the seventh space: H, D, F, K, L, G, I.

19. (D) – Plug in the new information and go from there. (Figure 2) L is fifth. What rules involve L? Rule 3 requires that L be given in a later class than F.

So F must be sometime earlier than fifth. Looking at our initial diagram, F can be second or third. (Figure 1) But when F is second, G must be fifth, so that will not work in this situation. Thus, F must be third and G must be sixth. The only remaining question is where can H, D, and I be? H is a free agent and can be anywhere. I must come later than D, so, by the initial analysis, I cannot be first, and D cannot be seventh.

(A) G must be sixth, and D must be first or second, so they are never consecutive.
(B) F must be third, and L must be fifth, so they are never consecutive.
(C) K must be fourth, and G must be sixth, so they are never consecutive.
(D) * D must be first or second, and H must be first, second, or seventh, so in certain permutations these two are consecutive.
(E) L must be fifth, and I must be second or seventh.

__	__	F	K	L	G	__
H/D	H/D/I					H/I

Fig. 2

20. (E) – Feel free to consult previous correct answers to help eliminate choices. You can also do the permutations, if your previous work is not understandable. In a "maximum" question, the correct answer will be one of the later (i.e., higher) numbers, so always start with choice (E).
(A) See (D).
(B) See (D).
(C) See (D).
(D) We can see from previous work in question 19 that H and I can be separated by four lectures, so there is no need to check for this number or for the lower numbers.
(E) * Can there be five lectures between H and I? They would have to be on opposite ends. I would have to be seventh, since D must be earlier than I. So if I is seventh and H is first, you could create the following permutation: H, G, D, K, F, L, I. This order does not violate any rules. There are other permutations that are also valid.

21. (A) – Create two diagrams, one with I third and the other with I fifth. When I is third, either F or G must be second. This leaves only the first space for D. H and L must be sixth or seventh. In the second permutation, when I is fifth, then F or G must be sixth and L must be seventh (in order to satisfy Rule 3). This leaves D and H to fill spaces one and two. This is all you need to answer the question.
(A) * In every permutation, L is later than G.
(B) In several permutations, K is given after F.
(C) There are permutations where D can be later than H.

(D) If H is first, then D must be second.
(E) Only in some permutations is G third.

D	f/g	I	K	f/g	h/l	h/l
d/h	d/h	f/g	K	I	f/g	L

Fig. 3

22. (B) – There are two ways you can approach this. You can do the three permutations where H comes after K. Alternatively, you can consult the answer choices and try to solve for the exception to each answer choice. Typically, this second approach is superior, since it requires less work. But this time the permutation route is just as efficient. H is the free agent, so this question is testing the effect of the new information on one of the other lectures. The initial analysis revealed that either D or H must be first.
(A) Try putting G third (and F sixth) and work H in later than K. It can be done: D, I, G, K, H, F, L.
(B) * The initial analysis answers this question. If you do the permutations, you also see that D must be first. Try putting D second, and you see that it does not work. Nor does putting D third. There is no point in trying to put D fifth, sixth, or seventh, since I must precede D, and there also needs to be space for F, G, and L. This is the correct answer.
(C) It is possible to put I second: D, I, F, K, H, G, L.
(D) It is possible to put L fifth: D, I, F, K, L, G, H.
(E) It is possible to put H seventh, as shown in (D).

23. (A) – Go back to the initial analysis. F and G can be second and fifth or third and sixth. Sketch out these two permutations and you see that there is no special effect on D and I, nor on H. What about L? L must be either sixth or seventh in the first permutation, and seventh in the second permutation. That is all that we can do with this information. Consult the answer choices.
(A) * D cannot be sixth because that would require I to be seventh, but L must be later than F, which is on space five. So D cannot be sixth.
(B) L can be sixth or seventh.
(C) G can be second or third.
(D) H is a free agent, so H is better able to move around than the others.
(E) I can be third.

__	G	__	K	F	__	__
					(L?)	
__	__	G	K	__	F	L

Fig. 4

Practice Test 3

Spend 35 minutes doing this practice test. When time is up, review the explanations to help you understand the questions that you did not answer correctly.

SECTION I

Time—35 minutes

23 Questions

Directions: Each group of questions in this section is based on a set of conditions. In answering some of the questions, it may be useful to draw a rough diagram. Choose the response that most accurately and completely answers each question and blacken the corresponding space on your answer sheet.

Questions 1–6

A grade-school teacher will assign students to a single row of consecutive work tables, numbered 1 through 5. Two of the students are morning-schedule students and five of the students are day-schedule students. Three of the students are boys, and four of the students are girls. The teacher will assign the children to tables in accordance with the following conditions:

No more than two students are assigned to a table.
Each morning student must share a table with a day student.
Boys cannot sit at a table with other boys.
Day students cannot be at three adjacent tables.

1. Which one of the following could be a complete and accurate list of the tables and assignments?

(A) 1: day boy; 2: day girl; 3: morning boy; 4: day girl and morning girl; 5: day boy and day girl.
(B) 1: day boy; 2: day girl and day boy; 3: empty; 4: morning girl and day boy; 5: morning girl and day girl.
(C) 1: morning girl and day girl; 2: day boy; 3: empty; 4: day girl and day boy; 5: day boy.
(D) 1: day boy; 2: day boy and day girl, 3: day boy and day girl, 4: empty; 5: morning girl and day girl.
(E) 1: day boy and morning boy; 2: day girl and morning girl; 3: empty; 4: day boy; 5: day girl and morning girl.

2. If a morning student is assigned to table 2, then which one of the following must be true?

(A) A girl is assigned to table 2.
(B) A morning student is assigned to table 4.
(C) A boy is assigned to table 2.
(D) A day student is assigned to table 4.
(E) A morning student is assigned to table 1.

3. Which one of the following must be true?

(A) A day student is assigned to table 1.
(B) A day student is assigned to table 3.
(C) A morning student is assigned to table 1.
(D) A morning student is assigned to table 2.
(E) A morning student is assigned to table 3.

4. If one morning girl is assigned to both table 1 and table 4, then which one of the following must be true?

(A) A boy is assigned to table 1 or table 2.
(B) A boy is assigned to table 5.
(C) A day boy is assigned to table 2.
(D) A day girl is assigned to table 1 or table 4.
(E) A day girl is assigned to table 4 or table 5.

5. If exactly one girl and no other student is assigned to table 4, then which one of the following could be true?

(A) Two day girls are assigned to table 1.
(B) A morning student is assigned to table 4.
(C) A day boy and a day girl are assigned to table 2.
(D) Two day girls are assigned to table 2.
(E) Two day boys are assigned to table 5.

6. If a day girl and no other student is assigned to table 1 and a morning boy is assigned to table 2, which one of the following pairs of students could be assigned to table 5?

(A) Morning girl and day boy.
(B) Morning girl and day girl.
(C) Morning boy and day boy.
(D) Day girl and day girl.
(E) Morning girl and morning girl.

GO ON TO THE NEXT PAGE

Questions 7–13

Employees of a restaurant are assigned to work shifts for the days the restaurant is open. The restaurant is open every day but Monday, and there are morning and evening shifts every day except Tuesday, when there is only an evening shift. All assignments of employees must conform to the following conditions:

All employees must work Friday and Saturday evening.
All employees must work at least two consecutive morning shifts.
If an employee works Wednesday morning and evening, the employee does not work Tuesday evening.
If an employee works two consecutive morning shifts, the employee must work the evening shift on the next day that the restaurant is open.
If an employee does not work Sunday morning and evening, the employee must work Friday morning.
If an employee works either of the shifts on Thursday, the employee does not work Saturday morning.

7. Which one of the following could be a complete and accurate weekly schedule for an employee?

(A) Wednesday morning, Wednesday evening, Thursday morning, Friday evening, Saturday morning, Saturday evening
(B) Tuesday evening, Friday morning, Friday evening, Saturday morning, Saturday evening
(C) Wednesday morning, Thursday morning, Friday morning, Friday evening, Saturday evening
(D) Tuesday evening, Wednesday morning, Thursday morning, Thursday evening, Friday evening, Saturday evening
(E) Tuesday evening, Wednesday morning, Wednesday evening, Thursday evening, Friday evening, Saturday evening, Sunday morning

8. If an employee is assigned to the morning shifts on Friday, Saturday, and Sunday, then the employee must also be assigned to which one of the following shifts?

(A) Tuesday evening
(B) Wednesday morning
(C) Thursday morning
(D) Wednesday evening
(E) Thursday evening

9. If an employee is assigned to the Wednesday morning shift and exactly one other morning shift, the employee must be assigned to which one of the following shifts?

(A) Tuesday evening
(B) Wednesday evening
(C) Friday morning
(D) Saturday morning
(E) Sunday evening

10. What is the maximum number of shifts that an employee may be assigned in a single week?

(A) six
(B) seven
(C) eight
(D) nine
(E) ten

11. Which one of the following CANNOT be true?

(A) An employee is assigned all five morning shifts.
(B) An employee is assigned both Wednesday and both Thursday shifts.
(C) An employee is assigned all six evening shifts.
(D) An employee is assigned the Thursday morning and Saturday evening shifts.
(E) An employee is assigned shifts only on Friday, Saturday, and Sunday.

12. If an employee is not assigned to the Thursday morning and Friday morning shifts, then which one of the following CANNOT be true?

(A) The employee is assigned the Wednesday morning and Wednesday evening shifts.
(B) The employee is assigned the Wednesday evening and Sunday evening shifts.
(C) The employee is assigned the Tuesday evening shift.
(D) The employee is assigned the Sunday evening shift.
(E) The employee is assigned the Sunday morning shift.

13. If an employee is assigned to exactly four shifts, then the employee must be assigned to which one of the following shifts?

(A) Tuesday evening
(B) Wednesday morning
(C) Thursday evening
(D) Friday morning
(E) Saturday morning

GO ON TO THE NEXT PAGE.

Questions 14–18

Customers at a spa schedule appointments for one of four treatments—kiwi, lime, mud, and nutrient—to be administered during each of six consecutive sessions, numbered one through six. Appointments for treatment sessions must meet the following requirements:

The kiwi treatment may only be scheduled once.
The mud treatment cannot be scheduled for sessions 5 or 6.
The same treatment cannot be scheduled for consecutive sessions.
If the kiwi or lime treatment is scheduled for session 5, the other treatment is scheduled for session 3, and if the kiwi or lime treatment is scheduled for session 3, the other treatment is scheduled for session 5.
Every set of five consecutive sessions must contain all four of the treatments.
No treatment is scheduled for more than two sessions.

14. Which one of the following CANNOT be true of the treatment schedule?

(A) The treatment given in session 1 is the same as the treatment given in session 4.
(B) The treatment given in session 3 is the same as the treatment given in session 5.
(C) The treatment given in session 5 is the same as the treatment given in session 1.
(D) The treatment given in session 6 is the same as the treatment given in session 4.
(E) The treatment given in session 3 is the same as the treatment given in session 4.

15. If the kiwi treatment is given in session 4, which one of the following is a complete and accurate list of the sessions, any one of which the lime treatment could be given?

(A) 1 and 2
(B) 2 and 3
(C) 1, 2, and 3
(D) 1, 2, 3, and 6
(E) 1, 2, and 6

16. If the same treatment is given during sessions 5 and 3, then which one of the following must be true?

(A) The nutrient treatment is scheduled for session 2.
(B) The lime treatment is scheduled for session 3.
(C) The kiwi treatment is scheduled for session 2.
(D) The lime treatment is scheduled for session 6.
(E) The mud treatment is scheduled for session 2.

17. When the lime treatment is not scheduled for sessions 2, 4, or 6, which one of the following must be true?

(A) The nutrient treatment is scheduled for session 6.
(B) The nutrient treatment is scheduled for session 4.
(C) The lime treatment is scheduled for session 1.
(D) The mud treatment is scheduled for session 2.
(E) The mud treatment is scheduled for session 4.

18. If the same treatment is given in session 1 and session 6, then which one of the following CANNOT be true?

(A) The nutrient treatment is scheduled for session 4.
(B) The mud treatment is scheduled for session 4.
(C) The mud treatment is scheduled for session 3.
(D) The kiwi treatment is scheduled for session 2.
(E) The lime treatment is scheduled for session 2.

GO ON TO THE NEXT PAGE

Questions 19–23

Engineers must perform six tasks—numbered 1 through 6—in consecutive order. The engineers that will perform the tasks belong to three work groups. The red group engineers are A and B and can perform tasks 1 through 3. The blue group engineers are E and F and can perform tasks 4 though 6. The green group engineers are T, S, and U, and can perform tasks 2 through 5. The following conditions govern:

Each task is performed by exactly one engineer.
At least one task is performed each day.
If one member of a work group performs a task during a day, no other member of that group performs a task that day.
An engineer performs no more than one task a day.

19. Which one of the following could be a complete and accurate list of the engineers that complete the six tasks in three days?

(A) A, T, S, U
(B) A, B, E, F
(C) T, S, E, F
(D) B, T, E
(E) A, S, U

20. If A is the only member of the red group to perform tasks and E is the only member of the blue group to perform tasks, what is the minimum number of days required to complete the six tasks?

(A) two
(B) three
(C) four
(D) five
(E) six

21. What is the minimum number of engineers required to complete the six tasks?

(A) one
(B) two
(C) three
(D) four
(E) five

22. If A, T, and E are the only engineers and they perform the tasks over three days, all of the following could be true EXCEPT?

(A) A performs only tasks 1 and 2.
(B) A performs only tasks 1 and 3.
(C) E performs only tasks 4 and 6.
(D) T performs only tasks 3 and 4.
(E) T performs only tasks 2 and 5.

23. If B, F, and S are the only engineers and they perform the tasks over three days, then which one of the following must be true if S performs task 2?

(A) B performs task 3.
(B) F performs task 4.
(C) S performs task 4.
(D) B performs at least two tasks.
(E) S performs at least two tasks.

S T O P

IF YOU FINISH BEFORE TIME IS CALLED, YOU MAY CHECK YOUR WORK ON THIS SECTION ONLY.
DO NOT WORK ON ANY OTHER SECTION IN THE TEST.

Answer key and explanations for Test 3

Answer Key

1. B
2. D
3. A
4. A
5. C
6. A
7. C
8. A
9. E
10. D
11. A
12. A
13. D
14. E
15. E
16. D
17. A
18. A
19. D
20. B
21. B
22. D
23. E

Table assignments

Line diagrams (which include simple lines and multiple lines) are the most frequently tested diagrams. This game uses a typical multiple-line diagram. This game is **nearly impossible to solve, until you make one important warranted conclusion, but more** on that in a moment. Skimming over the conditions, you see that there are a total of seven students (three boys and four girls) who have two schedules (two morning students and five day students). Since no more than two students are assigned to a table, each table must have zero, one, or two students. The vital rule is that the day students cannot sit at three consecutive tables. This bumps up against the fact that there are five day students. Do some quick counting and quick sketching and you see that it is difficult to schedule the five day students without assigning them to three consecutive tables. In fact, the only way to accomplish this is to assign no day students to Table 3. This intertwines with the rule that each morning student must share a table with a day student. Since day students cannot sit at Table 3, this means that morning students cannot sit at Table 3. So, Table 3 must always remain empty. If you fail to make this warranted conclusion, the questions are virtually impossible to answer. What if you failed to make this warranted conclusion? If you used rule violator answer elimination to arrive at the correct answer for question 1, that may have helped you see that Table 3 is empty. Also, three of the answer choices in question 1 show Table 3 as being empty, so that gives you a big hint that Table 3 is always empty. You must be clever about mining the answer choices for these kinds of hints. Figure 1 shows the two possible permutations for the schedules. Note that the order of both of these permutations can be reversed, because of the mirroring effect. Graphing the genders would create far too many permutations, so do not do it right now.

```
D|__          D|__          x|x          D|M          D|M
  ?D-----------?D

D|D           D|M           x|x          __|__        D|__
                                            ?M ________?M

Or

Day:
         ___    ___    X    ___    ___
Morn:                  X
```

Fig. 1

1. (B) – As is normal for the first question, use each rule to eliminate one answer choice. Start with the first rule and see if it is violated in any of the answer choices. Then do the same for each of the other rules.

   (A) This choice violates Rule 2 by having a morning student alone. It also places a morning student alone at a table and at Table 3, which must be left empty.

(B) * This permutation does not violate any rules. If you did not make the warranted conclusion about Table 3, this correct answer should have put you on the right track.
(C) This choice does not follow the initial set-up requirement that there be four girls and two morning students. It also has only one morning student. It also has only six students, instead of seven.
(D) This choice violates Rule 4 by having three day students in a row. It also only has one morning student.
(E) Two boys cannot share a table, Rule 3. This choice also has three morning students.

2. (D) – Doing many permutations is an inefficient use of time, so solve this question by trying to disprove each of the five answer choices. When a morning student is at Table 2, there must also be a day student at that table. Looking at the initial analysis in figure 1 for guidance, we see that there are three possibilities: first, that the other morning student is at Table 1; second, that the other morning student is at Table 4; and third, that they are at Table 5. Wherever the second morning student ends up, be sure to pair him or her with a day student. Now we must consider the four other day students. One of them must be paired with the second morning student. This leaves three day students to fill two tables. So one table must have one day student, while the other has two. The genders should not be important for this question.
(A) We can make no conclusions about gender, since we have no starting point to work from.
(B) As discussed above, you cannot know where the second morning student will end up.
(C) See (A).
(D) * Yes, it must be true that a day student (at least one, but maybe two) is assigned to Table 4. Actually, it must be true that at least one day student is assigned to tables 1, 2, 4, and 5.
(E) The second morning student can be at tables 1, 4, or 5.

3. (A) – For "must be true" questions, look for the choice that must always be correct, not just sometimes correct. Since this question adds no new information, you should be able to answer it using the initial analysis. The analysis you did for question 2 should also help.
(A) * Looking at the analysis done for questions 1 and 2, you can see that there must always be at least one day student at tables 1, 2, 4, and 5.
(B) No one is ever assigned to Table 3.
(C) The two morning students can be at tables 1, 2, 4, or 5.
(D) See (C).
(E) See (C).

4. (A) – Now we have four new pieces of information to keep track of. If a morning student is at tables 1 and 4, then a day student must be at both of those tables, but you already knew that. The three remaining day students must be allocated two to one table and one day student by him or herself. Pay special attention to the assignment of the three boys. Since they must be split up, three of the four tables must have a boy, but we can't know exactly which ones. That ambiguity is eliminated by the correct answer choice, which addresses the two possible permutations.

(A) * We know that boys must be at three of the four tables. Since this answer choice encompasses two of the four tables, it must be correct. At least one boy is at Table 1 or 2. Note that this is the same conclusion you could have reached at the initial analysis stage, but sometimes you will only realize certain conclusions once you begin answering the questions.

(B) A boy must be at three of the four tables, so a boy is not required for Table 5.

(C) We know that at least one boy must be at table 2 or 5, but we do not know which.

(D) It is possible to limit the day girls to tables 2 and 5.

(E) It is possible to limit the day girls to tables 1 and 2.

5. (C) – If a single girl is at Table 4, then the three boys must be at the other three tables. The three remaining girls will also be spread among the other three tables. Also, the single girl at Table 4 must be a day student, since morning students cannot be alone at a table. This narrows the possible tables for the two morning students to 1, 2, and 5. (Figure 2) We do not know exactly where the morning and day students are.

(A) Table 1 must have a boy and a girl.

(B) The girl at Table 4 must be a day student.

(C) * Yes, a boy and a girl are at Table 2, so it is possible to have a day boy and a day girl at Table 2.

(D) Table 2 must have a boy and a girl.

(E) Table 5 must have a boy and a girl. Also, Rule 3 prohibits two boys from being at the same table.

g|b g|b x|x Dg|x g|b

Fig. 2

6. (A) – Since a single day girl is assigned to Table 1, this is a similar situation to that in question 5, with regard to the boy/girl assignments. Since a morning boy is at Table 2, you now know that the girl at Table 2 is a day girl. You now have one morning student and three day students left to assign, as well as two boys and two girls. All of them must be at tables 4 and 5. (Figure 3) The answer choices for this question end up being very easy to eliminate.

(A) * We know that a girl and boy must be assigned to Table 5, and there is no reason they cannot be a morning girl and day boy.
(B) We need a boy/girl mix at Table 5.
(C) See (B).
(D) See (B).
(E) See (B).

Dg|x	Dg|Mb	x|x	g|b	g|b
				(1 M, 3 D)

Fig. 3

Restaurant shifts

This game uses a slight variation on the schedule matrix. Rule 1 is easy to graph. (Figure 1) Rule 2 cannot be effectively graphed, so make a note off to the side that each employee must work two consecutive morning shifts. The other rules pose a dilemma. A comprehensive diagram would be difficult to execute, because the conditions are all "if-then" statements, which do not lend themselves to a simple diagram. Rather than attempting to create the elaborate symbols needed to accurately reflect these four conditions, it is better to use very rudimentary symbols (figure 1) as mere place-keepers. Then return to the text of the rules when necessary. The arrows cannot perfectly convey the rules, rather, they are visual reminders that when, for example, an employee works Tuesday night, this will effect the Wednesday shifts.

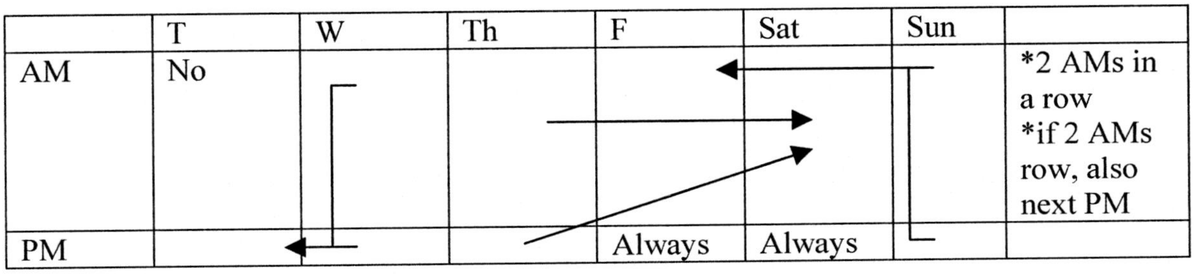

	T	W	Th	F	Sat	Sun	
AM	No						*2 AMs in a row *if 2 AMs row, also next PM
PM				Always	Always		

Fig. 1

7. (C) – Use each of the rules to eliminate the answer choices that violate them. The remaining answer choice is the correct answer.
   (A) This violates Rule 6, because an employee cannot work on both Thursday and on Saturday morning. It also violates Rule 5.
   (B) This violates Rule 4, because when an employee works Friday and Saturday mornings, he or she must also work Sunday evening.
   (C) * This is permitted.
   (D) This violates Rule 5, because when an employee does not work on either of the Sunday shifts, he or she must work Friday morning.
   (E) This violates Rule 3, because an employee who works both Wednesday shifts cannot also work Tuesday evening. It also violates Rule 2.

8. (A) – Look at the rules that specifically affect the morning shift. When the employee works two morning shifts in a row, he or she must also work the next evening shift that the restaurant is open. Since this employee works Saturday and Sunday morning, he or she must also work Tuesday night. If you chose to work further, you would see that the employee must also have the Sunday evening shift (because he or she worked the Friday and Saturday morning shifts), that there can be at most only one Wednesday shift (because there is a Tuesday evening shift), and that there cannot be any Thursday shifts (because of the Saturday morning shift). It was not necessary to do all this work; that is why it is a good idea to quickly check the answer choices after

you have made the first warranted conclusion. Often it is unnecessary to do the full analysis in order to answer the question.

(A) * Yes, Tuesday evening is a required shift when an employee works Saturday and Sunday mornings.

(B) Neither shift on Wednesday is required, although the employee could do one Wednesday shift.

(C) The employee cannot be assigned to either of the Thursday shifts because they work Saturday morning.

(D) See (B).

(E) See (C).

	T	W	Th	F	Sat	Sun	
AM	xxxxxxx	(Can only be 1 Wed.)	No	Yes	Yes	Yes	*2 in a row *if 2 row, also next PM
PM	Must	“”	No	Yes	Yes	Must	

Fig. 2

9. (E) – This one is a challenge. Always look to the rules that affect the new information given in the question stem. There must be two consecutive morning shifts, due to Rule 2. Since in this case one of them is Wednesday, the other must be Thursday. The effect of Rule 4 would require a Friday evening shift (but that was already given). When an employee has a shift on Thursday, the employee cannot have a Saturday morning shift, due to Rule 6 (but you already knew there was no Saturday morning shift). More relevant for your analysis, since this employee does not work Friday morning, he must work on at least one of the Sunday shifts, Rule 5. Since Sunday morning was already ruled out, the employee must work Sunday evening.

(A) You cannot know if Tuesday evening is assigned.

(B) Like (A), you cannot know if Wednesday evening is assigned.

(C) Friday morning cannot be assigned, because this question limits the employee to two morning shifts, which were already assigned.

(D) See (C).

(E) * Sunday evening must be assigned. If an employee does not work either of the shifts on Sunday, then they are supposed to work Friday morning, Rule 5. Here, since this employee does not work Friday morning, he must work at least one Sunday shift, and the evening shift is the only one available.

10. (D) – Remember, with maximum questions, the correct answer is usually the greatest or second greatest number. There are a total of eleven possible shifts. Do not try to find all the permutations. Instead, look at the rules that have an

exclusionary effect. For example, if both Wednesday shifts are assigned, then the Tuesday evening shift is not, so this knocks it down to ten shifts. Next, if there is one (or two) Thursday shifts, there is no Saturday morning shift. You are now down to nine shifts. Can you stop here? For example, there is a shift Sunday morning, but since there is no shift on Saturday morning, then it is not required that there be a Tuesday evening shift, which suits this analysis just fine.

(A) Since at least four shifts must be assigned, due to Rules 1 and 2, this is a pretty crummy answer choice.
(B) See the analysis.
(C) See the analysis.
(D) * Yes, there are only two shifts that cannot be assigned when all the others are assigned.
(E) See the analysis.

11. (A) – Use a combination of previous work and new analysis to solve this question. You can't solve for anything until you look at the answer choices.

(A) * Could an employee be assigned to five morning shifts? Focus on the relevant conditions. If the employee works two consecutive mornings, he or she must also work the following evening, which would require that the employee work Tuesday night. This is not a problem, as long as the employee doesn't also work Wednesday night. But, when the employee works Thursday morning, he or she cannot work Saturday morning, due to Rule 6. So the employee cannot work all five mornings. This analysis is similar to that done for question 10.
(B) When you graph this you can see that there is no conflict if the employee does the Wednesday and Thursday shifts.
(C) This is interesting. When the employee does the Tuesday evening shift, he or she cannot also do the Wednesday morning shift, but that is okay. When the employee works the Thursday evening shift, he or she cannot also work the Saturday morning shift, but that is okay. The Thursday and Friday morning shifts are still available to satisfy Rule 2.
(D) Thursday morning has no conflict with Saturday evening.
(E) The employee could have both Friday shifts, both Saturday shifts, and also Sunday evening. This would satisfy all the rules.

12. (A) – Simply plug in the new information. Since the Thursday and Friday morning shifts are now "off the table", Rule 2 must be satisfied by having the employee work Saturday and Sunday morning. Rule 4 then requires that the employee work Tuesday evening. Since the employee works Tuesday evening, Rule 3 requires that the employee not work both Wednesday morning and evening. There are more warranted conclusions you could make, but this is sufficient analysis to answer the question.

(A) * Correct. The employee could work one shift on Wednesday, but not both, because of Tuesday evening.
(B) It is okay for the employee to work Wednesday evening, so long as he or she doesn't also work Wednesday morning. It is also okay for the employee to work Sunday evening.
(C) The employee must be assigned the Tuesday evening shift.
(D) The employee can be assigned the Sunday evening shift.
(E) The employee must be assigned the Sunday morning shift.

13. (D) – If the employee is assigned to four shifts, then Rules 2 and 4 will be the ones to focus on. We already know the employee works Friday and Saturday evenings. The two required morning shifts must be consecutive, Rule 2. If they were Wednesday and Thursday, then the Friday evening shift would be required. So far, no problem. The problem comes from Rule 5; since there are no Sunday shifts, the Friday morning shift is required. So that doesn't work. On the other hand, if the two morning shifts are Thursday and Friday, then the no-Sunday shifts rule is satisfied. The two morning shifts cannot be on Friday and Saturday or Saturday and Sunday, because of Rule 4. So the required shifts are Thursday and Friday morning.
(A) See the analysis.
(B) See the analysis.
(C) See the analysis.
(D) * Correct.
(E) See the analysis.

Spa treatments

After spending a few rounds in the ring with the LSAT, you are probably ready for a spa treatment yourself. This simple-line diagram only has four members, yet there is something scheduled for each of six sessions. So obviously some will repeat. Could, for example, one spa session be used three or four times? Once you read the Rule 6, you learn this is not the case. Start with the easy rules. The only two rules you can graph are Rules 2 and 4. (Figure 1) Note that the parentheses around K and L tell us that it is not required for K or L to be in these spaces. If it were required that K or L be in these spaces, they would be above the line and there would be no parentheses. The other three rules you will have to keep in the back of your mind. Rule 3 is a "no neighbors" rule, do not put the same treatment twice in a row. Rule 5 is an interesting rule. It requires every set of five sessions to have one of each of the four treatments. So sessions 1–5 must have all four treatments used once and one treatment used a second time. The same is true for sessions 2–6. This is an important rule that you must run as a final check on every answer choice. Using this insight, you might have made the warranted conclusion that K cannot be first or sixth. Rather than attempt to draw more warranted conclusions, it is more efficient to go directly to the questions. You could waste a lot of time doing unnecessary permutations that will not be tested.

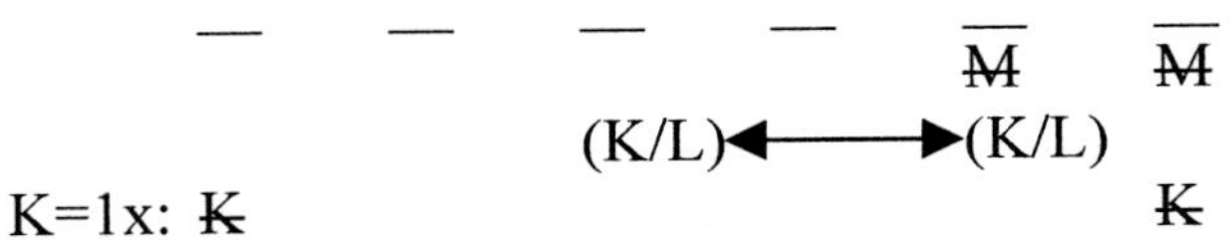

__ __ __ __ __ __

~~M~~ ~~M~~ (under spaces 5 and 6)

(K/L)◄——►(K/L) (under spaces 3 and 5)

K=1x: ~~K~~ (under space 1) ~~K~~ (under space 6)

Every series of five must have all four members

Fig. 1

14. (E) – Straying from the norm, this first question is not phrased like a typical rule violation answer elimination question. As it turns out, rule violator answer elimination is still the best way to answer this question. Try to find one valid permutation that will disprove each of the five answer choices, and eliminate your way to the correct answer.
    - (A) Try using M—MNLMKN. This does not violate any rules.
    - (B) Since M won't work (since it can't be on space 5) and L and K won't work (due to Rule 4), try using N—LMNKNL. This does not violate any rules.
    - (C) Since M won't work (due to Rule 2) and K won't work (due to Rule 1), try using N—NKMLNL. This does not violate any rules.
    - (D) Neither M nor K will work. Try L—NKMLNL. This does not violate any rules.
    - (E) * A quick scan of the answer choices before starting would have saved you a great deal of work. Since the same treatment can't be given twice in a row, this cannot be true.

15. (E) – With this new information, you should focus on Rules 1 and 3. (Figure 2) There is only one K, so it has been used it up. Also, since K is on space 4, you cannot put L on space 3 or 5. This eliminates three answer choices. Focusing on space 5, we see that N must be on space 5, and so can't also be in space 6. Building on this, M cannot be in space 6, so only L is left for space 6. The correct answer will list space 6 but not space 3. You could stop working now, since only one answer choice remains.
(A) L can be on either space 1 or 2, but also must be on space 6.
(B) L cannot be on space 3.
(C) L cannot be on space 3.
(D) L cannot be on space 3.
(E) * This is the correct choice.

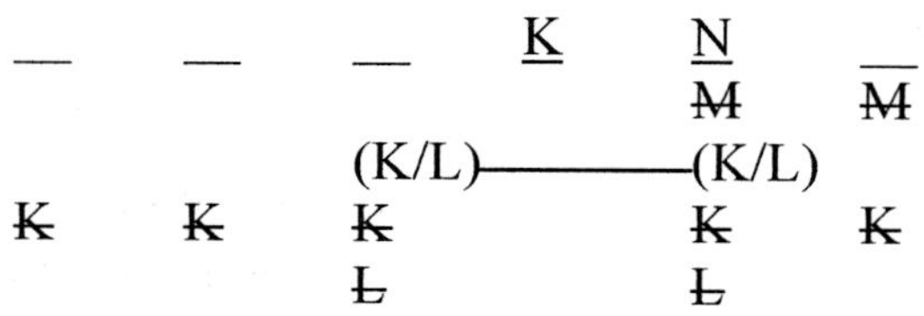

__	__	__	K	N	__
				~~M~~	~~M~~
		(K/L)	———	(K/L)	
~~K~~	~~K~~	~~K~~		~~K~~	~~K~~
		~~L~~		~~L~~	

Fig. 2

16. (D) – You could review the work for question 14 to see if there are any insights, or you can charge ahead and apply the rules. You know that neither L nor K can be on 3 or 5. You also know that M cannot be on space 5, so it cannot be on space 3 and space 5. This leaves only N. Once N is on spaces 3 and 5, it cannot appear again, Rule 6. Now what? Remember that rule you are keeping in the back of your mind? The one that says each treatment must appear in every set of five appointments? This is where it pays off. Make sure that every set of five sessions has all four treatments. If, for example, you were to put K in space 6, then the first five spaces would not contain a K (because there is only one K). This is bad. The same analysis applies to K being in space 1. So L must be in space 6. L must also be in space 1, so as to have an L in the first five appointments. This leaves K and M to split spaces 2 or 4 between them. (Figure 3)
(A) N must be in spaces 3 and 5.
(B) L cannot be in space 3.
(C) K may be in space 2 or 4.
(D) * L must be in 1and must be in 6.
(E) M may be in space 2 or 4.

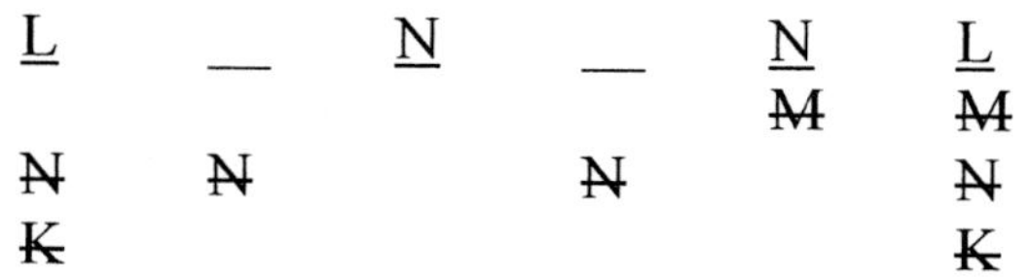

L	__	N	__	N	L
				~~M~~	~~M~~
~~N~~	~~N~~		~~N~~		~~N~~
~~K~~					~~K~~

Fig. 3

17. (A) – This one should be graphed. There seems to have been lots of activity at space 6 in previous questions. If L is not in space 6, and M is not in space 6, can K can in space 6? No, for the reason discussed in the previous question; K can't be in space 6 because of Rule 5. So N must be in space 6. Checking the answer choices, this is one of them. If you didn't catch this and had continued to work the permutations, you would have seen that there were many possibilities, since the members all had multiple possible locations.
(A) * It must be true that N is in space 6.
(B) Although N could be in space 4, so could M.
(C) L could be in space 1, but so could M or N.
(D) In some permutations M is in space 2, but this is not required.
(E) M or N could both be in space 4.

18. (A) – Once again you can use the analysis from question 16. You know that neither M nor K can be in space 1 and 6. So graph for N and for L. (Figure 4) First, if L is first and sixth, then K cannot be on space 3 or 5, due to Rule 4 and Rule 6. This means that only N can be on space 5. Also, either M or N must be on space 3. Check this against some answer choices before doing more work. This work shows that M can be in either space 3 or 4, eliminating two choices, (B) and (C). Also, K can be in space 2, so this eliminates (D). You know that N cannot be in space 4 in this permutation, but that may not be true for other permutations, so solve for those now. So, if instead of L, N is in space 1 and 6, then N cannot be in space 4, so that means that (A) is the correct answer, N can never be in space 4.
(A) * See the analysis.
(B) See the analysis.
(C) See the analysis.
(D) See the analysis.
(E) See the analysis.

L	K/M/N	M/N	K/M	N	L
		~~K~~	~~N~~		

Fig. 4

Engineering tasks

The final game is yet another line problem, and a quirky one. There are a total of six people in three groups who must be assigned to six open slots. Another thing to think about is that the same engineer can appear multiple times, as long as he or she doesn't appear twice on the same day (Rule 4). The setup information is easy to diagram. (Figure 1) Casting about for warranted conclusions, you might have realized that the tasks could be done in as few as three days or as many as six days. Also, as few as two engineers could be used, or all six could be used, depending on the number of days that the tasks are done in. There is no easy way to diagram this information. One warranted conclusion worth making is that either A or B must do task 1 and either E or F must do task 6. There is no other "eureka" insight, so go to the questions.

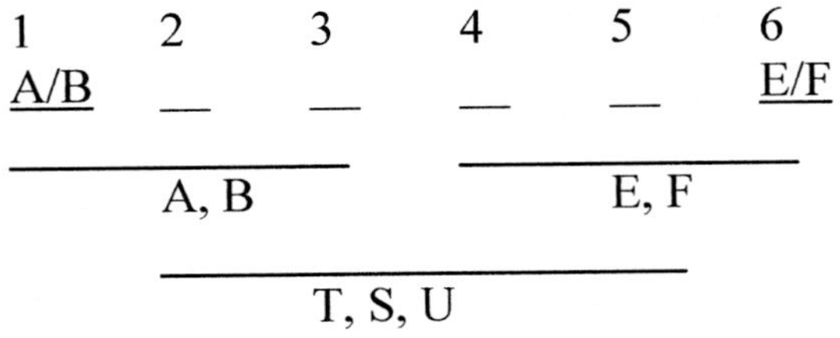

```
1      2      3      4      5      6
A/B    __     __     __     __     E/F
_____________        ______________
     A, B                 E, F
       _______________________
              T, S, U
```

Fig. 1

19. (D) – This question cannot be completely answered using rule violation elimination. Instead, work the permutations, while keeping an eye out for rule violations.
(A) Since this choice does not contain either an E or F, it is false, because either E or F is required for task 6.
(B) This group cannot do the six tasks in three days; they would require six days to do the tasks because of Rule 3.
(C) Since this choice does not contain either an A or B, it is false, because either A or B is necessary for task 1.
(D) * These three engineers can perform all six tasks over a three-day period. B,T || B,T,E || E
(E) See (A).

20. (B) – If you had done the initial analysis, you would know that the minimum number of days is three. You also know from question 19 that they can do it in three days. If you did not do the analysis, start with the two named members. If you use only A and E, then it would require six days. That is almost certainly a wrong answer in a question that asks for a minimum. Could you add more members and do it in three days? If you added T, for example, the tasks could be done in three days. Could the tasks be done in two days by adding more members? No, adding a fourth member would require you to add additional days to avoid violating Rule 3.
(A) See the analysis.
(B) * Correct, one possible order would be: A,T || A,T,E || E.

(C) See the analysis.
(D) See the analysis.
(E) See the analysis.

21. (B) – Once again, if you had done the initial analysis, you would know that the minimum number of engineers is two. If you did not do the analysis, start with the lowest number. Is it possible to use only one engineer? Of course not, no single engineer can do all six tasks. Is it possible to use two engineers? Yes, if one is from the red group and one is from the blue group, and only one task is performed each day for six days.
(A) See the analysis.
(B) * Correct, a possible order would be: A || A || A || E || E || E.
(C) See the analysis.
(D) See the analysis.
(E) See the analysis.

22. (D) – This question provides detailed limitations. Despite this, there are many possible permutations. Start with the easy information. A and E must fill spaces one and six, respectively. The next important thing is to realize that the first day holds either one or two tasks. From there, the permutations become too numerous, so go to the answer choices.
(A) Try to put A on tasks 1 and 2. It is possible to do: A || A,T,E || T,E.
(B) Try to put A on tasks 1 and 3. It is possible as well: A,T || A,T || T,E
(C) E can do tasks 4 and 6. A,T || T,E || T,E
(D) * If T only does tasks 3 and 4, then the six tasks cannot be finished in three days.
(E) T can do tasks 2 and 5. A,T || A,E,T || E

23. (E) – This question is similar to the previous question, but with a bit more information and a slightly different analysis. S can perform task 2 on the first day or the second day. Again, B and F must do tasks 1 and 6. Just a few of the possible permutations are shown in figure 2. Because of the large number of permutations, it is better to stop after doing a few permutations and eliminate some answer choices. Don't invest too much time trying to find every permutation.
(A) As you can see below, B is not required to do task 3.
(B) As you can see, F is not required to do task 4.
(C) Similar to (B), S is not required to do task 4.
(D) It is possible for B to do only one task: B,S || S,F || S,F
(E) * Yes, in one of the permutations S does three tasks, but S can never do just one task.

B|| S B F|| S F

B	S||	B	F||	S	F
B	S||	S	F||	S	F
B	S||	B	S	F||	F

Fig. 2

Practice Test 4

Spend 35 minutes doing this practice test. When time is up, review the explanations to help you understand the questions that you did not answer correctly.

SECTION I

Time—35 minutes

24 Questions

Directions: Each group of questions in this section is based on a set of conditions. In answering some of the questions, it may be useful to draw a rough diagram. Choose the response that most accurately and completely answers each question and blacken the corresponding space on your answer sheet.

Questions 1–6

Nine volunteers—G, H, I, J, K, L, M, N, and O—are available to staff a telephone help line during a four day pledge drive that runs Monday, Tuesday, Wednesday, and Thursday. There is a morning and afternoon shift on each day. Exactly one volunteer staffs the help line during each shift, and a volunteer may work only one shift during the pledge drive. The following conditions apply:

If J works during the pledge drive, J must be immediately followed by two morning shifts that are assigned to K and L.

If both N and O work in the pledge drive, O works earlier in the week than N.

G and N can only work morning shifts.

K cannot work on Tuesday.

If M and L work in the pledge drive, the days they work are separated by exactly one day.

1. Which one of the following could be the work schedule in order from Monday morning to Thursday afternoon?

(A) Mornings: G, H, L, K
Evenings: M, J, O, I
(B) Mornings: G, J, K, L
Evenings: H, I, M, O
(C) Mornings: N, J, K, L
Evenings: O, M, I, H
(D) Mornings: J, L, K, N
Evenings: O, G, H, I
(E) Mornings: G, K, L, N
Evenings: J, H, O, I

2. If H does not work during the pledge drive, then which one of the following could be the schedule for Tuesday morning and Tuesday afternoon respectively?

(A) L and O
(B) O and J
(C) G and K
(D) O and M
(E) O and N

3. If J works during the pledge drive, then which one of the following is a pair of students who could both work on Tuesday?

(A) H and M
(B) K and O
(C) H and I
(D) L and H
(E) L and G

4. If H and I work on the same day, each of the following could be true EXCEPT:

(A) K works Monday morning.
(B) J works Tuesday afternoon.
(C) M works Wednesday afternoon.
(D) N works Thursday morning.
(E) O works Tuesday morning.

5. If J works Monday morning, then which one of the following must be true?

(A) N works Thursday.
(B) I works Tuesday.
(C) M works Thursday.
(D) H works Thursday.
(E) O works Wednesday.

6. If two of the morning shifts are filled by H and I, then which one of the following could be true?

(A) K works Wednesday morning.
(B) N works Monday morning.
(C) L works Thursday morning.
(D) O works Wednesday afternoon.
(E) J works Monday afternoon.

GO ON TO THE NEXT PAGE.

Questions 7–11

A law review editor must assign law students to a research project. The editor must select from the following nine students: three male first-year students, two female first-year students, two male second-year students, and two female second-year students. The assignment of students to the project must satisfy the following conditions:

At least one male first-year is assigned.
As least two female students are assigned.
If a female second-year student is assigned, then at least two male first-year students are assigned.
The number of female students assigned is equal to or greater than the number of male students assigned.

7. Which of the following lists is an acceptable assignment of students to the project?

(A) Female first-year, female first-year, male first-year, male first-year, male second-year
(B) Female first-year, female second-year, male first-year, male second-year
(C) Female first-year, female second-year, male first-year, male first-year
(D) Female first-year, female first-year, male second-year, male second-year
(E) Female second-year, male first-year, male first-year

8. Each of the following could be true about the selection of students EXCEPT:

(A) All the females are assigned to the project.
(B) All the males are assigned to the project.
(C) Exactly one male is assigned.
(D) No female second-year students are assigned.
(E) No female first-year students are assigned.

9. If exactly three males are assigned to the project, then which one of the following must be true?

(A) At least two male first-year students are assigned.
(B) At least one male second-year student is assigned.
(C) Exactly one male second-year student is assigned.
(D) At least two female first-year students are assigned.
(E) Exactly two female first-year students are assigned.

10. What is the maximum number of students that can be assigned to the project?

(A) five
(B) six
(C) seven
(D) eight
(E) nine

11. If the editor only assigns to the project students from a single class years, then which one of the following could be a complete and accurate list of the students assigned to the project?

(A) Male first-year, female first-year
(B) Male first-year, male first-year, female first-year, female first-year
(C) Male first-year, male first-year, male first-year, female first-year, female first-year
(D) Male second-year, female second-year, female second-year
(E) Male second-year, male second-year, female second-year, female second-year

GO ON TO THE NEXT PAGE.

Questions 12–18

A football coach is scheduling the upcoming season of eight games against seven opposing teams—J, K, L, M, N, O, and P. The coach schedules exactly one opposing team for each game. The following scheduling conditions apply:

Exactly one opposing team is scheduled for two games.
Exactly two games separate the games that are played by team L and team P.
All games against team O must be earlier than any game against team K.
The first game against team J must be played in the first half of the season.

12. Which one of the following lists the opposing teams, in the order they are scheduled, from game 1 to game 8?

(A) L, M, O, P, J, K, N, M
(B) N, O, J, P, K, N, M, L
(C) O, K, J, L, M, O, P, N
(D) M, J, L, O, K, P, M, J
(E) N, J, P, O, M, L, O, K

13. Which one of the following teams CANNOT play game 2 and game 5?

(A) O
(B) K
(C) J
(D) N
(E) L

14. If P is the only team that plays a game between the games played by teams O and J, then all of the following could play fourth EXCEPT:

(A) K
(B) L
(C) M
(D) O
(E) P

15. If team O plays in the second game and the seventh game, then which one of the following is a complete and accurate list of teams, any one of which could play game 5?

(A) N
(B) M, N
(C) M, N, K
(D) M, N, J
(E) M, N, J, K, L, P

16. If the games played by teams M and N are separated by exactly one game, which is played by team K, then which one of the following could be true?

(A) L plays game 3.
(B) L plays game 8.
(C) P plays game 6.
(D) O plays game 6.
(E) P plays game 4.

17. If O is played after P and is separated by exactly two games that are played by two different teams, then which one of the following must be true?

(A) K plays game 7.
(B) L plays game 2.
(C) L plays game 1.
(D) M plays game 1.
(E) P plays game 1.

18. Which one of the following is a complete and accurate list of teams, any one of which can play game 1 and game 8 in the same season?

(A) M, K
(B) J, N
(C) M, N, L
(D) M, N, J
(E) M, N, K

GO ON TO THE NEXT PAGE

Questions 19–24

In each of six consecutive classrooms numbered 1–6, students will demonstrate exactly one of three science projects—astronomy, biology, and chemistry—and exactly one of three art projects—dance, etching, and folk music. The following requirements are the only ones used in making the assignment of projects to classrooms:

No project is demonstrated in two consecutive rooms.
No project that is demonstrated in room 1 is also demonstrated in room 5.
Biology is demonstrated in room 1, but not in room 6.
Only etching is demonstrated in exactly three rooms.
Astronomy and etching are never demonstrated in the same room.

19. Which one of the following could be the order of art projects demonstrated, in order from room 1 to room 6?

(A) Folk music, etching, dance, etching, dance, etching
(B) Etching, folk music, etching, dance, folk music, dance
(C) Folk music, etching, dance, etching, folk music, etching
(D) Etching, dance, etching, dance, etching, folk music
(E) Etching, etching, dance, folk music, dance, etching

20. If Astronomy is demonstrated in room 2, then which one of the following could be true?

(A) Chemistry is in room 5.
(B) Etching is in room 2.
(C) Dance is in room 4.
(D) Astronomy is in room 3.
(E) Astronomy is in room 4.

21. Which of the following must be true?

(A) Chemistry is in room 3.
(B) Dance is in room 1.
(C) Astronomy is in room 4.
(D) Etching is in room 5.
(E) Etching is in room 6.

22. If etching is not in room 3, then which one of the following are pairs of rooms that CANNOT hold the same science and art projects?

(A) Rooms 3 and 6
(B) Rooms 1 and 3
(C) Rooms 1 and 4
(D) Rooms 2 and 5
(E) Rooms 4 and 6

23. Which of the following must be true?

(A) In at least one room, biology is demonstrated with etching.
(B) In at least one room, etching is demonstrated with chemistry.
(C) Etching is demonstrated in room 1 and room 4.
(D) Chemistry is not demonstrated in a room that is next to a room in which biology is demonstrated.
(E) Folk music is demonstrated in exactly two rooms.

24. If folk music is demonstrated only in room 1, then which one of the following must be true?

(A) Etching is demonstrated in room 3, and astronomy is demonstrated in room 5.
(B) Dance is demonstrated in room 3, and chemistry is demonstrated in room 3.
(C) Biology is demonstrated in room 1 and room 3.
(D) Dance is demonstrated in room 2 and room 5.
(E) Chemistry is demonstrated in room 2, and dance is demonstrated in room 3.

S T O P

IF YOU FINISH BEFORE TIME IS CALLED, YOU MAY CHECK YOUR WORK ON THIS SECTION ONLY.
DO NOT WORK ON ANY OTHER SECTION IN THE TEST.

Answer key and explanations for Test 4

Answer Key

1. A
2. A
3. D
4. B
5. C
6. D
7. C
8. B
9. A
10. D
11. B
12. E
13. E
14. B
15. B
16. E
17. C
18. D
19. A
20. C
21. E
22. A
23. B
24. E

Telephone staffing

This game requires a typical schedule matrix because there are four days and two time slots per day. An important rule is that if J works, the next two mornings must be assigned to K and L. This creates a block of three letters that plays a key role in the questions. Note that there are eight time slots but nine people. This means that one person will not be used. This makes the puzzle much more complex because this "wild-card" prevents you from making as many warranted conclusions as you could if there were eight people for eight time slots. In fact, the only warranted conclusion you can make is that that J cannot be on Wednesday or Thursday. Figure 1 shows this, as well as the two rules that we can graph. Note that there are two free agents, I and H.

If J, then K/L next two AMs
If N and O, O < N
G & N only work mornings
K cannot work on Tuesday
If M and L, M _ L / L _ M

	Mon	Tue	Wed	Thu	
AM					
PM					~~G N~~
		~~K~~	~~J~~	~~J~~	

Fig. 1

1. (A) – As you would expect, use each rule to eliminate one answer choice. Start with the first rule and see if it is violated in any of the answer choices. Then do the same for each of the other rules.
(A) * This is correct since it does not violate any rules.
(B) This choice does not separate M and L, so it violates Rule 5.
(C) N must be later than O, Rule 2.
(D) G cannot be in the afternoon, Rule 3.
(E) By Rule 4, K cannot work on Tuesday.

2. (A) – H does not work, so you know who the eight members are. This simplifies things immensely, since you know, for example, that J must be scheduled, as must L and M and the others. Even so, there are still too many possible permutations to just start solving them blindly, so work with the answer choices.
(A) * Follow the arrows in figure 2 to see the chain of conclusions. When L is Tuesday morning, J is on one of the two Monday shifts and K is on Wednesday morning. Because of L, M has to be in one of the two Thursday shifts. Next, since O is on Tuesday afternoon, the only morning slot available for N is on. This means M must be Thursday afternoon.

This leaves Monday morning for G, Monday afternoon for J, and Wednesday afternoon for I. This is answer choice is valid.

(B) If J is Tuesday, then L must be Wednesday morning and K must be Thursday morning. But this leaves only one morning open, yet you are required to place both N and G in morning slots.

(C) K cannot be on Tuesday, by the rules.

(D) If O and M occupy Tuesday, then there is not room left to accommodate J, K, and L.

(E) This is the same analysis as (D). Also, N cannot work in the afternoon.

	Mon	Tue	Wed	Thu	
AM	G	~~L~~	K	N	
PM	J	O	I	M	~~G~~ ~~N~~
		~~K~~	~~J~~	~~J~~	

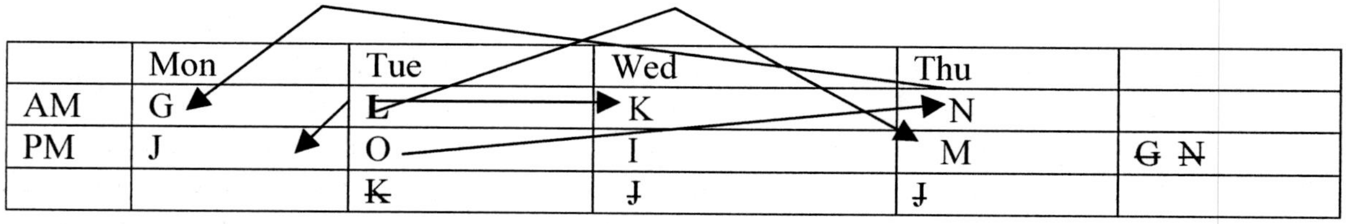

Fig. 2

3. (D) – This question has a similar focus to the previous question. The impact of J, K, and L will be important. In fact, if you review the diagram used in the previous question, you can see how moving O to Wednesday afternoon and putting H on Tuesday afternoon will work. If you didn't have this insight, you can, of course, still work the permutations for each answer choice.

(A) If M works on Tuesday, then L must be on Thursday. But this is not allowable because it does not leave enough space for J and K.

(B) K cannot work on Tuesday.

(C) If H and I work on Tuesday, then there is not enough space for J, K, and L.

(D)* Correct. There are a few ways this can work. For example, if L works on Tuesday morning and H works on Tuesday afternoon, then J must be working Monday, afternoon is okay. (As is turns out, J will have to work Monday afternoon.) K works on Wednesday morning. M must work on Thursday, because of L. There are two morning slots left for N and G, and either I or O can fill in the remaining afternoon slot (as long as N is placed before O).

(E) G cannot work in the afternoon. L has to work in the morning when J is working.

4. (B) – This is a tough question because H and I are both free agents, so you don't know exactly which day they are on, and it is a "could be true EXCEPT" question. Definitely, do not try to do the permutations until you look at the answer choices.

(A) This one is a little tricky. K can work Monday morning, provided J does not work during the week. By eliminating J, you now know who the eight members are and can graph accordingly. (Figure 3a) Both N and G must be used, so they will take two morning slots, and either H or I will take the fourth morning slot. Assign N to Thursday morning because of O. Now, it is important to keep M and L separated. You can do that by putting one of them on Tuesday afternoon and the other on Thursday afternoon. This allows H and I to have Wednesday. G and O fill the remaining slots.

(B) * This is the credited answer choice. If J works Tuesday afternoon and L works Wednesday morning and K works Thursday morning, then H and I are forced to be Monday. Because of L, you cannot use M now. So you must use N and G, but there is only one available morning slot open for both N and G. So, it does not work to have L on Wednesday morning. What if K and L switch, and K is Wednesday morning and L is Thursday morning? Initially, there is no problem. H and I can work Monday. The problem arises that you must fill three slots, Tuesday morning and Wednesday and Thursday afternoon. Four members remain—N, G, M, and O. If you use N on Tuesday morning you can't use O, because there is now no way to satisfy Rule 3. But if you use N, you have only an afternoon slot for G, which doesn't work either. If you use G and not N, then G must be Tuesday morning, but then M cannot be appropriately separated from L. You reach an impasse. (Figure 3b)

(C) If M works Wednesday afternoon and L also worked, L would have to work on Monday, so J would not work this week. There are several permutations that work. (Figure 3c)

(D) Again, N can be Thursday morning if J is not used. Simply keep G in the morning slot, separate L and M, and give H and I a full day. (Figure 3d)

(E) This is possible. (Figure 3d)

	Mon	Tue	Wed	Thu	
AM	K	G	H	N	
PM	O	M	I	L	~~G~~ ~~N~~
		~~K~~	~~J~~	~~J~~	

Fig. 3a

	Mon	Tue	Wed	Thu	
AM	H		K	L	
PM	I	J			~~G~~ ~~N~~
		~~K~~	~~J~~	~~J~~	

Fig. 3b

	Mon	Tue	Wed	Thu	
AM	K	G	N	H	
PM	L	O	M	I	~~G~~ ~~N~~
		~~K~~	~~J~~	~~J~~	

Fig. 3c

	Mon	Tue	Wed	Thu	
AM	G	O	H	N	
PM	K	L	I	M	~~G~~ ~~N~~
		~~K~~	~~J~~	~~J~~	

Fig. 3d

5. (C) – J plays a role again in this question. J is Monday morning. K can never be on Tuesday. Thus, L is Tuesday morning (which means that M, if working, is Thursday), and K is Wednesday morning. Either N or G must be Thursday morning. The remaining members are H, I, O and M. There are only four members to fill four spaces, so all of them must be used. Since H and I are free agents, you don't know which of them will be used, or if both of them will be used. Check the answer choices.
(A) N can work Thursday, but it is equally likely that G works Thursday.
(B) I is a free agent, so anything that is true of I is just as true for H. Therefore, I cannot be the correct answer to this must be true question.
(C) * M must work Thursday afternoon.
(D) Like choice (B), H is a free agent, so it a poor choice for a must be true question. Furthermore, M must work Thursday afternoon and either G or N must work Thursday morning. So H cannot work Thursday.
(E) Like H and I, O can work on Monday, Tuesday, or Wednesday afternoon.

	Mon	Tue	Wed	Thu	
AM	J	L	K	G/N	
PM	~~M~~	~~M~~	~~M~~		~~G~~ ~~N~~
		~~K~~	~~J~~	~~J~~	

Fig. 4

6. (D) – This question is intricate, but doable. Start by filling up the morning shifts. If H and I take two of the morning shifts, could L and K fill the other two? No, because at least one of N and G must have a morning shift. Since L and K cannot fill two morning shifts, J is not used in this week. That means that you know the eight members; everyone except J is included. Since there are eight members to fill eight spaces, the two other morning shifts must be taken by G and N. So, the morning shifts must be filled by H, I, N, and G. Remember to keep O earlier than N. The only other concern is to keep L and M appropriately separated. Neither of these poses much trouble.
(A) Since the four morning slots are already filled, K cannot fill one.
(B) The problem with N working Monday morning is that O could not be earlier than N.

(C) See (A).

(D) * This is possible. O can work Wednesday afternoon, as long as N works Thursday morning. H, I, and G can fill the other three morning slots in any order. K must work Monday afternoon; and either L or M will do Tuesday afternoon; the other one will do Thursday afternoon.

(E) J does not work at all.

Law review assignment

This game uses a simple-line diagram and some grouping rules. There is one major twist: you are never told how many students are assigned. As it turns out, the number varies depending on the situation. Start with the set-up. There are nine students to choose from. Of those nine, there are three male 1Ls and two each of the other three types. Rule 1 provides the first anchor. Rule 2 provides the second anchor. A simple, yet effective diagram is shown in figure 1a. Since the number of students varies, this is not the only possible diagram; it is just one of the possibilities. Rules 3 and 4 are more complex. Rule 3 is a conditional rule, so you might prefer to not graph it. If you did graph it, your diagram might look like figure 1b. Rule 4 is not conditional and is in fact quite important. The number of female students must equal or exceed the number of male students. Since there are four female students, this establishes a theoretical maximum of eight students. Thus, you will never use all nine students. This is an important conclusion. There are too many permutations to effectively graph this rule. Instead, you will need to check every answer choice against this rule to make sure there are not too many males. There are no additional useful warranted conclusions to be made at this point, so move to the questions.

```
1L
--    __    __
M     F     F
```

Fig. 1a

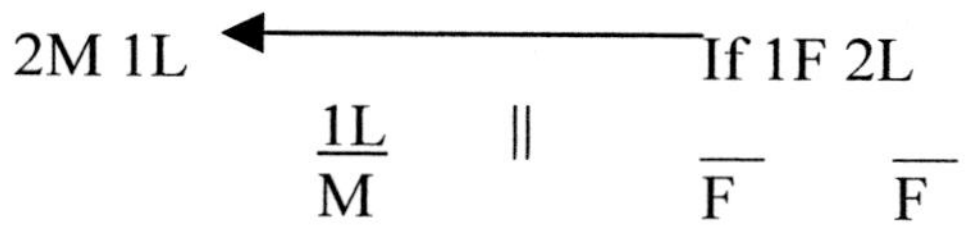

```
2M 1L <---------------------- If 1F 2L
          1L     ||
          --          __      __
          M           F       F
```

Fig. 1b

7. (C) – Use each of the rules to eliminate the answer choices that violate them. The remaining answer choice is the correct answer.
   (A) This choice is wrong because it violates Rule 4, the number of females must equal or exceed the number of males.
   (B) This violates Rule 3, because if a female 2L is selected, then two male 1Ls must be selected.
   (C) * This is a permissible assignment.
   (D) This violates Rule 1, because there must be at least one male 1L.
   (E) This violates Rule 2 and Rule 4.

8. (B) – Since there is no new information and this is an EXCEPT question, the most efficient approach is to dive right into the answer choices.
   (A) Can all four females be assigned? Yes, as long as at least two male 1Ls are also assigned.

(B) * Can all five males be assigned? No. As was determined in the initial analysis, the maximum number of males is four, since Rule 4 dictates that the number of females must equal or exceed the number of males.
(C) It is possible to have one male. The permutation is: F1L, F1L, M1L.
(D) As seen in (C), it is not necessary to use a female 2L.
(E) It is possible to not use any female 1Ls. That permutation would be: F2L, F2L, M1L, M1L.

9. (A) – This question turns out to be more complex than it initially appears. When there are exactly three males, there must be either three or four females. When there are three or four females, there must be one or two female 2Ls. When there is a female 2L, there must be at least two male 1Ls. (Figure 2). You do not know the identity of the third male, nor whether the second female is a 1L or 2L, nor do you know if there is even a fourth female at all.
(A) * This is required, as discussed in the analysis.
(B) It could be that the third male is a 2L, but that is only a 50/50 chance.
(C) See (B).
(D) At least one female 1L is assigned, but there need not be a second one.
(E) See (D).

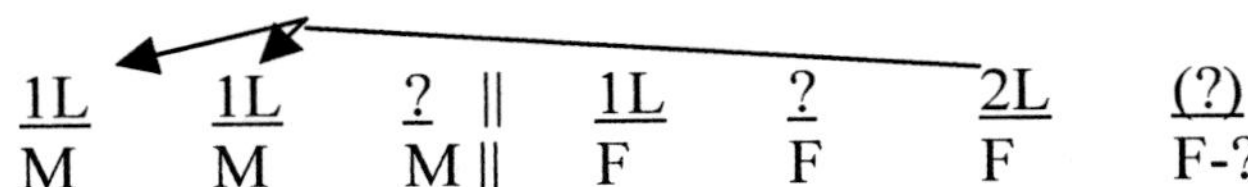

Fig. 2

10. (D) – This question can be answered quickly if you did the initial analysis. The effect of Rule 4 is that there is a maximum of eight students—four females and four males.
(A) See the analysis.
(B) See the analysis.
(C) See the analysis.
(D) * See the analysis.
(E) See the analysis.

11. (B) – This new information limits you to using either the 1Ls or the 2Ls. You know that a male 1L must be used, so the editor must use the 1Ls, not the 2Ls. This eliminates (D) and (E). You can quickly eliminate the invalid choices.
(A) There must be at least two females, per Rule 2.
(B) * This is a valid assignment.
(C) This does not work; it violates Rule 4.
(D) See the analysis.
(E) See the analysis.

Football schedule

This simple-line puzzle uses several simple-line rules. It uses a definite-order rule (Rule 2), a possible location rule (Rule 4), and a greater-than/less-than rule (Rule 3). The diagrams for these rules are familiar by now, and should need no special elaboration. The set-up is pretty clear—eight dashes. The only quirk is that there are seven members, but eight slots to fill. Even if you did not catch this at first, Rule 1 made it clear. This quirk makes the diagram more flexible, which means there are more possible permutations. As such, permutations should only be done when solving a specific question. Take special note of Rule 2. It says that exactly two games separate L and P. On the surface this looks easy to diagram, you simply draw L _ _ P or L _ _ P. But when you think this rule through to its logical extent, you realize that theoretically there may be two Ls or two Ps. If so, you would need to separate the *second* L or P according to the dictates of Rule 2. In a normal line diagram, with six or seven dashes, it would be likely that you could limit L and P to just a few possible locations. That is not so in this bigger diagram; there are simply too many places where L and P can be. The diagram and the rules are depicted in figure 1. Note that Rule 4 requires that first game played by J must be in the first half of the season. If J plays a second game, there is no restriction. Because of this, we cannot put negative Js under the fifth through eighth dashes.

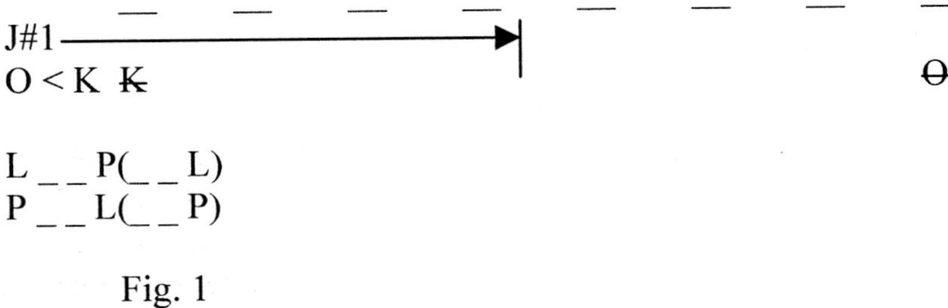

Fig. 1

12. (E) – This possible order question is no different than any other. Start with the first rule and work your way down.
(A) The first appearance of J must be in games 1–4, per Rule 4.
(B) This violates Rule 2, because it puts P and L too far apart.
(C) This violates Rule 3, by putting an O later than K.
(D) This violates Rule 1 and the initial set-up, since both M and J are used twice and N is not used at all.
(E) * This is a valid permutation.

13. (E) – Before trying to figure out who can be in both game 2 and game 5, look at the answer choices. You will note that team L is listed. Perhaps you remembered that L and P must be separated by two games. If so, you would realize that L cannot be in both games 2 and 5. Even if you didn't do this quick analysis, solving the permutations for each answer choice takes relatively little time.
(A) O is possible: LOJPOKMN.

(B) K is possible: OKJPKMLN.
(C) J is possible: OJPKJLMN.
(D) You really should not have checked for N, since N is a free agent. Regardless, N is possible: ONJPNKLM
(E) * This does not work, this diagram (_ L _ P L _ _) violates Rule 2.

14. (B) – Now there is an OPJ block or a JPO block. Three limiting factors potentially come into play. P must keep two spaces from L, O must be earlier than K, and if this is the only J in the schedule, it must be before game 5. Once again, since this is a "could be true EXCEPT" question, it has many possible permutations, so solve only for the answer choices.
(A) K can be fourth: OPJKLMNM.
(B) * L cannot be fourth. If L is fourth, then P must be first or seventh. Obviously P cannot be first if it is in the middle of a block of three members. Can P be seventh? If P is seventh, then either J or O is sixth and the other is eighth. Either way, O would now be later than K, which is always prohibited.
(C) J can be fourth: MNLJJPOK.
(D) O can be fourth: MJPOKLMN.
(E) P can be fourth: LNJPOKLM.

15. (B) – Once you jot down O in spaces 2 and 7 (and thus K in space 8), this becomes easy, since P and L must follow Rule 2. There are two possibilities depicted in figure 2. In neither one does P or L fill space 5. M and N are going to be fine anywhere. Can J go on space 5? No. Why not? Because the first J must be used in spaces 1–4. You cannot have a second J, because there are already two Os. K cannot be on space 5 because of O in space 7, so K is in space 8.
(A) N can be in space 5, but so can M.
(B) * Yes, either M or N can be in space 5. Remember, they are both free agents, and both of them share the same analysis.
(C) K cannot be fifth.
(D) J cannot be fifth.
(E) K cannot be fifth. Neither L nor P can be fifth.

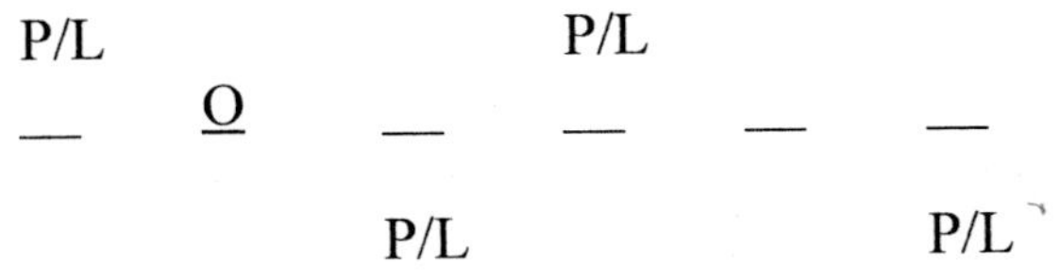

P/L			P/L				
__	O	__	__	__	__	O	K
		P/L			P/L		

Fig. 2

16. (E) – This time there is an MKN block. It doesn't matter for purposes of analysis whether it is MKN or NKM, since M and N are interchangeable. You know that K must be later than all Os, so try placing the block on space 1. That does not work, because of O. Try starting the block on space 2. Now you could fit in O, but the problem is that you also need to fit J into spaces 1–4. So, try starting the block on space 3 instead. A new problem comes up; there is not enough room for L _ _ P. Try starting the block on space 4 and you run into the same problem. We are running out of options. Starting on space 5, you can fit the block. Finally. Also, you can fit the block if you start on space 6. (Figure 3) When the block starts on space 5, the outcome is largely determined. L and P must take spaces 1 and 4, J and O must take spaces 2 and 3, and one member must double up and fill space 7. On the other hand, when the block starts on space 6, there are more possibilities. L and P can be on 1 and 4 or 2 and 5, but, never on space 3. Move to the answer choices.

(A) Neither L nor P can be in space 3.
(B) Since P and L must be separated by two spaces, L cannot be in space 8 in the first diagram below, since the latest P can appear is fourth.
(C) No matter what, space 6 is filled by M or K.
(D) See (C).
(E) * Yes, it is possible that P plays game 4.

L/P	J/O	J/O	L/P				?
__	__	__	__	M	K	N	__
__	__	__	__	__	M	K	N

Fig. 3

17. (C) – This new information should be combined with Rules 2 and 3 to make a compound rule: L _ _ P _ _ O (O< K). Graph this and see what emerges. Starting with L on space 1 works fine. Starting with L on space 2 does not, because of O<K. Go to the answers.

(A) K can only be on space 8.
(B) L can only be on space 1.
(C) * L must be on space 1.
(D) See (C).
(E) P must be on space 4.

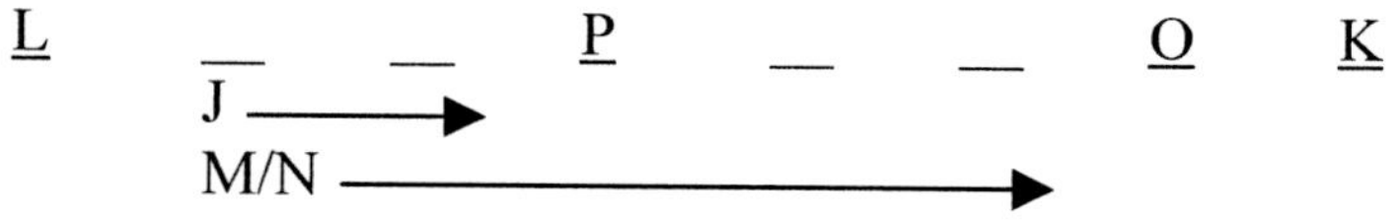

Fig. 4

18. (D) – Before jumping in, a quick glance will confirm that M and N, the free agents, appear in all the answer choices. And we know that M and N have the same analysis. That aside, the real issue is now, can L, J, or K appear first and last? A quick analysis will show you that K certainly cannot be first, because of O. Can L be first? Yes, if P is fourth. Can L also be eighth in the same season? This would require P to be fifth. But there cannot be two Ls and two Ps. So L cannot be first and eighth. By process of elimination, you find that only J can be first and last. Remember, Rule 4 merely requires that the first J appear in spaces 1–4.

(A) See the analysis. You could have quickly eliminated this choice because it contains K.

(B) See the analysis.

(C) See the analysis. You could have quickly eliminated this choice because it contains L.

(D) * See the analysis. After eliminating choices (A), (C), and (E), it was only necessary to compare (B) and (D). Since these choices both contain N and J, there was no need to check for N and J. This answer is correct, because just like N, M can play game 1 and game 8.

(E) See the analysis. You could have quickly eliminated this choice because it contains K.

Project demonstrations

This final game requires a large multiple-line diagram. At first glance, it looks like a very easy simple-line problem, since there are six rooms and six members. Once you read the rules and realize that there will be two members per room, the diagram suddenly becomes much more complex. There are several ways to diagram this puzzle. The simplest diagram is shown in figure 1. Use two parallel lines of six dashes. Rule 1 is easy to understand, if not to diagram; it is a "no neighbors" rule. Just make sure the same member is never in two consecutive rooms. Rule 2 is a pretty common rule and is easy to diagram. Rule 3 is easy to diagram, and this is the only anchor rule. Combining Rules 2 and 3, you see that B cannot be on day 5, so mark that as well. Rules 4 and 5 are difficult to diagram. Can we draw any warranted conclusions? If etching is in exactly three rooms, which rooms could they be? E could be rooms 1, 3, and 6 (not 5, because of Rule 2), or 2, 4, and 6, or 1, 4, and 6. So E can never be in room 5 and must always be in room 6. That is very helpful and should be diagrammed. Now turn to Rule 4. E and A cannot be in the same room. This means that A cannot be in room 6. Because neither A nor B is in room 6, then C must be in room 6. Due to Rule 1, C cannot be in room 5. Since neither B nor C can be in room 5, then A must be in room 5. Is there any more you can do? You know that E is the only member that is used three times. Could any of them be used four times? No, because of the effect of Rule 1, there can be no neighbors. Could any of them be used zero times? No, because this would force the other two members of the same line to appear three time (not allowed because of Rule 4) or more than three times (not allowed because of Rule 1). So each project must be used one or two times. This is probably as many warranted conclusions as you need to make.

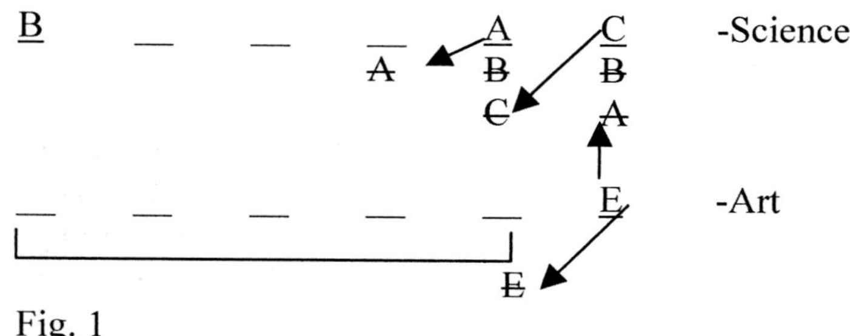

Fig. 1

19. (A) – Using the rules to eliminate choices is the most efficient technique.
    (A) * This is a possible order.
    (B) This choice only shows two Es, violating Rule 4.
    (C) This choice shows the same project in rooms 1 and 5, violating Rule 2.
    (D) This choice also shows the same project in rooms 1 and 5.
    (E) This choice is incorrect because Rule 1 prohibits using the same project twice in a row.

20. (C) – Plugging the new information into figure 2 allows you to fill several blanks. When A is in room 2, then E is not. Also, A cannot be in rooms 3 and 4, due to Rule 1. In order to accommodate three Es, you must place one in

room 1, and the second in room 3 or 4. That is as much as you can determine, but it is enough to answer the question.

(A) A is always in room 5.
(B) Since A is in room 2, E is not, by Rule 5.
(C) * Yes, D, a free agent, could be in room 2, 3, or 4.
(D) A cannot be in room 3, per Rule 1.
(E) A is in room 5, so it cannot be in room 4, per Rule 1.

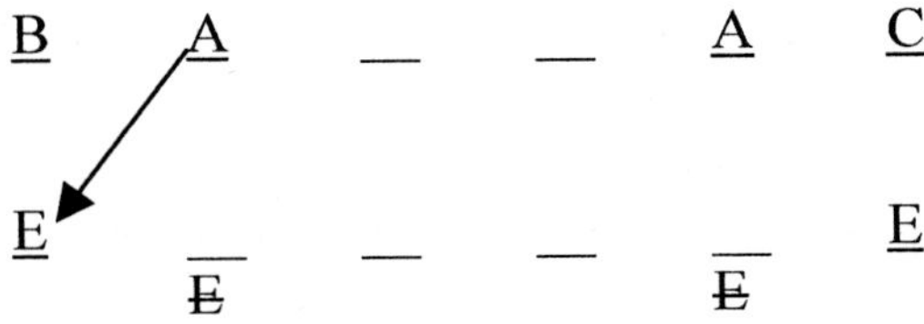

Fig. 2

21. (E) – The initial analysis answers this question.
(A) C may or may not be in room 3.
(B) D is not required to be in room 1, as seen in the previous question.
(C) This is always false. Since A must be in room 5, it can never be in room 4.
(D) Because A is in room 5, E can never be in room 5.
(E) * Correct. E must always be in room 6, because of the impact of several rules.

22. (A) – By removing one of the possibilities for etching, this choice reduces the number of permutations. Since room 3 is not available now, E must be in room 4. You can't know whether the third E is in room 1 or 2. Both possibilities are diagrammed below. (Figure 3) As the diagrams show, a great deal of flexibility remains.
(A) * Yes. In both permutations, E and C must be in room 6. But E cannot be in room 3, due to the new requirement. So the same pair cannot be in rooms 3 and 6.
(B) In the second permutation shown below, you can see that B and D could both be in rooms 1 and 3.
(C) It is possible for B and E to be in rooms 1 and 4.
(D) It is possible for A and D to be in rooms 2 and 5.
(E) It is possible for C and E to be in rooms 4 and 6.

B	A/C	A/B/C	B/C	A	C
E	D/F	D/F ~~E~~	E	D/F ~~E~~	E

B	C	A/B	B/C	A	C
D/F	E	D/F ~~E~~	E	D/F ~~E~~	E

Fig. 3

23. (B) – Once again, the initial analysis and the work done up to this point is sufficient to answer this question.
    (A) Consulting the initial analysis, or the previous question, you can see that it is not required that B and E be in the same room.
    (B) * Yes. In room 6, both C and E must be demonstrated—no matter what.
    (C) Although E can be in rooms 1 and 4, this is only one of the possible permutations.
    (D) There are several permutations where B and C are neighbors.
    (E) F and D must split three rooms, but sometimes D will be used twice; sometimes F will be used twice.

24. (E) – When F is only in room 1, D must fill the two remaining rooms. When E is not in room 1, it must be in rooms 2, 4, and 6. So D is in rooms 3 and 5. Organize the science projects, A, B, and C. Rule 4 specifies that there must be two of each. A cannot be in the same room as etching, so the two A projects must be in rooms 3 and 5. B is in room 1, so it cannot be in room 2, thus it must be in room 4. The series of steps is depicted in figure 4. You can now consult the diagram to answer the question.
    (A) E is not in room 3.
    (B) C is not in room 3.
    (C) B is not in room 3.
    (D) D is not in room 2.
    (E) * C is in room 2, and dance is in room 3.

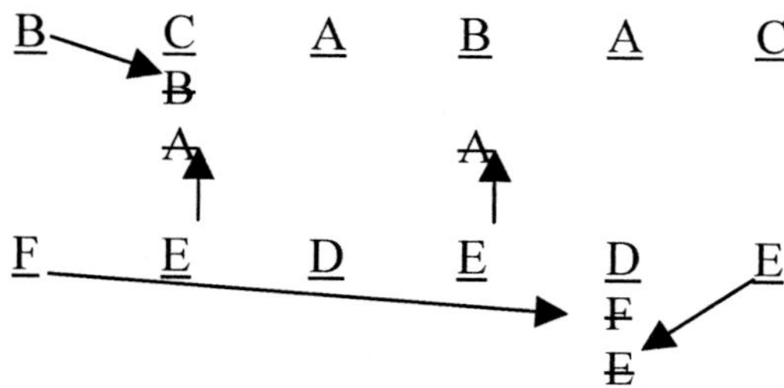

Fig. 4

Practice Test 5

Spend 35 minutes doing this practice test. When time is up, review the explanations to help you understand the questions that you did not answer correctly.

SECTION I

Time—35 minutes

23 Questions

Directions: Each group of questions in this section is based on a set of conditions. In answering some of the questions, it may be useful to draw a rough diagram. Choose the response that most accurately and completely answers each question and blacken the corresponding space on your answer sheet.

Questions 1–5

For seven radio commercials the station manager must schedule a play list. The seven commercials—F, G, H, I, J, K, and L—are each played one at a time and only once in the play list. The station manager must schedule the commercials in accordance with the following requirements:

Exactly two commercials must separate H and J.
G must be played at some time before I.
G must be played after K.
I is played only after L is played.

1. Which one of the following is an acceptable play list for the commercials from first to last?

(A) K, G, F, J, I, L, H
(B) F, L, H, K, G, J, I
(C) H, K, L, J, I, F, G
(D) K, F, G, H, L, J, I
(E) G, H, K, J, I, L, F

2. If L is played after F, each of the following could be true EXCEPT:

(A) G is played fifth.
(B) L is played second.
(C) K is played sixth.
(D) F is played third.
(E) I is played sixth.

3. If K is played third, and L is played fourth, which one of the following CANNOT be true?

(A) G is played sixth.
(B) J is played fifth.
(C) H is played second.
(D) F is played first.
(E) J is played first.

4. If F is played seventh, which one of the following must be true?

(A) The earliest L can be played is second.
(B) The latest K can be played is third.
(C) The earliest J can be played is second.
(D) The latest H can be played is fifth.
(E) The latest G can be played is fourth.

5. If all the requirements remain unchanged and a new commercial, T, is added and is played later than exactly four of the commercials and earlier than exactly three of the commercials, then each of the following could be true, EXCEPT:

(A) F is played first or eight.
(B) I is the only commercial played between T and H.
(C) H is played second.
(D) J is played earlier than K and later than L.
(E) G is played seventh.

GO ON TO THE NEXT PAGE

Questions 6–12

A design committee must select at least two of the following seven features to offer on a newly designed car. The features are: airbags, CD player, heated seats, navigation system, performance tires, roof rack, and sunroof. The designers must select features using the following requirements:

If a sunroof is offered with the car, then heated seats cannot be offered.

If the car is offered with a navigation system and a CD player, then a roof rack cannot also be offered.

If the car is offered with a CD player, then it must also be offered with an airbag.

If the car is not offered with performance tires, then it must be offered with a roof rack.

6. Which of the following is a list of the features that could be selected for the car?

(A) airbags, navigation system, roof rack
(B) airbags, CD player, heated seats, roof rack, sunroof
(C) airbags, CD player, navigation system, performance tires, roof rack
(D) CD player, performance tires, roof rack
(E) airbags, navigation system, heated seats

7. If a roof rack is not selected for the car, then which one of the following is a list of the features that could be selected?

(A) airbags, CD player, heated seats, performance tires
(B) airbags, CD player, navigation system, sunroof
(C) airbags, CD player, heated seats, navigation system, sunroof
(D) airbags, CD player, navigation system, heated seats
(E) CD player, navigation system, performance tires, sunroof

8. If performance tires are selected for the car, what is the maximum number of additional features that could be selected?

(A) two
(B) three
(C) four
(D) five
(E) six

9. If a CD player is selected, what is the minimum number of features that the car must contain?

(A) one
(B) two
(C) three
(D) four
(E) five

10. Each of the following could be a complete list of the features selected for the car EXCEPT:

(A) airbags, performance tires
(B) airbags, CD player, performance tires
(C) airbags, CD player, navigation system
(D) sunroof, performance tires
(E) heated seats, navigation system, roof rack

11. If exactly five features are selected for the car, which of the following could be a pair of features, both of which must be selected?

(A) airbags, sunroof
(B) airbags, performance tires
(C) CD player, heated seats
(D) performance tires, sunroof
(E) CD player, roof rack

12. Suppose that a new feature, fog lights, must be selected when either airbags or a CD player, or neither, are selected, but cannot be selected if both airbags and a CD player are selected. If all the other conditions remain unchanged, which of the following could be a list of the features selected?

(A) airbags, heated seats, fog lights
(B) airbags, CD player, heated seats, navigation system, roof rack
(C) airbags, navigation system, performance tires, roof rack, sunroof
(D) airbags, fog lights, navigation system, performance tires, roof rack, sunroof
(E) airbags, CD player, heated seats, fog lights, navigation system, performance tires

GO ON TO THE NEXT PAGE.

Questions 13–18

A company must appoint an advisory board. The company must select the members of the board from three groups: workers—A, B, C and D; managers—F, G, and H; and shareholders—R and S. Exactly six members must be appointed to the board, unless three managers are appointed, then exactly seven members must be appointed to the board. The appointments to the board must follow these rules:

If D is appointed to the board, G must be appointed to the board.

If B is appointed to the board, C cannot be appointed to the board.

If R or G is appointed to the board, the other must be appointed to the board.

There must be at least as many workers appointed to the board as shareholders appointed to the board.

13. Which one of the following could be a complete and accurate list of the members that are appointed to the board?

(A) A, B, D, F, G, S
(B) A, C, D, F, R, S
(C) A, B, C, F, H, S
(D) C, F, G, H, R, S
(E) B, D, G, H, R, S

14. Which one of the following must be true?

(A) R must always be appointed to the board.
(B) S must always be appointed to the board.
(C) D must always be appointed to the board.
(D) From at least one of the groups, exactly one member is appointed.
(E) From at least two of the groups, exactly two members are appointed.

15. If exactly two managers are appointed, then which one of the following must be appointed to the board?

(A) A
(B) B
(C) D
(D) G
(E) H

16. Each of the following could be true EXCEPT:

(A) Exactly one shareholder is appointed.
(B) Exactly one manager is appointed.
(C) A is not appointed.
(D) F is the only manager appointed.
(E) R is the only shareholder appointed.

17. If the three managers are appointed, all of the following could be true EXCEPT:

(A) Exactly one shareholder is appointed.
(B) Exactly two shareholders are appointed.
(C) Exactly three workers are appointed.
(D) Exactly two workers are appointed.
(E) Exactly one worker is appointed.

18. If neither B nor C is appointed, each of the following must be appointed to the board EXCEPT:

(A) A
(B) D
(C) G
(D) F
(E) S

GO ON TO THE NEXT PAGE.

Questions 19–23

On a residential street, there are exactly four houses on each side of the street. Each house is constructed from exactly one type of building material—brick, wood, or adobe. Each house has exactly one building style—split-level, ranch, or Tudor. On the north side of the street, from west to east, are houses 1, 2, 3, and 4. On the south side of the street, from west to east, are houses 5, 6, 7, and 8. The houses on the north side of the street face the houses on the south side of the street, such that house 1 faces house 5, house 2 faces house 6, house 3 faces house 7, and house 4 faces house 8. The following conditions also apply:

On each side of the street, there must be at least one house of each style and material.
A house cannot be of the same style or material as a house that is next to it or directly across the street from it.
There is exactly one brick house on each side of the street.
House 3 is a ranch.
House 8 is a Tudor.
House 5 is made of brick.

19. Which one of the following could be an accurate list of the house styles and building materials for houses 5, 6, 7, and 8, in that order?

(A) Tudor, brick: ranch, adobe: split-level, adobe: Tudor, wood.
(B) ranch, brick: Tudor, adobe: split-level, brick: Tudor, wood.
(C) ranch, brick: Tudor, wood: split-level, adobe: Tudor, wood.
(D) ranch, brick: split-level, wood: ranch, adobe: Tudor, wood.
(E) split-level, brick: Tudor, wood: split-level, adobe: Tudor, wood.

20. If house 6 is made of adobe, each of the following could be true EXCEPT:

(A) House 4 is a wood split-level.
(B) House 5 is a brick Tudor.
(C) House 6 is an adobe split-level.
(D) House 7 is a wood split-level.
(E) House 8 is an adobe Tudor.

21. Which one of the following must be true?

(A) House 1 is made of wood.
(B) House 2 is a split-level.
(C) House 4 is a split-level.
(D) House 4 is made of brick.
(E) House 5 is a ranch.

22. If there are exactly three ranch houses, then which one of the following must be true?

(A) House 2 is a Tudor.
(B) House 5 is a split-level.
(C) House 5 is a Tudor.
(D) House 6 is a split-level.
(E) House 1 is a Tudor.

23. If house 2 is made of wood, for how many of the eight houses can the exact building material be determined?

(A) four
(B) five
(C) six
(D) seven
(E) eight

S T O P

IF YOU FINISH BEFORE TIME IS CALLED, YOU MAY CHECK YOUR WORK ON THIS SECTION ONLY. DO NOT WORK ON ANY OTHER SECTION IN THE TEST.

Answer key and explanations for Test 5

Answer Key

1. B
2. C
3. E
4. B
5. C
6. A
7. A
8. C
9. C
10. C
11. B
12. D
13. E
14. A
15. D
16. D
17. E
18. D
19. C
20. C
21. C
22. A
23. C

Commercial play list

This simple line game makes extensive use of greater-than/less-than rules. The only slightly complex rule is that two members must separate H and J. Despite this, the diagram is easy. The questions add a bit of complexity to make up for the simplicity of the diagram. With greater-than rules, always combine the rules to make a larger block of members. In this set, we can combine G, I, and K to make one such block. Drop a line below I and graph L < I. Since the H/J rule does not tie-in directly with the rest of the members, just place it above them so that it is easy to see. Finally, note that F is the free agent that can be anywhere. On the diagram, you can depict where I, G, K, and L cannot be. (Figure 1) It would not be worth your time to do any permutations, so go to the questions.

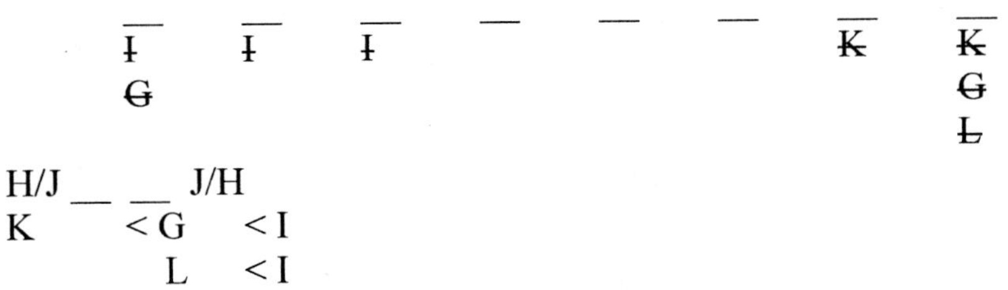

__	__	__	__	__	__	__	__
~~I~~	~~I~~	~~I~~				~~K~~	~~K~~
~~G~~							~~G~~
							~~L~~

H/J __ __ J/H

K < G < I

L < I

Fig. 1

1. (B) – In simple line games it is easy to use rule violation to eliminate the incorrect answer choices.
(A) L must be before I, as shown on the diagram. This violates Rule 4.
(B) * This is a possible play list.
(C) This choice has G later than I, which contradicts Rule 2.
(D) H and J are supposed to be separated by two other commercials, Rule 1.
(E) G is supposed to be later than K, Rule 3.

2. (C) – If F is played before L, then F must also be played before I. The earliest I can be played is fifth. You still do not know exactly where F is. Since this is a "could be true EXCEPT" question, try to make each of the five choices work.
(A) It is possible to make G fifth: J, F, K, H, G, L, I.
(B) It is possible to make L second: F, L, J, K, G, H, I.
(C) * There is no way to make K sixth, since G and I must be later than K.
(D) It is possible to make F third: J, K, F, H, G, L, I.
(E) I can be played sixth: K, G, F, H, L, I, J.

3. (E) – With two slots now occupied by this new KL block, you need to consider the effect this will have on the H and J block. (Figure 2) Because of overlap conflicts, no longer can H or J be first, sixth, or seventh. They must be second and fifth. G and I must be later than K and L, so they will fill spaces six and seven. F fills the remaining space.

(A) G must be sixth.
(B) J can be fifth or second.
(C) H can be second or fifth. Remember, J and H share the same analysis.
(D) F must be first.
(E) * Yes. J cannot be first.

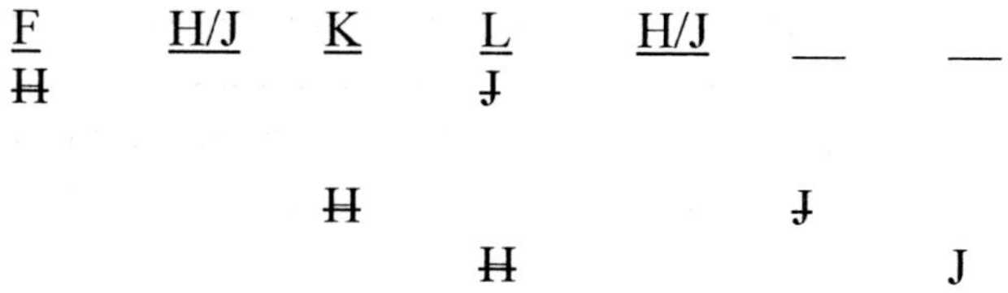

1	2	3	4	5	6	7
F	H/J	K	L	H/J	__	__
~~H~~			~~J~~			
		~~H~~			~~J~~	
			~~H~~			J

Fig. 2

4. (B) – When F is seventh, the other members still have a lot of flexibility. As such, instead of trying to solve all the permutations, go to the answer choices and try to disprove each of them.
(A) Try putting L first. There are several permutations that allow L to be first. For example: LJKGHIF.
(B) * Yes. Try putting K fourth. After trying to do this a few different ways, you realize it cannot be done because there are only two spaces between K and F. That adequately accommodates G and I, but then there is nowhere for the second half of the J and H block.
(C) Can J be first? Yes: JKLHGIF.
(D) Can H be sixth? Yes: KLJGIHF.
(E) Can G be fifth? Yes: JKLHGIF.

5. (C) – A new member is added. Does this mean that there are now seven or eight slots to fill? The way the rules are written, it means there are now eight slots, because there are eight commercials played only once and one at a time. If you were uncertain, the way the question is written makes it clear that there are eight spaces. Now that you have determined there eight slots, what next? The H and J block has been useful before, so start with that. With T on the fifth space, H and J cannot be in space 2 or space 8. Since this is an EXCEPT question, this would be a good time to check the answer choices. As it turns out, this is the only analysis you need to do.
(A) F can be first or eighth; F is a free agent, so F can be anywhere.
(B) This choice has TIH as a block. This is a workable permutation: LKGJTIHF.
(C) * Correct, H cannot be second.
(D) J can be before K and later than L: LFJKTHGI.
(E) G can be seventh. Remember, there are eight spaces now, so G can be seventh and I can be eighth.

Car features

This game requires a mono-group selection diagram. The clue that it requires this kind of diagram is that the rules are a series of if-then statements. For Rule 1, if S is offered, then H is not. Rule 2 requires a little more creativity. If both N and C are offered, then R is not. We can show this relationship by drawing lines from C and N that meet and then go to R. Rule 3 is easy to diagram using an arrow from C to A in the "offered" column. Rule 4 is the rule that many test-takers fail to use properly. Rule 4 says that when P is not used, R must be used. So P is important when it is *not* listed in an answer choice. A minimum of two features must be offered. The maximum number of features offered is five. If you prefer, you could use a single line diagram instead of the two-column format. (Figure 2)

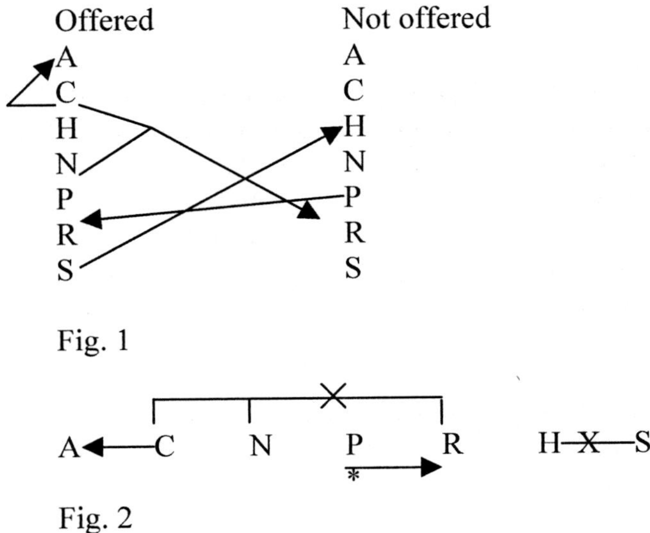

Fig. 1

Fig. 2

6. (A) – Use each of the rules to eliminate the answer choices that violate them. The remaining answer choice is the correct answer.
(A) * This is a possible order. A does not require C, we are not required to use S or H, and since there is no P, we must have an R.
(B) This violates Rule 1, because S and H are mutually exclusive.
(C) This violates Rule 2, because N and C cannot be grouped with R.
(D) This violates Rule 3, because C requires A.
(E) This violates Rule 4, because at the least, P or R must be selected.

7. (A) – Because R is not selected, P must now be selected. This eliminates a few choices. Since R is not selected, Rule 2 is irrelevant. See what the answer choices contain.
(A) * This is a possible selection of features.
(B) This choice does not contain the requisite P.
(C) This choice is incorrect because it contains both H and S.
(D) There must be a P, since there is no R.

(E) Whenever C is present, A must be present.

8. (C) – In this question, P is selected. Thus, R may or may not also be selected. Counting the rest of them, we see A, C, N, S/H, R. The only remaining conflict is that C, N and R cannot be together. So, we can have A, C, N, S/H. This yields four features in addition to P.
(A) See the analysis.
(B) See the analysis.
(C) * Correct. In addition to P, four features (A, C, H, and N) can be selected.
(D) See the analysis.
(E) See the analysis.

9. (C) – When C is selected, A must also be selected. That is the easy part. Must any other feature also be selected? Yes, either P or R must be selected.
(A) When C is selected, A must be selected.
(B) When C and A are selected, P or R must also be selected.
(C) * Correct, at least three features must be selected when C is selected.
(D) See the analysis.
(E) See the analysis.

10. (C) – With this question you are looking for basic conflicts, or lack thereof, in the answer choices. Remember, there must always be at least P or R.
(A) A and P are fine, since A does not require C and the presence of P satisfies Rule 4.
(B) C, A, and P are fine, just as in choice (A).
(C) * A, C, and N do not have any internal conflicts. However, as you determined in the initial analysis, there must be a P or R in every answer choice. Since this answer choice has both C and N, there cannot be an R; but it must have a P. P's absence makes this answer choice incorrect.
(D) S and P is also an acceptable selection. There is no requirement that A or C be selected.
(E) This contains no conflicts and satisfies Rule 4.

11. (B) – This time you must work at it from the opposite end, trying to fill a predetermined number of slots—five in this case. There are seven members to choose from. Can you select all the members except H and S? No, because of Rule 2. Can you use both H and S? No, because of Rule 1. Therefore, you know that S and H are mutually exclusive. So that leaves the other five to consider for the remaining four spaces. Remember, P and R can both be selected at the same time. The only remaining conflict is that the presence of C and N prohibits R. Here is the scorecard: S and H are 50/50 possibilities,

neither of them must be selected, but one of them must. A must be selected. (Figure 3)
(A) See the analysis. S may be used, but is not *required.*
(B) * Correct. See the analysis.
(C) See the analysis. H has the same analysis as S. Also, C is not required.
(D) P must be used, but S is not required.
(E) See the analysis. R cannot be used with C in this situation

	A	C/N	P	R	S/H
or					
	A	C	N	P	S/H

Fig. 3

12. (D) – It is not difficult to incorporate this new rule into the diagram. The important thing is that F cannot be selected if both C and A are selected. So you can have AF or F without A or C. You cannot have ACF. You cannot have CF, because Rule 3 requires A whenever C is present. So eliminate any choices with CF or ACF.
(A) This does not work because it lacks P or R.
(B) This does not work because Rule 2 prohibits CNR.
(C) In this choice, there is an A, but not an F.
(D) * This is a possible selection. There are no conflicts.
(E) This is unworkable because it has ACF.

Board appointments

Use a multi-group selection diagram. Rules 1–3 are easy to understand and easy to graph. (Figure 1) Rule 4 is slightly more complex. There must be at least as many workers as shareholders, so the number of workers is equal to or greater than the number of shareholders. Note that the D to G arrow is a one-way arrow. The rest are two-way arrows. The quirk of this puzzle came in the set-up. A typical selection grouping set-up would simply declare that there were six spaces to be filled. This set-up said that there are six spaces, except when all three managers are selected. In that case, there are seven spaces to fill. It is difficult to diagram this twist (figure 1), so you might prefer to keep it in the back of your mind. This rule is certain to feature in at least one question. Try a few permutations to see if there are any additional conclusions to be made. What if there is one shareholder? Then there would have to be three workers and two or three managers. What if there are two shareholders? Then there would have to be two workers and three managers, or three workers and one manager. So there must be at least two workers and at least one manager. After doing a few permutations, it becomes apparent that G must always be appointed. This means that R must also be appointed. Even if you did not make this initial conclusion right away, the questions would have quickly alerted you to this fact.

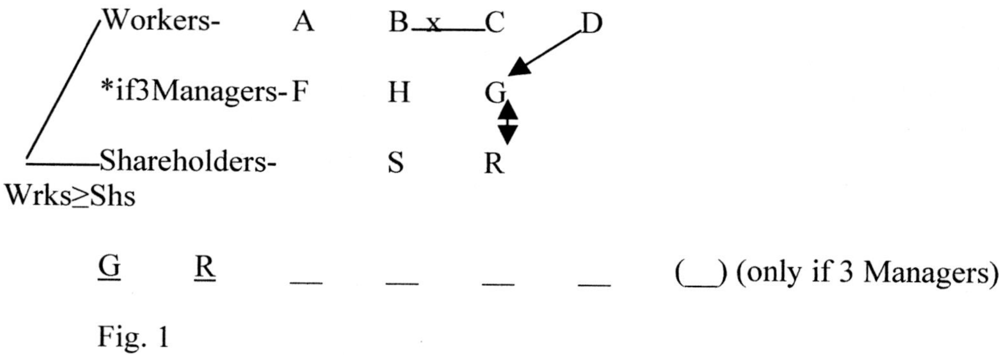

Fig. 1

13. (E) – Start with the first rule and work your way down.
    (A) When G is appointed, so is R, see Rule 3.
    (B) This runs afoul of Rule 1; the appointment of D requires the appointment of G.
    (C) This violates Rule 2 because it contains both B and C.
    (D) This violates the initial set-up. When all three managers are appointed, we need a seventh member, either A or S. This also violates Rule 4 because it has only one worker.
    (E) * This is a permissible permutation.

14. (A) – If you did not do the initial analysis, now you will try to disprove each of these answer choices.

(A) * Correct. Try as you might, there is no way to get a permissible permutation that does not include R. If you did not discover this during the initial analysis, you should add this insight to the initial diagram now.
(B) It is possible to create one permutation that omits S: A, B/C, D | G, H | R.
(C) D is not required: A, B | G, H | R, S.
(D) It is possible to use exactly two people from each group: A, B | G, H | R, S.
(E) It is possible to use three, three, and one: A, B, D | F, G, H | R.

15. (D) – If the two managers selected were H and F, then there could not be R, just S. This would leave three spaces to fill, but the workers could not fill these three spaces because B and C are mutually exclusive, and D requires that you also use G, and thus R. Therefore, the two managers must be G and either H or F. Since G is used, R is used. It is not required that you use D, since the one-way arrow goes from D to G. Apart from G, F/H, and R, you can't be sure. If S is used, then you only need two workers, so you don't need D. If you don't use S, then you must use three workers: A, B/C, and D. (Figure 2)
(A) A could be selected, but it is not required.
(B) B could be selected, but C is just as likely.
(C) As discussed, D is not required.
(D) * G must be used, as was determined.
(E) H and F share the same analysis, and neither is required.

Fig. 2

16. (D) – This is another question with no new information. You can see why the initial analysis is so important.
(A) As you learned in earlier questions, it is possible to select just one shareholder.
(B) It is possible to have one manager: A, B, D | G | R, S.
(C) It is not necessary to use A: B, D | G, H | R, S.
(D) * Can F be the sole manager? No. If F is the only manager chosen and both shareholders are chosen, then three workers must be chosen, and when three workers are chosen, D must be one of them. This then requires selecting G, a manager.
(E) As discussed in question 14, it is possible for R to be the only shareholder.

17. (E) – When all three managers are selected, four more people must be selected. This can be accomplished by selecting two workers and two

shareholders, or three workers and one shareholder. R must be selected in either case. D is not required to be selected if there are only two workers selected.

(A) See the analysis, it is possible to select just one shareholder, R.
(B) See the analysis.
(C) See the analysis.
(D) See the analysis.
(E) * It is impossible to select one worker and still have the required seven people.

18. (D) – If neither B nor C is selected, then both A and D must be selected, because of Rule 4 and the requirement that there be at least six members. Because D is selected, G must be selected. Now things get interesting. Either F or H can be selected (and there will be six members), or both F and H can be selected (and there will be seven members). But neither F nor H is required. Finally, both R and S are selected, regardless of whether there are six or seven members.

(A) Yes, A must be selected.
(B) Yes, D must be selected.
(C) Yes, G must be selected.
(D) * No. Either F or H must be selected, but neither is required.
(E) Yes, S must be selected.

House line-up

This game requires a multiple-line diagram. The lengthy set-up paragraph tries to eliminate any ambiguity, even though the set-up is pretty easy to understand. There are two parallel rows of four dashes. On each dash, you must leave space for two things: the style of the house and the building material. (Figure 1) Rules 4–6 are easy to diagram and result in several warranted conclusions. Rule 3 can be noted off to the side of the lines. Also, since Rule 6 places the lone brick house on the south side in space 5, you can make the warranted conclusion that houses 6, 7, and 8 are not brick. The ~~B~~ symbol makes this clear. Rule 1 does not lend itself to a symbol; so just keep in mind that every style and material must be used at least once on each side of the street. Now, it is time to apply Rule 2, the "no neighbors" rule and draw some warranted conclusions. House 3 is a ranch, so houses 2, 4, and 7 cannot be ranches. Use an ~~R~~ to denote this. So far, things are going well. Next, house 8 is a Tudor. Place a ~~T~~ symbol in 4 and 7. Now, draw a warranted conclusion. Since houses 4 and 7 cannot be ranch or Tudor, they must be split-levels. Since house 7 is a split-level, house 6 cannot be a split-level. Do this same analysis every time you get new information about a house. Interestingly, there is never any link between house styles and type of materials. For example, there is no rule that says, "Tudor houses cannot be made of adobe." Why is this worth noting? Since there is no link, the house styles and material types exist totally independently of each other, so in effect we are dealing with two independent multiple lines: one for house styles, the other for house materials. So when the time comes to solve a question that focuses on materials, you do not need to determine the styles, and vice versa. You could even make two separate diagrams.

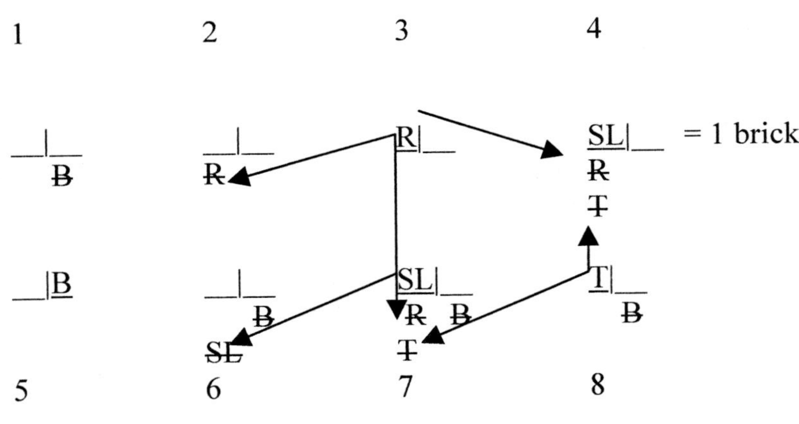

Fig. 1

19. (C) – Since there are six rules, at least two of the rules will not be used to eliminate an answer choice.

(A) Rule 2 says there cannot be two adobe houses next door to each other.

(B) There cannot be two brick houses on the same side of the street, Rule 3.

(C) * This looks like a possible set-up. If you can eliminate the remaining choices, there is no need to check this choice.

(D) This is wrong because house 7 is always a split-level. Also, house 3 is a ranch, so it is not possible to have a facing house, house 7, be a ranch, see Rule 2.

(E) This violates Rule 1, because there must be at least one ranch house on the south side of the street.

20. (C) – Using the new information that house 6 is adobe, you can fill in quite a few of the blanks. (Figure 2) Since house 6 is adobe, house 7 cannot be adobe. Since house 7 is not adobe and it cannot be brick, it must be wood. This means house 8 cannot be wood, and it also cannot be brick, so it must be adobe. Now determine the effect on the north side of the street. Going back to house 6, since house 6 is adobe, house 2 cannot be adobe. Since house 7 is wood, house 3 is not wood. Since house 8 is adobe, house 4 cannot be adobe. This should be enough work to answer the question.

(A) House 4 must be a split-level, and it could be brick or wood.

(B) House 5 must be brick, but we don't know what style it is.

(C) * House 6 must be adobe, but it cannot be a split-level, because house 7 is a split-level.

(D) House 7 must be a wood split-level.

(E) House 8 must be an adobe Tudor.

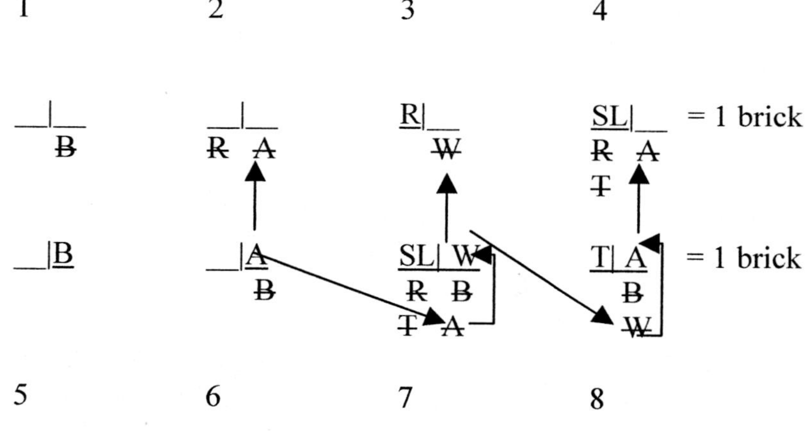

Fig. 2

21. (C) – Using the extensive initial analysis contained in figure 1, it is easy to find the must be true answer.

(A) You know nothing about house 1.

(B) You know only that house 2 is not a ranch.

(C) * Correct. House 4 must be a split-level, because house 3 is a ranch and house 8 is a Tudor.

(D) House 4 must be a split-level, but it is not necessarily brick.

(E) House 5 could be any of the three styles.

22. (A) – Now there are three ranch houses. One of them is house 3. Where might the other two be? Because of Rule 1, the only places these two other ranch houses can be are house 1 and house 6. They cannot be houses 1 and 5, because this would violate Rule 2. Knowing where all three ranches are allows you to fill in several more gaps. Since 1, 3, and 4 are two ranches and a split-level, house 2 must be a Tudor, Rule 1. Since house 6 is a ranch, house 5 cannot be a ranch, and so must be a split-level or Tudor. It is not necessary to make conclusions about the materials.
(A) * Yes, house 2 must be a Tudor.
(B) House 5 can be a Tudor or a split-level.
(C) See (B).
(D) House 6 must be a ranch.
(E) House 1 must be a ranch.

1	2	3	4	
R	**T** ~~R~~	R	SL ~~R~~ ~~T~~	= 1 brick
—	**R** ~~SL~~	SL ~~R~~ ~~T~~	T	= 1 brick
5	6	7	8	

Fig. 3

23. (C) – A simple set of dashes will be sufficient. (Figure 4) When house 2 is wood, houses 1, 3, and 6 are not wood, Rule 2. House 5 is brick, so house 1 and house 5 are not brick. Thus, house 1 and house 6 must be adobe. Because house 6 is adobe, house 7 is not adobe. Since house 7 is not adobe or brick, house 7 is wood. Since house 7 is wood, house 8 is not wood. Since house 8 is not wood and is not brick, house 8 is adobe. Since house 8 is adobe, house 4 is not adobe. So, the only houses you don't know for certain the material are houses 3 and 4. Of the eight houses, you can determine six.
(A) See the analysis.
(B) See the analysis.
(C) * Yes, See the analysis. Remember, the correct answer for a "maximum" question is typically one of the three highest numbers, while the answer for a "minimum" question is typically one of the three lowest numbers.
(D) See the analysis.

(E) See the analysis.

1	2	3	4
A ~~B~~ ~~W~~	**W**	~~W~~	~~A~~
B	A ~~B~~ ~~W~~	W ~~B~~ ~~A~~	A ~~B~~ ~~W~~
5	6	7	8

Fig. 4

Practice Test 6

Spend 35 minutes doing this practice test. When time is up, review the explanations to help you understand the questions that you did not answer correctly.

SECTION I

Time—35 minutes

23 Questions

Directions: Each group of questions in this section is based on a set of conditions. In answering some of the questions, it may be useful to draw a rough diagram. Choose the response that most accurately and completely answers each question and blacken the corresponding space on your answer sheet.

Questions 1–5

A television series must be scheduled once a week for a nine-week period. Each of the eight episodes—A, B, C, D, E, F, G, and H—must be scheduled at least once, and each episode appears on the same day of the week. The following conditions govern the scheduling of the episodes:

A is separated from B by no more than two other episodes.

At least one other episode must separate C and D, and C must precede D.

G must be scheduled for the week after D.

C is scheduled for some week after A is scheduled.

H is scheduled for the second and ninth weeks.

1. Which one of the following is an acceptable schedule of episodes, in order from the first week to the ninth week?

(A) A, H, B, C, D, G, E, F, H
(B) B, H, C, A, D, G, F, E, H
(C) B, H, C, E, D, G, A, F, H
(D) A, H, C, B, E, D, G, F, H
(E) B, H, A, C, F, D, E, G, H

2. The greatest number of episodes that can separate episodes G and B is

(A) three
(B) four
(C) five
(D) six
(E) seven

3. If episode B is shown in the first week and episode C is shown in the fifth week, how many possible schedules could there be for the nine episodes?

(A) two
(B) three
(C) four
(D) five
(E) six

4. If episode F is shown in the seventh week, then which one of the following must be true?

(A) Episode A is shown in the third week.
(B) Episode B is shown in the first week.
(C) Episode C is shown in the third week.
(D) Episode E is shown in the fourth week.
(E) Episode G is shown in the fifth week.

5. If episode G is shown in the eighth week, then which one of the following could be true?

(A) Episode E is shown in the third week, and episode F is shown in the fourth week.
(B) Episode E is shown in the fourth week, and episod B is shown in the fifth week.
(C) Episode C is shown in the third week, and episode E is shown in the fifth week.
(D) Episode B is shown in the first week, and episode D is shown in the sixth week.
(E) Episode F is shown in the fifth week, and episode D is shown in the sixth week.

GO ON TO THE NEXT PAGE

Questions 6–12

Four students—Williams, Xi, Ybarra, and Zoë—cooperate by each typing the lecture notes for the two classes they all share—Anthropology and Biology. Each student types the notes for exactly two classes a week. Each class meets once per day on Monday, Tuesday, Wednesday, and Thursday. The typing of the notes conforms to the following conditions:

A student may type notes for only one class a day.
Xi and Ybarra do not type notes for classes that meet the same day.
Zoë does not type notes for Anthropology classes.
Williams does not type notes for classes that meet on Thursday.

6. Which one of the following could be the list of students who type the class notes, in order from Monday to Thursday?

(A) Anthropology: Williams; Biology: Xi
Anthropology: Williams; Biology: Ybarra
Anthropology: Ybarra; Biology: Zoë
Anthropology: Xi; Biology: Zoë
(B) Anthropology: Xi; Biology: Williams
Anthropology: Ybarra; Biology: Zoë
Anthropology: Williams; Biology: Zoë
Anthropology: Xi; Biology: Ybarra
(C) Anthropology: Xi; Biology: Williams
Anthropology: Ybarra; Biology: Zoë
Anthropology: Xi; Biology: Zoë
Anthropology: Williams; Biology: Ybarra
(D) Anthropology: Xi; Biology: Williams
Anthropology: Zoë; Biology: Ybarra
Anthropology: Williams; Biology: Xi
Anthropology: Zoë; Biology: Ybarra
(E) Anthropology: Xi; Biology: Ybarra Zoe
Anthropology: Williams; Biology: Zoë Ybarra
Anthropology: Ybarra; Biology: Williams
Anthropology: Xi; Biology: Zoë

7. If Williams types notes for a class on Tuesday and a class on Wednesday, then which one of the following must be true?

(A) Ybarra types the notes for Anthropology on Monday.
(B) Zoë types the notes from Biology on Monday.
(C) Williams types the notes from Biology on Wednesday. ✓
(D) Xi types the notes from Anthropology on Thursday.
(E) W types the notes from Anthropology on Wednesday.

8. Which one of the following must be true?

(A) Xi types notes from a class on Wednesday.
(B) Zoë types notes from a class on Tuesday.
(C) Ybarra types notes from a class on Monday.
(D) Williams types notes from a class on Wednesday.
(E) Zoë types notes from a class on Thursday.

9. Each of the following is possible EXCEPT:

(A) Williams types notes from Anthropology on Tuesday and on Wednesday.
(B) Zoë types notes from Biology on Monday and Wednesday.
(C) Xi types notes from Biology on Monday and Wednesday.
(D) Ybarra types notes from Biology on Monday and Anthropology on Tuesday.
(E) Williams types notes from Anthropology on Tuesday and Biology on Wednesday.

10. Which one of the following cannot be true?

(A) Williams types notes from Biology on Tuesday and Anthropology on Wednesday.
(B) Ybarra attends Anthropology on Tuesday and Biology on Wednesday.
(C) Ybarra types notes from Biology on Wednesday and Biology on Thursday.
(D) Zoë types notes from Biology on two consecutive days.
(E) Xi types notes for Anthropology on two consecutive days.

11. If Williams and Ybarra type notes from the classes on Monday, each of the following could be true, EXCEPT:

(A) If Xi types notes from a Wednesday class, Ybarra types notes from a Thursday class.
(B) If Williams types notes from a Tuesday class, Zoë types notes from a Tuesday class.
(C) If Zoë types notes from a Tuesday class, Xi types notes from a Tuesday class.
(D) If Williams types notes from a Tuesday class, Zoë types note from a Wednesday class.
(E) If Ybarra types notes from a Thursday class, Xi types note from a Wednesday class.

GO ON TO THE NEXT PAGE.

Questions 12-18

A wildlife photographer is arranging photographs of her work for display on a wall. There are six photographs to be mounted in a straight line from left to right. There is one photograph each of an alligator, a bat, a donkey, an eagle, a falcon, and a lion. Each of the photographs is either a sepia print or a black and white print. The photographer arranges the photographs consistent with the following conditions:

A sepia print cannot have sepia prints on both sides of it.
There are at least four sepia prints.
The falcon photograph is either second or fifth.
The alligator photograph is either second or fifth.
The lion photograph is not next to the alligator photograph.
The donkey photograph is a black and white print.
If the third photograph is sepia, the fourth is black and white, and if the third photograph is black and white, the fourth is sepia.

12. Which one of the following would be a possible arrangement of photographs, from first to last?

(A) Sepia eagle, black and white lion, sepia alligator, black and white donkey, sepia falcon, sepia bat
(B) Black and white bat, sepia falcon, sepia lion, black and white donkey, sepia alligator, sepia eagle
(C) Sepia bat, sepia alligator, sepia eagle, black and white donkey, black and white falcon, sepia lion
(D) Sepia lion, black and white falcon, sepia bat, black and white donkey, sepia alligator, black and white eagle
(E) Sepia eagle, sepia falcon, black and white bat, sepia lion, sepia alligator, black and white donkey

13. If the lion is the first photograph and the donkey is the sixth photograph, then which one of the following must be true?

(A) The falcon photograph is a sepia print.
(B) The lion photograph is a black and white print.
(C) The bat photograph is a black and white print.
(D) The bat photograph is a sepia print.
(E) The eagle photograph is a sepia print.

14. Which one of the following must be false?

(A) The lion photograph is sixth.
(B) The second and fifth photographs are sepia prints.
(C) The second and fifth photographs are black and white prints.
(D) The donkey photograph is sixth.
(E) The lion photograph is a sepia print.

15. If the lion photograph is sixth and is a black and white print, then which one of the following must be true?

(A) The eagle photograph is a black and white print.
(B) The bat photograph is first.
(C) The alligator photograph is a sepia print.
(D) The falcon photograph is second.
(E) The donkey photograph is fourth.

16. Which one of the following CANNOT be true?

(A) The alligator and the lion are the same type of print.
(B) The lion and the falcon are the same type of print.
(C) The second and third photographs are black and white prints.
(D) The first and fifth photographs are sepia prints.
(E) The first and fourth photographs are different types of print.

17. If the first and second photographs are sepia prints, then which one of the following could be true?

(A) The fourth photograph is a donkey photograph and a sepia print.
(B) The sixth photograph is an eagle photograph and a sepia print.
(C) The fourth photograph is a falcon photograph and sepia print.
(D) The fifth photograph is a bat photograph and a sepia print.
(E) The third photograph is a lion photograph and a sepia print.

18. If the alligator photograph is second and is a black and white print, then which one of the following could be true?

(A) The bat photograph is a sepia print and is hung to the left of the eagle photograph, which is a sepia print.
(B) The eagle photograph is a black and white print and is hung to the left of the donkey photograph, which is a black and white print.
(C) The eagle photograph is a sepia print and is hung to the left of the lion photograph, which is a black and white print.
(D) The lion photograph is a sepia print and is fourth.
(E) The donkey photograph is a black and white print and is third.

Questions 19–23

A homeowner must paint all four walls of a bedroom using the following three paint colors—red, white, and tan. Each paint color is available in two types of finish—latex or satin. The homeowner adheres to the following restrictions when painting the room:

Each wall has exactly one color and one finish.
A wall cannot be the same color as any wall that touches it.
If there is more than one wall with a latex or a satin finish, then any wall that has that finish must touch at least one other wall with that finish.
There is no tan latex paint.
There is exactly one red wall.

19. Which one of the following could be an accurate description of the colors and types of finish for the walls starting with the north wall?

(A) North: red satin; West: white latex; South: white satin; East: tan satin.
(B) North: tan satin; West: red latex; South: tan satin; East: white satin.
(C) North: white latex; West: tan latex; South: red latex; East: tan satin.
(D) North: white satin; West: red latex; South: tan satin; East: white latex.
(E) North: red latex; West: white latex; South: red satin; East: tan satin.

20. If exactly one wall has a satin finish, then which one of the following must be true?

(A) The north wall is painted with red latex.
(B) The south wall is painted with white latex.
(C) Exactly three walls are painted white.
(D) Exactly one wall is painted tan.
(E) Exactly two walls are painted tan.

21. If there is exactly one wall with a latex finish and exactly one tan wall, then which one of the following must be true?

(A) There is exactly one red latex wall.
(B) There is at least one red satin wall.
(C) There is exactly one white satin wall.
(D) There are exactly two white satin walls.
(E) There is at least one white satin wall.

22. If there are two walls with a satin finish, then which one of the following must be true?

(A) Any red wall has a satin finish.
(B) Any white wall has a satin finish.
(C) There are two tan walls.
(D) There are two white walls.
(E) A red wall touches a tan wall.

23. Suppose that the restriction that there is exactly one red wall is suspended. If all other conditions remain unchanged, all of the following could be true EXCEPT:

(A) The walls are painted red and white, and there are two satin finishes and two latex finishes.
(B) The walls are painted red and white, and there are two satin finishes and two latex finishes.
(C) The walls are painted red and tan, and there are three satin finishes and one latex finish.
(D) The walls are painted tan and white, and there are three satin finishes and one latex finish.
(E) The walls are painted tan and white, and there are two satin finishes and two latex finishes.

S T O P

IF YOU FINISH BEFORE TIME IS CALLED, YOU MAY CHECK YOUR WORK ON THIS SECTION ONLY.
DO NOT WORK ON ANY OTHER SECTION IN THE TEST.

Answer key and explanations for Test 6

Answer Key

1. D
2. D
3. C
4. C
5. C
6. A
7. B
8. E
9. B
10. C
11. B
12. B
13. A
14. C
15. C
16. C
17. B
18. A
19. B
20. D
21. E
22. D
23. E

Television line-up

This game uses a typical simple-line diagram with a few unusual features. There are nine spaces instead of the typical six or seven spaces. There are only eight members; normally there is the same number of members as there are spaces to fill. In this game, one member will be used twice, which is also unusual for a simple line. The biggest problems are created by Rules 1 and 2; more on that in a moment. All that aside, the puzzle is not too difficult. When diagramming, always start with the easiest rules, the anchors. Here, H is second and ninth. This simplifies the diagram immensely, since you now know that the other members are all used exactly once. Members C, A, and D all have limiting relationships. Combine these rules into a block you can apply to the diagram. Rules 1 and 2 are a little quirky. Rule 1 says that A and B have no more than two spaces between them. Note that A could be before or after B; this is very tricky. The next one is really tricky. Rule 2 says C is followed by one or more episodes before D. What exactly does this mean? It means that if, for example D is on week six, C must be on week four or earlier. This is different from Rule 1, where A and B are separated by (up to) two weeks, that is, zero, one, or two spaces could separate A and B. These unique rules require some creative diagramming to capture the variability of the placements. If you are still confused, review Rules 1 and 2 until you understand how they are different. You can always turn to the answer choices for guidance as well. Rule 3 is easy; G is immediately after D. Rule 4 is easy; C is after A. This combination of rules is listed below. (Figure 1) We can make some warranted conclusions at this point. G can never be earlier than sixth. Also, D can never be first, second, third, or eighth. A can never be later than C. Since there is at least one space after C but before the DG block, A can never be later than fourth.

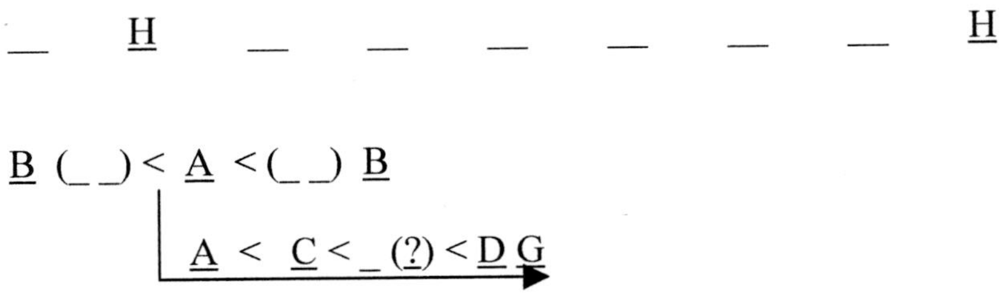

__ H __ __ __ __ __ __ H

B (_ _) < A < (_ _) B

A < C < _ (?) < D G

Fig. 1

1. (D) – Usually the first question in the set should be answered by using each rule to eliminate one answer choice. Start with the first rule and check if it is violated in any of the answer choices. Then do the same for each of the other rules.
   (A) This violates Rule 2, because at least one other episode must be between C and D.
   (B) This violates Rule 4 because it shows A later than C.
   (C) This violates Rule 1 and Rule 4.
   (D) * This is a valid permutation.
   (E) This violates Rule 3 because it separates D and G.

2. (D) – Remember, with largest number, or maximum number, questions, always start with the largest number and work down.
(A) Always start with the largest number and work down until you find the correct answer.
(B) Always start with the largest number and work down until you find the correct answer.
(C) Always start with the largest number and work down until you find the correct answer.
(D) * This is possible: B H A C E F D G H.
(E) This is impossible because there are not seven spaces between space one and space eight; there are only six spaces. Remember, H occupies space nine, so that space is not available for G or B.

3. (C) – This question requires you to invest some time to find all the possible permutations. When B is first, A can be third or fourth. When C is fifth, the only way to accommodate D and G is to put them seventh and eighth. Solving for A on space three, we find two permutations. (Figure 2) Solving for A on four, we find two more permutations, again involving E and F, the free agents. Thus, there are four permutations.
(A) See the analysis.
(B) See the analysis.
(C) * See the analysis.
(D) See the analysis.
(E) See the analysis.

B H A E/F C F/E D G H

B H E/F A C F/E D G H

Fig. 2

4. (C) – With F on seven, you know a little bit, but not much. What can be eighth? Not A, B, or C, due to space constraints. Nor can D or G, because of the effect of Rule 3. Thus, only E, the other free agent, can be on space eight. Now things are becoming clearer. You must accommodate the block of C, D, and G. You can put G sixth, D fifth, B fourth, C third, and A first. Can it be done any other way? No. Because of the interplay of all the rules, this is the only permutation that works.
(A) See the analysis. If A were third, then there would not be room to accommodate all the other members.
(B) See the analysis.
(C) * This must be true.

(D) E must be eighth.
(E) G must be sixth.

5. (C) – This question follows a similar line of inquiry as the previous question. Putting G eighth requires D to be seventh. C cannot be sixth. C can be fifth, fourth, or third. (Figure 3) From there you can find several permutations.
(A) E can be third, but not when F is fourth.
(B) E can be fourth, but not when B is fifth.
(C) * C can be third when F is fifth.
(D) B can be first, but D must always be seventh because G is eighth.
(E) F can be fifth, but D must always be seventh.

__	H	__	__	__	__	D	G	H
A/B	H	E/F	B/A	C	F/E			
A/B	H	B/A	E/F	C	F/E			
E/F	H	F/E	A	C	B			
A	**H**	**C**	**B**	**E/F**	**F/E**			

Fig. 3

Class order

This game requires a common multiple-line diagram. It is not a simple line because each day (with two classes each) has a special relationship that governs what can be within that day. Once you get your bearings, it is not difficult to create the diagram. Either of the two diagrams shown below will work. (Figure 1) The rule regarding Z is easy to depict, as is the rule regarding W. It should be easy to remember to not put X and Y on the same day. The best way to make warranted conclusions is to check the spaces with the most activity underneath them. For Thursday Anthropology, neither Z nor W is allowed. Thus, either X or Y must do that class. Since the other one now cannot be on Thursday, the only member available for Thursday Biology is Z.

Mon			Tue			Wed			Thur	
__	__	||	__	__	||	__	__	||	X/Y	Z
Ant	Bio		Ant	Bio		Ant	Bio		Ant	Bio
~~Z~~			~~Z~~			~~Z~~			~~Z~~	
									~~W~~	~~W~~

~~XY~~

Or

	Mon	Tue	Wed	Thur
Anth ~~Z~~				
Bio				
X≠Y				~~W~~

Fig. 1

6. (A) – Use each rule to eliminate an answer choice. The remaining answer choice is the correct answer.
(A) * This is a valid permutation.
(B) This violates Rule 2 because it has X and Y on the same day.
(C) This violates Rule 4 because it has W on Thursday.
(D) This violates Rule 3 because Z is in Anthropology.
(E) This violates Rule 2 because X and Y are on the same day.

7. (B) – Start by graphing the new information. (Figure 2) When W is on Tuesday and Wednesday, then Z must be on Monday and Thursday, because this is the only way to keep X and Y on different days. You don't know exactly which classes W, X, and Y do on Tuesday and Wednesday, but you know that Z does Biology on Monday and Thursday.
(A) Y can be in Anthropology on Monday, but so can X.
(B) * Z must be in Biology on Monday.
(C) W is on Wednesday, but you don't know which class.

(D) X and Y are very flexible.
(E) See (C).

Mon			Tue		Wed		Thur
__ ? Z	||		__ __ W/X/Y	||	__ __ W/X/Y	||	X/Y Z

Fig. 2

8. (E) – This question can be answered using the initial analysis.
   (A) Since X and Y can be on any of the four days and they share the same analysis, this would be a very poor choice.
   (B) Z must be on Thursday and one other day; you don't know which one.
   (C) See (A).
   (D) W must appear twice in the first three days, but you cannot determine what days those are.
   (E) * Z must always be on Thursday, as you learned from the initial analysis, or by doing the previous two questions.

9. (B) – Which of the following answer choices are not possible? First, check the answer choices against the initial diagram, and then work through each answer choice if necessary.
   (A) W can be in either class on Tuesday and Wednesday, Z would then be in Monday and Thursday, and X and Y would be adequately separated.
   (B) * If Z were to be on Monday and Wednesday, this would require that W be on Thursday, or that X and Y are on the same day, neither of which is permitted.
   (C) X and Y are poor members to focus on, since they are pretty flexible and share the same analysis. X can be in Biology on Monday and Wednesday, Z would be in Biology on Tuesday and Thursday, and W could be anywhere except Thursday.
   (D) See (C).
   (E) Having W on Tuesday and Wednesday would still allow Z to be on Monday and Thursday.

10. (C) – Once again, there is no new information. Work with the answer choices.
   (A) This choice is similar to choice (E) in question 9, and the analysis is the same.
   (B) If Y is in Biology on Wednesday, this still permits Z to be in Biology on any two of the three other days, so this could be true.
   (C) * This one is tricky. If Y is in Biology on the last two days of the week, this would force Z to be in Biology the first two days of the week. W

would have to be on two of the first three days of the week. So, for Anthropology on the fourth day of the week, only X would be available, but X is not permitted to be with Y on the same day.

(D) This is a possibility. Z could be on Wednesday and Thursday.

(E) It poses no problem to have X in Anthropology. Your choices are limited when it comes to Biology, not Anthropology.

11. (B) – Simply plug in the new information. (Figure 3) It does not matter exactly where W and Y are. You now must use one W, two Xs, one Y, and one Z. There is very little else you can diagram. You must work with the answer choices to solve this question.

(A) It is necessary to keep X and Y on different days. This could be true.

(B) * If the second W and Z are both on Tuesday, this would cause both X and Y to be on Wednesday.

(C) It would be okay for Z and X to be on Tuesday.

(D) Actually, it is necessary that either W or Z is on Tuesday and the other is on Wednesday.

(E) If Y is on Thursday, this would require that X be on Wednesday.

Mon			Tue			Wed			Thur	
__	__	||	__	__	||	__	__	||	Y/X	Z
W & Y										

Fig. 3

Portrait line-up

This game requires a standard multiple-line diagram. The animal name and the print type (sepia or black and white) are the two variables for each of the six spaces. The language in the set-up paragraph may have seemed non-standard, for example, the six spaces were not explicitly named. The language of a game can vary; don't get too set in your ways, because the LSAT is always ready to throw a curve ball. Rules 3 through 7 are pretty easy to graph. (Figure 1) Rule 3 can be depicted by placing an F with parenthesis, and a line connecting spaces two and five. Rule 4 combines with Rule 3. You now know that spaces two and five are always the alligator or the falcon. You cannot incorporate Rule 5 into the diagram, because the location of the alligator is not fixed. So make a simple note below the diagram that the lion and the alligator are not next to each other. Rule 6 (the donkey photograph is a black and white print) must also be noted below the diagram. Finally, Rule 7 is similar to Rules 3 and 4. The effect of Rule 7 is that the prints for spaces three and four are always the opposite. If one is sepia, the other is black and white, and vice versa. Rule 1 is a little different from what you are used to seeing. Rule 1 says that there cannot be three sepia prints in a row, because then one sepia print would have a sepia print on either side. If you think this rule through, you realize that it is permissible to have two sepia prints in a row, for example, in space one and space two. Such an order would not violate Rule 1. Rule 2 feeds off Rule 1. When there four sepia prints, there are two black and white prints. Do a bit more diagramming and you will see that there is no way to have five sepia prints, since this would violate Rule 1. What is the minimum number of sepia prints? Four, due to Rule 2. Since there are always four sepia prints and two black and white prints, this limits the number of permutations for the prints. You could have solved for them right away, but it is more efficient to wait and see if the questions require it. The permutations are shown in figure 2.

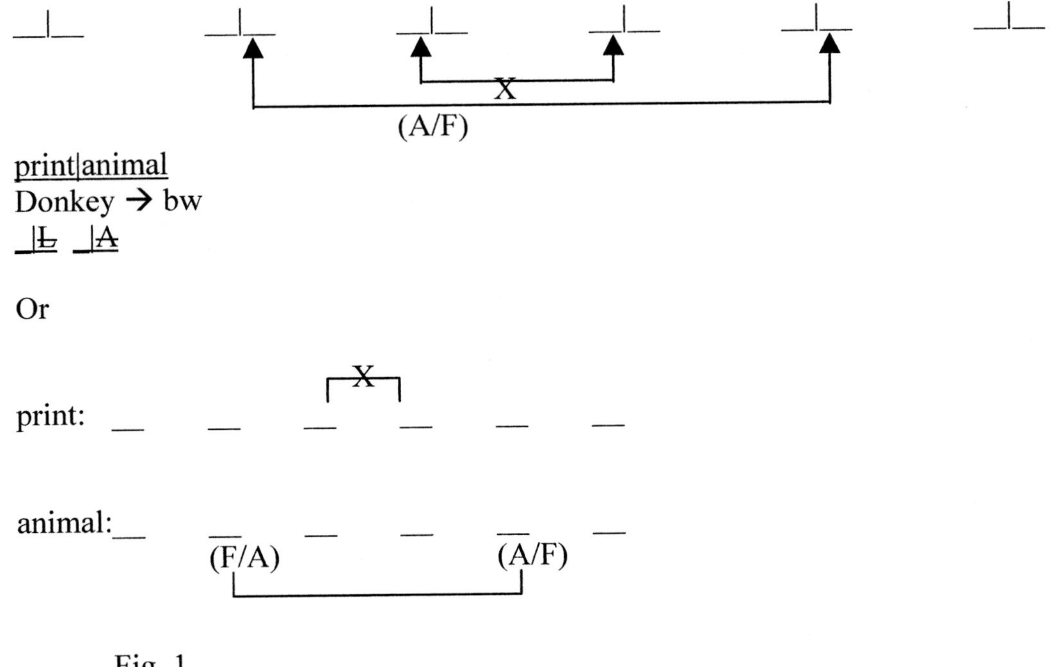

Fig. 1

S	S	B	S	B	S
S	S	B	S	S	B
S	B	S	B	S	S
B	S	S	B	S	S

Fig. 2

12. (B) – As is normal, you should use each rule to eliminate an answer choice. Since there are more than four rules in this diagram, not all of them will be used.
    (A) This is wrong, because either the alligator or the falcon must be in space two, by Rules 3 and 4. Here the lion is in space two.
    (B) * This is possible. Make a note of this order for future reference.
    (C) This violates Rule 1 by putting three sepia prints in a row.
    (D) This violates Rule 2 because it only has three sepia prints.
    (E) This violates Rule 5, because the lion and the alligator are next to each other.

13. (A) – You can start your analysis with the animals or the prints. Try starting with the animals. Since the lion is first, the alligator cannot be second because the alligator and the lion cannot be next to each other. Thus, the falcon must be second and alligator must be fifth. The eagle and the bat have no restrictions, so they will fill spaces three and four. What about the print types? Since one of the black and whites has been used (in space six, with the donkey), the second black and white must be placed in such a way that it prevents three sepias in a row. This means the black and white must be third. (Figure 2) The rest of the prints are sepia.
    (A) * Yes, the falcon photograph must be a sepia print, because the two black and white prints were used elsewhere.
    (B) The lion must be a sepia print, not black and white.
    (C) The bat can be either a sepia print or a black and white, since the bat photograph can be third or fourth.
    (D) See (C).
    (E) The eagle has the same analysis as the bat in this question.

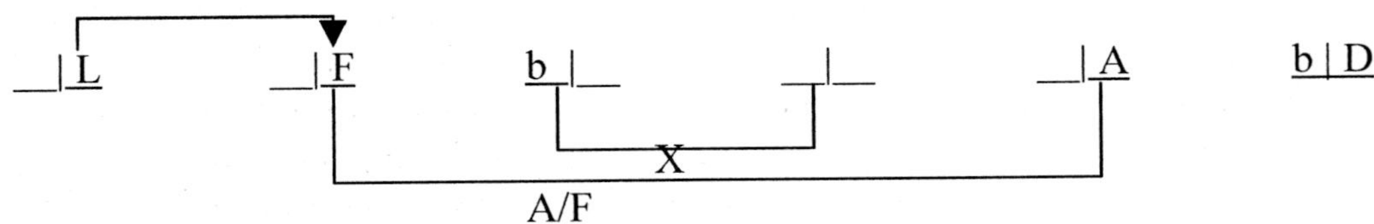

Fig. 3

14. (C) – We should be able to answer this question using the initial diagram and the correct answers from the previous two questions.

(A) There is no reason the lion photograph cannot be sixth, so long as the falcon photograph is fifth.

(B) As we saw in the previous question, it is possible that the second and fifth photographs are both sepia prints.

(C) * It is not possible for the second and fifth to both be black and white. Why? Because if they were, then the third and fourth photographs would be sepia, and they are not permitted to be the same type.

(D) As we saw in the previous question, the donkey can be sixth.

(E) The lion photograph can be a sepia print, see question 13

15. (C) – This was a tricky one. If the lion photograph is sixth and is a black and white print, then where must the other black and white photograph (the one of the donkey) be? It must be third in order to prevent three sepia prints from being in a row. Also, the falcon must be fifth, the alligator must be second, and the bat and eagle will fill the remaining two spaces.

(A) The lion and the donkey are the only black and white prints.

(B) Either the bat or the eagle is first.

(C) * The alligator must be second, and the second photograph must be a sepia print. This must be true.

(D) The falcon photograph must be fifth.

(E) The donkey photograph is third; otherwise there would be three sepia prints in a row.

16. (C) – Since there is no new information, you can answer this question using previous analysis. Check previous correct answer choices for clues. If you cannot answer this question using prior analysis, graph each answer choice. The one that is not graphable is the credited answer.

(A) You should have skipped checking this one, since it is unlikely that these two could not both be sepia prints. If you had eliminated the other answer choice, then it would be worth checking this one, but chances are this is possible. You could have also checked your work from question 13.

(B) See (A).

(C) * If you did the print permutations at the start, you would know that this cannot be true. Even if you did not do the permutations, it would be easy to figure out that putting black and white prints on second and third would leave three sepia prints in a row, which would violate Rule 1.

(D) Checking the initial permutations, or figure 3 from question 13, you can see that the first and fifth photographs can both be sepia prints.

(E) Again, checking the analysis with the initial permutations, or solving for this, would reveal that the first and fourth photos can be different types.

(Interestingly, this only works if sepia is first and the black and white is fourth. It doesn't work the other way around.)

17. (B) – If the first two photographs are sepia prints, then the third must be a black and white (because of Rule 1) and the fourth must be a sepia (because of Rule 7). It cannot be determined whether the fifth or sixth will be the second black and white photograph. That should be sufficient analysis to answer the question.
    (A) This cannot be true, because the donkey is a black and white print, but the fourth print must be sepia.
    (B) * This can be true. The eagle photograph is a free agent, and the sixth photograph can be sepia or black and white.
    (C) The fourth photograph cannot be the falcon, by Rule 3.
    (D) The fifth photograph cannot be the bat, by Rules 3 and 4.
    (E) The third photograph cannot be a sepia print.

18. (A) – Once you know the position of the alligator, then you know the position of the falcon, and roughly where the lion is as well. (Figure 4) Now things get tricky. Since the second photograph is black and white, where must the other black and white print be? Not third, because this would make for three sepias in a row on fourth, fifth, and sixth. It would be okay to have the other black and white print fourth. How about putting it fifth or sixth? No, because then both the third and fourth photographs would be sepia prints, violating Rule 7. So the other black and white print is the fourth photograph. The first, third, fifth, and sixth are all sepia prints. Now what? The donkey is a black and white print, so the donkey must be fourth, since that is where the other black and white print is. Since the donkey is fourth, the only place the lion can be is sixth. Now you know everything except where the bat and eagle are.
    (A) * The bat and the eagle are interchangeable on spaces one and three, so this could be true. The wording of this choice—"to the left of"—is a little odd, but is not difficult to understand.
    (B) It is true that the eagle is to the left of the donkey, but the eagle must be a sepia print.
    (C) It is true that the eagle is a sepia print and is left of the lion, but the lion must be a sepia print.
    (D) The lion must be sixth.
    (E) The donkey must be fourth.

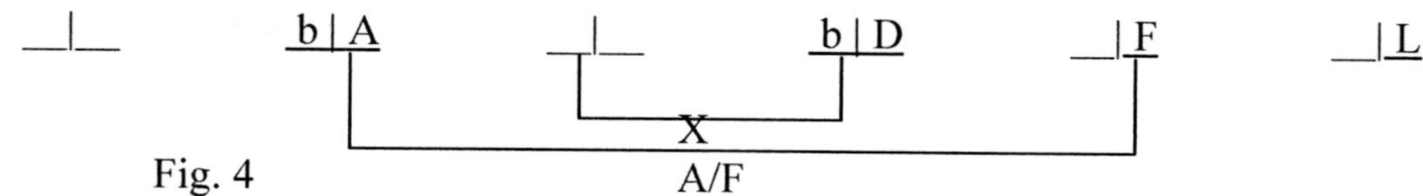

Fig. 4

Painting the room

This game harkens back to a type of puzzle that was occasionally tested in the early 1990s. It is called a table puzzle because the scenario often involves people sitting around a table and it is your job to seat them according to the rules. Although this puzzle is rarely tested, it is always possible that it will make an appearance. To ensure the best score, you must prepare for these rare puzzles as well as the common ones. How do you diagram this type of puzzle? Sometimes the LSAT will actually provide a picture or partial diagram in the set-up paragraph if it would be too confusing otherwise. In this game, no picture was provided because it is easy to visualize what a room with four walls looks like. (Figure 1) Rule 1 clarifies that a wall will not have two different colors or finishes. Rule 2 says that a wall cannot be the same color as a neighboring wall. This is the "no neighbors" rule, like in simple line games. Rule 2 allows you to make a warranted conclusion. Since there is one red wall (Rule 5), the other three walls must either be two white and one tan, or one white and two tan. (Figure 1) Anything else runs afoul of Rule 1, which prohibits neighboring walls from being the same color. Rule 3 is a bit unusual. It requires that, if there are two or more walls with the same finish, then those two, or three, walls *must* neighbor each other. For example, there cannot be two satin walls on opposite sides of the room and two latex walls on opposite sides of the room. Thinking through the permutations, you realize that all four walls can be satin. Not all four walls can be latex, because at least one wall is tan and tan walls cannot be latex. Also, there can be three satin and one latex wall, or three latex and one satin wall. Finally, there can be two latex and two satin walls, but if there are, make sure to observe Rule 3. It is fairly easy to graph the permutations for the finishes, but it is probably unnecessary. (Figure 2) Do not be misled by the locations (for example, red at the top of the diagram). A common mistake test-takers make on table games is to forget that there are no fixed positions. A diagram can be read in the clockwise or counter-clockwise direction and can start at the top, bottom, or sides, unlike a line, which has definite positions (first, second, third, etc.).

Possible paint colors: R, W, T, W or R, T, W, T

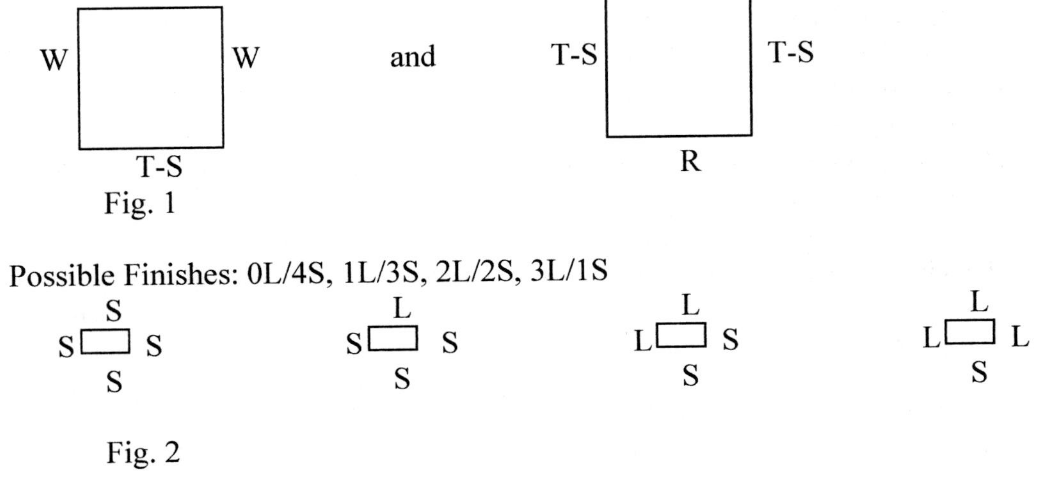

Fig. 1

Fig. 2

19. (B) – Even when the game is a bit different or unusual, you should be able to use answer elimination to eliminate the wrong answers.
(A) Per Rule 2, neighboring walls cannot be the same color.
(B) * This is a valid order.
(C) This choice contains a tan latex, which violates Rule 4.
(D) This choice splits the two latex and two satin walls so that they don't touch each other, thus violating Rule 3. It also places two white walls next to each other, violating Rule 2.
(E) This violates Rule 5, because it contains two reds.

20. (D) – If there is one satin wall and three latex walls, then which walls must be which? If the single red wall were satin, then there could be no tan walls (Rule 4 prohibits tan latex); so three walls would need to be white. But this would run afoul of Rule 2, since the three whites would neighbor each other. Could the single satin wall be white? Again, there would be the problem of three white walls. So, the satin wall must be the tan wall, which must separate the two white walls. (Figure 3)
(A) Although the red wall must be latex, it does not have to be the north wall. Remember, unless the question stem introduces a fixed position, there is no way to know exactly which walls are which color.
(B) Again, like (A), there is no reason any particular color must be on the north or south wall.
(C) This is false, as you learned during the analysis.
(D) * This is true. The only solution is to have two white walls, one tan wall, and one red wall.
(E) See (D).

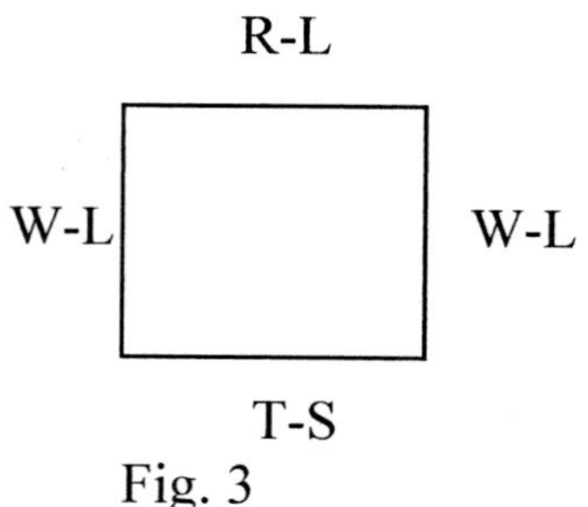

Fig. 3

21. (E) – This question approaches the same issue as the previous question, but from a slightly different angle. The single tan wall is clearly satin. There are two possible diagrams you could create. First, the latex wall could be the red wall and the two white walls would be satin. Second, the latex wall is one of the white walls, and the other white wall is satin and the red wall is satin. Since this is a must be true question, look for an answer choice that is compatible with both of the possible diagrams.
(A) There is a 50/50 chance the red wall is latex.

(B) This has the same analysis as (A), there is a 50/50 chance the red wall is satin.
(C) There could be one or two white satin walls.
(D) This has the same analysis as (C).
(E) * Correct, it must be true that there is at least one white satin wall.

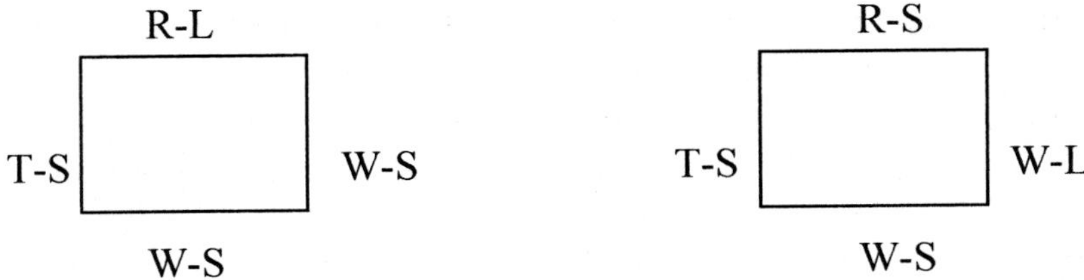

Fig. 4

22. (D) – Remember to keep the two satin walls next to each other. Can the two satin walls both be tan? No, because Rule 2 requires that the two tan walls not touch each other. Can the satin walls be a red wall and a white wall? No, because there must be one tan wall, and tan walls must be satin. Can the satin walls be a red wall and a tan wall? No, because the two remaining walls would be white and latex. The white walls are not permitted to touch, but the two latex walls must touch, so this is impossible. Finally, can the two satin walls be tan and white? Yes, this would allow for these two walls to touch each other, while allowing the white latex wall and red latex walls to touch each other without violating Rule 2. (Figure 5)
(A) See the diagram. The red wall must be latex.
(B) See the diagram. One of the two white walls must be latex.
(C) There cannot be two tan walls, as discussed in the analysis.
(D) * There must be two white walls.
(E) The tan wall must keep the two white walls separated, so the tan wall cannot touch the red wall.

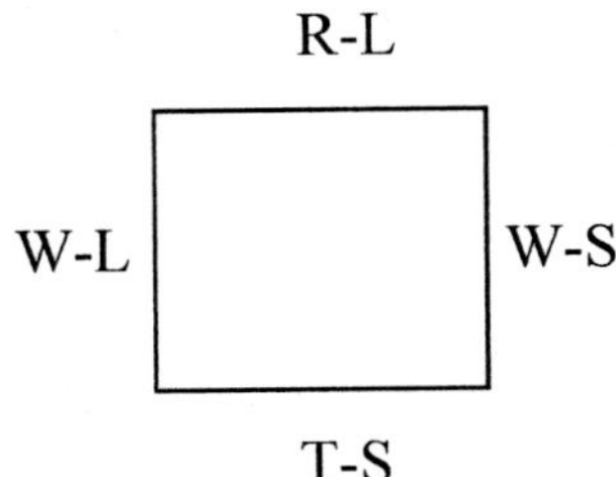

Fig. 5

23. (E) – Sometimes the final question suspends or modifies one of the conditions. This requires you to go back and rethink the warranted

conclusions, as well as your initial diagram. This set did not have much of a diagram to begin with, so it is not difficult to adjust for this change in the rules. But when the diagram is intricate and the analysis contains many intermediate steps, it can be too time-consuming to re-do the entire diagram. In this question, you are told that Rule 5 no longer applies. What does that mean? It means there can be zero red walls. It also means there can be two red walls. It also means there still can be one red wall. So all the previous diagrams are valid, but there are several new possibilities. If you graphed them, you would realize that there could be two tan/two white, two red/two tan, two red/two white, two red/one white/one tan. Rather than diagram all these permutations, review the answer choices for guidance, since this in an EXCEPT question.

(A) There cannot be three red walls or three white walls (because of Rule 2). Could there be two red walls and two white walls? Yes, red and white have no limitations with respect to the finish, so this can be true. (Figure 6)

(B) Similar to (A), red and white have no special limits with respect to finish.

(C) Can there be two tan satin walls, one red satin wall, and one red latex wall? Yes, the red and tan walls would alternate.

(D) Similar to (C), the two tan walls could be satin, leaving the satin and latex for the white walls.

(E) * This is not possible. Although it is okay to have the two white walls facing each other and the two tan walls facing each other, if there were two latex walls, then one of the tan walls would have to be latex, violating Rule 4.

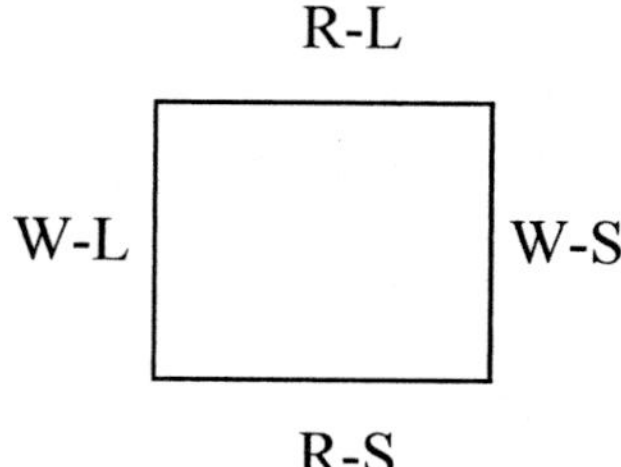

Fig. 6

Practice Test 7

Spend 35 minutes doing this practice test. When time is up, review the explanations to help you understand the questions that you did not answer correctly.

SECTION I

Time—35 minutes

23 Questions

Directions: Each group of questions in this section is based on a set of conditions. In answering some of the questions, it may be useful to draw a rough diagram. Choose the response that most accurately and completely answers each question and blacken the corresponding space on your answer sheet.

Questions 1–6

A veterinarian employed by the city zoo feeds the same animals every morning. The animals—falcons, gorillas, hyenas, iguanas, kangaroos, monkeys, and okapis—are fed one at a time and exactly once every morning. To ensure the animals are fed in an acceptable order, the following requirements must be satisfied:

The gorillas are fed second or sixth.

If the kangaroos are fed earlier than the hyenas, then the falcons must be fed later than the okapis. If the kangaroos are fed later than the hyenas, then the falcons must be fed earlier than the okapis.

Exactly two animal groups must be fed between the feedings of the hyenas and the gorillas.

The falcons must be fed immediately before or immediately after the gorillas.

The hyenas are fed earlier than the okapis or monkeys, but not both.

1. Which one of the following could be the feeding schedule in order from first to seventh?

(A) Kangaroos, iguanas, hyenas, okapis, falcons, gorillas, monkeys
(B) Falcons, gorillas, okapis, hyenas, kangaroos, monkeys, iguanas
(C) Iguanas, gorillas, monkeys, falcons, hyenas, kangaroos, okapis
(D) Monkeys, iguanas, hyenas, kangaroos, falcons, gorillas, okapis
(E) Okapis, gorillas, falcons, iguanas, hyenas, monkeys, kangaroos

2. Which one of the following animals CANNOT be fed fifth?

(A) Iguanas
(B) Monkeys
(C) Kangaroos
(D) Okapis
(E) Falcons

3. If the kangaroos are fed immediately after the okapis, then which one of the following must be true?

(A) The gorillas are fed second.
(B) The kangaroos are fed second.
(C) Either the iguanas or the monkeys are fed fourth.
(D) Either the hyenas or the falcons are fed third.
(E) Either the kangaroos or the monkeys are fed seventh.

4. Which one of the following could be an accurate partial list of the order in which the animals are fed?

(A) First: falcons; second: gorillas; third: kangaroos
(B) Second: gorillas; third: falcons; fourth: okapis
(C) Fourth: kangaroos; fifth: hyenas; sixth: okapis
(D) First: monkeys; second: okapis; third: hyenas
(E) Fifth: falcons; sixth: gorillas; seventh: kangaroos

5. The exact feeding order of all seven animals can be determined if which one of the following is known?

(A) The monkeys are first, and the kangaroos are sixth
(B) The monkeys are first, and the gorillas are sixth.
(C) The kangaroos are second, and the okapis are fourth.
(D) The falcons are third, and the iguanas are fourth.
(E) The falcons are third, and the okapis are sixth.

6. Which one of the following is a complete and accurate list of the times, any one of which the kangaroos could be fed?

(A) First, second, sixth, seventh
(B) First, fourth, sixth, seventh
(C) First, second, third, fifth, seventh
(D) First, second, fifth, sixth, seventh
(E) First, second, fourth, sixth, seventh

GO ON TO THE NEXT PAGE

Questions 7–11

Brenda is selecting music for a party. She must select a total of six songs from among three dance songs—F, G, and H—three pop songs—M, N, and O—and three rock songs—W, X, Y. Two songs must be selected from each song type. The selection of songs must also satisfy the following conditions:

G and H cannot both be played at the party.
M and G cannot both be played at the party.
If N is played, then O must be played.
If X and M are both played, then X must be played earlier in the party than M.
If W and H are both played, then W is played immediately before H is played.
Either M or O is played first.
Either X or Y is played fifth.

7. Which one of the following could be a complete and accurate order of songs played, from first to sixth?

(A) O, N, G, X, Y, H
(B) M, F, N, H, X, Y
(C) M, O, H, W, Y, F
(D) O, X, M, F, Y, H
(E) N, O, Y, F, X, H

8. If M is played first, then which one of the following could be true?

(A) X is third.
(B) W is third.
(C) G is sixth.
(D) H is second.
(E) N is fourth.

9. Which one of the following songs must be played at the party?

(A) H
(B) G
(C) M
(D) O
(E) W

10. If M is played second, then which one of the following songs CANNOT be played?

(A) F
(B) H
(C) N
(D) W
(E) Y

11. If N is not played and Y and is not played, how many possible song orders can be played?

(A) one
(B) two
(C) three
(D) four
(E) five

GO ON TO THE NEXT PAGE.

Questions 12–17

Six students must participate in a committee—either the dance committee or the parade committee—to organize the homecoming weekend activities. Each of the six students—Quinton, Robert, Sutall, Tijkman, Valse, and Xi—will be on one of the committees. The participation of the students will be in accordance with the following conditions:

If Quinton is on the parade committee, Tijkman is on the dance committee.
Valse is on the parade committee if Tijkman is on the parade committee.
Xi and Valse are always on different committees.
Sutall in on the dance committee if Tijkman is on the dance committee.
At least two students must participate in each committee.

12. Which one of the following could be a complete and accurate assignment of students to committees?

(A) Dance: Sutall, Tijkman, Xi
Parade: Quinton, Robert, Valse
(B) Dance: Robert, Tijkman, Xi
Parade: Quinton, Sutall, Valse
(C) Dance: Sutall, Tijkman, Valse, Xi
Parade: Quinton, Robert
(D) Dance: Robert, Sutall, Xi
Parade: Quinton, Tijkman, Valse
(E) Dance: Quinton, Valse
Parade: Robert, Sutall, Tijkman, Xi

13. Which one of the following CANNOT be a pair of students on the parade committee?

(A) Quinton and Robert
(B) Quinton and Sutall
(C) Tijkman and Robert
(D) Tijkman and Sutall
(E) Robert and Xi

14. If there are exactly two students on the parade committee, then which one of the following must be true?

(A) Tijkman is on the parade committee.
(B) Sutall is on the dance committee.
(C) Quinton is on the parade committee.
(D) Robert and Xi are on the dance committee.
(E) Tijkman and Sutall are on the dance committee.

15. Each of the following could be a complete list of the students on the parade committee EXCEPT:

(A) Quinton, Robert, Valse
(B) Sutall, Robert, Tijkman, Valse
(C) Quinton, Valse
(D) Tijkman, Valse
(E) Quinton, Sutall, Valse

16. If Xi is on the parade committee, then which one of the following must be true?

(A) Quinton is on the parade committee.
(B) Robert is on the dance committee.
(C) Tijkman is on the dance committee.
(D) Valse is on the parade committee.
(E) Sutall is on the parade committee.

17. If there are exactly two students on the dance committee, then which one of the following could be true?

(A) Xi is on the parade committee.
(B) Quinton is on the dance committee.
(C) Tijkman is on the dance committee.
(D) Quinton is on the parade committee.
(E) Robert is on the dance committee.

GO ON TO THE NEXT PAGE

Questions 18–23

Whenever a company takes delivery of a new computer, the software technician must load at least one program from each of the following three categories: word processing programs—F, G, H; database programs—O, P, R; internet browsers—T, U, W. When the software technician loads the programs, the following requirements must be satisfied:

An equal number of programs from each category must be loaded on the computer.
T and P are not both loaded on the same computer.
If R is loaded on a computer, U must also be loaded.
O must be loaded on a computer if F is loaded on the computer.
R is not loaded if P is loaded on the computer.

18. Which one of the following is an acceptable list of software programs to be loaded onto an employee's computer?

(A) G, H, T
(B) F, P, U
(C) F, G, O, T, U, W
(D) G, H, O, P, U, W
(E) F, G, O, R, T, W

19. If R and W are loaded onto an employee's computer, then which one of the following must also be loaded onto the computer?

(A) F
(B) G
(C) O
(D) T
(E) H

20. If P is the only database program loaded onto an employee's computer, how many possible combinations of programs could be added to that computer?

(A) two
(B) three
(C) four
(D) five
(E) six

21. If two browsers are loaded onto an employee's computer, all of the following could be true, EXCEPT:

(A) T and U are loaded.
(B) R and O are loaded.
(C) P and O are loaded.
(D) F and G are loaded.
(E) T and W are loaded

22. If F and T are loaded onto an employee's computer, each of the following could be true, EXCEPT:

(A) O is the only database program loaded onto the computer.
(B) G or H is loaded onto the computer.
(C) O is loaded onto the computer.
(D) P is loaded onto the computer.
(E) U is loaded onto the computer.

23. If the condition that requires that an equal number of programs from each category must be selected is suspended, and all other conditions remain unchanged, what is the greatest number of programs that can be loaded onto an employee's computer?

(A) five
(B) six
(C) seven
(D) eight
(E) nine

S T O P

IF YOU FINISH BEFORE TIME IS CALLED, YOU MAY CHECK YOUR WORK ON THIS SECTION ONLY.
DO NOT WORK ON ANY OTHER SECTION IN THE TEST.

Answer key and explanations for Test 7

Answer Key

1. D
2. C
3. C
4. B
5. A
6. E
7. D
8. B
9. D
10. C
11. B
12. A
13. B
14. B
15. E
16. C
17. B
18. D
19. C
20. C
21. E
22. D
23. D

Feeding time

This simple line game had enough twists to keep you on your toes. These twists made this game very time-consuming. Most of the rules were easy enough, but Rules 2 and 5 required serious analysis. Rule 1 is the easiest rule, so it is the one to start with. G must be second or sixth. This is easily diagrammed. (Figure 1) To keep things clearer, for demonstration purposes we have used two separate lines, one for each possibility, but it is fine if you used one line. Skip Rule 2 and go to Rule 3, which ties into Rule 1. Rule 3 says: H _ _ G or G _ _ H. Thus, you can conclude that H must be third or fifth. Rule 4 requires that F must be on either side of G. This is more difficult to graph, but you could use a slash to indicate that F is only a 50% possibility, or you could put an (F) under the appropriate spaces. Both methods are shown below. Now return to Rule 2. Things are about to get complicated. If K is before H, then O is before F. If K is after H, O is after F. This is too variable to diagram, so it is better to make a note of the rule below the diagram. Even though this is phrased as an "if" rule, in reality it is a permanent rule, since K must always be either before or after H. So this rule always applies. Because this rule affects four of the seven members, it will play a role in every question. Finally, Rule 5 is a bit unusual. It says that H is before either O or M, but not both of them. So, either H is before O (and after M) or H is before M (and after O). This is too difficult to put on the diagram, so make a note of it underneath.

F/?	G	?/F	__	H	__	__
(F)		(F)				

__	__	H	__	F/?	G	?/F
				(F)		(F)

if K < H, then O < F
or
if H < K, then F < O

M < H < O
or
O < H < M

Fig. 1

1. (D) – Although this is a complicated game, you can still use answer elimination. Starting with Rule 1, check each rule against each answer choice.
   (A) Rule 5 does not allow H to be before both O and M.
   (B) G and H must be separated by two spaces, by Rule 3.
   (C) F must be immediately before or after G, by Rule 4.
   (D) * This is a possible order. It violates no rules.
   (E) This choice violates Rule 2. It has H before K, but O before F.

2. (C) – Before doing each permutation, is there any answer choice that is easy to eliminate? First, look at the correct answer from question 1. You see that F is fifth. This allows you to eliminate answer choice (E). Next, I is a free agent, so I is unlikely to be prohibited in the fifth space. Now, the quickest way to find the correct answer is to do the permutations for the remaining three answer choices.

(A) Since I is a free agent, you should not have checked this answer choice until you checked the other choices. It is possible to place I fifth. If I is fifth, clearly H is not fifth, so H is third. Therefore, G is sixth and F is seventh. Since F is seventh, it is impossible for K to be after H, so K will have to be first or second. Also, either M or O will have to be fourth. The other one will have to be first or second. For example: KMHOIGF.

(B) If M is fifth, H must be third, G must be sixth, and F must be seventh. Because F is after O, K must be before H. K will have to be first or second. I must be fourth. O cannot be fourth because of Rule 5. O must be first or second. For example: KOHIMGF.

(C) * K cannot be fifth. If K were fifth and G were sixth and so F were seventh, then H would be before K, but when H is before K, F must be before O. This can't happen if F is seventh.

(D) O has the same analysis as M. For example: MKHIOGF

(E) This choice was eliminated using the correct answer from question 1.

3. (C) – You are provided with an O K block. Rules 2 and 5 will be relevant. Where might the O K block fit? If G is second and the O K block is third and fourth, H would be fifth, and F would be first. This would run afoul of Rule 2. (Figure 2a) If G is second and the block is sixth and seventh, this will work. (Figure 2b). Try the mirror image of both of these and you find a similar result, the O K block can be first and second too. (Figure 2c) I and M can fill the remaining spaces in a variety of ways.

(A) Although G can be second, it can also be sixth. This choice was for people who did not think about the alternate option.

(B) Again, K can be second, but it can also be seventh.

(C) * This is true. Either I or M must be fourth.

(D) Although either H or F can be third, so could I or M.

(E) M cannot be seventh.

F G O K H __ __ – no!

Fig. 2a

F/? G ?/F __ H O K

Fig. 2b

O K H __ F/? G ?/F

Fig. 2c

4. (B) – Although this question asks only about part of the order, you must solve for the validity of the whole order. There is no short cut; you must work through all the rules for each answer choice.
   (A) If you have the block of F G K starting on space one, then K is before H. Whenever K is before H, F is supposed to be after O, which is not the case here. See Rule 2.
   (B) * If you have a block of G F O starting on space two, then space five must be H. Since O is after F, K must be after H, by Rule 2. Also, M must be after H, by Rule 5. I must fill the first space. (Figure 3)
   (C) If K H O are fourth, fifth, and sixth, then K is before H. This means F is supposed to be after O. But F cannot be seventh, since it must be next to G, which is second.
   (D) An M O H block violates Rule 5 because both M and O precede H.
   (E) With F G K at the end of the series, K is after H, and this would require that F be before O, which clearly can't happen because there is now no place for O to go, except before F.

I G F O H K/M M/K

Fig. 3

5. (A) – There is no easy short cut for this question. It requires diligently working though the answer choices. But if it becomes clear that there is more than one permutation, you can stop examining an answer choice since it is not the one you want.
   (A) * If K is sixth and M is first, then G must be second, F must be third, and H must be fifth. Since H is fifth, O must be seventh. The remaining space, space four, is filled with I. (Figure 4)
   (B) This is similar to, but not the same as, choice (A). If M is first and G is sixth, there are several possible orders. One is MKHOIGF, another is MKHIOGF, and a third is MIHKFGO.
   (C) If K is second and O is fourth, then H must be third and M must be first. G must be sixth, but F can be fifth or seventh, and I can be fifth or seventh.
   (D) This too looks like figure 4. If F is third and I is fourth, then G must be second and M must be first. H must be fifth, but K can be sixth or seventh, as can O.
   (E) There are two possibilities when F is third and O is sixth: MGFIHOK and IGFMHOK.

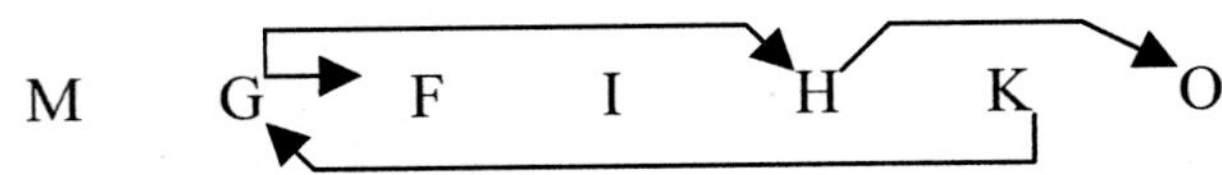

Fig. 4

6. (E) – Before doing anything else, compare the five answer choices, looking for similarities and differences. You can see that most of the choices contain "first" and "second", so there is no point checking for those, simply assume they are true. Choice (B) does not have "second". Because (B) is an oddball choice, you should eliminate it. The remaining four choices all have "seventh", so there is no point checking that either. Three of the four choices have "sixth", so there is little point in checking that yet. Now consult the answer choices from previous questions. In question 2, you learned that K cannot be fifth, so eliminate choices (C) and (D). Of the remaining two choices, the only difference is "fourth." In question 1(D), you learned that K can be fourth. So this eliminates choice (A). As you can see, you can often answer this kind of question without doing much, or any, new work.
(A) See the analysis.
(B) See the analysis.
(C) See the analysis.
(D) See the analysis.
(E) * See the analysis.

Song selection

At first, this game looked like it was going to be a standard multi-group selection game, in which you select a small final group from the members of three initial groups. But, then it threw in conditions that contain time/space limitations like “first” and “fifth” and “earlier” and “immediately before”. At that point it became clear that this game requires both a grouping diagram and a line diagram. Fortunately, executing a grouping diagram and a line diagram is pretty straightforward for a well-trained LSAT taker like you. The first step is to get both diagrams started. The grouping diagram is the more important one. The first three rules are relevant to the grouping diagram and are easily diagrammed using one-way and two-way arrows. (Figure 1) Rules 4 and 5 deal with conditional situations, and are not so easily diagrammed. You may choose to use dotted lines to connect M and X and W and H. Or you may choose to place stars by these members, just to remind yourself of their special rule. Either way you choose to do it, it will be necessary to refer to these rules or their respective notes under the diagram. The final two rules are easily diagrammed on a simple line. (Figure 2) Remember, even if you use X on space five, you can still use Y elsewhere. The same applies to M and O. Now it is time to determine if there are any warranted conclusions that should be made. You are told there are exactly two selected from each song type. You can combine this with the other rules and conclude several things. Since dance songs G and H are mutually exclusive, dance song F must be used. For the pop songs, if N is used, then so is O. M and N cannot be used together, because this would activate Rule 3. So O is always used. For rock, you know that either X or Y must be used, but Rule 7 made this explicit. Penciling out permutations, you realize that M cannot be first if X is fifth. Also, when M is first and Y is fifth, then F, H, O, and W must all be used, and there are only a few permutations. When O is first, there are many more possible permutations. Instead of wasting time doing permutations you might not need, go to the questions now.

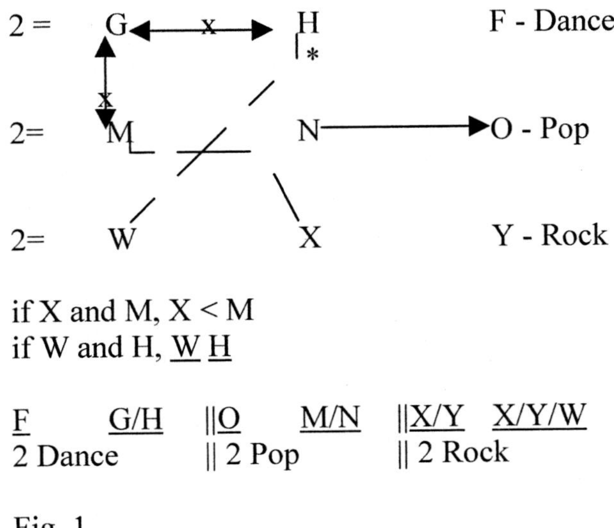

Fig. 1

M/O	__	__	__	X/Y	__
1	2	3	4	5	6

Fig. 2

7. (D) – Use each of the rules to eliminate the answer choices that violate them. The remaining answer choice is the correct answer.
   (A) This choice is wrong because it violates Rule 1, by having both G and H.
   (B) This violates Rule 3, because it contains N, but not O. This also violates Rule 4 because when X and M are both played, X must be played before M.
   (C) This violates Rule 5, because when H and W are played, W must be immediately before H.
   (D) * This is a possible order.
   (E) This violates Rule 6, because neither O nor M is first.

8. (B) – After plugging in the new information you discover quite a few things. As discussed in the initial analysis, when M is first, X cannot be included in the play list at all. So W and Y must be played, and Y must be fifth. Also, when M is played G is not, therefore, F and H are played. When both H and W are played, W must immediately precede H. So there are four possible permutations. (Figure 3)
   (A) As determined in the analysis, X cannot be played.
   (B) * W can be third or second.
   (C) G cannot be played at all, as was determined in the analysis.
   (D) H can be third or fourth, but not second. Because W and H are present, H must come immediately after W, and the earliest W can appear is second.
   (E) M and N cannot both be played, because when N is played, O must be played. That would make for three pop songs. But, there can only be two pop songs.

M	W	H	F/O	Y	O/F
1	2	3	4	5	6

M	F/O	W	H	Y	O/F
1	2	3	4	5	6

Fig. 3

9. (D) – You can use the initial analysis and correct answers from the two previous questions since there is no new information in this question. Referring to previous work usually eliminates several incorrect answers. If

two or three answer choices remain, only then should you solve for those answer choices. Consulting the work from questions 7 and 8, you can see that it is definitely not necessary to use G. Eliminate choice (B). Consulting the correct answer from question 7, you see that it is definitely not necessary to use W. Eliminate choice (E). Although you could spend time pondering how the relationship of G and M affects this question, it is more efficient to simply do the permutations for the three remaining answer choices.

(A) H is not required. It is possible to form a play list without H: O, N, F, G, X, Y.
(B) G is not required, as proven in question 7.
(C) It is possible to form a play list that does not include M: O, F, H, N, Y, X
(D) * There is no way to form a play list without including O.
(E) See (C).

10. (C) – M plays a big role in this game because it has relationships with several other members. It actually is not necessary to diagram this question to figure out the correct answer. If M is second, then O must be first. Because two pop songs have now been used, N cannot be used. If you did not make this connection, it is still possible to diagram the possibilities. If M is second, O must be first. Since X cannot be played, Y must be played fifth. This leaves space three for W, space four for H, and space six for F. (Figure 4)

(A) F is in figure 4. When M is played, F must be played, because G is no longer available.
(B) Like F, H must be played, because G cannot be played.
(C) * N cannot be played, because O and M are played.
(D) W must be played. Because M is second, X cannot be played (because of Rule 4). This means that W and Y must be played.
(E) See (D).

O	M	W	H	Y	F
1	2	3	4	5	6

Fig. 4

11. (B) – Because N is not played, M and O must be played. Because M is played, G is not played. Therefore F and H must be played. Because Y is not played, X and W are. Because M and X are both played, X must be played before M. Since either X or Y must be fifth, X must be fifth, and M must be sixth. Finally, W and H must be played as a block. Since this question specifically asks for the number of permutations, do as many as you can and count them up. (Figure 5)

(A) See the analysis.
(B) * See the analysis.
(C) See the analysis.

(D) See the analysis.
(E) See the analysis.

O	W	H	F	X	M
1	2	3	4	5	6

O	F	W	H	X	M
1	2	3	4	5	6

Fig. 5

Committee selection

Since all six members of the beginning group will be assigned to one of the two committees, this is a variation of the mono-group selection diagram. The rules are easy to diagram. (Figure 1) Rule 1 requires a one-way arrow from Q to T. Rule 2 requires an arrow from T to V. Rule 3 requires two arrows, one from V in the parade column to X in the dance column, and one from V in the dance column to X in the parade column. Rule 4 requires an arrow from T to S in the dance column. Now consider the occupancy limits. There must be at least two students on each committee, due to Rule 5. You can conclude that there are two members on the parade committee and four on dance, or three on parade and three dance, or four on parade and two on dance. Since V and X are mutually exclusive, reserve one space in each committee for them.

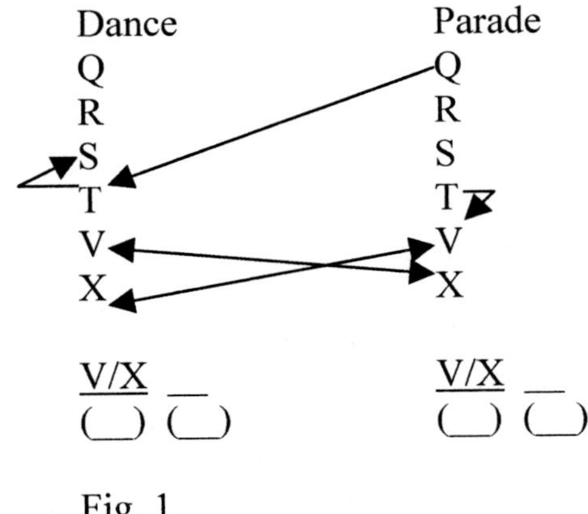

Fig. 1

12. (A) – To make the most efficient use of your time, start with the first rule and work your way down the list of rules, eliminating answers as you go.
(A) * This is a possible order. None of the rules were violated.
(B) This violates Rule 4, because T is on dance and S is on parade.
(C) This violates Rule 3, because X and V are not split up.
(D) This violates Rule 1, because Q is on parade and T is on parade.
(E) This violates Rule 2, because T is on parade and V is on dance.

13. (B) – Look at the parade column. You see that Q and T cannot both be on the parade committee. You also see that if T is on parade, then V must also be on parade, which would prevent X from being on parade. This should be sufficient analysis, go to the questions.
(A) It is possible to put Q and R together on parade. When Q is on parade, T (and S) must be on dance. X and V must always be split between the two. R is the free agent. So it is QRV (or QRX) on parade and STX (or STV) on dance.
(B) * It is not possible to put Q and S on the parade committee. When Q is on parade, T is on dance. When T is on dance, S is supposed to be on dance as well.

(C) It is possible to put T and R on parade. With T on parade, so must V. The other three could be on dance.
(D) With T (and S) on parade, so must V be on parade. The others can be on dance.
(E) R is a free agent, so it is unlikely R would run into any problems. When X is on parade, V must be on dance. Since V is on dance, T cannot be on parade, and so must be on dance. With T on dance, so must S. VTS is on dance. RXQ can be on parade.

14. (B) – This question uses a slightly different approach. It focuses on the occupancy instead of the individuals. Even so, the individuals will determine the result. It is best to form the possible two-person parade committees. Remember that V or X must always take one of the two spaces on parade. This simplifies things immensely. While doing the permutations, we learn that Q, R, or T can be the second member of parade. S cannot be the second member of parade, because this would push T into dance, and when T is on dance, S must also be on dance. (Figure 2)
(A) T may or may not be on parade.
(B) * Yes, S must be on dance, because of the effect of Rule 4.
(C) Q may or may not be on parade.
(D) R and X may or may not be on dance.
(E) Although S must be on dance, it is not necessary for T to also be on dance.

Parade		Dance			
Q	X/V	T	S	R	V/X
R	V/X	Q	T	S	V/X
T	V	Q	R	S	X

Fig. 2

15. (E) – Lacking new information, you need to work closely with the answer choices. Glancing at the parade column in the initial diagram, we see that Q and T cannot both be on parade. Keep that in mind. Although this question asks about the parade committee, make sure to consider the effect of each answer choice on the dance committee as well.
(A) If QRV is on parade, then TSX are on dance and no rules are violated.
(B) If SRTV is on parade, then QX are on dance and no rules are violated.
(C) If QV is on parade, SRTX are on dance and no rules are violated.
(D) If TV is on parade, QRSX are on dance and no rules are violated.
(E) * If QSV is on parade, RTX is on dance. This is invalid because when T is on dance, S is supposed to be on dance as well. So, this choice violates Rule 4.

16. (C) – Consulting figure 1, when X is on parade, the first effect is that V is on dance. When V is on dance, T is no longer able to be on parade (Rule 2), so T is on dance. When T is on dance, S must also be on dance (Rule 4). So far, VTS is on dance. Can Q or R be with VTS? Yes, one of them can be with VTS. The other must be with X on parade, in order to meet the two-student minimum. Can both Q and R be with X? Yes, there is no reason they cannot both be with X.
(A) Q may or may not be on parade.
(B) R may or may not be on dance.
(C) * Correct. Because X is on parade, V must be on dance. Because V is on dance, T cannot be on parade, and so T must be on dance.
(D) V must be on dance, so this is 100% false.
(E) S can never be on parade, because T must be on dance.

17. (B) – Again, the question focuses on the occupancy, but the analysis must focus on the members. Before doing permutations, you know that either V or X must take one of the two spaces on dance. Start your analysis there. (Figure 3) If V is on dance, then T must also be on dance, because of Rule 2. But then a problem crops up. Both spaces on dance are now taken, but S is supposed to be with T when T is on dance. So you now know that V is not on dance, V is on parade. If X on dance, the issue with T is the same, so T cannot be on dance because of S. Can Q be on parade with T? No, because of Rule 1. So Q must be on dance with X. This fills the two spaces, and you can stop the analysis now.
(A) X must be on dance, not parade.
(B) * Correct. Q must be on dance.
(C) T cannot be on dance.
(D) Q must be on dance, not parade.
(E) R must be on parade, not dance.

Parade	Dance
~~X~~	~~V T~~
V T R S	X Q

Fig. 3

Software groups

This game requires a multi-group selection diagram. There are three groups from which you must choose certain members. This puzzle has a small twist on the classic diagram. Normally, a fixed number of members must be selected; five or six is typical. In this puzzle, there is a minimum of three—at least one member must be taken from each of the three categories. Another factor also influences the size of the ending group. Rule 1 requires that an equal number of programs must be selected from each category. So, you can conclude that if one program is selected from each category then there are a total of three programs. Furthermore, if two programs are selected from each category that would mean there are a total of six programs. Can three programs from each category be selected? No. Because of Rule 2 and Rule 5, you cannot select three from each category to get a total of nine members, because these two rules establish a practical maximum of eight members. So, going back to Rule 1, there are either three or six members in the final group. The basic diagram requires positive one-way arrows and negative two-way arrows. (Figure 1) Given the large number of possible permutations, it is not advisable to do permutations in advance of the questions.

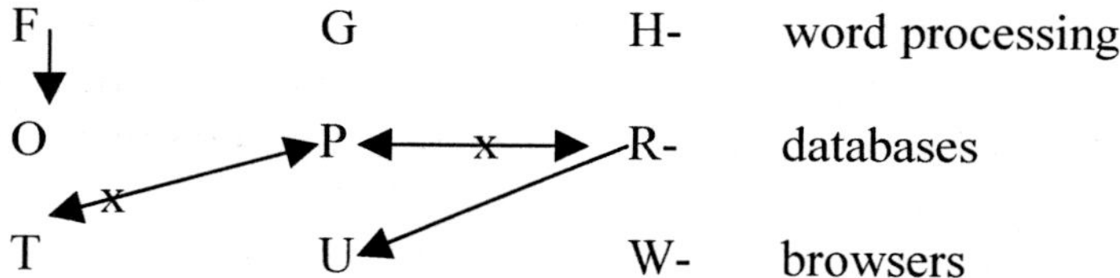

Fig. 1

18. (D) – Using the rules to eliminate choices is, as usual, the most efficient technique.
    (A) This violates the initial set-up requirement that at least one program be selected from each of the categories.
    (B) This choice has F without O, violating Rule 4.
    (C) This choice shows two from the word processing group, one from databases, and three from browsers, violating Rule 1.
    (D) * This choice is valid.
    (E) This choice is invalid, because Rule 3 requires U to be selected when R is selected.

19. (C) – Plugging the new information into figure 2 allows you to fill several of the blanks. When R is selected, U must be selected. U and W are two of the browsers. Since two browsers are selected, two databases and two word processing programs must be selected. Of the databases, when R is selected, P cannot be selected, thus O is selected. R and O are the two databases. Finally, you must select two programs from word processors F, G, and H. All three are equally valid.
    (A) F, G, and H have each a 50/50 chance of being selected.

(B) See (A).
(C) * Correct. O must be selected because P is not selected and there must be two databases.
(D) T can never be selected, because W takes the first browser slot and U takes the second slot.
(E) See (A).

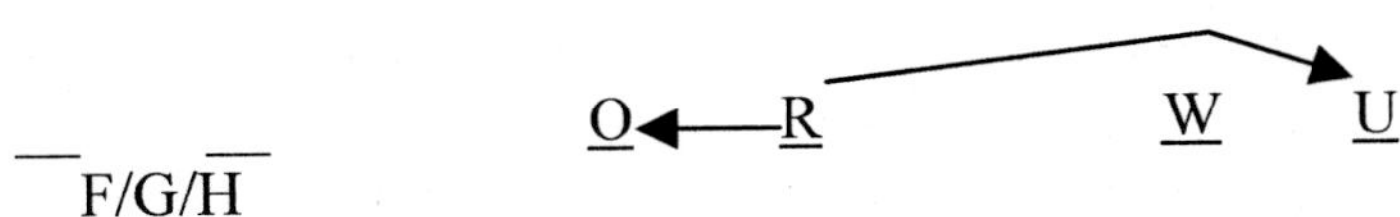

Fig. 2

20. (C) – If there is only one database, then a total of three programs are selected. Since P is the only database, R is not used and O is not used. When O is not used, F cannot be used. G and H are wide-open free agents for the first slot. When P is used, T cannot be used. U and W can be used for the third slot. Note that the R to U link is a one-way arrow. This means U can be selected even if R is not. Do the permutations and count them up. (Figure 3) There are four.
(A) See the analysis.
(B) See the analysis.
(C) * See the analysis.
(D) See the analysis.
(E) See the analysis.

G	P	U
G	P	W
H	P	U
H	P	W

Fig. 3

21. (E) – Since there are now two browsers, there must be a total of six programs. The quickest method is to review the answer choices for potential issues. If you don't see any possible issues, only then should you solve each permutation.
(A) It could be true that T and U are selected: GHORTU
(B) It could be true that R and O are selected, see (A).
(C) It could be true that P and O are selected, when W and U are selected.
(D) It could be true that F and G are selected; there are no restrictions on F, G, and H.
(E) * T and W cannot be selected. If you skimmed the answer choices and the initial diagram, you might have noticed that T, W, and U have quite a few

arrows pointing at them. This makes them interesting to us. If T and W are used, then P cannot be used, so R and O must be used. This causes a problem, because when R is used, U is supposed to be used. T and U can be selected or W and U can be selected. But T and W cannot. (Figure 4)

___	___	R	O	T	W – no!
___	___	R	O	T	U
___	___	P/R	O	W	U
F/G/H					

Fig. 4

22. (D) – This new information gives us quite a bit to work with. When F is selected, so is O. So the three programs could be FOT. But there could also be six programs. When T is selected, P is not selected. (Figure 5) When there are six programs, the absence of P means that R must be selected. Once R is selected, U must be selected. G and H are equally likely.

(A) It could be true that O is the only database program, if there are three programs.
(B) It could be true that either G or H is loaded.
(C) It must be true that O is loaded.
(D)* It cannot be true that P is loaded when T is loaded.
(E) It could be true that U is loaded.

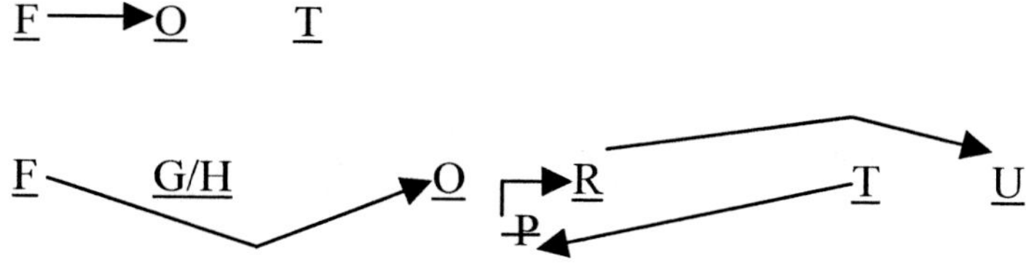

Fig. 5

23. (D) Rule modification questions are very difficult if they force you to go back and re-examine your entire diagram and all the warranted conclusions. In this case, the rule suspension is not difficult. Determine the maximum number. Examine the mutually exclusive members, P and T, and P and R. We can use the other eight members together, if we exclude P.

(A) See the analysis.
(B) See the analysis.
(C) See the analysis.
(D) * See the analysis.
(E) See the analysis.

Practice Test 8

Spend 35 minutes doing this practice test. When time is up, review the explanations to help you understand the questions that you did not answer correctly.

SECTION I

Time—35 minutes

24 Questions

Directions: Each group of questions in this section is based on a set of conditions. In answering some of the questions, it may be useful to draw a rough diagram. Choose the response that most accurately and completely answers each question and blacken the corresponding space on your answer sheet.

Questions 1–6

The manager of a grocery store is arranging a blind taste test of eight different sodas—F, G, H, J, K, L, M, and N. The sodas are to be arranged on a table in eight spaces, numbered 1–8 from left to right, and there will be exactly one soda per space. The manager must arrange the sodas according to the following conditions:

Sodas M and N cannot be placed next to each other on the table.

Sodas G and M must be placed next to each other on the table.

Soda J must be placed in space number 6.

Soda K must be placed in a lower-numbered space than soda H.

Soda L must be placed immediately to the right of soda H.

1. Which one of the following is an acceptable arrangement of sodas from space 1 to space 8 on the table?

(A) G, M, K, H, L, F, J, N
(B) F, K, H, L, M, J, N, G
(C) K, M, G, F, N, J, H, L
(D) N, M, G, K, F, J, H, L
(E) F, K, G, M, H, J, N, L

2. If soda K is placed in space 5, then which one of the following must be true?

(A) Soda M is in space 1.
(B) Soda N is in space 1.
(C) Soda G is in space 2.
(D) Soda F is in space 2.
(E) Soda L is in space 8.

3. Which one of the following CANNOT be true?

(A) Soda L is in space 7.
(B) Soda K is in space 1.
(C) Soda M is in space 5.
(D) Soda G is in space 4.
(E) Soda N is in space 2.

4. If Soda H is placed in space 2 and soda F is placed in space 4, then which one of the following could be true?

(A) Soda M is in space 1.
(B) Soda N is in space 3.
(C) Soda G is in space 7.
(D) Soda L is in space 7.
(E) Soda N is in space 8.

5. If Soda K is in space 2 and soda L is in space 5, then how many different ways can the manager arrange the sodas on the table?

(A) 1
(B) 2
(C) 3
(D) 4
(E) 5

6. There is only one possible option for how the sodas may be arranged on the table if which one of the following is true?

(A) Soda M is in space 1 and soda N is in space 3.
(B) Soda G is in space 3 and soda L is in space 8.
(C) Soda K is in space 4 and soda F is in space 5.
(D) Soda L is in space 3 and soda M is in space 7.
(E) Soda N is in space 3 and soda K is in space 5.

GO ON TO THE NEXT PAGE

Questions 7–12

A teacher must select two teams to compete in a math contest with other schools. The available students are Alan, Ben, Carl, and Desi, who are boys, and Tamika, Ursula, Val, and Wendy, who are girls. The students must be divided into two teams of four students each—Team 1 and Team 2—and no student can be on both teams. Each team must include at least one boy, and the formation of the teams must conform to the following conditions:

Alan and Val must be on the same team.
If Ben is on a team, then Tamika must also be on that team.
If Wendy is on Team 1, then Carl must be on Team 2.
If Desi is on Team 2, then Tamika must be on Team 2.

7. Which one of the following lists of students is an acceptable assignment of students to Team 1?

(A) Alan, Carl, Val, and Wendy
(B) Ben, Carl, Tamika, and Ursula
(C) Ben, Desi, Tamika, and Wendy
(D) Alan, Ben, Desi, and Wendy
(E) Tamika, Ursula, Val, and Wendy

8. If Wendy and Carl are on the same team, then which one of the following must be true?

(A) Desi is on Team 1.
(B) Alan is on Team 1.
(C) Val is on Team 1.
(D) Ursula is on Team 2.
(E) Tamika is on Team 2.

9. If Desi in on Team 2, then which one of the following could be true?

(A) Alan is on Team 2.
(B) Ben is on Team 1.
(C) Carl is on Team 2.
(D) Tamika is on Team 1.
(E) Val is on Team 2.

10. Which one of the following cannot be true?

(A) Alan and Ben are both on Team 1.
(B) Tamika is on Team 1 and Carl is on Team 2.
(C) Ben is on Team 1 and Val is on Team 2.
(D) Carl and Wendy are both on Team 2.
(E) Alan is on Team 1 and Wendy is on Team 2.

11. If Alan is on Team 2, then which one of the following must be true?

(A) Carl is on Team 1.
(B) Desi is on Team 1.
(C) Tamika is on Team 2.
(D) Ursula is on Team 2.
(E) Wendy is on Team 2.

12. Suppose that the condition that requires at least one boy on each team no longer applies. What is the maximum number of girls that could be on Team 2?

(A) 0
(B) 1
(C) 2
(D) 3
(E) 4

GO ON TO THE NEXT PAGE.

Questions 13–19

A tennis pro schedules two individual lessons per day, one in the morning and one in the afternoon, on Monday, Tuesday, and Friday. His students include novice players—Jones, Kimpton, Levin, and Mayer—and advanced players—Perkins, Rose, Sari, and Tosca. No student has more than one lesson. Schedules follow these rules:

Two novice players are not scheduled on the same day.
If Rose is scheduled for a lesson, then Sari is also scheduled for a lesson, but they cannot be scheduled on consecutive calendar days.
Jones can be scheduled only on Friday.
Mayer can only be scheduled for a morning session.
If both Levin and Tosca are scheduled, then Tosca must be scheduled for a lesson that is at some time after Levin's lesson.
The appointments scheduled for Monday morning and Tuesday afternoon must be different levels of players.

13. Which one of the following could be the schedule for the week, listing morning and afternoon lessons respectively?

(A) Monday: Rose and Levin; Tuesday: Kimpton and Tosca; Friday: Sari and Jones
(B) Monday: Mayer and Levin; Tuesday: Perkins and Tosca; Friday: Rose and Jones
(C) Monday: Sari and Kimpton; Tuesday: Mayer and Rose; Friday: Jones and Perkins
(D) Monday: Jones and Tosca; Tuesday: Mayer and Sari; Friday: Kimpton and Perkins
(E) Monday: Mayer and Rose; Tuesday: Levin and Tosca; Friday: Jones and Sari

14. If Rose is scheduled for an appointment on Tuesday, then each of the following could be true EXCEPT:

(A) Perkins is scheduled for Monday morning.
(B) Sari is scheduled for Monday afternoon.
(C) Tosca is scheduled for Tuesday morning.
(D) Levin is scheduled for Tuesday morning.
(E) Kimpton is scheduled for Tuesday afternoon.

15. If the tennis pro schedules Jones for an appointment, then which one of the following CANNOT be true?

(A) Levin is not scheduled for an appointment.
(B) Mayer is not scheduled for an appointment.
(C) Perkins is scheduled for Tuesday afternoon.
(D) Rose is scheduled for Friday afternoon.
(E) Kimpton is scheduled for Friday afternoon.

16. Which one of the following must be true?

(A) At most, three novice players can be scheduled.
(B) At least three novice players must be scheduled.
(C) At most, four novice players can be scheduled.
(D) No more than two advanced players can be scheduled.
(E) No more than three advanced players can be scheduled.

17. If Kimpton is scheduled for Tuesday afternoon and Levin is scheduled at some time during the week, then which one of the following players CANNOT be scheduled for an appointment on Monday?

(A) Levin
(B) Perkins
(C) Rose
(D) Sari
(E) Tosca

18. If Tosca is scheduled for an appointment on Monday morning, then which one of the following must be true?

(A) Mayer is not scheduled for an appointment.
(B) Kimpton is not scheduled for an appointment.
(C) Levin is not scheduled for an appointment.
(D) Rose is not scheduled for an appointment.
(E) Sari is not scheduled for an appointment.

19. Which one of the following conditions, if added to the conditions already in place, would make it impossible for the tennis pro to make an acceptable schedule of appointments?

(A) Both Levin and Mayer are scheduled for appointments.
(B) Jones is not scheduled for an appointment.
(C) Neither Jones nor Levin is scheduled for an appointment.
(D) Sari is not scheduled for an appointment.
(E) Both Kimpton and Mayer are scheduled for an appointment.

GO ON TO THE NEXT PAGE

Questions 20–24

In an island chain, there are exactly six islands: K, L, M, N, O, and P. To reach one island from another island, a visitor must travel across a bridge connecting those two islands. Each island is connected to at least one other island by a bridge, and only one bridge can connect the same pair of islands. The following information is known about the islands and the bridges that connect them:

K is connected by a bridge to N.
L is connected by a bridge to M, and L is connected by a bridge to P.
O is connected by a bridge to N.
A visitor may not return to an island once they have left it.

20. A visitor could visit each of the six islands if there was a bridge connecting which of the following two islands?

(A) K and O
(B) K and L
(C) L and N
(D) O and P
(E) M and P

21. A visitor who does not start at island K, but wants to visit that island, must visit which one of the following islands?

(A) L
(B) M
(C) N
(D) O
(E) P

22. If no new bridges are added, then which one of the following is the maximum number of islands that a visitor could visit?

(A) 1
(B) 2
(C) 3
(D) 4
(E) 5

23. If a bridge is added that connects island L with island N, then which one of the following pairs of islands would require the fewest number of visits to other islands in order for a visitor to visit that pair?

(A) K and P
(B) M and N
(C) M and O
(D) K and M
(E) O and P

24. If a new bridge is built to connect island L with island O and a visitor uses that bridge, the visitor CANNOT visit both of the islands in which one of the following pairs?

(A) K and N
(B) M and P
(C) N and P
(D) O and K
(E) O and M

S T O P

IF YOU FINISH BEFORE TIME IS CALLED, YOU MAY CHECK YOUR WORK ON THIS SECTION ONLY.
DO NOT WORK ON ANY OTHER SECTION IN THE TEST.

Answer key and explanations for Test 8

Answer Key

1. C
2. E
3. A
4. C
5. D
6. E
7. C
8. A
9. C
10. A
11. B
12. D
13. E
14. B
15. E
16. A
17. E
18. C
19. D
20. D
21. C
22. C
23. B
24. B

Taste Test

This game requires a straightforward simple-line diagram. Simple lines are the most frequently tested games, so you have to be able to do them with ease. The rules are easy to understand and diagram. The diagram should reflect this simplicity. You will place eight items in a horizontal line. The only rule you can definitively place on the diagram is Rule 3. The other rules cannot yet be placed on the diagram, but Rules 4 and 5 can be combined. This combination will be very useful later. Rule 1, affecting M and N, and Rule 2, affecting G and M, are easy to depict. Once you have diagrammed, or attempted to diagram, each rule, the next step is to make warranted conclusions about what can and cannot be true. Start with the three-letter block K < H L. Can you place H on space 1? No, because this would not allow space for K. Can L be on space 1 or 2? No, for the same reason. Looking at the other end of the line, can K be on spaces 7 or 8? No. Can H be on space 8? No. Finally, can L be on space 7? No, because space 6 is already occupied, so H cannot be placed there. How about H on space 5? No, for the same reason. Add all this new information to your diagram. (Figure 1) There do not appear to be easy warranted conclusions involving G, M, or N. Remember, just as important as making warranted conclusions is knowing when to stop making conclusions and move on to the questions.

K < H L
G M or M G
~~M N~~

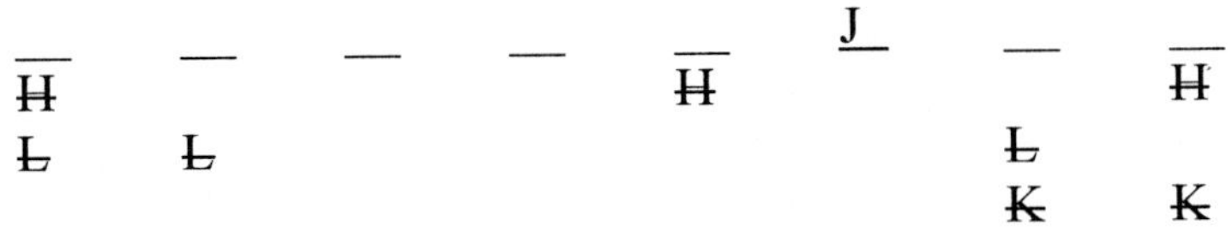

__	__	__	__	__	J	__	__
~~H~~				~~H~~			~~H~~
~~L~~	~~L~~					~~L~~	
						~~K~~	~~K~~

Fig. 1

1. (C) – Use each rule to eliminate one of the answer choices. Start with the first rule and see if it is violated in any of the answer choices. Then do the same for each subsequent rule. Since (C) is the only choice left, it must be correct.
(A) Rule 3, J must be in space 6, is violated.
(B) Rule 2, G and M must be next to each other, is violated.
(C) * This is possible.
(D) Rule 1, M and N cannot be next to each other, is violated.
(E) Rule 5, L must be immediately to the right of H, is violated.

2. (E) – When you get a piece of new information—K is in space 5—consider what you know about that member. The combination rule tells you that K must be in a lower-numbered space than H, and L must be immediately to the right of H. So, if you put K in space 5, then the only spaces available to H and L are spaces 7 and 8. The diagram would look like the diagram below. (Figure 2) Thus, choices (A) – (D) are all things that COULD be true, but (E) is the only one that must be true. Always distinguish between "could be true"

and "must be true" questions. In "must be true" questions, some of the wrong answer choices will be possible permutations, but not required permutations. This is a fine point that confuses many test-takers. Permutations that could be true are not the same as permutations that must be true.
(A) See the analysis.
(B) See the analysis.
(C) See the analysis.
(D) See the analysis.
(E) * See the analysis.

__ __ __ __ K J H L

Fig. 2

3. (A) – For "cannot be true" questions, look for a clear violation of the rules. If you did a good job making the warranted conclusions, this should be easy. Even if you did not make the warranted conclusion, this answer is still easy to find. When looking at the answer choices, focus on the members that have restrictions, instead of on free agents like F. Since L is immediately to the right of H, L cannot be in space 7, because J must be in space 6. This prevents H from being in space 6. Choices (B)–(E) are all things that could happen. The only certainty is that J is in space 6, so a choice like (A) that focuses on a space near space 6 is more likely to be correct.
(A) * See the analysis.
(B) See the analysis.
(C) See the analysis.
(D) See the analysis.
(E) See the analysis.

4. (C) – When H is in space 2 and F is in space 4, K must be in space 1 (due to Rule 4) and L must be in space 3 (due to Rule 5). (Figure 3) Since G and M must be next to each other, they go in spaces 7 and 8, though not necessarily in that order. Thus (C) could be true; G could be in space 7. The other answer choices cannot be true—which is always the case with the four incorrect answer choices for "could be true" questions.
(A) See the analysis.
(B) See the analysis.
(C) * See the analysis.
(D) See the analysis.
(E) See the analysis.

K H L F N J G/M M/G

Fig. 3

5. (D) – Diagram the new information. If K is in space 2 and L is in space 5, then H is in space 4 and J is in space 6. (Figure 4) Once again, since G and M must be next to each other, they must be in spaces 7 and 8, though not necessarily in that order. Since M and N are separated, N could be in space 1 or space 3, just as F could be in either of those two spaces. Thus, there are four options for placing the sodas: N in space 1, F in 3, G in 7 and M in space 8; the same placement for N and F but M in 7 and G in 8; then two more options with F in 1 and N in 3. (D) is the correct response.

(A) See the analysis.
(B) See the analysis.
(C) See the analysis.
(D) * See the analysis.
(E) See the analysis.

N/F K F/N H L J M/G G/M

Fig. 4

6. (E) – With this time-consuming question, focus on the members that are limited by the rules. Ignore free agents, like F, which have no restrictions. In choice (E), placing K in space 5 forces H and L into spaces 7 and 8. With N in space 3, M must be in space 1 to keep them apart. Once M is in space 1, G must be in space 2. The only remaining member is F and the only remaining space is 4. The other answer choices determine only a partial order, not the whole order.

(A) The completed diagram for this choice is M G N _ _ J H L
(B) The completed diagram for this choice is _ _ G _ _ J H L
(C) The completed diagram for this choice is _ _ _ K F J H L
(D) The completed diagram for this choice is K H L _ _ J M G
(E) * The completed diagram is M G N F K J H L

Math Teams

This game requires a multiple-line diagram and use some grouping rules. The two teams each have four members. Draw two parallel lines with four dashes each. Each team must have at least one boy. As it turns out, this is not a difficult restriction to work with. Reserving a space for a member of one of the groups is common in a double-line diagram. All the rules are depicted in figure 1. A and V are together. The effect of Rule 2 is that B and T are always together, since all eight students are selected. None of the rules provide a fixed anchor. The next challenge is to determine if there are any warranted conclusions that will anchor any of the members. There are no immediately apparent warranted conclusions to be made, so the best thing to do is to quickly move to the questions.

AV
BT
If W 1, then C 2
If D 2, then T 2 (and so is B)

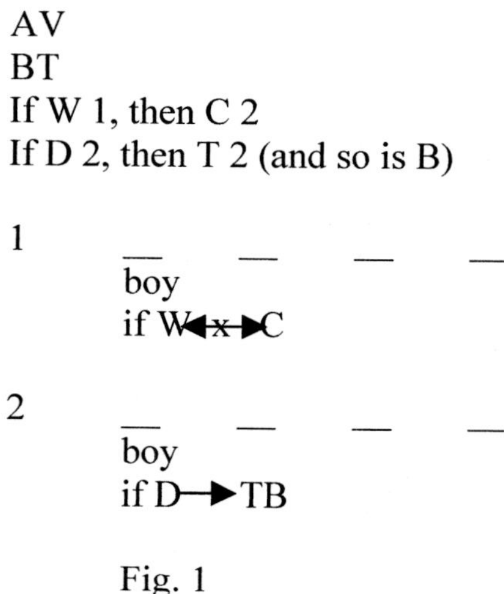

Fig. 1

7. (C) – Use each rule and eliminate the answer choices that violate them until only one choice remains. In this case, however, pay attention to who would remain available to staff Team 2, since that might be where the violation occurs.
   (A) Using Rule 3, since Wendy is on Team 1, Carl must be on Team 2. This choice violates Rule 3.
   (B) Using Rule 4, if Desi is on Team 2, then Tamika must be on Team 2 as well, but in this choice Tamika is on Team 1 and Desi is not, which means that Desi would have to be on Team 2. Rule 4 is violated.
   (C) * Choice (C) is the only choice left and hence the correct answer.
   (D) This choice violates Rule 1.
   (E) This choice violates Rule 1 since it does not show Alan and Val on the same team. It also violates the initial setup by having a team with no boys on it.

8. (A) – Start by looking at the rule that affects Wendy and Carl. If Wendy and Carl are on the same team, then they must be on Team 2, since if Wendy were

on Team 1 then Carl would be on Team 2. Draw this on your diagram. (Figure 2) Next, since Alan and Val must be together, and Ben and Tamika must be together, you have two options. (Figure 3) In both options Desi and Ursula must be on team 1, so (A) is the correct choice. As you will see in question 10, you could not have Alan, Val, Ben and Tamika together on Team 1, since Desi would then be on Team 2, which would require Tamika to be on Team 2 as well.
(A) * See the analysis.
(B) See the analysis.
(C) See the analysis.
(D) See the analysis.
(E) See the analysis.

__	__	__	__
boy			
C	W	__	__
boy			

Fig. 2

Team 1: Ben, Tamika, Desi, Ursula
Team 2: Carl, Wendy, Alan, Val

Team 1: Alan, Val, Desi, Ursula
Team 2: Carl, Wendy, Ben, Tamika

Fig. 3

9. (C) – If Desi is on Team 2, then so must Tamika (Rule 4). Furthermore, once Tamika is on Team 2, then Ben must be as well, because of Rule 2. Since there is now only one space remaining on Team 2, Alan and Val must be on Team 1, since they must be together. Thus, your diagram would look like figure 4. As long as Carl and Wendy are not both on Team 1, any other arrangement is fine, so Carl could be on Team 2, as stated in answer choice (C). All of the wrong answers on this "could be true" question are things that cannot be true.
(A) See the analysis.
(B) See the analysis.
(C) * See the analysis.
(D) See the analysis.
(E) See the analysis.

Team 1: Alan, Val, ?, ?
Team 2: Desi, Ben, Tamika, ?

Fig. 4

10. (A) – As discussed in question 8, Alan and Ben cannot both be on Team 1, since Alan must go with Val, and Ben must go with Tamika, that would complete Team 1, and the remaining members would all have to be on Team 2. This would violate a rule, since Desi would then be on Team 2, but Tamika would not. Thus, (A) cannot be true. When a question that does not add new information (such as this one) appears late in the set, check your previous work to see if some of the answer choices have already been shown to be possible. That way you can quickly eliminate those choices, and you will only need to try the ones that remain. You could have used the work from question 8 to eliminate choices (B)-(E).
(A) * See the analysis.
(B) See the analysis.
(C) See the analysis.
(D) See the analysis.
(E) See the analysis.

11. (B) – The same warranted conclusion is often tested in more than one question. As you have already seen, if Alan is on Team 2, then so is Val. Ben and Tamika have to be on Team 1; if they were with A and V on Team 2, then Wendy and Carl would be together on Team 1, which would violate Rule 4. Once Tamika is on Team 1, then Desi cannot be on Team 2. Desi must be on Team 1, so (B) must be true. (Figure 5) (A), (D), and (E) all could be true, but none of them must be true.
(A) See the analysis.
(B) * See the analysis.
(C) See the analysis.
(D) See the analysis.
(E) See the analysis.

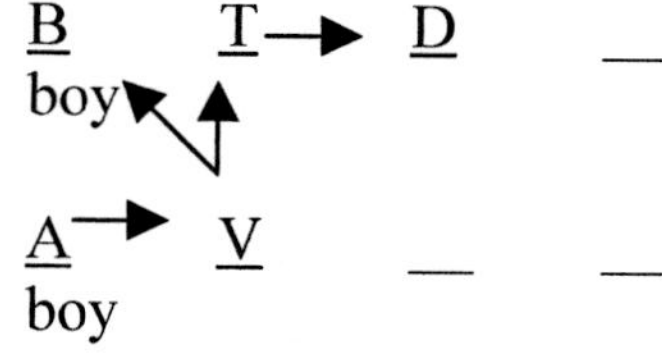

Fig. 5

12. (D) – Although this question suspended one of the rules, this had little practical effect on the diagram. Can you put four girls on Team 2? No. Val must always be with Alan, so the maximum number of girls on Val's team would be three. Since Val and Tamika can never be together, as discussed in

previous questions, the maximum number of girls that could be together on a team is three, answer choice (D). One such possibility is shown in figure 6. When a question asks for the maximum number, normally the correct answer is the second or third highest number. Avoid the highest number and lowest two numbers (0, 1, and 4 in this example), since those are usually wrong.
(A) See the analysis.
(B) See the analysis.
(C) See the analysis.
(D) * See the analysis.
(E) See the analysis.

Team 1: Ben, Tamika, Desi, Carl
Team 2: Alan, Val, Wendy, Ursula

Fig. 6

Tennis Pro

This game requires a matrix or a grid. When the setup discusses days of the week and an AM and PM time slot, a schedule matrix is normally the best diagram. Start with the basic diagram. You need three days and two time slots per day. Note that the days are Monday, Tuesday, and Friday. Because there is a two-day gap, you can be certain that at least one question will concern "consecutive" days or somehow manage to make this gap relevant. Now you are ready for the rules. Rule 1 is not yet graphable, so mark it with a star and move on. Rule 2 is not graphable, so mark it also. Rule 3 can be graphed by showing the days Jones cannot be. Similarly, Rule 4 can be graphed by showing that Mayer cannot be in the afternoon. Rule 5 is not graphable, so mark it. Rule 6 can be graphed by using a line to connect the Monday morning box with the Tuesday afternoon box. (Figure 1) This puzzle is made more difficult because only six of the eight members will be used. (If you did not realize this, the first question alerted you to this fact.) This open-ended situation makes it very unlikely that you can make warranted conclusions. Thus, it is more efficient to go directly to the questions and let them guide you in the right direction. With a complicated game like this, you need to keep track of the rules, especially the several rules that you were not able to diagram.

	Mon	Tue	X	Fri	
AM			X		
PM			X		~~M~~
	~~J~~	~~J~~	X		

Fig. 1

13. (E) – This possible order question is easier to answer than it initially appears. Start with the first rule and work your way down. Rule 1 says that we cannot schedule two novices on the same day, so choice (B) is out. Rule 2 says that if Rose is scheduled then so is Sari, but they cannot be consecutive days, so (C) is out. Rule 3 requires that Jones can only be scheduled on Friday, so (D) is out. Rules 4 and 5 are not violated. Finally, Rule 6 says that the appointments scheduled for Monday morning and Tuesday afternoon must be different types of players, so (A) is out. Choice (E) is the only one left and is thus the correct answer.
(A) See the analysis.
(B) See the analysis.
(C) See the analysis.
(D) See the analysis.
(E) * See the analysis.

14. (B) – Always recheck the rules when a member is mentioned in the question stem. What do you know about Rose? Rule 2 states that if Rose is scheduled for an appointment, then Sari must be scheduled as well, but they cannot be scheduled for consecutive calendar days. Thus, since Rose is scheduled for an appointment on Tuesday, Sari cannot be scheduled for either appointment on

Monday, so (B) cannot be true. When the question asks "All of the following could be true EXCEPT", it is asking for what cannot be true.
(A) See the analysis.
(B) * See the analysis.
(C) See the analysis.
(D) See the analysis.
(E) See the analysis.

15. (E) – Even in a difficult game like this one, it is possible to use the new information in the question and follow a chain of deductions to the correct answer. You are told that Jones is scheduled. What do the rules tell us about Jones? If Jones is scheduled, he is scheduled on Friday. That doesn't seem to help us much. What else do you know about Jones? He is a novice player, and Rule 1 states that you cannot schedule two novice players on the same day, so it cannot be true that a second novice player has a lesson on Friday. Reviewing the setup paragraph, we see that the novices are Kimpton, Levin, and Mayer. Checking the answer choices, we see that Kimpton cannot be scheduled for Friday afternoon, so (E) is correct. Always use the information you are given in question by first looking at those rules that affect the member.
(A) See the analysis.
(B) See the analysis.
(C) See the analysis.
(D) See the analysis.
(E) * See the analysis.

16. (A) – Since we did not make any initial warranted conclusions about what must be true when we created the initial diagram, go back to the rules. All of these answer choices discuss novice or advanced players, so focus on the two rules that effect those groups. The first rule is the vital one. Since you cannot have two novice players scheduled on the same day, and there are only three days of appointments, then you can have a theoretical maximum of three novice players, and thus (A) must be true. If you are uncertain, double-check it by trying to put four novices in the weekly schedule. It does not work. Choice (B) is tricky, because you could have three novice players, but you aren't required to have three. You could have four advanced players and two novices. Again, you should double-check this, because sometimes we overlook things and double-checking can catch any errors.
(A) * See the analysis.
(B) See the analysis. It is possible to have two novice players. (Figure 2)
(C) See the analysis.
(D) See the analysis. See (B).
(E) See the analysis. See (B).

	Mon	Tue	X	Fri	
AM	S	P	X	J	
PM	T	K	X	R	~~M~~
	~~J~~	~~J~~	X		

Fig. 2

17. (E) – If Kimpton is on Tuesday afternoon, there could not be a novice player on Monday morning, according to Rule 6. Thus, Levin would have to be either Monday afternoon or sometime on Friday. Now look at the other rule that affects Levin. Tosca must be scheduled (if at all) after Levin, Rule 5. Either way, the result of Rule 5 is that you could not have Tosca on Monday, if Tosca is scheduled. The fact that the earliest Levin can be scheduled is Monday afternoon means that Tosca cannot be scheduled on Monday morning. (E) is correct.
(A) See the analysis.
(B) See the analysis.
(C) See the analysis.
(D) See the analysis.
(E) * See the analysis.

18. (C) – Just like the previous question, this one focuses on how Rule 5 affects Tosca and Levin. If Tosca were scheduled for Monday morning, then it would be impossible for Tosca to be after Levin. Thus, to avoid violating Rule 5, the tennis pro would not schedule Levin, so (C) must be true. Notice once more that the answer choice associated with Tosca and Levin turned out to be the credited answer. This is typical.
(A) See the analysis. It would be impossible to make a conclusion about Mayer based on the evidence provided.
(B) Kimpton must be scheduled for Tuesday afternoon because novices Levin, Mayer, and Jones are not eligible, yet Tuesday afternoon must contain a novice.
(C) * See the analysis.
(D) Rose and Sari have much the same analysis in this scenario, so whatever is true of one will probably prove true of the other.
(E) See (D). It is common for two answer choices to reflect both aspects of the same issue.

19. (D) – This is a very frustrating question. To make the best of this bad situation, glance at the five answer choices to see if you can identify any "issues." Focus on members that have restrictions. Since Kimpton is a free agent and Mayer is a partially free agent, you can probably safely ignore

answer choice (E). Now work through the choices. For (A), check the rules that affect Levin and Mayer. It does not appear, at least initially, that it will create problems if we schedule both of them. Before spending the time to graph a permutation for (A), check the other choices. Checking (B), it is unlikely that not scheduling Jones will create any problems. As it is, Jones is only allowed on Friday anyway. Checking (C) requires a bit more work. If you remembered from question 18 that Levin is not required, nor is Jones, then you could have eliminated (C). If not, a little analysis will bring you to the same conclusion. Jones can probably be safely left off the schedule, as was decided when working on (B). Can Levin be left off the schedule? This would leave only two novice players, but you determined in question 16 that this is okay. So choice (C) is probably wrong. For choice (D), if you don't schedule Sari, then you can't schedule Rose, so that leaves only two advanced players (and four novices). Since you cannot have two novice players on the same day, it is impossible to have all four of the novice players during the three-day week. So if Sari is not scheduled, then it is impossible to make an acceptable schedule of appointments, and (D) is the credited response. You could have diagrammed out each answer choice to find the correct answer, but that would have wasted a great deal of time. It was more efficient to work through the rules.

(A) See the analysis.
(B) See the analysis.
(C) See the analysis.
(D) * See the analysis.
(E) See the analysis.

Island Bridges

The LSAT doesn't just test lines and groups. Occasionally, a different puzzle type will appear. Map puzzles are one type of rarely tested puzzle. The map concept is not difficult to understand, nor is the diagram difficult to execute. Pay attention to the details and wording of the questions and this puzzle will pose no difficulty at all. A simple, intuitive diagram depicts Rules 1–3, and Rule 4 is easy to remember. (Figure 1)

Fig. 1

20. (D) – K, N, and O are connected, and L, M, and P are connected, but there is, as of yet, no way to travel between both groups of islands. Since you can only visit each island once, a connection between O and P would allow for a continuous trip from, say, M>L>P>O>N>K. Any of the other suggested connections would either require going through an island more than once—(B) and (C)—or they fail to actually connect the two groups—(A) and (E). Thus, (D) is correct.
(A) See the analysis.
(B) See the analysis.
(C) See the analysis.
(D) * See the analysis.
(E) See the analysis.

21. (C) – The initial diagram shows the answer already. The only way in or out of island K is through island N since it is the only island connected to K. Thus, to visit K, one has to go through N to get there, and (C) is correct.
(A) See the analysis.
(B) See the analysis.
(C) * See the analysis.
(D) See the analysis. It is not necessary for a visitor to first visit island O. The visitor could start on island N and go to island K, never visiting island O.
(E) See the analysis.

22. (C) – This question also plays on the number of connections. You have the two groups, each with three islands, and no bridge connecting those groups. So, if no new bridges are added, a visitor could go to a maximum of three islands, answer choice (C).

(A) See the analysis.
(B) See the analysis.
(C) * See the analysis.
(D) See the analysis.
(E) See the analysis.

23. (B) – Adding a bridge between L and N makes a whole new series of possible connections. (A), (C), (D), and (E) would all require a visit to two intermediate islands to reach the destination island, whereas a visitor could now go from M to N with only one stop, on island L, so (B) has the fewest connections.
(A) See the analysis.
(B) * See the analysis.
(C) See the analysis.
(D) See the analysis.
(E) See the analysis.

24. (B) – Looking at the diagram, L is now connected to O, but it is also connected to M and P. If you used the bridge connecting L and O, then you cannot go to both M and P, since that would require two visits to island L. Choice (B) is the credited response.
(A) See the analysis.
(B) * See the analysis.
(C) See the analysis.
(D) See the analysis.
(E) See the analysis.

Practice Test 9

Spend 35 minutes doing this practice test. When time is up, review the explanations to help you understand the questions that you did not answer correctly.

SECTION I

Time—35 minutes

24 Questions

Directions: Each group of questions in this section is based on a set of conditions. In answering some of the questions, it may be useful to draw a rough diagram. Choose the response that most accurately and completely answers each question and blacken the corresponding space on your answer sheet.

Questions 1–6

On the Greenville High School basketball team, there are eight players: Guards—Avery, Boone, and Childs; Forwards—Jackson, Kemper, and Lewis; and Centers—Shultz and Thompson. The Greenville coach must select five of these players to play in a game against a rival team. The selection of players must conform to the following conditions:

No more than two forwards can be selected.
If Avery is selected, then Shultz must be selected.
If Kemper is selected, then Boone is not selected.
Shultz and Thompson cannot both be selected.
Childs cannot be selected unless Jackson is selected.

1. Which one of the following is an acceptable selection of players to play in the game?

(A) Avery, Boone, Jackson, Lewis, Thompson
(B) Boone, Childs, Kemper, Lewis, Shultz
(C) Avery, Boone, Childs, Jackson, Shultz
(D) Avery, Childs, Kemper, Lewis, Shultz
(E) Avery, Jackson, Kemper, Lewis, Shultz

2. Which one of the following CANNOT be true?

(A) Avery is selected.
(B) Boone is selected.
(C) Childs is not selected.
(D) Jackson is not selected.
(E) Thompson is not selected.

3. If Shultz is not selected to play in the game, then which one of the following must be true?

(A) Avery is selected.
(B) Childs is selected.
(C) Kemper is selected.
(D) Lewis is not selected.
(E) Thompson is not selected.

4. Which one of the following could be true of the players selected to play in the game?

(A) Both Avery and Thompson are selected.
(B) Neither Boone nor Childs are selected.
(C) Kemper is the only forward selected.
(D) Both centers are selected.
(E) All of the guards are selected.

5. If Lewis is not selected to play in the game, then how many different combinations of players can the coach select to play in the game?

(A) 1
(B) 2
(C) 3
(D) 4
(E) 5

6. Suppose that the rule that no more than two forwards can be selected to play in the game is suspended. If all of the forwards are selected to play in the game, then the remaining players must include at least one player from which one of the following pairs?

(A) Childs and Schultz
(B) Avery and Boone
(C) Avery and Thompson
(D) Childs and Thompson
(E) Boone and Schultz

GO ON TO THE NEXT PAGE

Questions 7–12

A farmer has made seven jars of preserves and must now place them on a shelf. The spaces on the shelf are numbered from 1 to 7 from left to right. The farmer made the following types of preserves—apple, cherry, date, fig, grape, lychee, and mango. Each type of preserves must be placed in exactly one of the numbered jars according to the following conditions:

The cherry preserves cannot be placed immediately next to the mango preserves.
The fig preserves must be placed to the right of the date preserves.
The lychee preserves must be placed to the left of the apple preserves.
The cherry preserves must be on one of the ends of the shelf.
If the fig preserves are placed in jar 3, then the lychee preserves must be placed in jar 5.

7. Which one of the following is an acceptable assignment of the preserves jars to spaces, from space 1 to 7?

(A) cherry, lychee, apple, mango, fig, date, grape
(B) apple, mango, date, fig, grape, lychee, cherry
(C) cherry, date, fig, grape, mango, lychee, apple
(D) date, lychee, grape, mango, apple, cherry, fig
(E) lychee, mango, grape, date, apple, fig, cherry

8. Which one of the following preserves jars CANNOT be placed in space 7?

(A) apple
(B) cherry
(C) date
(D) fig
(E) grape

9. If the cherry preserves are placed to the left of the lychee preserves and the fig preserves are placed in space 3, then which one of the following could be true?

(A) The grape preserves are placed in space 6.
(B) The apple preserves are placed in space 4.
(C) The mango preserves are placed in space 2.
(D) The date preserves are placed in space 4.
(E) The lychee preserves are placed in space 6.

10. If the mango preserves are placed in space 6, then which one of the following is a complete and accurate list of preserves any one of which could be placed in space 7?

(A) apple, date, grape
(B) apple, cherry, grape
(C) fig, lychee
(D) fig, grape
(E) apple, fig, grape

11. If the cherry preserves must be immediately next to the fig preserves, which one of the following must be true?

(A) The apple preserves are placed in space 5.
(B) The date preserves are placed in space 5.
(C) The grape preserves are placed in space 5.
(D) The lychee preserves are not placed in space 5.
(E) The mango preserves are not placed in space 5.

12. Which one of the following placements of the preserves in the numbered spaces would allow for only one possible assignment of preserves to spaces?

(A) The apple preserves are placed in space 2, and the grape preserves are placed in space 5.
(B) The mango preserves are placed in space 2, and the fig preserves are placed in space 3.
(C) The lychee preserves are placed in space 2, and the date preserves are placed in space 6.
(D) The grape preserves are placed in space 2, and the cherry preserves are placed in space 7.
(E) The date preserves are placed in space 2, and the lychee preserves are placed in space 5.

GO ON TO THE NEXT PAGE.

Questions 13–18

Three couples composed of women and men respectively—Carrie and Bob, Fiona and Greg, and Paula and Quincy—will dine at a new restaurant. The restaurant serves three different categories of food, which include the following items: Salads—house or romaine; Entrées—duck or trout; and Desserts—watermelon or ice cream. A diner may not order more than one item from each category. Each of the diners must order at least one item, and their order must conform to the following conditions:

No couple orders all of the same items.
Greg orders the duck.
If Paula orders an entrée, then she does not order a dessert.
Bob and Quincy both order salads, but not the same salads.
If a diner orders a house salad, then they also order ice cream.

13. Which one of the following is an acceptable assignment of items ordered to diners?

(A) Bob: house salad, ice cream; Carrie: duck; Fiona: romaine salad, duck: Greg: romaine salad, duck; Paula: romaine salad, watermelon; Quincy: romaine salad, duck, watermelon
(B) Bob: house salad, ice cream; Carrie: duck, watermelon; Fiona: house salad, trout, ice cream; Greg: house salad, duck, ice cream; Paula: romaine salad, trout; Quincy: romaine salad, duck
(C) Bob: romaine salad, trout; Carrie: house salad, ice cream; Fiona: house salad, duck; Greg: duck, ice cream; Paula: romaine salad, trout; Quincy: house salad, ice cream
(D) Bob: romaine salad, duck, watermelon; Carrie: romaine salad, trout; Fiona: duck; Greg: duck, ice cream; Paula: duck; Quincy: romaine salad, trout, watermelon
(E) Bob: house salad, trout, ice cream; Carrie: duck; Fiona: romaine salad, duck; Greg: duck, ice cream; Paula: house salad, trout, ice cream; Quincy: romaine salad, duck

14. If Bob orders the romaine salad, then which one of the following must be true?

(A) Carrie orders the trout
(B) Fiona orders the duck
(C) Greg orders the watermelon
(D) Paula orders the ice cream
(E) Quincy orders the ice cream

15. If each of the diners orders a dessert, then each of the following diners could order the duck EXCEPT:

(A) Bob
(B) Carrie
(C) Fiona
(D) Greg
(E) Paula

16. If all of the women order house salads, then the maximum number of people who could order the trout is:

(A) 1
(B) 2
(C) 3
(D) 4
(E) 5

17. If exactly one diner orders ice cream, then which one of the following CANNOT be true?

(A) Bob orders ice cream.
(B) Carrie orders ice cream.
(C) Greg orders watermelon.
(D) Paula orders watermelon.
(E) Quincy orders ice cream

18. If each of the diners orders an entrée, then the minimum number of items ordered is:

(A) 6
(B) 7
(C) 8
(D) 9
(E) 10

GO ON TO THE NEXT PAGE

Questions 19–24

A bank manager must change the four-letter security code of the bank vault every day after the bank closes. The code is set as QRST for the first business day. The same code change cannot be used on consecutive days. Each day after the bank closes the manager must change the code in exactly one of three ways:

Change 1 – Each letter in the code is moved one space to the left, with the far left letter moving to the far right.
Change 2 - The letters Q and T change places, and the letters R and S change places.
Change 3 - The letters Q and R change places, and the letters S and T change places.

19. After one code change, the new code could be:

(A) QSRT
(B) QTSR
(C) TSRQ
(D) RQST
(E) SRQT

20. If on day 3 the code is SRQT, then the manager could have made which of the following two changes?

(A) Change 1 followed by Change 2.
(B) Change 1 followed by Change 3.
(C) Change 2 followed by Change 3.
(D) Change 3 followed by Change 1.
(E) Change 3 followed by Change 2.

21. If the bank manager decides not to use Change 1 at any time, then on day 3 the security code must be:

(A) QSRT
(B) RTSQ
(C) STQR
(D) TQRS
(E) TSRQ

22. How many different codes could there be after two changes have been made?

(A) 1
(B) 2
(C) 3
(D) 4
(E) 5

23. If no change is used twice in a series of three changes, then on day 4 the security code must be:

(A) QRST
(B) QTSR
(C) RSQT
(D) RTSQ
(E) TQRS

24. Suppose that a fifth letter, U, is added to the security code after T in the initial code, but all other conditions remain the same. Which one of the following could be the security code on day 2?

(A) QRSTU
(B) STQRU
(C) URSTQ
(D) RSTUQ
(E) TRSQU

S T O P

IF YOU FINISH BEFORE TIME IS CALLED, YOU MAY CHECK YOUR WORK ON THIS SECTION ONLY.
DO NOT WORK ON ANY OTHER SECTION IN THE TEST.

Answer key and explanations for Test 9

Answer Key

1. C
2. D
3. B
4. E
5. B
6. A
7. E
8. C
9. A
10. E
11. D
12. B
13. B
14. E
15. E
16. D
17. B
18. D
19. C
20. A
21. C
22. C
23. E
24. D

Greenville Basketball

This game requires a classic multi-group selection diagram. There are two varieties of grouping games. In the first variety, you *assign* all of the members to two to four ending groups. In the second variety, like this game, you *select* a few members from each of the starting groups for inclusion in a single ending group. This game is the second variety, because there are three starting groups, from which you must choose some members to fill the ending group. The diagram for this game is fairly simple. List the members of each group on separate lines and use arrows to show the relationships. (Figure 1) Rule 1 limits the ending group to 0, 1, or 2 forwards. You will come back to this rule when it is time to make warranted conclusions. Rule 2 requires a positive one-way arrow from Avery to Schultz. Rule 3 requires a negative two-way arrow between Boone and Kemper. Rule 4 requires a negative two-way arrow between Schultz and Thompson. Rule 5 is subtle. Childs cannot be selected unless Jackson is selected. So a positive one-way arrow must go *from* Childs *to* Jackson. (Figure 1)

Turn your attention to the rules that affect Avery/Schultz and Childs/Jackson. These are one-way arrows. Thus, if Childs is selected, then Jackson must also be selected. But if Jackson is selected, it is not required that Childs be selected. Next, Boone and Kemper are mutually exclusive, as are Schultz and Thompson. Finally, write next to the forwards that 0, 1, or 2 of them can be used. This is an unusual game, since we were able to diagram all the rules.

Once the rules are diagrammed, make conclusions. Let's start with the forwards. We know there cannot be three forwards, per the rules. Can there be zero forwards? If there were no forwards, this would require all three guards (okay, so far) and both centers (this is not allowed). So there must be one or two forwards. You can cross off the zero in the diagram. (Figure 2) Next, must there be zero or one centers? If there were zero centers, then, following the Avery/Schultz arrow, Avery could not be on the team, so the five spaces would have to be filled by the remaining five players, which is not allowed, because Boone and Kemper are mutually exclusive. Thus, there must be one, and only one, center. Note this below the fifth dash. (Figure 2) Let's review the conclusions we have made so far. Schultz or Turner occupies one space; there are one or two forwards, and thus two or three guards. Making these warranted conclusions is vital to organizing the information into a usable format. But just as important as making warranted conclusions is knowing when to stop making conclusions and move on to the questions.

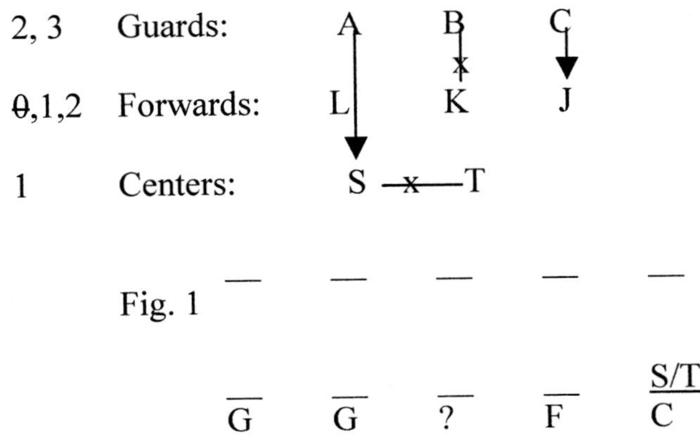

Fig. 1

				S/T
G	G	?	F	C

Fig. 2

1. (C) – With "acceptable arrangement" questions, the wrong answers violate the rules. Typically, each of the four incorrect responses clearly violates exactly one rule. That is, Rule 1 will be violated in only one answer choice, Rule 2 will be violated in only one answer choice, and so on. The best strategy is to start with Rule 1, eliminate the answer choice that violates it, and then proceed down the list of rules until you have thrown out the four incorrect responses. Then only the correct answer remains.
(A) This violates Rule 2, since you have Avery without Shultz.
(B) This violates Rule 3, since you have both Kemper and Boone.
(C) * This is the only choice that works.
(D) Rule 5 is violated since it has Childs without Jackson.
(E) This violates Rule 1 since it has more than two forwards.

2. (D) – This is a typical early question in a logic game, and one that can be very difficult if not approached properly. Fortunately, there are two approaches that would work. First, at the time you made the initial warranted conclusions, you would have seen that certain members cannot be together. You cannot have both Kemper and Boone, and you cannot have both Shultz and Thompson. Since you must get rid of one player from each of those pairs, this leaves only four players. Of those remaining four players, only Jackson must be selected. Jackson must be selected if Childs is selected, and Jackson must be selected if Childs is not selected. (D) is correct, Jackson must be selected. If you failed to use the first approach, there was a second approach, which is actually much easier to use. The second approach requires that you use the correct answer from the question 1 to eliminate choices (A), (B), and (E). In question 1, Avery, Boone, Childs, Jackson, and Schultz was a possible grouping. So in question 2, we know that Avery and Boone can be selected, and that it is possible for Thompson to not be selected. This process of elimination leaves choices (C) and (D). We know that Childs and Jackson can be selected, but we don't yet know which of them must be selected. So try to form teams that don't include them. You can form a team without using Childs. That team would be Avery, Boone, Jackson, Larson, and Schultz. You can't form a team without Jackson.
(A) See the analysis.
(B) See the analysis.
(C) See the analysis.
(D) * See the analysis.
(E) See the analysis.

3. (B) – Hypothetical questions are generally easier than questions that do not provide new information. You know that Shultz is not selected, so start with

him. Based on Rule 2, without Shultz, Avery cannot be selected. This leaves you with six players remaining, but you cannot select all three forwards. So to get the required five players, you must select Boone, Childs, and Thompson plus two of the forwards. Since Boone must be selected, Kemper cannot be, so the team selected to play must be Boone, Childs, Jackson, Lewis, and Thompson. Hence, (B) is the correct response.

(A) See the analysis.
(B) * See the analysis.
(C) See the analysis.
(D) See the analysis.
(E) See the analysis.

4. (E) – Like the second question, you might hold off on this question until after you have completed some easier questions. Perhaps doing one of the other questions will show you that one of these choices could be true. Here, the first four choices all violate the rules in some way, while in (E) you could have all three guards. Once you have Avery, you must have Shultz, and once you have Childs, you must have Jackson; so the team selected to play would be Avery, Boone, Childs, Jackson, and Shultz. This selection does not violate any of the rules, thus, (E) could be true.

(A) This choice runs afoul of Rule 2, because Avery requires Schultz and Schultz is incompatible with Thomas.
(B) The initial analysis revealed that at least two guards are required.
(C) If Kemper is the only forward, then Avery and Childs are required, as is Schultz, but the fifth space cannot be filled.
(D) This violates Rule 4.
(E) * See the analysis. One of the initial conclusions was that up to three guards can be selected.

5. (B) – Remember, information you learn from one question can often be used in other questions. If you answered question 4 correctly, then you know that you could have a team without Lewis that includes Avery, Boone, Childs, Jackson, and Shultz. That is one possibility. Another possibility is that a team could include Kemper instead of Boone, and include the other four players named above. Using the same reasoning as in question 2, including Thompson precludes having Shultz and Avery, and since you cannot have both Kemper and Boone, you would fall short of the five players needed. Thus, if Lewis is not selected, only these two possibilities will work. (B) is correct. The other way to solve this question would have been to solve for all the permutations, which can be time-consuming, although it was not this time, since there were only two permutations.

(A) See the analysis.
(B) * See the analysis.
(C) See the analysis.

(D) See the analysis.
(E) See the analysis.

6. (A) – Even when a question eliminates or suspends one of the rules, it does not create an entirely new game, but you do need to be careful about which initial warranted conclusions you keep and which you discard. All the other rules still apply. So, if you have all three forwards—Jackson, Kemper, and Lewis—then you cannot have Boone, because of Rule 3. While there is no explicit rule that says you *must* select a center, in this case you must because not doing so would mean that the remaining two players would be Avery and Childs, but if Avery is selected you must select Shultz. Thus, you must select one of the two centers. If Thompson is selected, and Shultz is not, then Avery is not selected and Childs must be the fifth player. If Shultz is selected instead of Thompson, then either Avery or Childs could be the fifth player. So the three options to complete the team are Childs and Thompson, Avery and Shultz, or Childs and Shultz. (Figure 3) In these three options, you must have at least either Childs or Shultz.
(A) * See the analysis.
(B) See the analysis.
(C) See the analysis.
(D) See the analysis.
(E) See the analysis.

```
J    L    K  →  __     __
                ~~B~~
                A      S
                A      T- no!
                C      S
                C      T
```

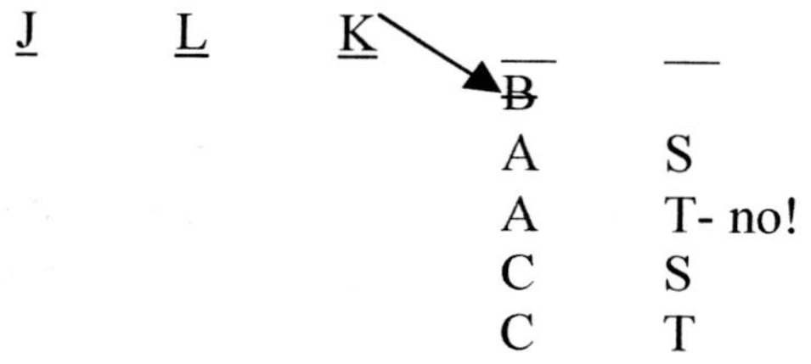

Fig. 3

Farmer's Preserves

Simple line games are the most common puzzle type. You will always see at least one simple-line game on an LSAT. Often there will be two, or maybe even three line games. This preserves game uses a traditional seven-space line. It is very easy to diagram the rules. (Figure 1)

Note the (C) on opposite ends of the line, Rule 4. The parentheses show that the cherry is not fixed in the spaces. The line that connects the two (C)s helps you to keep track of the cherry preserves. Next, note the one-way arrow from (F) under space 3 to (L) under space 5, Rule 2. This reminds us that the fig is not required to be in space 3, but that if it is in space 3, then L must be in space 5. Even if lychee is in space 5, this does not automatically require that fig be in space 3. That is why this is a one-way arrow. Finally, note the three conditions that we could not place on the diagram but that we were able to create shorthand notations for. Although we cannot diagram Rules 2 and 3, we can make a warranted conclusion that F, D, A, and L cannot be in certain spaces. (Figure 1) Beyond this, there are no obvious warranted conclusions, so go directly to the questions.

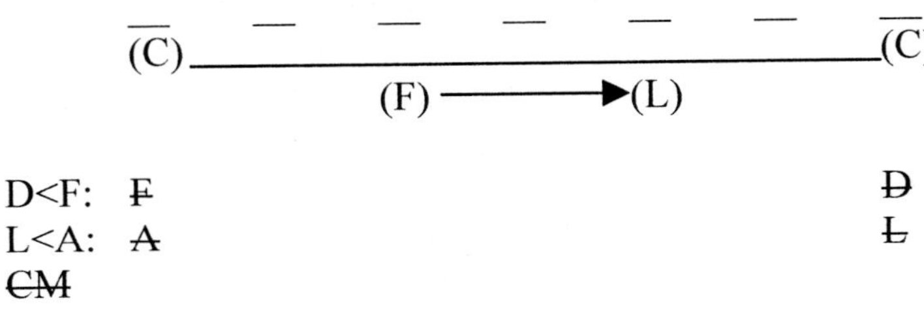

Fig. 1

7. (E) – Use each rule to eliminate the answer choice that violates it. The remaining answer choice is the correct answer. Start with Rule 1 and see if it is violated in any of the answer choices. Work your way down the list of rules until only one choice remains.
   (A) This choice is wrong because is violates Rule 2, since the fig preserves are to the left of the date preserves.
   (B) This violates Rule 3, because the lychee preserves are to the right of the apple preserves.
   (C) Rule 5 is violated; the fig preserves are in space 3 but the lychee preserves are not in space 5.
   (D) This violates Rule 4; the cherry preserves are not on either end of the shelf.
   (E) * This does not violate any of the rules.

8. (C) – If you did the initial analysis properly, then you already have the answer to this question. Simply consult figure 1. If you did not, this question might appear difficult, but it was actually quite simple. What would preclude one of the preserves from being placed in space 7? If it is one of the preserves that

must be to the left of another preserve. Both the date and lychee preserves fit this criterion, so (C) is the correct response.
(A) See the analysis.
(B) See the analysis.
(C) * See the analysis.
(D) See the analysis.
(E) See the analysis. Note, the grapes are a free agent, so that makes this a very unlikely answer choice.

9. (A) – When a question stem gives you two pieces of information, often the second piece is more helpful. Here, since the cherry preserves are to the left of the lychee preserves, you can quickly deduce that the cherry preserves are in space 1. That doesn't tell you much about the rest of the jars. Consult figure 2 as you follow along with the rules. The second piece of information is that the fig preserves are in space 3, so Rule 5 kicks in—the lychee preserves must be in space 5. Also, because of Rule 2, the date preserves must be in space 2. Right away that eliminates choices (D) and (E). Also, since the apple preserves are to the right of the lychee preserves, (B) cannot be true. And since you know that the date preserves are in space 2, choice (C) (mango preserves in space 2) cannot be true. On this question, there is no restriction that prevents the grape preserves from being in space 6, so (A) is correct.
(A) * See the analysis. Always be aware of what members are free agents.
(B) See the analysis.
(C) See the analysis.
(D) See the analysis.
(E) See the analysis.

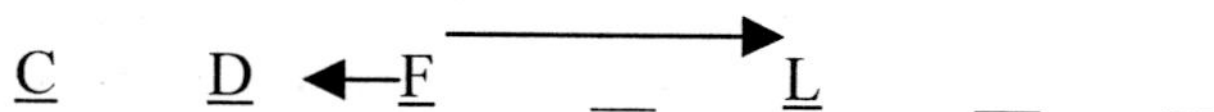

Fig. 2

10. (E) – With the mango preserves in space 6, the cherry preserves must now be in space 1, since they cannot be next to the mango preserves. That eliminates answer choice (B). You learned in the initial analysis and in the second question that neither the date nor the lychee can be in space 7. Often the deductions made for early questions can be very useful for later questions. Eliminate answer choices (A) and (C). Of the remaining three types of preserves, any of them could be in space 7. Note that the question asks for a *complete* and accurate list. In answer choice (D), either the fig or grape preserves could be in jar 7, but so could the apple preserves, so (E) is the credited answer.
(A) See the analysis.

(B) See the analysis.
(C) See the analysis.
(D) See the analysis.
(E) * See the analysis.

Fig. 3

11. (D) – If the cherry preserves must be next to the fig preserves, then they must be in spaces 7 and 6 respectively, since the cherry preserves must be on one of the ends of the shelf and the fig preserves must be somewhere to the right of the date preserves, Rule 2. If you tried to put the cherry preserves in space 1 and the fig preserves in space 2, there would be nowhere to put the date preserves to the left of the fig preserves. Review the rules to find one that is relevant. Rules 1 and 2 are no longer relevant, because they cannot possibly be violated anymore. Rule 3 can be violated. Any of the remaining preserves may or may not be in space 5, except the lychee preserves, since they must be to the left of the apple preserves. The only choice that *must* be true is (D), the lychee preserves are not in jar 5.
(A) See the analysis.
(B) See the analysis.
(C) See the analysis.
(D) * See the analysis.
(E) See the analysis.

12. (B) – You certainly could solve this question by trying every answer choice to see which one works. But the smarter method is to look for the answer choice that seems to most limit the possibilities. It is the one that is most likely to result in a single permutation. There are no rules regarding the grape preserves, so (A) and (D) are unlikely to be correct, though you may still need to check them. But do so later, and only if necessary. Furthermore, placing the lychee and date preserves means that the apple and the fig preserves respectively must be somewhere to their right, but we don't know exactly where, so (C) and (E) are probably not right, although they could be. (B) should be tempting because it provides some significant limitations. Once the mango preserves are in space 2, then the cherry preserves must be in space 7 (since they cannot be next to the mango yet must be on one end of the shelf). Also, once the fig preserves are in space 3, then the lychee preserves must be in space 5 (Rule 5) and the date preserves must be in space 1, since they must be to the left of the fig preserves. Finally, since the apple preserves must be to the right of the lychee preserves, they must be in space 6, and the only

remaining space for the grape preserves is space 4. (B) is the correct response.

(A) See the analysis.
(B) * See the analysis.
(C) See the analysis.
(D) See the analysis.
(E) See the analysis.

Couples Dining

This puzzle requires a matrix diagram. Matrix puzzles are much less common than they once were. Typically, a matrix game will be a schedule matrix. In the schedule matrix, there will be three to five days, each with a morning and an afternoon time slot. However, this game requires a plain matrix. This plain matrix is a grid with people's names on one axis and the types of food on the other axis. The diagram for this game is quite elaborate. Rule 1 is confusing, so leave it alone for now. Rule 2 is easy, Greg orders duck. Rule 3 is easy; make a two-way negative arrow in Paula's column. Rule 4 is not too hard to diagram. Connecting the two relevant boxes with a line will remind you that Bob and Quincy order salads, but different salads. You can diagram Rule 5 in much the same way, connecting salads and desserts and including a short explanatory note. (Figure 1)

Greg orders duck, so he will not also order the trout. There are two ambiguities that you need to clarify before moving on. The setup says that each diner orders at least one item. Does this mean that they order at least one item from each of the three categories, or at least one item total? When the language of the setup leaves you wondering, feel free to check the answer choices. The first question usually asks about possible orders, so you can review those answer choices. Doing so reveals that some people order only one or two items. This clears up that ambiguity. The second ambiguity results from Rule 1. It says that no couples order all of the same items. Does this mean that if Bob orders romaine salad and watermelon that Carrie cannot order trout and watermelon? No. Reviewing the answer choices again, we learn that Carrie cannot also order romaine salad and watermelon, nor can she order romaine salad, watermelon, and trout. The moral of the story is that sometimes a rule is ambiguous. When it is, look to the answer choices for guidance.

Now that those ambiguities are cleared up, are there any warranted conclusions to make? The diagram is still quite empty, which makes it less likely that you can make warranted conclusions. Since there are no obvious warranted conclusions yet, go directly to the questions.

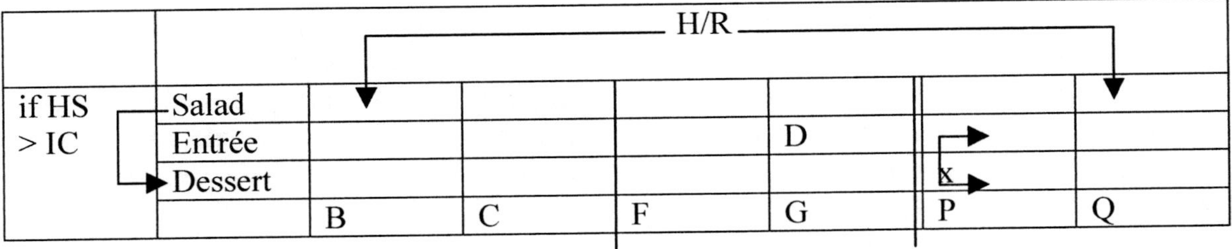

Fig. 1

13. (B) – This "possible order" question is no different from any other. Start with the first rule and work your way down. Regarding ambiguous language, sometimes a rule is unclear, as was the case with Rule 1. The ambiguity is resolved once you review the answer choices, so never let ambiguous language stop you, keep moving forward to resolve the ambiguity.
(A) Rule 1 is violated, because Fiona and Greg order the exact same items.

(B) * This does not violate any rules.
(C) Rule 5 is violated, because Fiona orders the house salad but does not order the ice cream.
(D) Rule 4 is violated, because Bob and Quincy both order the romaine salad.
(E) Rule 3 is violated, because Paula has both an entrée and a dessert.

14. (E) – What do you know about Bob? You know that both he and Quincy order salads, but not the same kind. Thus, if Bob orders the romaine salad, then Quincy must order the house salad, and due to Rule 5, Quincy must also order ice cream. So (E) is correct. This is classic deductive reasoning. The hypothetical information (if Bob orders the romaine salad) allows you to deduce a new fact (that Quincy orders the house salad), which in turn allows you to deduce a second fact (that Quincy orders ice cream). If you ever get stuck on a question in logic games, ask yourself if you have missed a deductive step or two.
(A) There is no way to know if Carrie orders an entrée or not.
(B) There is no way to know if Fiona orders an entrée or not.
(C) There is no way to know if Greg orders a romaine salad, in which case he could order (but would not be obligated to order) watermelon.
(D) There is no way to know if Paula orders a dessert or not.
(E) * Because Quincy orders a house salad, he must order ice cream.

15. (E) – This is a classic example of the contrapositive, a negative two-way arrow. When you have an if-then rule like the one affecting Paula, reverse and negate the terms to form the contrapositive, which must also be true. The original rule is: if Paula orders an entrée, then she does not order a dessert. When you reverse and negate the terms you get: if Paula orders a dessert, then she does not order an entrée. Here, since all of the diners order dessert, Paula also orders dessert; thus, from the contrapositive, she does not order an entrée. Thus, Paula cannot order the duck (or trout), and (E) is the credited answer. If you created a good diagram, you would have seen the arrow in the Paula column that connects the desserts and the entrees, and you would have known to focus on Paula. Use your diagram, that is why you go to the trouble of making it.
(A) See the analysis.
(B) See the analysis.
(C) See the analysis.
(D) See the analysis. Rule 2 stated that Greg must order duck.
(E) * See the analysis.

16. (D) – If all of the women order house salads, then they also order ice cream, by virtue of Rule 5. By the same reasoning used in the previous question, Paula then cannot order an entrée. You also know from Rule 2 that Greg

orders the duck, not the trout. Hence, the maximum number of diners who could order the trout is four, that is, everyone except Paula and Greg. The only remaining rule to watch out for is that no couple orders exactly the same items, but as long as Bob orders a romaine salad instead of the house salad that Carrie orders, that rule will not be triggered.

(A) See the analysis.
(B) See the analysis.
(C) See the analysis.
(D) * See the analysis.
(E) See the analysis.

17. (B) – What do the rules say about ice cream? Rule 4 states that anyone who orders the house salad also orders ice cream. Both Bob and Quincy order salads, but not the same kind; one of them orders the house salad and one of them orders the romaine salad. Since only one person orders ice cream in this question, it must be either Bob or Quincy, whichever one orders the house salad. So only one house salad and one ice cream are ordered, they are ordered by the same person, and that person must be Bob and Quincy. Thus, either (A) or (E) could be true, but Carrie definitely cannot order the single ice cream, thus (B) is the credited choice.

(A) See the analysis.
(B) * See the analysis.
(C) We don't know anything about who orders watermelon.
(D) We don't know anything about who orders watermelon.
(E) See the analysis.

18. (D) – With maximum and minimum questions, start with either the smallest number and work your way up (with a minimum question) or start with the largest number and work your way down (with a maximum question). Each diner will order an entrée. That equals six items. Is anyone required to order something else besides an entrée? Yes, Bob and Quincy both must order salads, so now there are eight items and you can eliminate choices (A) and (B). Finally, when either Bob or Quincy orders the house salad he must also order ice cream. That is now nine items. Eliminate answer choice (C). There are no other rules that require one of the diners to order anything else, so nine is the minimum number of items ordered.

(A) See the analysis.
(B) See the analysis.
(C) See the analysis.
(D) * See the analysis.
(E) See the analysis.

Vault combinations

This game may seem strange, and it is. Once in a very rare while, one of the four games is an oddball game that is not one of the common types. Although these games look unusual, the same strategy is required. That is, apply the rules, make conclusions, and everything will work out.

What are the chances you will see this exact kind of multiple rounds game on your test? The chances are very slim. Even so, it helps to be exposed to all the possibilities. The dilemma with multiple rounds game is always, should you do the permutations, or not? To help you decide, look at the questions. Most of these questions focus on day 3. So the smartest thing to do is to create series, starting on day 1 with QRST, and then changing this twice to reach day 3, using all the possible combinations of changes. See figure 1 for a partial example. Now you have all the information about days 2 and 3. When a question asks about day 4, you can do the necessary work at that point. Be very careful of the wording of the questions. Some questions ask about what the code must be during the day, while others ask about what the code change must be after the bank closes. Just be very careful so you don't misread the question.

Day 1 start- QRST
Day 2 #1- RSTQ
Day 3 #2- SRQT

QRST	QRST	QRST	QRST	QRST
#1- RSTQ	#2- TSRQ	#2- TSRQ	#3- RQST	#3- RQTS
#3- QTSR	#1- SRQT	#3- STQR	#1- QTSR	#2- STQR

Fig. 1

19. (C) – You are told that the bank security code begins as QRST on the first day, so after one change there are three possibilities: if change 1 is used, the code would be RSTQ, if change 2 is used the code would be TSRQ, and if change 3 is used the code would be RQTS. (Figure 2) The only one of these possibilities that appears in the answer choices is TSRQ.
(A) See the analysis.
(B) See the analysis.
(C) * See the analysis.
(D) See the analysis.
(E) See the analysis.

	QRST		QRST		QRST
Change: #1-	RSTQ	#2-	TSRQ	#3-	RQTS

Fig. 2

20. (A) – This question asks you to work backwards. Multiple rounds games always have questions that ask you to work backwards. That is why solving for the permutations at the beginning can save time. If you do have to work backwards, how should you do it? It is frustrating to learn how to do it under timed conditions, so learn now. You know the code on day 3 and you must determine how the code could have gotten there from QRST. There were two changes. Start by trying change 1, which yields RSTQ. Now do change 2, which yields SRQT. Change 1 followed by change 2 gives you the code from the question stem, so (A) is correct. Notice that if you did change 2 first you would have TSRQ, and if you then did change 1 you would have SRQT, the same code from the question stem. This was a key deduction for this game—it doesn't matter what order you do two changes; they end up yielding the same result. Remember this conclusion, it will prove useful in later questions.
(A) * See the analysis.
(B) See the analysis.
(C) See the analysis.
(D) See the analysis.
(E) See the analysis.

21. (C) – Since change 1 is not used, the only way to get to day 3 is to use change 2 and change 3 (or change 3 and change 2). Starting with QRST and remembering that the order of the changes doesn't matter (the helpful deduction from the previous question), use change 2 first (TSRQ) and change 3 second (STQR), and you get answer choice (C). Again, if you did change 3 first (RQTS) and change 2 second (STQR), you would get the same answer.
(A) See the analysis.
(B) See the analysis.
(C) * See the analysis.
(D) See the analysis.
(E) See the analysis.

22. (C) – This is a perfect example where making the big deduction early on pays off. In all logic games, there are certain warranted conclusions that can be deduced. Here, it was the deduction that the order of the changes doesn't matter—when you use the same two changes in either order you get the same result. If you didn't make this deduction, you may have thought there were six possibilities for reaching day 3: 1+2, 1+3, 2+1, 2+3, 3+1, and 3+2. However, since the order the changes are done doesn't matter, there are only three possible ways to reach day 3: 1+2, 1+3, and 2+3. Choice (C) is the credited answer. Or, if you had done all the permutations at the outset, this question would have been even easier to answer, just look at the permutations.
(A) See the analysis.
(B) See the analysis.
(C) * See the analysis.

(D) See the analysis.
(E) See the analysis.

23. (E) – Some logic games are one-trick ponies that continually test your understanding of the same deduction. That is the case here. If no change is used twice, then on day 4 you must have used change 1 once, change 2 once, and change 3 once. Again, the order the changes are doesn't matter to the final result; start with change 1 (RSTQ), then do change 2 (SRQT), then do change 3 (TQRS), and you will finish with the correct response, choice (E).
(A) See the analysis.
(B) See the analysis.
(C) See the analysis.
(D) See the analysis.
(E) * See the analysis.

24. (D) – Don't panic when a new rule or member is added. Just do what you've done in the rest of the game and incorporate the new member. Here, if U is added after T in the initial code, then it would be QRSTU. Changes 2 and 3 will not affect, or move, U. Change 1 moves *all* the letters one space to the left and takes the far left letter to the far right. That would make the code RSTUQ, answer choice (D).
(A) See the analysis. This choice shows no change at all.
(B) See the analysis. This choice would have Q and S swap and R and T swap. None of the three changes do this.
(C) See the analysis. This choice would have U and Q swap and no others.
(D) * See the analysis.
(E) See the analysis. This choice would have Q and T swap, but not R and S.

Practice Test 10

Spend 35 minutes doing this practice test. When time is up, review the explanations to help you understand the questions that you did not answer correctly.

SECTION I

Time—35 minutes

23 Questions

Directions: Each group of questions in this section is based on a set of conditions. In answering some of the questions, it may be useful to draw a rough diagram. Choose the response that most accurately and completely answers each question and blacken the corresponding space on your answer sheet.

Questions 1–5

During a tax year, the county of Oakridge raises revenue through property taxes on buildings located in at least one of the following special taxing districts—A, B, C, E, J, and R. Buildings may be located in more than one taxing district. The following conditions apply to the location of the taxing districts:

No building that is located in district B is also in district A.

At least some buildings that are located in district E are also located in district B.

All buildings that are located in district C are also located in district B.

If a building is located in district A, then it is also located in district J.

1. Each of the following could be true EXCEPT:

(A) At least one building in district R is also in districts A and E.
(B) At least one building in district A is also in district C.
(C) At least one building in district J is in district R.
(D) All buildings in district C are also in district E.
(E) All buildings in district E are also in district J.

2. If during a tax year a building is located in district E, then each of the following is a complete and accurate list of the other districts that the building could also be located in EXCEPT:

(A) A, R
(B) B, C, R
(C) A, J, R
(D) B, C, J
(E) B, C, J, R

3. If a building is not located in district B during the tax year, then which one of the following districts could it be located in during the tax year?

(A) A and C
(B) C and E
(C) A and R
(D) E, J, and R
(E) A, E, and R

4. If a building is located in district A, what is the maximum number of districts the building could be located in?

(A) two
(B) three
(C) four
(D) five
(E) six

5. If all buildings in district C are also in district R, which one of the following must be true?

(A) No building in district A is also in district R.
(B) No building in district E is also in district R.
(C) Some buildings in district B are also in district R.
(D) Some buildings in district E are also in district R.
(E) Some buildings in district A are also in district R.

GO ON TO THE NEXT PAGE

Questions 6–11

Twelve tons of metal alloys must be shipped from the foundry to a factory in exactly four shipments. There are two tons of duralium, two tons of magnalium, four tons of pewter, and four tons of steel to be shipped. Each metal alloy is shipped in exactly one-, two-, three-, or four-ton units. The composition of the shipments must satisfy the following conditions:

Each of the four shipments must have exactly two, four, or six tons of alloy.
If a shipment contains at least one ton of magnalium, then it must contain at least one ton of pewter.
If a shipment contains at least one ton of duralium, then it must contain at least one ton of steel.
The first and fourth shipments contain no pewter.

6. Which one of the following could be an accurate list of the alloys shipped in shipments 1 and 2?

(A) Shipment 1: one ton duralium, one ton steel
Shipment 2: one ton duralium, one ton magnalium, one ton steel
(B) Shipment 1: two tons steel
Shipment 2: one ton magnalium, one ton pewter
(C) Shipment 1: one ton magnalium, one ton pewter, one ton steel
Shipment 2: one ton magnalium, one ton pewter
(D) Shipment 1: two tons steel
Shipment 2: one ton magnalium, one ton pewter, two tons steel
(E) Shipment 1: one ton duralium
Shipment 2: one ton magnalium, three tons pewter

7. If there is exactly one ton of duralium in shipment 4, then which one of the following must be true?

(A) There is exactly one ton of duralium in shipment 1.
(B) There are exactly two tons of pewter in shipment 3.
(C) There is at least one ton of magnalium in shipment 2.
(D) There are exactly two tons of steel in shipment 1.
(E) There is at least one ton of steel in shipment 1.

8. If exactly two tons of pewter are in shipment 3, then which one of the following must be true?

(A) There is no duralium in shipment 2 and two tons of steel in shipment 2.
(B) There is no magnalium in shipment 2 and no duralium in shipment 2.
(C) There is one ton of duralium in shipment 1.
(D) There are two tons of pewter in shipment 2.
(E) There are two tons of magnalium in shipment 3.

9. If the number of tons of duralium in shipment 2 is equal to the number of tons of magnalium in shipment 2, then which one of the following must be true?

(A) There is no steel in shipment 3.
(B) There is one ton of duralium in shipment 1
(C) There are three tons of pewter in shipment 3.
(D) There are two tons of steel in shipment 1.
(E) There are two tons of magnalium in shipment 2.

10. If shipment 3 contains exactly two tons of alloy, then which one of the following must be true?

(A) There is at least one ton of steel in shipment 3.
(B) There is at least one ton of duralium in shipment 4
(C) There is at least one ton of pewter in shipment 3.
(D) There is at least one ton of magnalium in shipment 2.
(E) There is at least one ton of steel in shipment 2.

11. What is the minimum and maximum number of shipments that must contain at least one ton of steel?

(A) 0 and 3
(B) 1 and 3
(C) 2 and 3
(D) 1 and 4
(E) 2 and 4

GO ON TO THE NEXT PAGE.

Questions 12-17

Students in the History class are required to meet with the teaching assistant once per semester. The teaching assistant offers meeting times on one day: one meeting time in the morning, one in the afternoon, and one in the evening. The students in the History class this semester are Frank, Gina, Harry, Jon, Kaspar, Leon, Marc, and Nino. The meetings with the teaching assistant must conform to the following conditions:

The teaching assistant will not meet with only one student at a time.
The teaching assistant must meet with at least one student in each of the available meeting times.
Frank and Jon cannot attend the same meeting.
Kaspar and Marc cannot attend the same meeting.
If Gina attends the morning meeting, then Kaspar must attend the evening meeting.
If Jon attends the afternoon meeting, then Harry must attend the afternoon meeting.
The number of students who meet in the morning must be the same as the number of students who meet in the evening.

12. Which one of the following is an acceptable arrangement of student meetings?

(A) Morning: Frank, Gina, Nino; Afternoon: Harry, Jon; Evening: Kaspar, Leon, Marc
(B) Morning: Jon; Afternoon: Frank, Gina, Harry, Leon, Marc, Nino; Evening: Kaspar
(C) Morning: Gina, Marc; Afternoon: Harry, Jon, Leon, Nino; Evening: Frank, Kaspar
(D) Morning: Harry, Leon, Nino; Afternoon: Frank, Gina, Kaspar; Evening: Jon, Marc
(E) Morning: Frank, Gina, Harry; Afternoon: Jon, Marc; Evening: Kaspar, Leon, Nino

13. If Jon and Kaspar meet the assistant in the afternoon, then which one of the following must be true?
(A) Frank attends the morning meeting.
(B) Marc attends the afternoon meeting.
(C) Leon attends the afternoon meeting.
(D) Exactly three people attend the morning meeting.
(E) Exactly four people attend the afternoon meeting.

14. If Gina meets the assistant in the morning and Leon and Nino meet the assistant in the evening, then how many different possible combinations of meetings could there be in the afternoon?

(A) 2
(B) 3
(C) 4
(D) 5
(E) 6

15. If Harry and Frank both meet the assistant in the morning, then which one of the following must be true?

(A) Jon meets in the evening.
(B) Kaspar meets in the morning.
(C) Leon meets in the morning.
(D) Marc meets in the afternoon.
(E) Nino meets in the afternoon.

16. If Gina and Leon are the only students who meet in the morning, then which one of the following CANNOT be true?

(A) Frank meets in the evening.
(B) Harry meets in the afternoon.
(C) Jon meets in the afternoon.
(D) Nino meets in the evening.
(E) Marc meets in the afternoon.

17. Suppose that the teaching assistant changes the conditions to allow for meeting with only one student in a given meeting. If all of the other conditions remain the same, what is the maximum number of students who could meet in the afternoon?

(A) 4
(B) 5
(C) 6
(D) 7
(E) 8

GO ON TO THE NEXT PAGE.

Questions 18-23

A car dealer has seven luxury cars in the showroom: a Bowie, a Faeri, a Jalar, a Le, a Mearcint, a Porti, and a Volant. The dealer must place the cars in one of seven showroom spaces that are numbered one to seven from left to right. Each showroom space must be filled with exactly one car. The following conditions apply to the placement of the cars in the showroom:

The Jalar must not be placed in a space adjacent to the Le.

The Bowie must be placed in a space adjacent to the Volant.

The Faeri must be placed in the first or the last space.

If the Mearcint is placed in the third space, then the Le must be placed in the fifth space.

18. Which one of the following is an acceptable placement of the cars in the showroom spaces from one to seven?

(A) Bowie, Volant, Mearcint, Jalar, Le, Porti, Faeri
(B) Faeri, Jalar, Mearcint, Porti, Le, Bowie, Volant
(C) Jalar, Faeri, Porti, Le, Volant, Bowie, Mearcint
(D) Faeri, Bowie, Mearcint, Porti, Le, Volant, Jalar
(E) Porti, Jalar, Mearcint, Volant, Bowie, Le, Faeri

19. If the Le is placed in space seven, then which one of the following must be false?

(A) The Faeri is in space one.
(B) The Bowie is in space two.
(C) The Jalar is in space three.
(D) The Mearcint is in space three.
(E) The Volant is in space two.

20. If the Jalar is placed in space one, then which one of the following must be true?

(A) The Bowie is in space two.
(B) The Faeri is in space six.
(C) The Mearcint is not in space three.
(D) The Porti is not in space five.
(E) The Volant is not in space six.

21. If the Faeri is in space one and the Mearcint is in space three, then which one of the following could be false?

(A) The Jalar is in space two.
(B) The Porti is in space four.
(C) The Mearcint and the Volant are not in adjacent spaces.
(D) The Bowie is in space six.
(E) The Faeri and the Porti are not in adjacent spaces.

22. If the Volant is in space seven, then which one of the following is a complete and accurate list of cars, any one of which could be in space four?

(A) Jalar, Le
(B) Le, Mearcint
(C) Jalar, Le, Mearcint
(D) Le, Mearcint, Porti
(E) Jalar, Le, Mearcint, Porti

23. If the car dealer wants to place the Faeri and the Porti as far apart as possible on the showroom floor, and then place the Jalar and Le as far apart as possible on the remaining spaces on the showroom floor, then which one of the following must be true?

(A) The Mearcint is in space five.
(B) The Jalar is in space two.
(C) The Faeri is adjacent to the Jalar.
(D) The Le is adjacent to the Porti.
(E) The Mearcint is adjacent to the Volant.

S T O P

IF YOU FINISH BEFORE TIME IS CALLED, YOU MAY CHECK YOUR WORK ON THIS SECTION ONLY. DO NOT WORK ON ANY OTHER SECTION IN THE TEST.

Answer key and explanations for Test 10

Answer Key

1. B
2. A
3. D
4. C
5. C
6. B
7. E
8. D
9. A
10. D
11. E
12. C
13. E
14. B
15. A
16. D
17. C
18. B
19. D
20. C
21. D
22. E
23. A

Taxing districts

Most games require one of the common diagrams, whether a simple line or a multiple line. Some games require a rare diagram, like a matrix or a grouping diagram. Occasionally, a game is completely different. This is one of those games. As always, you want a diagram that organizes the information. Most of the rules in this game are very normal grouping rules. But Rule 2 is atypical. It says that some buildings in district E are also in district B. We do not have a diagramming tool that can capture this, so put an asterisk next to E, and an arrow connecting E to B. The grouping diagram is helpful, but a visual aid would be nice too. With atypical puzzles like this, you must be creative. The easiest way to visualize these rules is to use a series of overlapping circles or boxes. This is called a Venn diagram. (Figure 1) The difficulty with, and the inherent weakness of, Venn diagrams is that it is easy to create a diagram that is valid but omits important information or creates the wrong impression. For example, the Venn diagram below shows that districts J and E are separate, but in fact, there is no reason that J and E can't overlap. Overall, the usefulness of a Venn diagram is debatable. For example, in the diagram below, R does not overlap with any other district. But the rules leave open three possibilities: that R does not overlap any other district; that it overlaps all of the other districts; or something in between. The same is true of J and E. Note that B and A have no buildings in common. Also, C, because it is a subset of B, also cannot overlap with A. Another thing to watch out for is that E may or may not overlap with some or all of C. Do not rely on the Venn diagram too much, since it will lead you astray if you do not double-check the rules when selecting an answer.

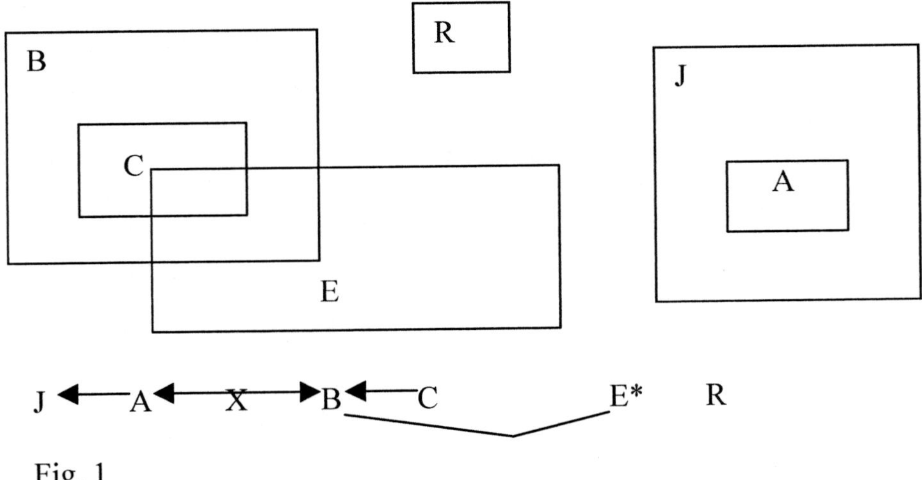

Fig. 1

1. (B) – Use the visual aid and the list of rules to narrow choices. Since R is a free agent, R will not be the correct answer in an EXCEPT question.
   (A) It could be true that a building in R is also in A and E. R is a free agent.
   (B) * It is not possible for a building to be in A and C, since no building in A can be in B, and all buildings in C are in B.
   (C) It could be true that there is one building in J that is also in R. R is a free agent.

(D) It is possible that all the buildings in C are also in E.
(E) It is possible that all the buildings in E are also in J.

2. (A) – Four of the answer choices are lists of districts that the building can be in. The other answer choice is not a listing of the districts that the building can be in. What do you know about district E? You know that district E shares at least one building with district B. Let's name that building "x". Building x could be in district B, but it is not required to be. Actually, building x could be in any of the other districts, or none at all. Shift your focus. What *combination* of districts could building x not be in during one tax year? It could not be in both B and A during the same year. It could not be in both C and A during the same year. Unfortunately, none of the answer choices contain A and C or A and B. You will need to try harder. Rule 4 requires that when a building is in district A, it must also always be in district J. Answer choice (A) shows district A but not district J, so choice (A) is not possible, and so is the credited answer choice. The other four choices are possible.
(A) * See the analysis.
(B) See the analysis.
(C) See the analysis.
(D) See the analysis.
(E) See the analysis.

3. (D) – When a building is not in B, it cannot be in C. This should be sufficient analysis to begin answering this question. Eliminate choices that contain district C. We can eliminate choices (A) and (B). Now, do more analysis. You notice that the three remaining choices all contain R, so there is no need to check for R. For choice (C) and (E), the building must be in J if it is in A.
(A) See the analysis.
(B) See the analysis.
(C) If the building is in district A, then it must also be in district J.
(D) * This is possible.
(E) See (C).

4. (C) – When a building is in district A, it must be in J and it cannot be in C or B. So, A, J, R, and E equals four districts as a maximum.
(A) See the analysis. For a maximum question, the lowest number is never the credited answer.
(B) See the analysis.
(C) * Correct.
(D) See the analysis.
(E) See the analysis. For a maximum question, the highest number is not usually the credited answer.

5. (C) – When a building is in C, it is also in B. Thus, these buildings are in C, B, and R. They may be in J or E. They cannot be in A. This question uses some tricky language in the answer choices to make them challenging.

(A) A building could still be in A and R; this would not be affected by the fact that all buildings in C are also in R.

(B) It is possible that there are no buildings that are in E and R. Remember, there is no requirement that a building in C be in E also.

(C) * This must be true. At least some buildings in B (at least those that are also in C) must be in R.

(D) See (B).

(E) It is possible that some buildings in A are also in R. The new information was that all buildings in C are in R, not that all buildings in R are in C.

Alloy shipments

This game requires a matrix diagram. As often happens with matrix diagrams, the questions focus on the occupancy of each of the columns and rows. With each question, pay close attention to the minimum and maximum number of tons. This matrix is a straightforward four-by-four grid. The alloy names are on the y-axis and the shipment numbers are on the x-axis. Next to each of the alloys, write the number of tons they have. (Figure 1) Rules 2 and 3 are one-way arrows, if there is a D, then there is an S, etc. Rule 4 is important. Since shipments 1 and 4 contain no pewter, you should have concluded (using Rule 2) that they also contain no magnalium. Rule 1 tells you that there are two, four, or six tons in each shipment. You can either mark this on the grid or try to remember it. You must allocate the twelve tons over exactly four shipments. How could this be done? Could you ship two, two, two, and six (not necessarily in that order)? It is mathematically possible to have three shipments of two tons each and one shipment of six tons. It is also possible to have two, two, four, and four (not necessarily in that order). There are many possible permutations, so don't waste time doing them, instead, go to the questions. But remember, if you have one shipment with four tons, then there will be a second shipment of four tons, and two shipments of two tons each.

	1	2	3	4	2/4/6 tons each ship.
D =2					
M =2	XX			XX	
P =4	XX			XX	
S =4					

Fig. 1

6. (B) – Use each of the rules to eliminate the answer choice that violates it. The remaining answer choice is the correct answer.
   (A) This choice is wrong because it violates Rule 1, since it has three tons in shipment 2.
   (B) * This does not violate any rules.
   (C) This violates the warranted conclusion from Rule 2, because it has M in shipment 1.
   (D) This is not a valid choice, because if you use all four tons of S in shipment 1 and 2, then there is none left for shipment 4, yet shipment 4 needs at least some D and some S.
   (E) This violates Rule 2, because it has D without S. It also violates Rule 1, because it only has one ton in shipment 1, not two tons.

7. (E) – If there is one ton of D in shipment 4, then there must be at least one ton of S in shipment 4 (Figure 2a) or three tons of S in shipment 4 (Figure 2b). There cannot be two tons of S. You don't know anything for certain as to how much M and P are in 2 and 3. You do know that you need to have at

least one ton of S in shipment 1 (or two tons, if there is no D in shipment 1). It is not necessary to have D in shipment 1.

(A) It is possible to not use any D in shipment 1, as long as there are two tons of S in shipment 1. (Figure 2a)

(B) Shipments 2 and 3 have a great deal of flexibility. It is possible to have one ton of M and one ton of P in shipment 3.

(C) Shipments 2 and 3 have a great deal of flexibility. It is possible to have zero tons of M and two tons of P in shipment 3. (Figure 2b)

(D) It is possible to have only one ton of S in shipment 1, as long as there is one ton of D in shipment 1. (Figure 2b)

(E) * It must be true that there is at least one ton of S in shipment 1. When you do both permutations, you find that there must be either one or two tons of S in shipment 1.

	1	2	3	4	2/4/~~6~~ tons each ship.
D =2	0	0	1	1	
M =2	XX	1	1	XX	
P =4	XX	2	2	XX	
S =4	2	1	0	1	

Fig. 2a

	1	2	3	4	2/4/~~6~~ tons each ship.
D =2	1	0	0	1	
M =2	XX	2	0	XX	
P =4	XX	2	2	XX	
S =4	1	0	0	3	

Fig. 2b

8. (D) – If there are two tons of P in shipment 3, then the other two tons of P must be in shipment 2. Since this is a "must be true" question, you could stop the analysis right here and go to the choices once you figure this out. But to be thorough, let's discuss the rest of the analysis for learning purposes. Since P is in both shipments, M can be in either or both shipments. You cannot tell anything specific about S and D and where they are, except of course that they must have at least some tonnage on shipments 1 and 4. Since this is a "must be true" question, the answer choice will be the warranted conclusion that you made.

(A) It could be true that shipment 2 has no D and two tons of S (Figure 2a), but it certainly is not required. (Figure 2b)

(B) Again, this could be true, but it is not required.

(C) It is possible to have one ton of D in shipment 1 (Figure 2b), but it is not required. (Figure 2a)

(D) * You know for certain that the remaining two tons of P can only be in shipment 2.

(E) M can have two tons in either shipment 2 or 3 (Figure 2b), or split between them. (Figure 2a)

9. (A) – Sometimes you just have to make up a number and plug it in. (Figure 3) If there is one ton of D in shipment 2, then there is one ton of M. Both D and M have one ton remaining. There must also be at least one ton of P and S in shipment 2. The remaining ton of M must be in shipment 3, as must be the remaining one or three tons of P. What about the remaining ton of D? Let's try it in shipment 1 (though the analysis is the same if you put it in shipment 4). This requires that at least one ton of S be in shipment 1. You have now used two of the four tons of S. The remaining two tons of S must be in shipment 4, in order for shipment 4 to meet its minimum requirement. If you are careful, it is possible to answer the question with this information. If you were not as confident, put two tons of D in shipment 2. You would eventually learn that S cannot be in shipment 3.

(A) * Yes, because you must use all four tons of S in shipments 1, 2, and 4, there is no S available for shipment 3.

(B) Although our diagram shows D on shipment 1, it could just as easily be true that D is on 4.

(C) There can be three tons of P or one ton of P in shipment 3.

(D) There can be two tons of S in shipment 1, but it is just as possible that the two tons of S are in 4.

(E) It is impossible to have two tons of M in shipment 2, since there would not be enough tons to fill the other shipments.

		1	2	3	4	2/4/6 tons
D	=2	1	1	0	0	
M	=2	XX	1 →	1	XX	
P	=4	XX	1 or 3 →	3 or 1	XX	
S	=4	1	1	0	2	

Fig. 3

10. (D) – If shipment 3 has exactly two tons, how could this come about? There are many possibilities. Maybe M supplied one ton and P supplied one ton. Maybe P supplied two tons. A third option is that P supplied one ton and S supplied one ton. Or maybe M and P did not supply anything to shipment 3, and instead D and S each supplied one ton. Instead of solving for a myriad of permutations, look at the answer choices and solve for the alternative—try to

disprove the answer choice. You can do this because this is a "must be true" question.

(A) It is possible to use no S in shipment 3, if S is in shipments 1 and 4.

(B) It is possible to have no D is shipment 4 if you use the two tons of D in one or two of the other three shipments.

(C) It is possible to have no P in shipment 3, instead putting it all in shipment 2. The diagram would look different than figure 4. The two required tons for shipment 3 would come from D and/or S. M and P would have zero tons in shipment 3. Their six tons would all be in shipment 2.

(D) * No matter what you do, at least one ton of M must be in shipment 2. Why? If you put no M in shipment 3, you must put two tons of M in shipment 2. If you put one ton of M in shipment 3, you must put one ton in shipment 2. You cannot put two tons of M in shipment 3, because then at least one ton of P would have to be in shipment 3, and that would be three tons, but this question limits you to two tons for shipment 3.

(E) S is quite flexible and is not required to put any alloy in shipment 2.

		1	2	3	4	2/4/6 tons
D	=2	2	0	0	0	
M	=2	XX	1	1	XX	
P	=4	XX	3	1	XX	
S	=4	2	0	0	2	

Fig. 4

11. (E) – Figure 4 shows that S can be in two shipments. Can all four tons of S be one shipment? No. If all four tons of S is used in one shipment, shipment 1 for example, then the two D tons must also be used in shipment 1, per Rule 3. Now no S or D remains for shipment 4. Shipment 4 must have at least two tons. So S must be in at least two shipments, shipments 1 and 4. That eliminates choices (A), (B) and (D). Can S be used in all four shipments? Yes. (Figure 5)

(A) See the analysis.

(B) See the analysis.

(C) See the analysis.

(D) See the analysis.

(E) * See the analysis.

		1	2	3	4	2/4/6 tons
D	=2	1			1	
M	=2	XX	1	1	XX	
P	=4	XX	2	2	XX	
S	=4	1	1	1	1	

Fig. 5

Student meetings

As with all games on the LSAT, there are extra deductions that must be made. Making these deductions is one of the two keys to success in the games. (Correctly diagramming the rules is the other key to success.) Here, there were three extra deductions that you should have made.

Whenever you are given an if-then rule, such as, "if Gina meets in the morning, then Kaspar meets in the evening," you can form the contrapositive of that statement by reversing and negating both terms. More plainly, the contrapositive of Rule 5 is, if Kaspar does not meet in the evening, then Gina does not meet in the morning (extra deduction 1), and the contrapositive of Rule 6 is, if Harry does not meet in the afternoon, then Jon does not meet in the afternoon (extra deduction 2).

The third deduction concerns the number of students who could meet in the different meeting times. These are the occupancy limits. There are eight students. No student can meet with the assistant individually. But at least one student must attend each of the meetings, and the same number of students must meet in the morning and the evening. Thus, there are only two possible scenarios: two students meet in the morning, four meet in the afternoon, and two meet in the evening; or, three students meet in the morning, two meet in the afternoon, and three meet in the evening (extra deduction 3). Recognizing these occupancy limitations makes this game much easier. A very simple diagram will keep track of the rules and the conclusions about the occupancy limits. (Figure 1)

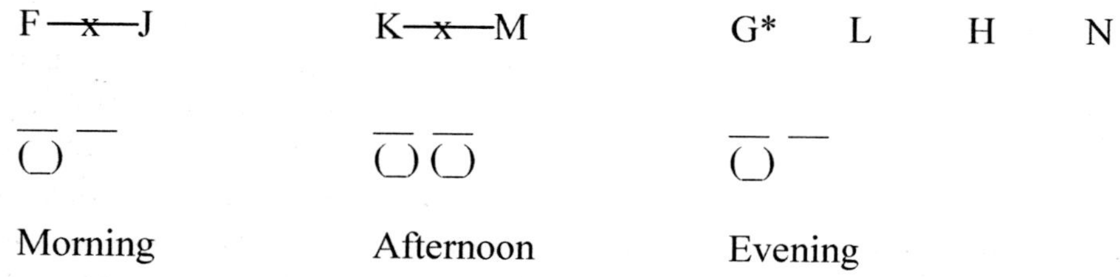

F—x—J K—x—M G* L H N

Morning	Afternoon	Evening
__ __ (_)	__ __ (_) (_)	__ __ (_)

Fig. 1

12. (C) – Eliminate answer choices that violate the explicit rules.
 (A) K and M cannot attend the same meeting, per Rule 4.
 (B) This violates Rule 1, because the teaching assistant will not meet with only one student. It also violates Rule 7, which says that the same number of students must meet in the morning and the evening.
 (C) * This does not violate the rules.
 (D) This violates Rule 7 because the number of students that meet in the morning must be the same as the number of students that meet in the evening.
 (E) This answer choice violates Rule 6. If J meets in the afternoon, then H meets in the afternoon.

13. (E) – What can you deduce using this new information? In this case, if J meets in the afternoon, then H meets in the afternoon, so that would mean that

you now have at least H, J, and K in the afternoon. The initial warranted conclusion about the number of students in each meeting (3,2,3 or 2,4,2), allows you to deduce that this time it must be the 2,4,2 order. Thus, there are four students in the afternoon meeting. Remember that things that could be true (the other four answer choices *could* be true) do not have to be true. Only (E) *must* be true.

(A) See the analysis. In this question, F and M have a similar analysis.
(B) See the analysis. See (A).
(C) See the analysis. L is a free agent, so it is a bad choice for a "must be true" question.
(D) See the analysis.
(E) * See the analysis.

14. (B) – Follow the chain of deductions. The question stem states that G meets in the morning and L and N meet in the evening. Rule 5 says that if G meets in the morning, then K meets in the evening. Mark this on the diagram. At this point, since there are three students in the evening meeting, it must be the 3,2,3 student set-up, which means that the evening session is now complete. Next, Rule 3 says that F and J cannot attend the same meeting. Try putting F in the morning and J in the afternoon and vice versa to see how many possibilities there are. In this scenario, when J meets in the afternoon, H must meet in the afternoon, and the only remaining student, M, must meet in the morning. Thus, with F in the morning and J in the afternoon, there is only one possibility. If you try the other scenario, with J meeting in the morning and F meeting in the afternoon, then either H or M could meet in either the morning or the afternoon. Thus, with J meeting in the morning and F meeting in the afternoon, there are two possibilities for the afternoon meeting, one with F and H and one with F and M. Thus, there are three possible arrangements for the afternoon meeting when G meets in the morning and L and N meet in the evening.

(A) See the analysis.
(B) * See the analysis. For questions that ask you for the number of possible permutations, the correct answer is usually one of the three-lowest numbers.
(C) See the analysis.
(D) See the analysis.
(E) See the analysis.

15. (A) – If H meets in the morning, remember the contrapositive of Rule 6. If J meets in the afternoon, then H meets in the afternoon, so the contrapositive is if H does not meet in the afternoon, then J does not meet in the afternoon. Furthermore, Rule 3 says that F and J cannot attend the same meeting, so that means that J cannot attend the morning meeting. Since J cannot attend the

morning meeting or the afternoon meeting, then he must attend the evening meeting.
(A) * See the analysis.
(B) See the analysis.
(C) See the analysis.
(D) See the analysis.
(E) See the analysis.

16. (D) – If G and L are the only students who meet in the morning, then you can deduce that it is the 2,4,2 order. Since G is in the morning, K is in the evening. (Rule 5) Now think about Rule 6. If H were to be in the second space in the evening, with K, then this would create problems with J in the afternoon. You can deduce that H must be in the afternoon. Also, M cannot be with K, so M is also in the afternoon. The unanswered question is where F and J (which are mutually exclusive) and N are. Since either F or J must be with K in the evening, then N must be in the afternoon.
(A) See the analysis.
(B) See the analysis. H must meet in the afternoon.
(C) See the analysis.
(D) * See the analysis.
(E) See the analysis. M must meet in the afternoon.

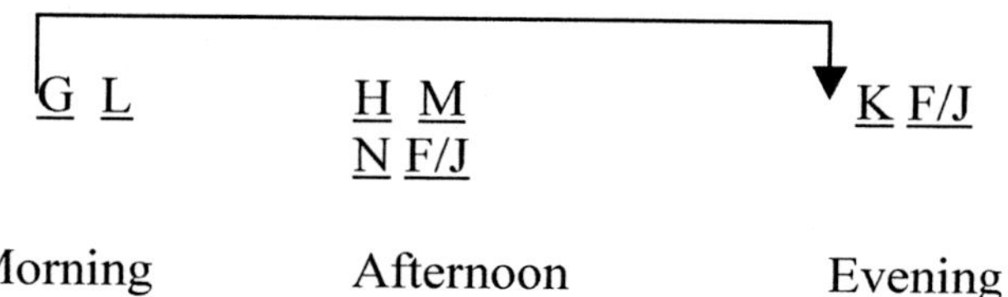

Fig. 2

17. (C) – Don't become unglued when a logic game changes a rule. It happens occasionally. The rest of the conditions or rules still apply. In this question, the only rule that changes is that it is now permissible for the teaching assistant to meet with just one student. However, the teaching assistant still has to meet with at least one student during each meeting time, so he must meet with at least one student in the morning and at least one student in the evening. Since there are eight total students, this leaves a maximum of six students that could meet in the afternoon. But would this violate any other rules? As long as the one student who meets in the morning is a member of the restricted mutually exclusive pairs of F/J and K/M, and the same is true for the evening, then no other rules would be violated. A sample diagram with six students meeting in the afternoon appears in figure 3.
(A) See the analysis.
(B) See the analysis.

(C) * See the analysis.
(D) See the analysis.
(E) See the analysis.

F	G H J K L N	M
Morning	Afternoon	Evening

Fig. 3

Car line-up

This game requires a simple line. As for the warranted conclusions, Rule 4 is a classic if-then statement. Given the rule that "if the Mearcint is placed in space three, then the Le is placed in space five," you can form the contrapositive (reverse and negate both terms) and say that if the Le is not placed in space five, then the Mearcint is not placed in space three. There are no other major deductions to be made, but pay attention to Rule 3. Since you know that there are only two options for F (space one or space seven), if you can eliminate one of those options on a given question (suppose the question stem says that V is in space one), then you know F must be placed in the other space (space seven in the example just given). This "two option" scenario is a normal feature of simple lines.

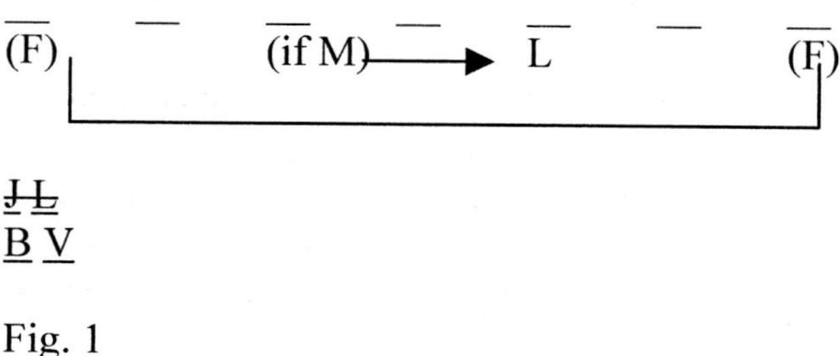

Fig. 1

18. (B) – With the "possible order" or "acceptable arrangement" question type, simply eliminate any answer choices that violate the rules and the one that's left is the correct response.
(A) This violates Rule 1, because J and L cannot be in adjacent spaces.
(B) * This is possible.
(C) This answer choice violates Rule 3, because F must be in one of the end spaces.
(D) This answer choice violates Rule 2. B and V must be in adjacent spaces.
(E) This answer choice violates Rule 4. If M is in space three, then L is in space five.

19. (D) – Often, early questions like this one test your grasp of the initial conclusions. Many students fail to make the extra deduction using Rule 4 (the contrapositive, discussed above, that if L is not in space five, then M is not in space three). This question tests whether you made that deduction. If you did, then clearly if L is in space seven (i.e., NOT in space five), then M cannot be in space three and thus answer choice (D) must be false. Whenever a question contains new information about a specific member, L in this case, always review the rules that name that member.
(A) See the analysis.
(B) See the analysis.
(C) See the analysis.
(D) * See the analysis.

(E) See the analysis.

20. (C) – This is a potentially time-consuming question because you may need to check each answer choice. Since J is in space one, F must be in space seven (F must be in an end space; remember the "two option" scenario discussed earlier). That is all you know so far. Can you make any other concrete deductions at this time? Not really, so check each answer choice to see if it is a must be true. Do this by checking whether it doesn't have to happen.
(A) Could B be in a space other than space two? Yes, put B in space three and V in space two, and no rules will be violated when you place the other members.
(B) You don't even have to try this answer choice because you already know that F is in space seven.
(C) * Could you put M in space three? Well, if you do, then according to Rule 4, L is in space five. Does this violate any of the rules? Yes, it does. According to Rule 2, B and V must be in adjacent spaces. Since you only have spaces two, four, and six still open, you don't have two adjacent spaces for B and V. Thus, M cannot be in space three and answer choice (C) must be true.
(D) It is possible to put the P in space five: JMBVPLF. So, it is not a must be true that P is not in space five.
(E) It is possible for V to be in space six: JPLMBVF.

21. (D) – This new fact allows you to complete nearly the entire diagram. If F is in space one and M is in space three, then from Rule 4 you know that L must be in space five. (Figure 2) Now, you need two adjacent spaces to place B and V, so they must go in spaces six and seven in either order. Continue down the list of rules to see if there are any rules you haven't used yet. Rule 1 says that J and L cannot be in adjacent spaces, so J must be in space two and the only remaining car, P, must be in space four. You have now filled in the entire diagram with the only uncertainly being whether B is in space six and V is in space seven, or vice versa.
(A) See the analysis.
(B) See the analysis.
(C) See the analysis.
(D) * This is the only choice that could be false. B could be in space seven and V could be in space six.
(E) See the analysis.

F	J	M	P	L	B/V	B/V
1	2	3	4	5	6	7

Fig. 2

22. (E) – Don't lose your cool; just look at the relevant space and determine which cars could be placed there without violating the rules. If V is in space seven, then B is in space six (Rule 2) and F is in space one (Rule 3). The only remaining rules are that J cannot be next to L, and if M is in space three, then L is in space five. As long as you separate J and L (on either spaces two and four, two and five, or three and five), and you have L in space five if M is in space three, then you will not violate any rules. A quick run through of the different possibilities shows that any of the four remaining cars (J, L, M, or P) could be in space four without violating the rules, so answer choice (E) is a complete and accurate list of cars, any one of which could be in space four.
(A) See the analysis.
(B) See the analysis.
(C) See the analysis.
(D) See the analysis.
(E) * See the analysis.

23. (A) – There are two new items of information. First, if the car dealer wants to put F and P as far apart as possible on the showroom floor, then he would put one of them in space one and one in space seven. Next, the dealer wants to put J and L as far apart as possible, so he would place one of them in space two and the other in space six. Would any rules be violated by any of these combinations? So far, no. Can you now make any further deductions? Since L is not in space five, then by the contrapositive of Rule 4, M cannot be in space three. But since only spaces three, four, and five remain, and you still need two adjacent spaces for B and V, that means that M must be in space five, and B and V are in spaces three and four, in either order. The only car whose exact placement can be determined is M, which must be in space five. The other answer choices are all things that could be true, but none of them must to be true.
(A) * See the analysis.
(B) See the analysis.
(C) See the analysis.
(D) See the analysis.
(E) See the analysis.

Practice Test 11

Spend 35 minutes doing this practice test. When time is up, review the explanations to help you understand the questions that you did not answer correctly.

SECTION I
Time—35 minutes
22 Questions

Directions: Each group of questions in this section is based on a set of conditions. In answering some of the questions, it may b useful to draw a rough diagram. Choose the response that most accurately and completely answers each question and blacken th corresponding space on your answer sheet.

Questions 1–6

A television news program has seven time slots during which will be broadcast five video segments—domestic news, entertainment news, international news, science update, and weather report. Each time slot must be filled with exactly one video segment and every video segment must be broadcast at least once. The video segments must be scheduled in accordance with the following requirements:

The entertainment news and the science update are each broadcast exactly one time.
No video segment is broadcast twice in a row.
The weather report cannot be broadcast until the international news has been broadcast at least once.
Domestic news cannot be broadcast immediately before or after the weather report.
Domestic news is the fourth broadcast.

1. Which one of the following could be the broadcast order?

(A) International news, weather report, international news, domestic news, science update, entertainment news, international news
(B) International news, science update, weather report, domestic news, entertainment news, international news, domestic news
(C) Science update, weather report, international news, domestic news, entertainment news, international news, domestic news
(D) International news, weather report, science update, domestic news, domestic news, international news, entertainment news
(E) Domestic news, science update, international news, domestic news, science update, weather report, entertainment news

2. Which one of the following cannot be true?

(A) Domestic news is broadcast three times.
(B) International news is broadcast three times.
(C) Weather report is broadcast two times.
(D) Domestic news is broadcast two times, and weather report is broadcast two times.
(E) International news is broadcast two times, and weather report is broadcast two times.

3. If either science update or entertainment news is the first broadcast and either science update or entertainment news is the seventh broadcast, then whic one of the following must be true?

(A) Domestic news is broadcast sixth.
(B) Entertainment news is broadcast first.
(C) International news is broadcast third.
(D) Science update is broadcast first.
(E) Weather report is broadcast second.

4. If science update is the second broadcast and entertainment news is third broadcast, then which one of the following CANNOT be true?

(A) Domestic news is broadcast first.
(B) International news is broadcast first.
(C) International news is broadcast fifth.
(D) Domestic news is broadcast sixth.
(E) Weather report is broadcast sixth.

5. If domestic news is broadcast seventh, then which one of the following must be true?

(A) International news is broadcast first.
(B) International news is broadcast third.
(C) Science update is broadcast third.
(D) Entertainment news is broadcast fifth.
(E) Weather report is broadcast sixth.

6. If weather report is broadcast exactly two times, then which one of the following must be true?

(A) International news is broadcast third.
(B) International news is broadcast two times.
(C) Science update is broadcast third.
(D) Domestic news is broadcast two times.
(E) Weather report is broadcast seventh.

GO ON TO THE NEXT PAGE

Questions 7–11

A pet shop employee must place six fish into three aquarium tanks. The fish include a blenny, a clown fish, a damselfish, a goby, a squirrelfish, a wrasse, and no others. No more than three fish can be placed in the same tank. When placing fish into the tanks the employee is limited by the following constraints:

The clownfish cannot be in the same tank as the damselfish or the wrasse.

If the goby is in the same tank as the blenny, then the squirrelfish is not in the same tank as the wrasse.

The damselfish cannot be in the same tank as the wrasse.

If the clown fish is with exactly two other fish, then the wrasse is alone.

If the wrasse is with the goby, then the squirrelfish is with the damselfish.

7. Which one of the following could be a complete and accurate listing of fish to tanks?

(A) Tank 1: clown fish and wrasse; tank 2: blenny, damselfish, and goby; tank 3: squirrelfish
(B) Tank 1: clown fish, goby and squirrelfish; tank 2: blenny and damselfish; tank 3: wrasse
(C) Tank 1: blenny, goby and damselfish; tank 2: clown fish; tank 3: squirrelfish and wrasse
(D) Tank 1: wrasse and blenny; tank 2: damselfish; tank 3: clown fish, goby and squirrelfish
(E) Tank 1: clown fish and squirrelfish; tank 2: blenny and damselfish; tank 3: goby and wrasse

8. If the damselfish is alone, then which one of the following must be true?

(A) The wrasse is alone.
(B) The wrasse is with exactly one other fish.
(C) The clown fish is alone.
(D) The clown fish is with exactly one other fish.
(E) The clown fish is with exactly two other fish.

9. If the clown fish is alone, then which one of the following could be true?

(A) The damselfish is with the goby and the blenny.
(B) The blenny is with the damselfish and the squirrelfish.
(C) The goby is with the squirrelfish and the wrasse.
(D) The squirrelfish is with the wrasse and no other fish.
(E) The blenny is with the damselfish and no other fish.

10. If there are exactly two fish in each tank, what is the maximum number of combinations in which the fish can be placed?

(A) three
(B) four
(C) five
(D) six
(E) seven

11. If the employee must place two fish in the tank with the wrasse, then which one of the following must be true?

(A) The clown fish is with the goby.
(B) The blenny is with the damselfish.
(C) The blenny is with the wrasse.
(D) The blenny is with the goby and the wrasse.
(E) The goby is with the squirrelfish and the wrasse.

GO ON TO THE NEXT PAGE.

Questions 12–16

A museum curator is hanging paintings for an exhibit. The five paintings will be hung in a single row from left to right. There is at least one of each of the following styles of paintings: portrait, landscape, and still life. Each painting is done in exactly one of the following three mediums: oil, latex, or watercolor. At least one painting is done in each of the three mediums. The following restrictions limit how the paintings may be arranged:

An oil painting is either a landscape or a portrait.
Latex paintings are landscapes.
There are at least two watercolors.
No paintings that hang next to each other may be of the same medium or style.
The fourth painting is an oil.
There are more still lifes than oils.

12. Which one of the following could be an accurate list of the styles and mediums of paintings, hung in order from left to right?

(A) Landscape, latex; still life, oil; portrait, watercolor; still life, oil; landscape, watercolor
(B) Still life, watercolor; still life, watercolor; landscape, latex; portrait, oil; landscape, watercolor
(C) Landscape, latex; still life, watercolor; landscape, oil; still life, watercolor; portrait, oil
(D) Still life, watercolor; landscape, latex; still life, watercolor; landscape, oil; portrait, latex
(E) Still life, watercolor; landscape, latex; still life, watercolor; portrait, oil; landscape, latex

13. If there are an equal number of latex and watercolors, which one of the following must be true?

(A) The first painting is a landscape.
(B) The fourth painting is a portrait.
(C) The second painting is a still life.
(D) The second painting is a watercolor.
(E) The fifth painting is a latex.

14. If there are more watercolors then either latex or oils, then which one of the following must be true?

(A) The first painting is a portrait.
(B) The second painting is a latex.
(C) The third painting is a still life.
(D) The fourth painting is a landscape.
(E) The fifth painting is a still life.

15. If the second painting is a watercolor, all of the following must be true, EXCEPT:

(A) The first painting is a landscape.
(B) The first painting is a portrait.
(C) The third painting is a latex.
(D) The fourth painting is a portrait.
(E) The fifth painting is a still life.

16. If there are an equal number of portraits and still lifes, then which one of the following must be true?

(A) There is an oil landscape.
(B) There is watercolor portrait.
(C) The third painting is a landscape.
(D) The fifth painting is a landscape.
(E) The fifth painting is a portrait.

GO ON TO THE NEXT PAGE

Questions 17–22

Each day during a five-day period (Tuesday to Saturday), a gym trainer will schedule a spinning class, a toning class, or a yoga class. The trainer will schedule each class at least once and will only schedule one class per day. One of the three classes requires the trainer to schedule 30 minutes, another class requires 45 minutes, and another class requires 60 minutes. The following requirements are the only ones used in scheduling the classes:

Spinning is scheduled exactly twice.
The trainer schedules different classes for Wednesday, Thursday, and Friday.
Yoga is not the longest class.
Wednesday's class is 45 minutes.
The trainer does not teach the same class on two consecutive days.

17. Which one of the following could be a complete and accurate class schedule for the week, beginning on Tuesday?

(A) Yoga, 30 minutes; spinning, 45 minutes; yoga, 30 minutes; toning, 60 minutes; spinning, 45 minutes
(B) Spinning, 30 minutes; yoga, 45 minutes; spinning, 30 minutes; toning, 60 minutes; spinning, 30 minutes
(C) Yoga, 60 minutes; toning, 45 minutes; spinning, 30 minutes; yoga, 60 minutes; spinning, 30 minutes
(D) Toning, 60 minutes; yoga, 45 minutes; spinning, 30 minutes; spinning, 30 minutes; toning, 30 minutes
(E) Toning, 45 minutes; toning, 45 minutes; spinning, 60; yoga, 30; spinning, 60

18. If spinning is on Wednesday, then which one of the following must be true?

(A) Spinning is on Friday.
(B) Friday's class is 30 minutes.
(C) Yoga is on Thursday.
(D) Thursday's class is 60 minutes.
(E) Saturday's class is 45 minutes.

19. Which one of the following CANNOT be true?

(A) Spinning is on Wednesday and Toning is on Saturday.
(B) Yoga is on Wednesday and Saturday.
(C) Spinning is on Wednesday and Toning is on Friday.
(D) Toning is on Wednesday and Saturday.
(E) Spinning is on Tuesday and Friday.

20. If there must be a yoga class the day before any toning class, each of the follow could be true, EXCEPT:

(A) Spinning is on Tuesday.
(B) Toning is on Saturday.
(C) Toning is on Thursday.
(D) Thursday's class is 60 minutes.
(E) Saturday's class is 30 minutes.

21. If there is exactly one 60 minute class, then which one of the following must be true?

(A) A yoga class is Tuesday.
(B) A yoga class is Tuesday or Thursday.
(C) A toning class is Thursday or Friday.
(D) A toning class is Thursday and Saturday.
(E) A spinning class is Wednesday and Saturday.

22. If a new 15 minute class, dance clas, is added and is always scheduled on Saturday, then which one of the following CANNOT be true?

(A) Yoga is 45 minutes.
(B) Yoga is scheduled for Tuesday.
(C) Toning is scheduled for Wednesday or Thursday.
(D) Toning is 60 minutes.
(E) Spinning is 45 minutes.

S T O P

IF YOU FINISH BEFORE TIME IS CALLED, YOU MAY CHECK YOUR WORK ON THIS SECTION ONLY. DO NOT WORK ON ANY OTHER SECTION IN THE TEST.

Answer key and explanations for Test 11

Answer Key

1. A
2. A
3. C
4. D
5. A
6. B
7. B
8. D
9. B
10. C
11. C
12. E
13. C
14. B
15. A
16. B
17. A
18. E
19. A
20. B
21. C
22. E

Television broadcasts

This simple line diagram has seven slots to be filled by five members. A game is more difficult when you must reuse members. As is typical, each member must be used at least once. Thus, each of the five members is used at least once, and one or two members are used more than once. Rule 1 further limits the options by declaring that E and S will be used exactly once. This means that only D, I, and W are eligible to be used multiple times. Rule 2, a "no neighbors" rule, will play a big role in several questions. There is no need to diagram this rule, just keep it in mind. When you diagram Rule 3 (W is not until after the first I), remember that W need not be later than *every* I, instead, W must not appear until at least one I has appeared. You can now make a warranted conclusion. Since W cannot appear until after I has made one appearance, W cannot be first. (Figure 1) Rule 4 prohibits D and W from being next to each other. (Figure 1) It is not a good use of your time to try to make additional warranted conclusions, so go to the questions.

	1	2	3	4	5	6	7
	__	__	__	D	__	__	__
$I^{\#1}$<W:	~~W~~						
~~D W~~:			~~W~~		~~W~~		

E=1
S=1

Fig. 1

1. (A) – For this question, use the rules to quickly eliminate four of the answer choices.
   (A) * This choice does not violate any rules.
   (B) This choice violates Rule 4 because it has W and D next to each other.
   (C) This choice violates Rule 3 because it has W preceding the first I.
   (D) This choice violates Rule 2 because it has two Ds next to each other.
   (E) This choice violates Rule 1 because it has two Ss.

2. (A) – Four of the choices are possible, one is not possible.
   (A) * D cannot be used three times. Look at figure 1. Notice that you would have to place one of the three Ds in space 1 or 2. The third D would have to be in space 6 or 7. Doing this prevents W from being placed anywhere on the diagram, because Rule 4 prohibits W and D from being next to each other. Although you could have made this conclusion at the initial analysis stage, doing so would have been an inefficient use of your time.
   (B) See the analysis.

(C) See the analysis.
(D) See the analysis.
(E) See the analysis.

3. (C) – This question places either S or E first, and the other one seventh. Since neither of these two videos have any rules that tie them into other members, it doesn't matter for our purposes which one is where. Figure 2 quickly fills up once we place S and E. Where can W be? Can W be second? No, because Rule 3 requires that I come before W. So W must be sixth. Which video can be fifth? Only I can be fifth; for various reasons, none of the other videos can be fifth. I must also be third, for the same reason. Since I is third, I cannot be second, so D is the only remaining video that can be second.
(A) D cannot be sixth.
(B) Either S or E can be first.
(C) * Yes, I must be third. It actually was not necessary to do the full analysis found in figure 2 to arrive at this conclusion. But the full analysis was quite easily accomplished, so the time wasted was minimal.
(D) See (B).
(E) W cannot be second.

	1	2	3	4	5	6	7
	S/E	D	I	D	I	W	S/E
$I^{\#1}<W$:	~~W~~	~~W~~					
~~D W~~:			~~W~~		~~W~~		

Fig. 2

4. (D) – By fixing the locations of S and E, this question greatly reduces the number of possible permutations. Since S and E are now "out of the picture," what can be fifth? Neither S nor E. Not D, Rule 2. Not W, Rule 4. Only I can be fifth. Can D be sixth or seventh? No, because W must be sixth or seventh, preventing D from being used next to it. Whatever space W does not take, I will take. But, I cannot be sixth, due to Rule 2, so W must be sixth and I must be seventh. (Figure 3)
(A) D could be first, and so could I.
(B) See (A).
(C) I must be fifth.
(D) * D cannot be sixth.
(E) W must be sixth.

	1	2	3	4	5	6	7
	__	S	E	D	I	W	I
$I^{\#1}$<W:	~~W~~						
~~D~~ ~~W~~:			~~W~~		~~W~~		

Fig. 3

5. (A) – If D is seventh, then W cannot be sixth. W can never be fifth, fourth, or third. This forces W to be second. Since W must be second, I must be first. That is enough analysis to answer this question.
(A) * See the analysis.
(B) It is possible that I is third, but either S or E could be third also.
(C) See (B).
(D) I, S, or E could be fifth.
(E) W could be sixth.

6. (B) By now, you should be familiar with where W can be. If W is used exactly two times, then W must be used second, and then either sixth or seventh. Since W is second, I must be first. Since W is either sixth or seventh and D cannot be next to W, D is used once and I and W are used twice.
(A) Maybe I is third, but S or E could also be third.
(B) * Yes, I must be used twice. We don't know exactly where, but we do know I must be used twice.
(C) S and E are always interchangeable.
(D) D cannot be used twice, as discussed in the analysis.
(E) W is seventh or sixth.

	1	2	3	4	5	6	7
	I	W	__	D	__	__	__
$I^{\#1}$<W:	~~W~~						
~~D~~ ~~W~~:			~~W~~		~~W~~		

Fig. 4

Fish tanks

This game requires a very simple diagram, but there is a lot of interaction among the various members. This complexity requires that you be on your toes to catch all the interactions. The key to this game is realizing the effect of Rules 1 and 3: C, D, and W must all be in separate tanks. This becomes the nucleus of the diagram. (Figure 1) The other three rules are conditional (if/then) rules, so they will not be much help for drawing warranted conclusions, but they will be useful once the questions provide more information to work with.

C____ D____ W____

If C+2 ————→ W+0

D + S ←—— If W + G

If G+B→~~SW~~

Fig. 1

7. (B) – Use each rule to eliminate the answer choice that violates that rule. The answer choice that is not eliminated is the correct answer.
   (A) This choice is wrong because it violates Rule 1, since it has C and W in the same tank.
   (B) * This does not violate any rules.
   (C) This violates Rule 2 because it has G and B together, but the S and W are also together.
   (D) This violates Rule 4 because it has C with two other fish, but W is not alone.
   (E) This violates Rule 5 because it has G and W together, but the S and D are not together.

8. (D) – If D is alone, then Rule 5 is relevant. Thus, W and G cannot be together. That means that G must be with C. Can another fish be placed in C's tank? No, because that would trigger Rule 4, requiring that W be alone. This would mean that four fish would have to be in C's tank, which is prohibited. (Figure 2)
   (A) W must have B and S.
   (B) W must have B and S.
   (C) C must have G.
   (D) * C must have G and no other fish.
   (E) If C had two other fish in its tank, then W would have to be alone. This would force S into C's tank, making for four fish in C's tank.

CG D WBS

If C+2 ————→ W+0

D + S ← If W + G

If G+B → ~~SW~~

Fig. 2

9. (B) – When C is alone, the two rules to focus on are Rule 2 (if G+B, then S is not with W) and Rule 5 (if W+G, then S is with D). A quick diagram reveals three valid permutations. (Figure 3)
   (A) D cannot be with both G and B, because of the effect of Rule 2.
   (B) * This could be true. The third permutation shows D, B, and S together in the same tank.
   (C) G, S, and W cannot be in the same tank. Rule 5 is the relevant rule.
   (D) None of the three permutations show the S and W alone in the same tank.
   (E) In none of the permutations are B and D in the same tank alone.

C	DG	WBS
C	DGS	WB
C	DBS	WG
	D + S ←	If W + G

If G+B → ~~SW~~

Fig. 3

10. (C) – The quickest way to answer this question is to do as many permutations as you can. (Figure 4) When doing permutations, stay organized by starting with C+B and trying both permutations. Both of those permutations are valid. Then move on to C+G, trying both permutations. Both of those permutations are valid. Finally, do C+S. You find that only one permutation works, CS/DG/WB. The other one (CS/DB/WG) does not work because of Rule 4; G cannot be with W when S is with C. So there are a total of five valid permutations.
    (A) See the analysis.
    (B) See the analysis.
    (C) * See the analysis.
    (D) See the analysis.
    (E) See the analysis.

C____	D____	W____
	D + S ←	If W + G
CB	DS	WG
CB	DG	WS

CG	DS	WB
CG	DB	WS
CS	DG	WB

Fig. 4

11. (C) – Now we must place two fish with W. (Figure 5) We must choose from either G and B, G and S, or B and S. Trying each of these, we find that it is possible to place G and B with W. It is also possible to place B and S with W. It is not possible to place G and S with W. Thus, we can conclude that B must be with W.
    (A) Although C can be with G, it is not required.
    (B) No. B must be with W.
    (C) * Yes. B must be with W.
    (D) Although W, G, and B can be together, it is not required.
    (E) The B must be with W, so this choice is incorrect.

C____	D____	W____	
	D + S ◄———	If W + G	
C	DS	WGB	
C	DB	WGS	- no
C	DG	WBS	
CG	D	WBS	

Fig. 5

Painting styles and mediums

The whole point of the logic games is to force you to make extra deductions. Sometimes you can make the conclusions immediately after reading the rules. Other times, as in this puzzle, you cannot make any warranted conclusions until the questions provide more information to serve as an anchor. Knowing when to stop trying to make conclusions and move on to the questions is the skill that separates experienced LSAT takers from novices.

The basic setup in this game is pretty easy: two parallel rows with five dashes each. Put the style of painting on the top line and the medium on the bottom line. The only rule that is easily graphed is Rule 5: the fourth painting is an oil. (Figure 1) The next relevant rule is Rule 1: oil paintings can only be landscapes or portraits. The rest of the rules cannot be easily diagrammed, so you must review the rules as you work through the questions.

```
Pt, Ls, Sl:   ___   ___   ___   Ls/Pt  ___
#Sl>#Oil

Oil, Lx, Wc:  ___   ___   ___   Oil    ___
                          O̶             O̶

If Lx → Ls
Wc=2+
```

Fig. 1

12. (E) – With "possible arrangement" questions the trick is to eliminate answer choices that violate the explicit rules.
(A) An oil painting cannot be a still life, Rule 1.
(B) Two neighboring paintings cannot have the same style, Rule 4.
(C) This answer choice has a watercolor in the fourth position. The fourth painting must be an oil, Rule 5.
(D) This violates Rule 2, because a latex painting must be a landscape.
(E) * This answer choice does not violate any rules.

13. (C) – There is at least one oil painting. If there is an equal number of latex and watercolors, how many are there? Do the math. If there were one latex, one watercolor, and three oils, this would not work for three reasons. First, there is no way to fit three oils on the diagram without violating Rule 4. Second, Rule 6 specifies there are more still lifes than oils, so this would mean there would have to be four still lifes, out of the five paintings. Third, Rule 3 specifies there are at least two watercolors. Thus, there are two latex, two watercolors, and one oil. There are two ways they can fit on the diagram and not violate the "no neighbors" rule, see figures 2a-b. Once you place the two latex, you know those two paintings will be landscapes, per Rule 2. Note that either the third or fifth painting must always be a landscape; this means that

the fourth painting can never be a landscape; it must be a portrait. There are only two more spaces to fill, and we know that there must be more still lifes than oils, so there must be two still lifes to fill the remaining two open spaces. Now that we have solved both permutations, use the diagrams to find the correct answer choice.

(A) See the diagrams, there is only a 50% chance that the first painting is a landscape.

(B) * Yes, in both permutations, the fourth painting is a portrait.

(C) See the diagrams, there is only a 50% chance that the second painting is a still life.

(D) See the diagrams, there is only a 50% chance that the second painting is a watercolor.

(E) See the diagrams, there is only a 50% chance that the fifth painting is a latex.

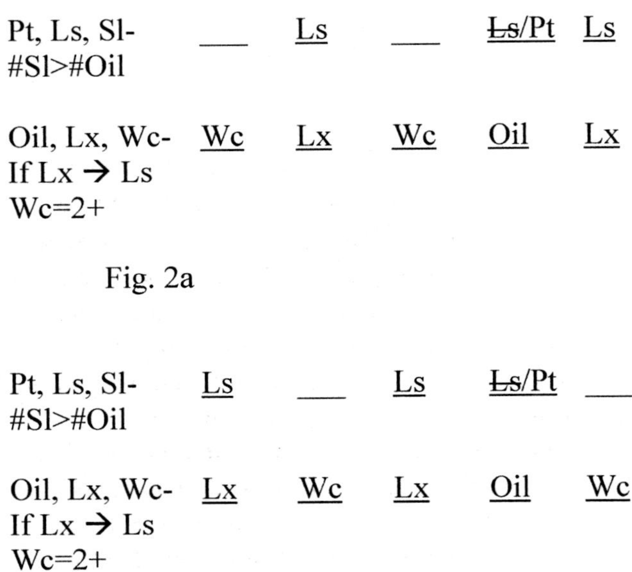

Fig. 2b

14. (B) – Like the previous question, this question tests your understanding of the minimum and maximum numbers of each style. We know there are at least two watercolors, per Rule 3. For there to be more watercolors than either latex or oils, there must be three watercolors, one latex, and one oil. Again, like the previous question, the next step is to place these three watercolors on the diagram. There is only one way to accommodate three watercolors to avoid having them neighbor each other. (Figure 3) Once we place the watercolors, the latex is put in the only available spot. The next step is to place the styles. The latex must be a landscape. More difficult, there must be at least two still lifes (since there is one oil). But could there be three still

lifes? There also must be at least one portrait, but could there be two? Before devoting time to diagramming the permutations, check the answer choices; you may already have enough information to answer the question.

(A) The first painting must be a watercolor.

(B) * Correct. The second painting must be latex.

(C) The third painting might be a still life.

(D) The fourth painting may be a landscape or a portrait.

(E) The fifth painting may be a still life, or it may be something else.

Pt, Ls, Sl- #Sl>#Oil	___	Ls	___	Ls/Pt	___
Oil, Lx, Wc- If Lx → Ls Wc=2+	Wc	Lx	Wc	Oil	Wc

Fig. 3

15. (A) – Follow the chain of conclusions to complete the diagram. (Figure 4a) The second painting is a watercolor. Rule 3 specifies there be at least two watercolors. Where can the other watercolor be? It can't be first or third (due to Rule 4). It can't be fourth. So it must be fifth. Next, the third painting can't be a watercolor or oil, due to Rule 4, so it must be latex. Since it is a latex, then it must be a landscape (Rule 2). Since the third painting is a landscape, the second and fourth are not. Since the fourth (oil) painting is not a landscape, then it must be a portrait (Rule 1). The diagram in figure 4a shows this. Now what? Step back and reconsider the rules. Rule 6 specifies there are more still lifes then oils. Right now the diagram has one oil, so if we were to have a second oil in space one, this would require there to be three still lifes, but, there is no way to place three still lifes on figure 4a. So there must be two still lifes and one oil. Since there is only one oil, the first painting cannot be an oil. Since it also cannot be a watercolor (Rule 4), therefore it must be a latex, and thus it must be a landscape. This forces the two still lifes into spaces two and five. (Figure 4b)

(A) * See the analysis.

(B) See the analysis.

(C) See the analysis.

(D) See the analysis.

(E) See the analysis.

Pt, Ls, Sl- #Sl>#Oil	___	___	Ls	~~Ls~~/Pt	___
Oil, Lx, Wc-	___	Wc	Lx	Oil	Wc

If Lx → Ls
Wc=2+

Fig. 4a

Pt, Ls, Sl:	Ls	Sl	Ls	Pt	Sl
#Sl>#Oil					
Oil, Lx, Wc:	Lx	Wc	Lx	Oil	Wc
If Lx → Ls					
Wc=2+					

Fig. 4b

16. (B) – Once again, pay attention to the numbers of each style of painting. In this question there is an equal number of still lifes and portraits. We know that there are more still lifes than oils (Rule 6), so there must be at least two still lifes. Since there are an equal number of portraits, then there must be two still lifes, and two portraits (and therefore, one landscape.) Since there is exactly one landscape, we now know several more facts. First, there is exactly one latex. Second, since the oil painting is not a landscape, it is a portrait. Now turn to the still lifes. There are two still lifes, so that means there is exactly one oil (Rule 6). We know now that there is exactly one oil and exactly one latex, so there must be exactly three watercolors. There is only one way to place the three watercolors. (Figure 6) Once we place the watercolors and latex, there are three spaces left to place two still lifes. The third painting must be a still life, because it can't be a landscape or portrait. The fifth painting cannot be a portrait or a landscape, so it must be the second still life. This leaves the first painting to be a portrait. (Figure 6)
(A) See the diagram, there is no oil landscape.
(B) * See the diagram, the first painting must be a watercolor portrait.
(C) The third painting is not a landscape because the second painting is a landscape.
(D) The fifth painting is not a landscape.
(E) The fifth painting is not a portrait because the fourth painting is a portrait.

Pt, Ls, Sl-	Pt	Ls	Sl	~~Ls~~/Pt	Sl
#Sl>#Oil					
Oil, Lx, Wc-	Wc	Lx	Wc	Oil	Wc
If Lx → Ls					
Wc=2+					

Fig. 6

Workout schedule

This diagram is similar to the previous game's diagram. It has five spaces, each of which has two variables. A multiple line will work well. Also similar to the previous game, there is very little we can do with the rules until we get to the questions. One thing that is a little different in this puzzle is that the Wednesday through Friday slots have to be different classes. This is a minor variation on the "no neighbors" rule. The [brackets] around those three days will remind us of this rule. The effect of this rule is that neither Thursday nor Friday will be a 45-minute class. Because of Rule 5, Tuesday will not be a 45-minute class either. Saturday may or may not be a 45-minute class. Were you confused by a possible ambiguity in the language of the setup? The way the setup was written might have caused you to wonder whether the three classes always stay the same duration during the week, or whether, for example, the toning class could be 30 minutes on Tuesday but 60 minutes on Friday. The way to resolve this kind of ambiguity is to look at the answer choices. Since the first question normally lists permutations, you can look at it for guidance. Here, answer choice 17(A), for example, shows that yoga is always 30 minutes and spinning is always 45 minutes, thus the ambiguity is resolved, the classes stay the same length during a week. Remember, the LSAT does not deliberately use ambiguous language to try and trick you. Instead, the LSAT uses the complex interconnecting rules to test your ability to discover unstated connections.

	T	[W	Th	F]	S
Y,T,S-	___	___	___	___	___
Time-	___	45	___	___	___

Y= 30 or 45
S= 2 times

Fig. 1

17. (A) – With the "possible order" or "acceptable arrangement" question type, simply eliminate any answer choices that violate the rules. The answer choice that remains is the correct response.
    (A) * This does not violate any rules.
    (B) This violates Rule 1 because is has spinning done three times.
    (C) This answer choice violates Rule 3, because yoga is not 60 minutes.
    (D) This answer choice violates Rule 2. Spinning cannot be on both Thursday and Friday.
    (E) This answer choice violates Rule 5. Toning can't be taught two days in a row.

18. (E) – Once the new information is placed on the diagram, this question is easy. (Figure 2) Spinning is on Wednesday. This means spinning is the 45-minute class. Spinning cannot be Tuesday, Thursday, or Friday. Since there

must be two spinning classes, the Saturday class must be a spinning class. Since spinning is 45 minutes, yoga is 30 minutes. Besides this, we don't know much about the other days.

(A) Spinning cannot be on Friday, because it is on Wednesday, see Rule 2.
(B) Friday's class could be 30 minutes, but it is not required to be.
(C) Yoga can be either Thursday or Friday.
(D) Thursday's class can be either 60 minutes (if toning) or 30 minutes (if yoga.)
(E) * Yes, spinning is 45 minutes, and the second spinning class must be Saturday.

	T	[W	Th	F]	S
Y,T,S-	___	Sp	___	___	Sp
Time-	___	45	___	___	45

Y= 30 or 45
S= 2 times

Fig. 2

19. (A) – This question requires more work than the previous one. Instead of providing an anchor in the question stem like the previous question did, it will provide an anchor in each answer choice. A small diagram next to each answer choices may be necessary to keep track of your work.

(A) * The previous question showed us that if the spinning class is on Wednesday, then the second one must be on Saturday. Fortunately, our work for the last question made this answer choice easy to verify.
(B) Yoga could be on Wednesday and Saturday.
(C) As we saw in question 18, this is a possible order.
(D) It is possible to have toning on Wednesday and Saturday, as long as one of the spinning classes is on Monday.
(E) It is possible to have spinning on Tuesday and Friday. Either toning or yoga would have to be Saturday.

20. (B) – The quickest route to the solution is to check all the permutations where yoga is the day before toning. (Figures 3a-b) The way the question is phrased, a yoga class must precede any toning class, but a yoga class is not necessarily followed by a toning class.

(A) Spinning can be Tuesday, figure 3b.
(B) * Toning cannot be on Saturday. Doing so would require a second toning to be during Wednesday, Thursday, or Friday. This would make a total of six classes for five spaces.

(C) Toning class can be Thursday, figure 3a.
(D) If toning or spinning is Thursday, the class can be 60 minutes.
(E) See the analysis.

	T	[W	Th	F]	S
Y,T,S-	Sp	Y	T	Sp	Y
Time-	___	45	___	___	45

Fig. 3a

	T	[W	Th	F]	S
Y,T,S-	Y	Sp	Y	T	Sp
Time-	30	45	30	60	45

Fig. 3b

21. (C) – If there is exactly one class that is 60 minutes, which class could it be? It can't be yoga, since yoga is either 30 or 45 minutes. It can't be spinning, because there are two spinning classes. So it must be the toning class that is 60 minutes, and there must be one toning class. This means that either yoga or spinning is on Wednesday. Figures 4a and 4b show the two possibilities. We do not know exactly which day the toning class will be conducted.
(A) There is a 50% chance that the yoga class will be on Tuesday.
(B) We do not know exactly where toning, the 60 minute class, will be.
(C) * Yes, the toning class must be Thursday or Friday.
(D) See (C).
(E) There is a 50% chance that the spinning class will be on Wednesday and Saturday.

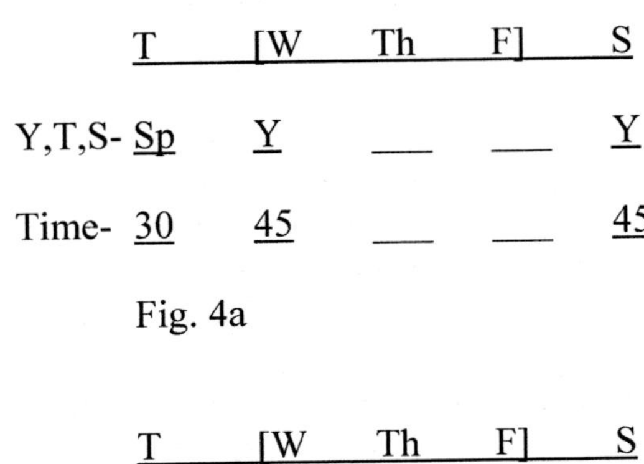

	T	[W	Th	F]	S
Y,T,S-	Sp	Y	___	___	Y
Time-	30	45	___	___	45

Fig. 4a

T	[W	Th	F]	S

Y,T,S-	Y	Sp	___	___	Sp
Time-	30	45	___	___	45

Fig. 4b

22. (E) – The addition of a dance class on Saturday simplifies our diagram. We now must place the two spinning classes in such a way that they do not violate the rules. The only way to do this is to place one of the spinning classes on Tuesday, and the other on either Thursday or Friday. (Figure 5) The next step is to realize that the spinning class is not 45 minutes. The rest of the diagram cannot be ascertained, so, before doing permutations, go to the answer choices.

(A) Yoga can be 30 minutes or 45 minutes.
(B) Yoga cannot be on Tuesday.
(C) Toning can be on Wednesday, Thursday, or Friday.
(D) Toning can be 30, 45, or 60 minutes.
(E) Spinning cannot be 45 minutes.

	T	[W	Th	F]	S
Y,T,S-	Sp	___	___	___	D
Time-	___	45	___	___	15

Fig. 5

Practice Test 12

Spend 35 minutes doing this practice test. When time is up, review the explanations to help you understand the questions that you did not answer correctly.

SECTION I

Time—35 minutes

22 Questions

Directions: Each group of questions in this section is based on a set of conditions. In answering some of the questions, it may b useful to draw a rough diagram. Choose the response that most accurately and completely answers each question and blacken th corresponding space on your answer sheet.

Questions 1–6

On a single day a tennis instructor must schedule lessons with each of six different students—Dunn, Fick, Green, Hines, James, and Xavier. The instructor meets with exactly one student at a time, and each lesson is exactly one hour long. The times available for scheduling the lessons are 9:00 AM, 10:00 AM, 11:00 AM, 12:00 noon, 1:00 PM, and 2:00 PM. The following conditions apply:

Xavier's lesson must be scheduled at some time before Fick's lesson.

James' lesson cannot be scheduled for 12:00 noon or later.

Hines' lesson must be scheduled at some time before Xavier's lesson.

There must be exactly one lesson scheduled between the lessons of Dunn and Fick.

1. Which one of the following is an acceptable assignment of students in order from 9:00 AM to 2:00 PM?

(A) Green, Xavier, James, Dunn, Hines, Fick
(B) Hines, Xavier, Fick, Green, Dunn, James
(C) James, Green, Hines, Xavier, Fick, Dunn
(D) Green, Hines, James, Dunn, Xavier, Fick
(E) Fick, James, Dunn, Hines, Xavier, Green

2. Which one of the following is a complete and accurate list of students, any one of whom could be scheduled for the first lesson of the day?

(A) Dunn, James, Xavier
(B) Dunn, Hines, Green
(C) Green, Hines, James
(D) Fick, Hines, James
(E) Green, James, Xavier

3. If James' lesson is scheduled for 11:00 AM and Fick's lesson is scheduled before Dunn's lesson, then which one of the following must be true?

(A) Hines' lesson is scheduled for 9:00 AM.
(B) Green's lesson is scheduled for 10:00 AM.
(C) Xavier's lesson is scheduled for 12:00 noon.
(D) Dunn's lesson is scheduled for 12:00 noon.
(E) Fick's lesson is scheduled for 1:00 PM.

4. If Hines' lesson is scheduled immediately before Green's lesson, then which one of the following could be true?

(A) Xavier's lesson is scheduled for 9:00 AM.
(B) Dunn's lesson is scheduled for 9:00 AM.
(C) James' lesson is scheduled for 10:00 AM.
(D) Xavier's lesson is scheduled for 10:00 AM.
(E) Green's lesson is scheduled for 11:00 AM.

5. If Xavier's lesson is scheduled before 12:00 noon, the which one of the following must be true?

(A) Hines' lesson is scheduled for 9:00 AM.
(B) Xavier's lesson is scheduled for 10:00 AM.
(C) Dunn's lesson is scheduled for 12:00 noon.
(D) Green's lesson is scheduled for 1:00 PM.
(E) Fick's lesson is scheduled for 2:00 PM.

6. Which one of the following CANNOT be true?

(A) Green's lesson is scheduled for 9:00 AM.
(B) Green's lesson is scheduled for 10:00 AM.
(C) Xavier's lesson is scheduled for 11:00 AM.
(D) Dunn's lesson is scheduled for 11:00 AM.
(E) Hines' lesson is scheduled for 12:00 noon.

Questions 7–11

The local chamber of commerce management committee consists of representatives from exactly three companies—Peterson Grocery, Quincy Stationary and Roberts Hardware. Management committee matters fall into five categories—internal, judicial, kitchen, local, and monetary. When these matters are up for a vote, the representatives of the three companies cast votes, and each company's representatives vote on exactly three of the five categories. Each category is voted on by at least one company's representatives. The following must obtain:

Peterson Grocery does not vote on judicial matters unless Roberts Hardware does also.
If Quincy Stationary votes on kitchen matters, then Peterson Grocery does not vote on local matters.
No company votes on both internal and local matters.
Roberts Hardware and Quincy Stationary cannot both vote on monetary matters.

7. Which one of the following could be an accurate list, for each of the companies, of the matters on which they vote?

(A) Peterson Grocery: internal, judicial, monetary; Quincy Stationary: internal, kitchen, local; Roberts Hardware: judicial, local, monetary.
(B) Peterson Grocery: judicial, local, monetary; Quincy Stationary: internal, judicial, monetary; Roberts Hardware: judicial, kitchen, local.
(C) Peterson Grocery: internal, judicial, kitchen; Quincy Stationary: internal, kitchen, monetary; Roberts Hardware: internal, kitchen, local.
(D) Peterson Grocery: kitchen, local, monetary; Quincy Stationary: internal, judicial, monetary; Roberts Hardware: judicial, kitchen, monetary.
(E) Peterson Grocery: judicial, local, monetary; Quincy Stationary: internal, kitchen, monetary; Roberts Hardware: internal, judicial, kitchen.

8. If Peterson Grocery votes on both judicial and local matters, then which one of the following could be true?

(A) Quincy Stationary votes on kitchen matters.
(B) Peterson Grocery votes on internal matters.
(C) Roberts Hardware votes on internal matters.
(D) All three companies vote on local matters.
(E) All three companies vote on kitchen matters.

9. If Quincy Stationary votes on both internal and kitchen matters, then which one of the following must be true?

(A) Roberts Hardware votes on local matters.
(B) Peterson Grocery votes on judicial matters.
(C) At most two companies vote on judicial matters.
(D) Only one company votes on monetary matters.
(E) All three companies vote on internal matters.

10. If Peterson Grocery votes on local matters, then which one of the following CANNOT be true?

(A) Peterson Grocery votes on kitchen matters.
(B) Peterson Grocery votes on judicial matters.
(C) Quincy Stationary votes on internal matters.
(D) Roberts Hardware votes on monetary matters.
(E) Roberts Hardware votes on local matters.

11. If all three companies vote on kitchen matters and Quincy Stationary is the only company that votes on judicial matters, then which one of the following could be true?

(A) Peterson Grocery and Roberts Hardware vote on only one common matter.
(B) Only one of the companies votes on monetary matters.
(C) Quincy Stationary votes on monetary matters.
(D) Peterson Grocery and Quincy Stationary vote on exactly two common matters.
(E) Roberts Hardware votes on neither internal nor local matters.

GO ON TO THE NEXT PAGE.

Questions 12–16

The six employees of a small company—Cal, Dave, Fred, Greg, Harrison, and Jake—may or may not eat lunch during a workday. Employees may eat lunch by themselves, or as part of a group, but only one group or a single employee will eat lunch during the workday. The following conditions must apply:

If Dave eats lunch, then Fred eats lunch with him.
Cal and Greg do not eat lunch together.
If Harrison eats lunch, then he does not eat alone.
Jake will not eat lunch unless exactly two people join him.
If only two people eat lunch, then Greg does not eat lunch.

12. Which one of the following could be a complete and accurate list of the employees who eat lunch during a workday?

(A) Cal, Dave, Fred, Jake
(B) Dave, Harrison
(C) Fred, Harrison, Jake
(D) Cal, Dave, Fred, Greg
(E) Fred, Greg

13. What is the maximum number of employees who can eat lunch together during a workday?

(A) 2
(B) 3
(C) 4
(D) 5
(E) 6

14. If Greg eats lunch, then which one of the following CANNOT be true?

(A) Both Fred and Jake eat lunch.
(B) Both Dave and Jake eat lunch.
(C) Neither Dave nor Jake eats lunch.
(D) Neither Harrison nor Fred eats lunch.
(E) Both Fred and Jake eat lunch.

15. If exactly four employees eat lunch, then which one of the following could be true?

(A) Harrison does not eat lunch.
(B) Cal eats lunch.
(C) Dave does not eat lunch.
(D) Jake eats lunch.
(E) Fred does not eat lunch.

16. If Jake eats lunch, then each of the following pairs of employees could eat lunch with him EXCEPT:

(A) Cal and Dave
(B) Cal and Harrison
(C) Dave and Fred
(D) Fred and Greg
(E) Greg and Harrison

GO ON TO THE NEXT PAGE

Questions 17–22

Exactly six volunteers—Mathias, Rolando, Santos, Ursula, Victor and Wilma—are available to serve as ushers at a charity event. Ushers are assigned to the event in pairs, and during the course of the event exactly four pairs will serve as ushers. There are four shifts numbered one through four, and when one pair of ushers finishes their shift, a new shift begins. No usher may work during consecutive shifts. The following conditions must apply:

Each of the six people available will serve as an usher on at least one shift.
Mathias cannot serve as an usher on either the second or third shifts.
Rolando serves as an usher on only one shift.
Santos must serve as an usher on at least one shift that is later than at least one of Ursula's shifts.
Wilma serves as an usher on the second shift.

17. Which one of the following could be an accurate list of ushers that serve on the four shifts from first to last?

(A) Mathias and Rolando; Santos and Wilma; Ursula and Victor; Mathias and Wilma.
(B) Victor and Ursula; Rolando and Wilma; Santos and Victor; Mathias and Victor.
(C) Mathias and Ursula; Rolando and Wilma; Santos and Victor; Mathias and Rolando.
(D) Ursula and Victor; Santos and Wilma; Mathias and Rolando; Santos and Victor.
(E) Santos and Victor; Ursula and Wilma; Rolando and Santos; Mathias and Ursula.

18. Which one of the following must be true?

(A) Exactly two of the ushers serve on only one shift.
(B) Exactly three of the ushers serve on only one shift.
(C) Exactly four of the ushers serve on only one shift.
(D) Exactly one usher serves on more than two shifts.
(E) Exactly three ushers serve on two shifts.

19. If Both Ursula and Wilma serve as ushers on two separate shifts, at least one of which they serve together, then which one of the following must be false?

(A) Mathias and Santos serve as ushers on the same shift.
(B) Mathias serves as an usher on the first shift.
(C) Victor serves as an usher on the first shift.
(D) Rolando serves as an usher on the second shift
(E) Victor and Rolando serve as ushers on the same shift.

20. Which one of the following could be true?

(A) Santos serves as an usher on the first shift only.
(B) Victor pairs with both Mathias and Wilma.
(C) Rolando pairs with both Santos and Ursula.
(D) Ursula serves as an usher on the last shift only.
(E) Wilma serves as an usher on the third shift.

21. If neither Victor nor Mathias serves as an usher on two shifts, then which one of the following could be a complete and accurate list of those volunteers who could serve as ushers on two shifts?

(A) Wilma only
(B) Ursula and Wilma
(C) Santos only
(D) Santos, Ursula and Wilma
(E) Rolando and Ursula

22. Suppose that Santos cannot serve his first shift as usher until after Ursula has finished all of her shifts, but all other conditions remain the same. If Ursula ushers twice, then which one of the following pairs of ushers CANNOT serve together?

(A) Rolando and Ursula
(B) Santos and Victor
(C) Mathias and Ursula
(D) Rolando and Wilma
(E) Mathias and Victor

S T O P

IF YOU FINISH BEFORE TIME IS CALLED, YOU MAY CHECK YOUR WORK ON THIS SECTION ONLY.
DO NOT WORK ON ANY OTHER SECTION IN THE TEST.

Answer key and explanations for Test 12

Answer Key

1. D
2. C
3. A
4. E
5. D
6. E
7. B
8. C
9. A
10. D
11. D
12. C
13. C
14. B
15. B
16. A
17. E
18. C
19. A
20. B
21. B
22. E

Tennis lessons

This easy simple line game has six slots, each to be filled by one member. Further simplifying the game, each member is used exactly once. A line game does not get any easier than this. You should combine Rule 1 and Rule 3 to create the chain of H < X < F. Rule 2 is self-explanatory: J cannot be 12:00, 1:00, or 2:00. (Figure 1) Rule 4 is slightly more complex. Rule 4 could be F __ D or it could be D __ F. Now, make warranted conclusions. Start with the chain of H < X < F. Because F must come after both H and X, F cannot be at 9:00 or 10:00. (Figure 1) Similarly, because H must come before both F and X, H cannot be at 1:00 or 2:00. But, H must also come before D, because only one student separates D and F. So, even if the order were D X F, H would have to be before D. So H cannot be at 12:00 either. What about X? X must, at a minimum, be after H and before F, so X cannot be at 9:00 or 2:00. If you still have difficulty seeing how these blocks affect the diagram, use your fingers to measure out the length of the three-letter block, and place your fingers on the diagram to help you visualize how they take up the spaces. Although you may have made other conclusions, the conclusions that are now on the graph are more than adequate to begin answering the questions.

9	10	11	12	1	2
__	__	__	__	__	__
			~~J~~	~~J~~	~~J~~
~~F~~	~~F~~		~~D~~	~~D~~	~~D~~
			~~H~~	~~H~~	~~H~~
~~X~~					~~X~~

Fig. 1

1. (D) – For this question, you can use the rules to quickly eliminate four of the answer choices.
   (A) This choice violates Rule 3 because it has X before H.
   (B) This choice violates Rule 2 because it has J at 2:00 PM.
   (C) This choice violates Rule 4 because it has F preceding D by only one hour.
   (D) * This choice does not violate any rules.
   (E) This choice violates Rule 1 because it has F before X.

2. (C) – Before checking the answer choices, consider how this question is written. It asks which of the answer choices contains students, any one of whom could be scheduled for the first lesson. So, all you need to do is eliminate one of the three students in an answer choice and you can eliminate the whole answer choice. Look at figure 1 for guidance. We know that neither F nor X can have the first lesson. Three of the answer choices contain

either F or X, so we can eliminate those three answer choices. Only answer choices (B) and (C) remain. H and G are in both of these answer choices, so there is no need to check them. You only need to check D and J.

(A) X cannot be first. (Figure 1) Nor, as it turns out, can D be first.

(B) D cannot be first, because if it were, then F would have to be third and J would have to be second. This would not leave space for H and X to precede F. You should add this new information to figure 1 for future reference.

(C) * Any of these three students are possible for the first lesson.

(D) F cannot be first. (Figure 1)

(E) X cannot be first. (Figure 1)

3. (A) – Simply create a new diagram with J at 11:00 AM. Now, consider figure 1 and where F and D may be. H and X must precede F, and F must precede D. So, the only place F will fit is 12:00 noon. D is at 2:00 PM. (Figure 2)

(A) * H must be at 9:00 AM.

(B) G must be at 1:00 PM.

(C) X must be at 10:00 AM.

(D) D must be at 2:00 PM.

(E) F must be at 12:00 noon.

9	10	11	12	1	2
H	X	J	F	G	D
			~~J~~	~~J~~	~~J~~
~~F~~	~~F~~		~~D~~	~~D~~	~~D~~
			~~H~~	~~H~~	~~H~~
~~X~~					~~X~~
~~D~~					

Fig. 2

4. (E) – H is now immediately before G. Add G to the chain of H < X < F to create a longer chain, H G < X < F, F _ D. What is the latest H and G could be? G could be at 10:00 AM, or G could be at 11:00 AM. G cannot be later than 11:00 AM. Quickly diagram these two permutations. (Figures 3a-b) Because J must be before 12:00 noon, the two permutations are easy to diagram.

(A) X must be at 1:00 PM.

(B) D must be at 12:00 noon.

(C) J must be at 11 :00 AM.

(D) X must be at 1:00 PM.

(E) * G could be at 11:00 AM.

9	10	11	12	1	2
H	G	J	D	X	F

Fig. 3a

9	10	11	12	1	2
J	H	G	D	X	F

Fig. 3b

5. (D) – If X is before 12:00 noon, then X can be either 10:00 AM or 11:00 AM. (Figure 1 reminds us that X cannot be 9:00 AM.) The quickest way to solve this question is to graph the permutations for X at 10:00 AM (figure 4a) and at 11:00 AM (figure 4b). In either case, G must be at 1:00 PM; all the other members are not fixed.
(A) H can be 9:00 AM or 10:00 AM.
(B) X can be 10:00 AM or 11:00 PM.
(C) D can be 12:00 noon or 2:00 PM.
(D) * G must be 1:00 PM.
(E) See (C).

9	10	11	12	1	2
H	X	J	F/D	G	F/D

Fig. 4a

9	10	11	12	1	2
J/H	J/H	X	F/D	G	F/D

Fig. 4b

6. (E) Because this question adds no new information, you should be able to answer it using the initial warranted conclusions, as well as any insights you gleaned while answering earlier questions.

(A) Figure 1 does not show that G cannot be at 9:00 AM, but a little more confirmation would be nice. A quick check of the previous correct answer choices—specifically question 1, answer choice (D)—shows that G can be at 9:00 AM.

(B) Figure 1 does not show that G cannot be at 10:00 AM, but a little more confirmation would be nice. A quick check of the work you did for question 4, answer choice (E) shows that G can be at 10:00 AM.

(C) In question 5, we saw that X can be at 11:00 AM.

(D) Figure 1 does not show that D cannot be at 11:00 AM, but none of the previous work we did shows that D can be at 11:00 AM. It is a simple matter to graph a permutation where D is at 11:00 AM. For example: H, J, D, X, F, G.

(E) * As we learned while making the warranted conclusions, H cannot be at 12:00 noon. (Figure 1)

Chamber of Commerce voting

This is a very difficult game. It is difficult to determine what diagram to use and how to modify it. A grouping diagram does not keep track of the rules. A matrix diagram does not work either. A modified line diagram appears promising, but it is still difficult to decide whether the three companies should serve as the main organizing principle of the diagram, or whether the five categories should serve as the main focus of the diagram. Either way you do it, the questions are solvable, but it is easier to use the five categories for the basic structure, and place the three company names on the dashes. (Figure 1) Rule 3 specifies that no company votes on both internal and local matters, so those two categories should be closely linked in the diagram. With this diagram, Rule 1 is easy to depict, though it is necessary to rephrase it in the positive to mean that if PG votes for judicial, then RH does too. (Figure 1) Rule 2 requires a bit more diagramming, but is easy enough to depict using this diagram. (Figure 2) Finally, Rule 4 is easy to depict. (Figure 2) Remember, each company votes three times.

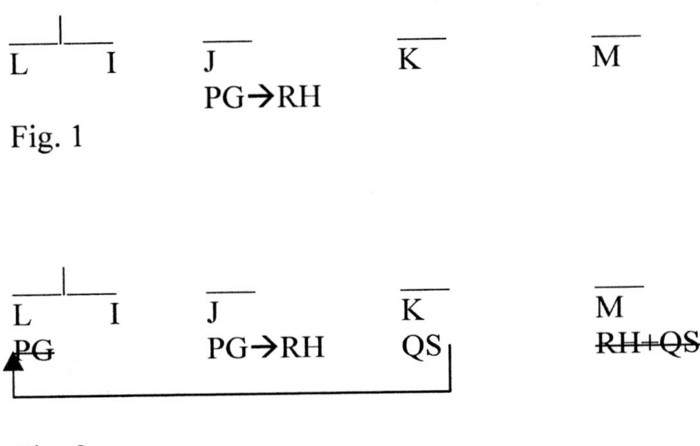

Fig. 1

Fig. 2

7. (B) – Use each rule to eliminate the answer choice that violates that rule. The answer choice that is not eliminated is the correct answer.
   (A) This choice is wrong since it shows QS voting on both internal and local matters, violating Rule 3.
   (B) * This does not violate any rules.
   (C) This violates Rule 1: it shows PG voting on judicial, but not RH.
   (D) This violates Rule 4: it shows both QS and RH voting on monetary.
   (E) This violates Rule 2: it has PG vote on local while QS votes on kitchen.

8. (C) – If PG votes on judicial, then RH votes on judicial as well, Rule 1. (Figure 3) If PG votes on local, then QS cannot vote on kitchen. PG also cannot vote on internal. Consider what you now know. There must be three PGs, but we don't know whether the third PG votes on kitchen or monetary. We don't know anything definite about RH either. We can conclude something about QS. We know there are three QSs available to vote on the

four spaces. One of the QSs will vote on either local or internal. The second QS must vote on judicial. The third QS must vote on monetary. Finally, since QS votes on monetary, RH does not. That should be sufficient analysis to answer the question.

(A) No, QS cannot vote on kitchen matters.
(B) PG cannot vote on internal matters because PG votes on local matters.
(C) * RH may vote on internal matters.
(D) No, not all three companies can vote on local matters, one of them must vote on internal matters in order to satisfy Rule 3.
(E) QS does not vote on kitchen matters.

~~QS~~
RH
PG|~~PG~~   PG
L   I   J   K   M
~~PG~~   PG→RH   QS   ~~RH+QS~~

Fig. 3

9. (A) – If QS votes on internal matters, then it does not vote on local matters. If QS votes on kitchen matters, then PG does not vote on local matters. This means that RH is the only one that can vote on local matters.

(A) * RH is the only one available to vote on local matters. The set-up specified that each matter is voted on by at least one company.
(B) This could be true, or it may not be.
(C) This could be true, or it may not be.
(D) This could be true, or it may not be.
(E) Because RH must vote for local matters, it cannot vote for internal matters.

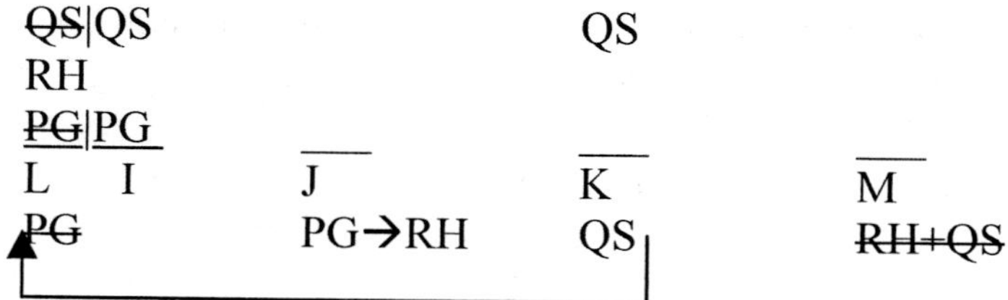

Fig. 4

10. (D) – If PG votes on local matters, then, due to the effect of Rule 2, QS does not vote on kitchen matters. This creates a situation similar to that in question 8, where the three QSs must be allocated. There must be a QS voting on judicial, another on monetary, and the third on either local or internal. Since

QS votes on monetary, Rule 4 specifies that RH does not vote on monetary. (Figure 5)

(A) See figure 5. There is no indication that PG cannot vote on kitchen matters.

(B) See figure 5. There is no indication that PG cannot vote on judicial matters.

(C) QS must either vote on internal matters or local matters.

(D) * See figure 5. Since QS must vote on monetary matters, RH cannot.

(E) We have no way of knowing whether RH will vote on local matters or internal matters.

? ? QS ~~QS~~ QS

~~RH~~

PG|~~PG~~ ___ ___ ___

L I J K M

~~PG~~ PG→RH QS ~~RH+QS~~

Fig. 5

11. (D) – Do each part of this question separately. Since QS votes on kitchen matters, then PG does not vote on local matters. Since PG does not vote on local matters or judicial matters, yet PG must vote twice more, PG must vote for internal matters and monetary matters. (Figure 6) Now consider QS, where might its third vote be? So far, we can't be sure. Now consider RH. RH must vote on exactly two more matters, and judicial is eliminated. So RH must vote on monetary and on either local or internal. Since RH votes on monetary, QS cannot.

(A) RH and PG must both vote on monetary and kitchen.

(B) See (A).

(C) QS cannot vote on monetary because RH must vote on monetary.

(D) * It is possible that PG and QS vote on two common matters, kitchen and local.

(E) RH must vote on either internal or local.

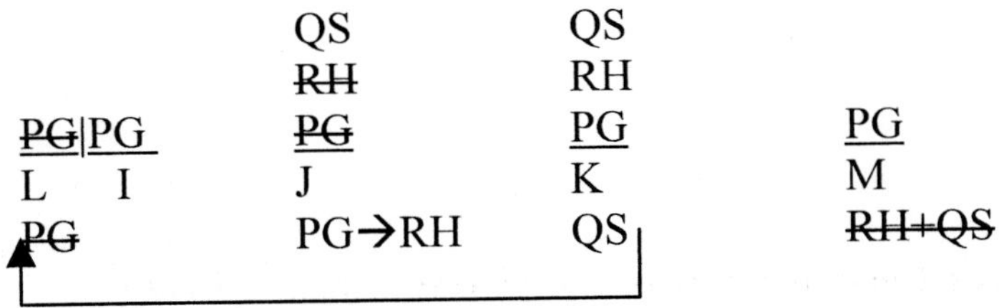

Fig. 6

Employee lunch groups

Logic games always require you to make extra deductions. With some games, you can make at least some deductions immediately after reading the rules. Other times, like in this game, you cannot easily make warranted conclusions until the questions provide more information to anchor the diagram. You cannot excel on the LSAT until you have developed an instinct for when to stop attempting to make conclusions and move to the questions. Although it is always possible to do permutations, it is usually a waste of precious time.

A standard mono-group selection diagram works well for this game. Include all the members in each column and use arrows to show the relationships created by the rules. G, H, and J all have certain restrictions. H cannot eat alone, so H eats with one or more employees. J eats with exactly two other employees. G either eats alone or with two or more employees. In other words, G does not eat with exactly one other employee; G eats with zero, two, or more other employees. All of this is noted under the main diagram.

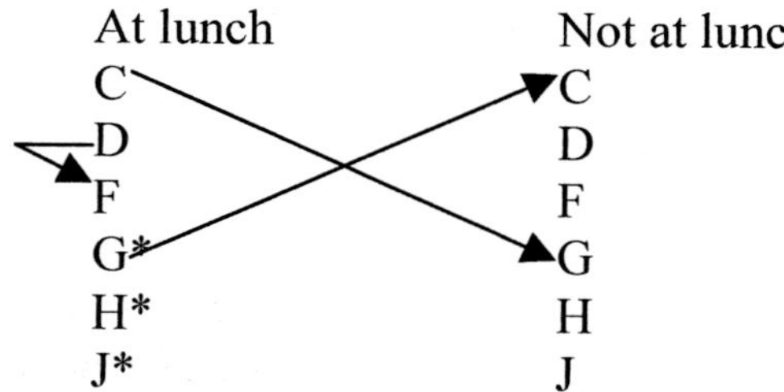

H + 1 or more
J + exactly 2.
G + 0, 2, or more

Fig. 1

12. (C) – With "possible arrangement" questions, simply eliminate answer choices that violate the explicit rules.
(A) J will not have lunch unless exactly two people join him, Rule 4.
(B) If D eats lunch, F eats with him, Rule 1.
(C) * This is viable lunch group; no rules are violated.
(D) This violates Rule 2, because C and G are together.
(E) This answer choice violates Rule 5.

13. (C) – What is the maximum number of employees who can eat together? Start with the highest number. Can all six eat together? No, because C and G are mutually exclusive. Can five eat together? No, because if J is eating, then exactly two others are permitted. Can four eat together? Yes, one possible group is CDFH.
(A) See the analysis.

(B) See the analysis.
(C) * See the analysis.
(D) See the analysis.
(E) See the analysis.

14. (B) – If G eats lunch, can G eat alone? Yes, G can eat lunch alone. Can G eat with exactly one other employee? No, Rule 5 prohibits this. Can G eat with two or three other employees? Yes. Keep this in mind while considering the answer choices.
(A) As long as G, F, and one other employee, like J, eat together, this is a possible lunch group.
(B) * Can both D and J eat lunch with G? G, J, and one other employee can eat lunch together, but if that third employee is D, then Rule 1 requires that F also join the group. But J is only allowed to eat with two other employees, so this cannot be true.
(C) If G eats alone, then neither D nor J eats lunch.
(D) See (C).
(E) It is possible that G, F, and J all eat lunch together.

15. (B) – If exactly four employees eat lunch, you should look at the work done for question 13. In that question, we learned that CDFH was a valid lunch group of four employees. It is also possible to substitute G for C. Keep this in mind while checking the answer choices.
(A) We know that that H can eat lunch. Must H eat lunch in a group of four? Yes, because it is not possible to substitute either G or J for H.
(B) * We know that C can eat lunch. We also know that C can be replaced by G.
(C) Similar to (A), D must eat lunch in a group of four.
(D) J can never eat lunch in a group of four, due to Rule 4.
(E) F must eat lunch in any group of four.

16. (A) – Starting with Rule 4, J must eat lunch with exactly two other employees. Four of the following pairs will be possible, one will not.
(A) * C and D cannot eat lunch with J. If D eats lunch, then F must also eat lunch. J cannot eat with three other employees.
(B) C and H can eat with J. Rule 2 specifies that H does not eat alone, so that is satisfied.
(C) D and F can eat with J. All rules are satisfied.
(D) F and G can eat with J. Just because F is present does not mean D must be.
(E) G and H can eat with J. Rule 5 specifies that G does not eat with exactly one other employee.

Volunteer ushers

This puzzle requires attention to detail. It has four time slots, with two spaces to fill for each time slot. The tricky part is that there are eight spaces to fill, and only six people to fill the spaces, so some of the volunteers will be used more than once. The setup specifies that no usher works on consecutive shifts. Rule 1 specifies that each of the six people will serve on at least one shift. Keeping both of these rules in the back of your mind, diagram the other rules. (Figure 1) Rule 2 is easy to diagram, simply note a negative M under the second and third shifts. Rule 3, R serves one shift, should be noted off to the side. Rule 4 is a complex rule. Make a brief note of it off to the side with an asterisk, and come back to the text of this rule as you work through the questions. Rule 4 is less precise then it appears. All it really says is that at least one S must be later than at least one U. Finally, Rule 5 is easy, place W in the second shift. What warranted conclusions can we make? Nothing too helpful, unfortunately. We know that W cannot be in the first or third shift. Now consider the occupancy issues. There are six volunteers for eight slots. Clearly, at least one person must be used more than once. Could one person be used three times, and the other five people be used once each? No, if one person, say, V, were used three times, then V would have to serve on two consecutive shifts, violating the setup which said that no usher works consecutive shifts. So we can conclude that two volunteers are used twice each, and the other four are used once each. Keep this in mind as you work through the questions.

1	2	3	4
___	W	___	___
___	___	___	___
	~~M~~	~~M~~	
~~W~~		~~W~~	

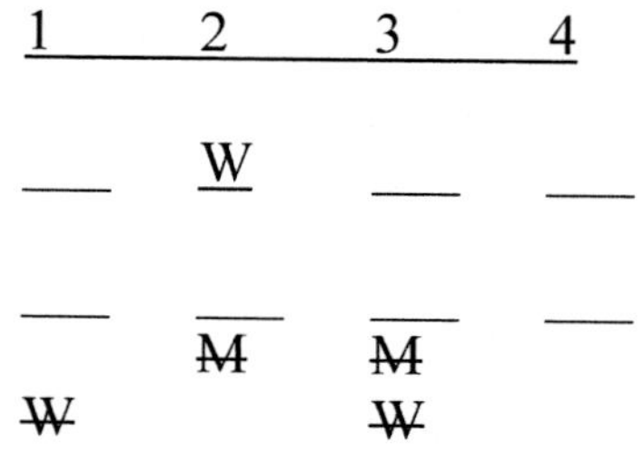

U<S*
R=1

Fig. 1

17. (E) – With the "possible order" or "acceptable arrangement" question type, simply eliminate any answer choices that violate the rules. The answer choice that remains is the correct response.
(A) This violates Rule 4 because it does not have an S later than a U.
(B) This violates the setup because it has V twice in a row.
(C) This answer choice violates Rule 3, because R is used twice.
(D) This answer choice violates Rule 2, because M cannot be in the third shift.
(E) * This answer choice does not violate any rule.

18. (C) – Since this question does not add any new information, we should be able to answer it using our initial analysis.

(A) In the initial analysis, we determined that four of the volunteers must serve on one shift.
(B) See (A).
(C) * Correct. Four of the ushers must serve on one shift.
(D) One usher cannot serve on three shifts, as discussed in the initial analysis.
(E) If three ushers were to serve on two shifts, then only two shifts would be left for the remaining three ushers, meaning that one usher would be without a shift.

19. (A) – This questions picks U and W to be the two ushers that serve two shifts each. The only place for a second W would be in the fourth shift. Where could the two Us be? U could be either first and fourth, or second and fourth. So U must be fourth and cannot be third. (Figure 2) Let's see if that is enough work to answer the question.
(A) * The only shift open to both M and S is the first shift. But putting S in the first shift violates Rule 4.
(B) M can serve on the first shift, as long as it is not with S.
(C) V can serve on the first shift.
(D) R can serve on the second shift.
(E) V and R could both serve on the third shift.

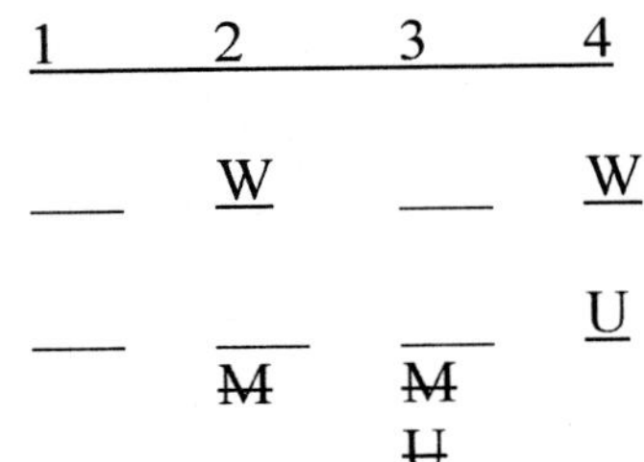

U<S*
R=1

Fig. 2

20. (B) – Each of the answer choices will require work.
(A) S cannot be on the first shift only, as discussed in question 19(A).
(B) * At first glance, nothing seems to prevent V from ushering with both M and W. For example, V could be in the second shift with W, and the fourth shift with M. Then we can fill the remaining shifts.
(C) R can only be on one shift, per Rule 3.
(D) Because of Rule 5, U cannot serve only on the fourth shift.
(E) W cannot be on the third shift because W is already on the second shift.

21. (B) – If neither V nor M (nor R) is used twice, then exactly two out of W, S, or U must be used twice. This eliminates answer choices (A), (C), and (D)

since they have too many or too few volunteers. We want an answer choice with two members, WS, WU, or SU. Of the remaining two answer choices, choice (E) contains R. This violates Rule 3, so we can eliminate choice (E). Remember, this question is asking about a possible permutation, so the correct answer choice must have exactly two members of the W, S, U group. This is a tricky phrasing.

(A) See the analysis.
(B) * See the analysis.
(C) See the analysis.
(D) See the analysis.
(E) See the analysis.

22. (E) – This slight change in the rules means that U must serve twice, and only then can S serve. To accommodate this, U must serve on the first and third shifts, and S must serve on the fourth shift. S cannot serve on any other shifts. (Figure 3a) There are still many permutations, so go to the answer choices.

(A) R and U could serve together, on the third shift, for example.
(B) S and V could be together in the fourth shift. V would also have to be in the second shift to make this work. (Figure 3b)
(C) M and U could be together. (Figure 3b)
(D) R and W could be together. M would be on the first and fourth shift, and V would be on the third shift.
(E) * Both M and V cannot be together because each of the four shifts has only one space available to hold either M or V, but not both. (Figure 3a)

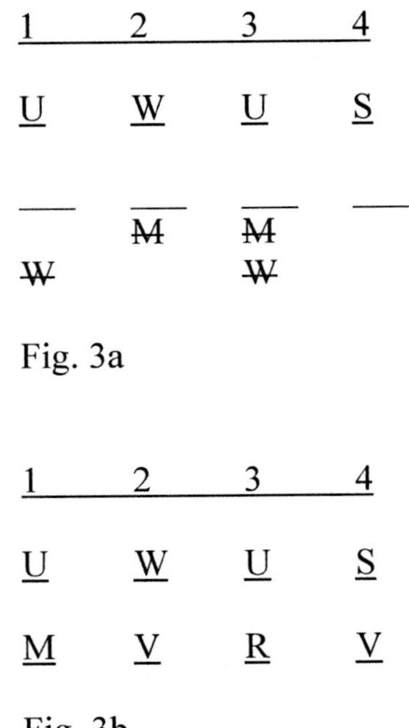

Fig. 3a

Fig. 3b

Practice Test 13

Spend 35 minutes doing this practice test. When time is up, review the explanations to help you understand the questions that you did not answer correctly.

SECTION I

Time—35 minutes

23 Questions

Directions: Each group of questions in this section is based on a set of conditions. In answering some of the questions, it may b useful to draw a rough diagram. Choose the response that most accurately and completely answers each question and blacken th corresponding space on your answer sheet.

Questions 1–6

A sporting goods store has six aisles, numbered 1 to 6. Each aisle features only one of the following six categories—basketball, darts, fishing, hunting, lacrosse, or mountain climbing. Each of the categories is featured on exactly one aisle. The following conditions must apply:

The dart aisle must be either aisle number 1 or aisle number 4.

The lacrosse aisle must be a lower-numbered aisle than the hunting aisle.

The hunting aisle must be a higher-numbered aisle than the basketball aisle, but a lower-numbered aisle than the fishing aisle.

1. Which one of the following could be an accurate list of products featured in the store from aisle 1 to aisle 6?

(A) basketball, hunting, lacrosse, darts, mountain climbing, fishing
(B) darts, basketball, fishing, lacrosse, hunting, mountain climbing
(C) basketball, lacrosse, darts, hunting, fishing, mountain climbing
(D) darts, lacrosse, basketball, hunting, fishing, mountain climbing
(E) mountain climbing, lacrosse, hunting, darts, basketball, fishing

2. Which one of the following categories of products CANNOT be featured on aisle 4?

(A) basketball
(B) fishing
(C) hunting
(D) lacrosse
(E) mountain climbing

3. If lacrosse products are featured on aisle 4, then each of the following must be true EXCEPT:

(A) Aisle 1 features dart products.
(B) Aisle 2 features basketball products.
(C) Aisle 3 does not feature fishing products.
(D) Aisle 5 does not feature mountain climbing products.
(E) Aisle 6 features fishing products.

4. Which one of the following categories of products can be featured on any one of the six aisles?

(A) basketball
(B) fishing
(C) hunting
(D) lacrosse
(E) mountain climbing

5. If the mountain climbing products are featured on a lower-numbered aisle than the dart products, then which one of the following must be true?

(A) The basketball products are featured on a lower numbered aisle than the mountain climbing products.
(B) The basketball products are featured on a lower numbered aisle than the lacrosse products.
(C) The dart products are featured on a higher numbered aisle than the fishing products.
(D) The dart products are featured on a higher numbered aisle than the lacrosse products.
(E) The fishing products are featured on a lower numbered aisle than the basketball products.

6. If the basketball products are featured on an aisle that numbered exactly two lower than the aisle on which th lacrosse products are featured, then which one of the following could be true?

(A) Aisle 1 features mountain climbing products.
(B) Aisle 3 features hunting products.
(C) Aisle 4 features lacrosse products.
(D) Aisle 5 features lacrosse products.
(E) Aisle 6 features mountain climbing products.

GO ON TO THE NEXT PAG

Questions 7–11

A numismatist has a collection of coins numbered 1 through 4. Each coin has two sides, heads and tails, and each side pictures one of the following U.S. presidents—Jefferson, Monroe, Polk or Taft. For each coin, the heads side of that coin is listed first when naming the presidents pictured on that coin. The following conditions must apply:

Each president is pictured on exactly two of the eight coin sides.

Coin 1 pictures Polk on at least one side.

Taft is not pictured on any two consecutively numbered coins.

Jefferson is not pictured on any coin numbered exactly one higher than a coin that pictures Monroe on either side.

If any coin pictures Taft on the tails side, then Jefferson must appear only on the heads side of any coin on which Jefferson is pictured.

7. Which one of the following could be an accurate matching of coins with the presidents that are pictured on them?

(A) Coin 1: Jefferson and Polk; Coin 2: Jefferson and Polk; Coin 3: Monroe and Taft; Coin 4: Monroe and Taft
(B) Coin 1: Jefferson and Polk; Coin 2: Jefferson and Taft; Coin 3: Monroe and Polk; Coin 4: Monroe and Taft
(C) Coin 1: Jefferson and Polk; Coin 2: Taft and Monroe; Coin 3: Jefferson and Polk; Coin 4: Monroe and Taft
(D) Coin 1: Taft and Monroe; Coin 2: Polk and Monroe; Coin 3: Taft and Polk; Coin 4: Jefferson on both sides
(E) Coin 1: Polk on both sides; Coin 2: Taft on both sides; Coin 3: Jefferson on both sides; Coin 4: Monroe on both sides

8. Which one of the following must be true?

(A) If Coin 1 pictures Polk on both sides, Coin 3 pictures Monroe on at least one side.
(B) If Coin 1 pictures Jefferson on one side, Coin 2 features Jefferson on one side.
(C) If Coin 2 pictures Monroe on both sides, Coin 4 features Jefferson on both sides.
(D) If Coin 2 pictures Taft on both sides, Coin 3 features Monroe on at least one side.
(E) If Coin 3 pictures Polk on at least one side, Coin 4 pictures Monroe on at least one side.

9. If Taft is pictured on both sides of Coin 2, then which one of the following CANNOT be true?

(A) Polk is pictured on both sides of Coin 1.
(B) Monroe is pictured on Coin 3.
(C) Monroe is pictured on consecutively numbered coins.
(D) Jefferson is not pictured on any coin that also pictures Polk.
(E) Jefferson is pictured on consecutively numbered coins.

10. Which one of the following CANNOT be true?

(A) Jefferson is pictured on the tails side of Coin 1 and Coin 4.
(B) Polk is pictured on the tails side of Coin 1 and Coin 3.
(C) Taft is pictured on both sides of Coin 4.
(D) Monroe is pictured on both sides of Coin 4.
(E) Jefferson is pictured on both sides of Coin 4.

11. If Polk appears on both sides of a single coin, then which one of the following could be the list of presidents that appear on the two sides of Coin 2?

(A) Monroe only
(B) Monroe and Taft
(C) Jefferson and Taft
(D) Jefferson only
(E) Taft only

GO ON TO THE NEXT PAGE.

Questions 12–17

Five high-school students serve as ambassadors to the Model United Nations. The five students are Ross, Selby, Turner, Voss and Wentis. There will be four ambassador meetings, and each meeting will be attended by exactly two ambassadors. Each of the five students attends at least one of the ambassador meetings, but no student will attend all four meetings. The following conditions must apply:

Ross and Selby do not attend any meeting together.
Turner and Wentis attend exactly one meeting together.
Voss attends only one meeting.

12. If Voss does not attend any meeting that either Ross or Selby attends, then which one of the following must be true?

(A) Ross attends exactly two meetings.
(B) Selby attends exactly two meetings.
(C) Turner attends only one meeting.
(D) Two students attend exactly one meeting.
(E) One student attends exactly three meetings.

13. If Ross attends exactly two meetings, then which one of the following pairs of students CANNOT attend the same meeting?

(A) Ross and Turner
(B) Voss and Selby
(C) Voss and Wentis
(D) Ross and Wentis
(E) Selby and Turner

14. Which one of the following could be true?

(A) Exactly one student attends only one meeting.
(B) Exactly two students attend two meetings.
(C) Exactly four students attend only one meeting.
(D) Exactly three students attend two meetings.
(E) Exactly two students attend three meetings.

15. If Voss and Wentis attend a meeting together and Wentis attends exactly three meetings, then each of the following must be true EXCEPT:

(A) Either Ross or Selby attends a meeting with Wentis.
(B) Turner attends exactly two meetings.
(C) Selby attends exactly one meeting.
(D) Ross attends a meeting with Turner.
(E) Wentis does not attend two meetings with the same ambassador.

16. If Turner only attends one meeting, then which one of the following CANNOT be true?

(A) Voss attends a meeting with Ross.
(B) Wentis attends a meeting with Selby.
(C) Both Ross and Selby attend exactly two meetings.
(D) Exactly three of the students attend only one meeting.
(E) Exactly one student attends three meetings.

17. If the condition that Voss attends only one meeting is changed so that Voss attends exactly three meetings, but all other conditions remain the same, then which one of the following could be true?

(A) Turner attends a meeting with Voss.
(B) Ross attends a meeting with Wentis.
(C) Selby attends a meeting with Turner.
(D) Voss does not attend a meeting with Selby.
(E) Exactly two students attend two meetings.

GO ON TO THE NEXT PAGE

Questions 18–23

A theater company will audition six actors for an upcoming play. The actors to be auditioned are Adams, Benz, Crow, Daly, Evans and Francis. The actors will audition one at a time, and each actor will audition for the lead role in the play. Additionally, some actors will also audition for a supporting role. The following must obtain:

Francis is the third actor to audition.
The fifth actor to audition will audition for only the lead role.
The theater company will audition Benz for both the lead and supporting roles.
Adams' audition must take place at some time before Evans' audition, but at some time after Crow's audition.

18. Which one of the following could be an accurate listing of auditions held on the first day?

(A) Benz, Crow, Francis, Daly, Evans, Adams
(B) Daly, Benz, Francis, Crow, Adams, Evans
(C) Francis, Crow, Daly, Benz, Adams, Evans
(D) Crow, Adams, Francis, Evans, Benz, Daly
(E) Adams, Crow, Francis, Benz, Evans, Daly

19. If Benz auditions at some time after Evans auditions, then which one of the following must be true?

(A) Daly auditions first.
(B) Crow auditions second.
(C) Adams auditions fourth.
(D) Evans auditions fifth.
(E) Benz auditions sixth.

20. If any actor that auditions before Adams will audition only for the leading role, then the maximum number of actors that could audition for both roles is:

(A) 1
(B) 2
(C) 3
(D) 4
(E) 5

21. If Daly must audition immediately before Crow auditions, then which one of the following could be false?

(A) Crow auditions at some time before Benz auditions.
(B) Francis auditions at some time before Adams auditions.
(C) Benz auditions at some time before Evans auditions.
(D) Adams auditions at some time after Daly auditions.
(E) Evans auditions at some time after Francis auditions.

22. If Daly's audition is the last audition to be conducted, then which one of the following CANNOT be true?

(A) Evans' audition is the fourth audition conducted.
(B) Adams' audition is the fourth audition conducted.
(C) Adams' audition is the second audition conducted.
(D) Crow's audition is the second audition conducted.
(E) Benz' audition is the first audition conducted.

23. If both Adams and Evans audition for both the lead and supporting roles, then which one of the following must be true?

(A) Benz's audition is the first audition conducted.
(B) Adams' audition is the second audition conducted.
(C) Crow's audition is the third audition conducted.
(D) Evans audition is the fourth audition conducted.
(E) Daly's audition is the fifth audition conducted.

S T O P

IF YOU FINISH BEFORE TIME IS CALLED, YOU MAY CHECK YOUR WORK ON THIS SECTION ONLY.
DO NOT WORK ON ANY OTHER SECTION IN THE TEST.

Answer key and explanations for Test 13

Answer Key

1. D
2. B
3. B
4. E
5. D
6. C
7. B
8. A
9. A
10. A
11. C
12. E
13. C
14. D
15. D
16. C
17. A
18. B
19. E
20. D
21. C
22. A
23. E

Sporting goods line

This easy line game has six slots, each to be filled by one member. Further simplifying your task, each member is used exactly once. This makes it a very easy line diagram. Rule 1 is a typical rule, and is easy to graph. Rules 2 and 3 are also typical greater-than rules, and are also easily graphed. When there are interconnected greater-than rules, you should combine the rules. Here you can combine them to create L/B < H < F. Next, determine where members cannot be. For example, H cannot be first or second, because both L and B must precede H. H also cannot be sixth, because F must come after H. F cannot be first, second or third, because L, B, and H must precede F. Also, F cannot be fourth, because D must be first or fourth. So, when D is first, or fourth, at a minimum L, B, and H must take up three spaces, pushing F out to space five. The free agent is M. The questions will now be easy to answer.

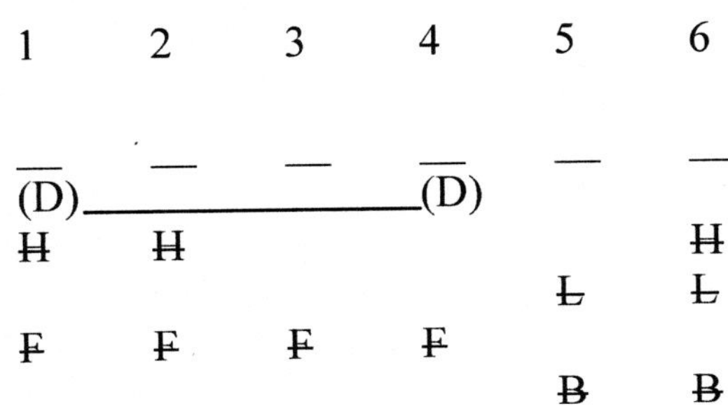

Fig. 1

1. (D) – In keeping with standard practice, use the rules to quickly eliminate four of the answer choices. Since there are only three rules, one of them will be used twice.
   (A) This choice violates Rule 2 because it has H before L
   (B) This choice violates Rule 3 because it has F before H.
   (C) This choice violates Rule 1 because it has D on space three.
   (D) * This choice does not violate any rules.
   (E) This choice violates Rule 3 because it has H before B.

2. (B) – This question is answerable using the initial analysis. If you failed during the initial analysis to conclude that F cannot be fourth, then you should add that information to your basic diagram once you learn it in this question.
   (A) B can be fourth. For example: D L M B H F.
   (B) * In the initial analysis you learned that F cannot be fourth.
   (C) H can be fourth. For example: D L B H M F.
   (D) See (A). L and B share the same analysis.
   (E) M is a free agent, and so can usually be anywhere in the diagram

3. (B) – Simply create a new diagram with L in the fourth space. D will now have to be first. H and F must come after L, so they will fill the fifth and sixth spaces, respectively. The second and third spaces are open for B and M. (Figure 2)
(A) Yes, the first space must have D.
(B) * The second space can have B or M.
(C) Yes, F cannot be in the third space.
(D) Yes, M cannot be in the fifth space.
(E) Yes, F must be in the sixth space.

1	2	3	4	5	6
D	__	__	L	H	F

Fig. 2

4. (E) – The only free agent is M. A quick glance at the figure 1 shows that five of the products—H, L, F, B, and D—are not permitted in certain aisles.
(A) See the analysis.
(B) See the analysis.
(C) See the analysis.
(D) See the analysis.
(E) * See the analysis.

5. (D) – Since M is now in a lower-numbered aisle than D, D must be in the fourth space. (Figure 3) M, L, and B must occupy the first three spaces while H and F occupy spaces five and six, respectively. That should be enough analysis to answer the question.
(A) We don't know exactly where the B, L, and M are.
(B) See (A).
(C) D must be fourth and F must be sixth.
(D) * Yes, D must be higher than L.
(E) No, F must be higher than B.

1	2	3	4	5	6
__	__	__	D	H	F

Fig. 3

6. (C) – Always be careful with rules that are phrased this way. Sometimes the rule is phrased, "exactly one member separates X and Y" or "X is in a space numbered two lower than Y." This means that there is one space between the two, and it is diagrammed like this: X _ Y. Occasionally, you will see a rule phrased as "X and Y are separated by two spaces." In that case, there are two empty spaces between them and it is diagrammed: X _ _ Y. In question 6, we are told that B is in an aisle numbered exactly two lower than L, so B _ L is the correct form. Where can B and L be? If B is first, L is third, D must be fourth and we can place all the products. (Figure 4a) If B is second, L is fourth, D is first, and we can place all the products. (Figure 4b)

(A) M cannot be first.
(B) H cannot be third.
(C) * L can be fourth.
(D) L cannot be fifth.
(E) M cannot be sixth.

1	2	3	4	5	6
B	M	L	D	H	F

Fig. 4a

1	2	3	4	5	6
D	B	M	L	H	F

Fig. 4b

Coin toss

This game requires a double line, and serious attention to detail. Rule 2 (Polk is on Coin 1) is the only rule that is easy to diagram. (Figure 1) Rule 5, if a T is on tails, then both Js are on heads. This can be graphed somewhat. Note the rest of the rules below the diagram. T cannot appear on consecutive coins, but can appear twice on the same coin. J is not immediately higher in number than M. It does not seem possible to draw warranted conclusions without getting bogged down in numerous permutations, so go directly to the questions.

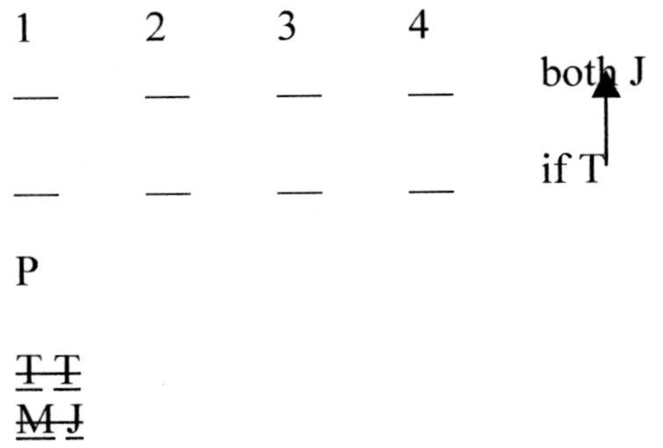

```
1    2    3    4
__   __   __   __      both J
                         ↑
__   __   __   __      if T

P

T T  (crossed out)
M J  (crossed out)
```

Fig. 1

7. (B) – Use each rule to eliminate the answer choice that violates that rule. The answer choice that is not eliminated is the correct answer.
(A) This violates Rule 3 because it shows T on consecutive coins.
(B) * This does not violate any rules.
(C) This violates Rule 4 because it shows J immediately after M.
(D) This violates Rule 2 because it does not have P on Coin 1.
(E) This violates Rule 5 because it shows a T and a J on tails.

8. (A) – When a "must be true" question does not add new information, but each of the five answer choices adds new information, it takes a great deal of work to find the correct answer. Skip this kind of question and come back to it after you have solved all the other questions and have a better feel for the game and the rules. For each of these answer choices you try to find at least one valid permutation to prove that the answer choice is not a "must be true."
(A) * If you had skipped this question and returned to it after doing question 12, then you could have used your work from question 12 to answer this. If P is on both sides of Coin 1, is it possible to not place an M on Coin 4? See figure 2. First, try placing both Ms on Coin 2. This would force both the Js to Coin 4. Then both the Ts would have to be on Coin 3. But this would violate Rule 5. Second, try placing both Ms on Coin 3. Both the Js would have to be on Coin 2 and both Ts on Coin 4. The same problem arises. Finally, try placing one M on Coin 2 and one M on Coin 4. The problem is that then J cannot be placed without violating Rule 4. As a

final check, make sure that M can be on Coin 3. Yes, M can be on Coin 3 and Coin 4, J can be on Coin 2 and Coin 3, and T can be on Coin 2 and Coin 4. Therefore, it must be true that if P is on both sides of Coin 1, M must be on Coin 3. This is a great deal of work just to answer one question. Make sure you do not get drawn into a question like this and waste valuable time.

(B) Yes, it is possible to have J on Coins 1 and 3, P on Coins 1 and 2, T on Coins 2 and 4, and M on Coins 3 and 4.

(C) It is possible to have both Ms on Coin 2, one J on Coin 4 and one on Coin 1, one P on Coin 4 and one on Coin 1, and both Ts on Coin 3.

(D) It is possible to have both Ts on Coin 2, both Ms on Coin 4, and J and P on Coins 1 and 3.

(E) It is possible to have P on Coins 3 and 1, M on Coins 2 and 3, both Ts on Coin 4, and J on Coins 1 and 2.

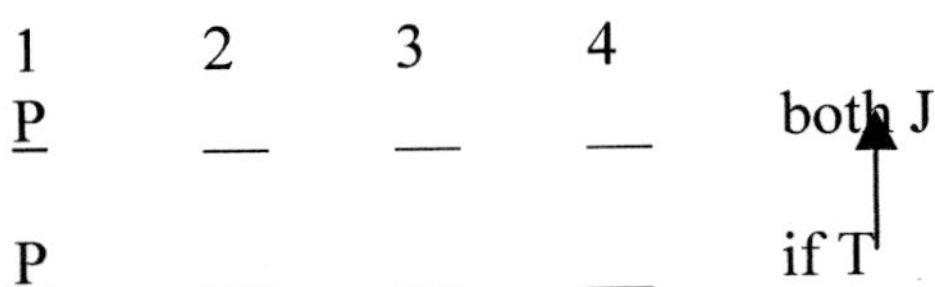

Fig. 2

9. (A) – Employing the new information about T, you now know that both Js must be heads. We can deduce that J must be heads on either Coin 1 and Coin 3 or Coin 3 and Coin 4. This still leaves the diagram a bit sparse, so go to the answer choices for more guidance.

(A) * P cannot be on both sides of Coin 1. If it were, then J and M would have to share Coin 3 and Coin 4, and then Rule 4 would be violated.

(B) M can be on Coin 3. (Figure 3)

(C) M can be on consecutive coins. (Figure 3)

(D) J can be on the same coin as P. (Figure 3)

(E) J can be on consecutive coins, Coin 3 and Coin 4.

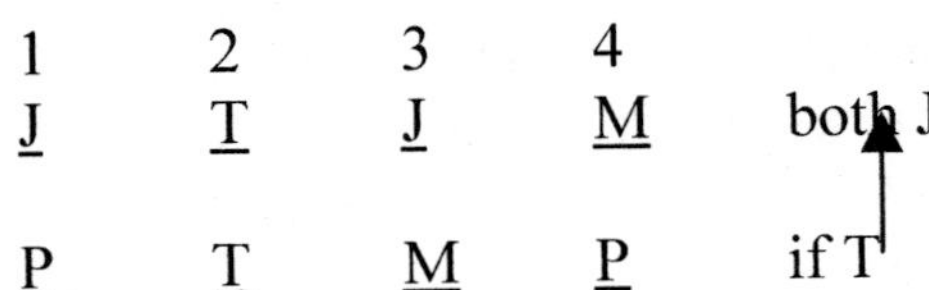

Fig. 3

10. (A) – Once again, a question with no new information. Fortunately, you only need to test the answer choice; if it makes one valid permutation, you can eliminate it. (Figure 4)

(A) * See figure 4. Both Ts would need to be heads to avoid violating Rule 5. The Ts could not be on consecutive coins, so T would need to be on Coins 2 and 4. The problem comes when you then try to place M. There is nowhere to place M without violating Rule 4.

(B) P can be on tails of Coins 1 and 3, as long as T is on tails of Coins 2 and 4, J is on heads of Coins 1 and 2, and M is on heads of Coins 3 and 4.

(C) T can be on both sides of Coin 4, as long as J is heads on Coins 1 and 2, P is tails on Coins 1 and 2, and M is on both sides of Coin 3.

(D) M can be on both sides of Coin 4, as long as T is on both sides of Coin 3, J is on heads of Coins 1 and 2, and P is on tails of Coins 1 and 2.

(E) J can be on both sides of Coin 4, as long as T is on heads of Coins 1 and 3, P is on tails of Coins 1 and 3, and M is on both sides of Coin 2.

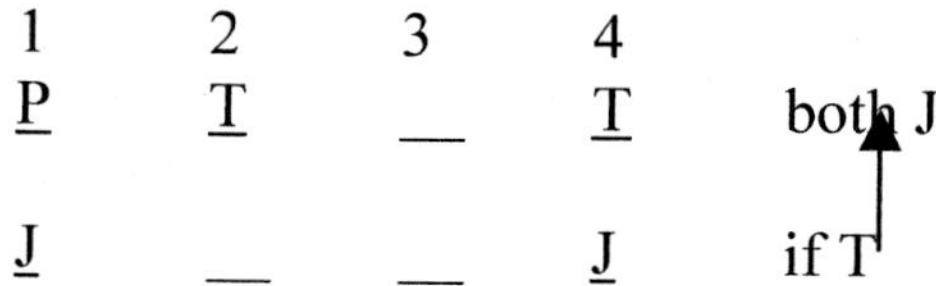

Fig. 4

11. (C) – Since there must be at least one P on Coin 1, this new information means that P must be on both sides of Coin 1. Plug the new information from each answer choice into figure 5.

(A) If M were to occupy both sides of Coin 2, then J would have to be on both sides of Coin 4. This would then require T to be on tails of Coin 3, which would violate Rule 5.

(B) If M and T are on Coin 2 (it doesn't matter which configuration) then both Js would have to be on Coin 4. But this will not work because the second M would have to be on Coin 3.

(C) * J and T can be on Coin 2. J could be heads and T could be tails. The second J could be on Coin 3 (heads). The second T could be tails on Coin 3. Both Ms could be on Coin 4.

(D) If both Js were on Coin 2, then both Ts would have to be heads on Coins 3 and 4. But Rule 3 specifies that T cannot be on two consecutive days.

(E) If both Ts are on Coin 2, then J has to be heads on Coins 3 and 4, but then the M on tails of Coin 3 will violate Rule 4.

1 2 3 4
P __ __ __ both J
P __ __ __ if T

Fig. 5

Student ambassadors

This game requires a basic diagram. There are four meetings, and each meeting has exactly two attendees. (Figure 1) It is not necessary to number the meetings, since neither the rules nor the questions refer to a specific meeting by its number. Begin by diagramming the rules. Rule 2 is the easiest to diagram: T and W attend exactly one meeting together. Since the specific meeting number is not relevant, just go ahead and put T and W in the first meeting. (Figure 1) Rule 1 says that R and S will not attend any meetings together. This can also be diagrammed. Place R in one of the open meetings and S in the other. (Figure 2) For Rule 3 it will be easy enough to keep in mind that V is used only once. Now, what warranted conclusions can you make? Always be thinking about the occupancy limits. We know that each student is used at least once, and no student is used more than three times. What if one student is used three times, what would that mean for the other students? There would be four students left to fill five open slots. So one of those four students would be used twice, and the other three would be used once. This could be noted as 1-3x/1-2x/3-1x. Now try some other numbers. It is not possible to have just one student used twice and the others all used just once, as this equals six. It is also not possible to have two students used twice and the other three used just once, as this equals seven. It is possible to have three students used twice, and two students used once, this equals eight. This could be noted as 3-2x/2-1x. Keep these two possible occupancy numbers in mind; they will be very helpful when answering some of the questions.

T	__	__	__
W	__	__	__

Fig. 1

T	R	S	__
W	__	__	__

Fig. 2

12. (E) – Plug the new information into the diagram. V will be in the meeting that does not have R or S. (Figure 3) Now what? We know that R, S, and V cannot appear again. That leaves T and W to fill the remaining three slots. In the initial analysis we determined that when three students (here it is R, S, and V) are each used once, then one student (here it is either T or W) is used three times, and the other student is used twice. We don't know exactly where T and W will be, but we should have enough information to answer the question.

(A) R cannot attend two meetings, because Rule 1 prevents R from attending a meeting with S, and this question said that R does not attend with V.
(B) S has the same analysis as R does in answer choice (A).
(C) T attends either two or three meetings.
(D) Three students, R, S, and V, attend exactly one meeting.
(E) * Correct, either T or W attends three meetings.

T R S V

W __ __ __

Fig. 3

13. (C) – R attends two meetings, but can't attend a meeting with S, so R attends the only open meeting. (Figure 4) What else can we conclude? S cannot attend any meetings with R. So S is used once. V will be used once, but we don't know where. Consider the occupancy limits. The occupancy limits are: 1-3x/1-2x/3-1x, or 3-2x/2-1x. So, for example, could T be used three times, R used twice, and W, S, and V each be used once? Certainly. Could, for example, T, R, and W each be used twice and S and V be used once? Certainly.
(A) Can R and T attend the same meeting? Yes.
(B) Can V and S attend the same meeting? Yes.
(C) * Can V and W attend the same meeting? No, there is no way to make this fit.
(D) R and W can attend the same meeting.
(E) S and T can attend the same meeting.

T R S R

W __ __ __

Fig. 4

14. (D) – Our initial analysis should be adequate to answer this question. Remember, the occupancy limits are: 1-3x/1-2x/3-1x, or 3-2x/2-1x.
(A) There is no way to make the numbers work if exactly one student attends one meeting. If one student attends one meeting and the other four attend two meetings, then this equals nine people for only eight slots.
(B) Again, the numbers don't add up. If two students attend two meetings, that fills four slots. Then three students are left to fill four slots, and this doesn't work.

(C) If four students attend one meeting, then there would be four more spaces to fill and only one student available to fill them.
(D) * If three students attend two meetings, this fills six slots. The remaining two students can each fill one slot, bringing us up to eight.
(E) If two students attend three meetings, this would fill six slots, leaving only two slots for the remaining three students.

15. (D) – If W attends three meetings and one is with V, then the diagram is fairly complete. (Figure 5) Doing a little more analysis, the final open slot cannot be a V (there is only one V), an R (S and R can't be together), an S (S and R can't be together), or a W (there are three already). It must be a T.
(A) Yes, either R or S must attend with W.
(B) Yes, T must attend two meetings.
(C) Yes, S attends one meeting.
(D) * No, R can attend a meeting with T, but it is just as possible that S is the one that attends the meeting with T.
(E) Yes, one student, W, attends three meetings.

T	V	S/R	R/S
W	W	W	__

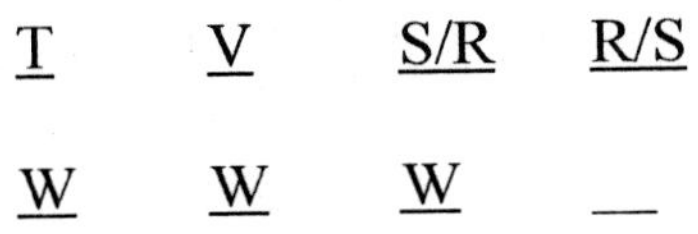

Fig. 5

16. (C) – If T attends only one meeting (the meeting with W), then the diagram is pretty open. (Figure 6) We do know where T cannot be.
(A) Can V attend a meeting with R? Certainly.
(B) Can W attend a meeting with S? Certainly.
(C) * Can R and S both attend two meetings? No. Looking at the diagram, we see that there are not enough open spaces for S and R to both attend two meetings. Doing so would violate Rule 1.
(D) Three students—for example, T, V, and R—could attend one meeting.
(E) Yes, W could attend three meetings.

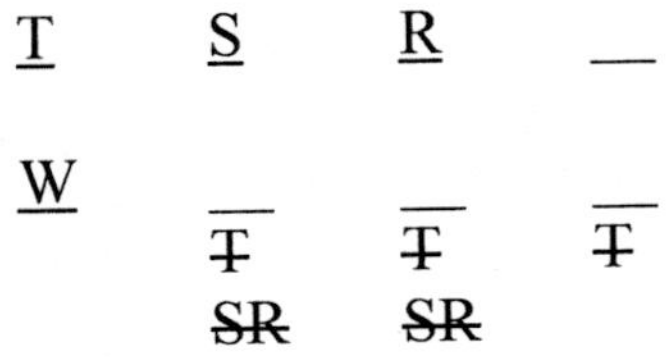

T	S	R	__
W	__	__	__
	~~T~~	~~T~~	~~T~~
	~~SR~~	~~SR~~	

Fig. 6

17. (A) – With V attending three meetings, the diagram is largely complete. (Figure 7)

(A) * Could T attend with V? Yes, T could fill the empty spot in figure 7.

(B) Could R and W attend the same meeting? No.

(C) Could S and T attend the same meeting? No.

(D) This answer choice has tricky wording. It is not a "could be true" that V does not attend a meeting with S. V must attend at least one meeting with S.

(E) Could it be true that exactly two students attend two meetings? Consider the occupancy limits. When one of the students, V, attends three meetings, then one student attends two meetings, and the other three students attend one meeting. Thus, this answer choice is wrong.

T	V	V	V
W	S	R	__

Fig. 7

Actor auditions

This game is a simple line with a few twists to make it interesting. It has six members, each of whom will fill one space. So far this is pretty easy. Complexity is added by the condition that some of the actors audition for a lead role only, while others audition for both a lead role and a supporting role. We must decide how to diagram this. Initially, it seems like two rows of two parallel dashes will be required. But after doing a bit of work with the questions, it turns out that a simple line is adequate. Start the diagram by placing F in the third space. (Figure 1) Next, incorporate Rule 2 under the fifth space by writing, "lead only" or something similar. Rule 3 cannot be graphed, since we don't know where B is, but we can make a warranted conclusion. B cannot be in the fifth space because the fifth space is reserved for lead auditions only. Note this under the fifth space. Finally, Rule 4 provides the chain of C < A < E. As with most simple lines, this chain of members allows us to draw conclusions about where A, C, and E cannot be. (Figure 1) This should be enough work, so move on to the questions.

	—	—	F	—	—	—
					lead only	
					~~B~~	
C<A<E	~~A~~					~~A~~
	~~E~~	~~E~~			~~C~~	~~C~~

Fig. 1

18. (B) – With "possible order" or "acceptable arrangement" questions, simply eliminate answer choices that violate the rules. The answer choice that remains is the correct response.
(A) This violates Rule 4 because it has A after E.
(B) * This answer choice does not violate any rule.
(C) This answer choice violates Rule 1, because F is supposed to be third.
(D) This answer choice violates the warranted conclusion that is based on the fact that B auditions for a supporting role and that Rule 2 specifies that the fifth actor does not audition for a supporting role.
(E) This violates Rule 4 because it has A before C.

19. (E) – This question extends the chain to C < A < E < B. Visualize how this chain might fit on the six dashes. B can no longer be first, second, or fourth. Also, B can't be fifth, as we learned earlier, so B must be sixth.
(A) D could be almost anywhere. That is the nature of a free agent.
(B) C could be first or second.
(C) A could be fourth or second.
(D) E could be fifth or fourth.

(E) * B must be sixth.

20. (D) – Once again, the chain plays a major role in answering a question. We want to maximize the number of actors that audition for both roles, so push A as far towards the beginning as you can. A can be second. (Figure 2) C cannot audition for both roles. We also know that the fifth actor, whoever that ends up being, cannot audition for both roles. Therefore, the second, third, fourth, and sixth actors can potentially audition for both roles.
(A) See the analysis.
(B) See the analysis.
(C) See the analysis.
(D) * See the analysis.
(E) See the analysis.

C A F __ __ __
*
~~B~~
~~A~~ ~~A~~
~~E~~ ~~E~~ ~~C~~ ~~C~~

Fig. 2

21. (C) – Now the chain becomes D C < A < E. How will this chain fit on the diagram? Since D and C must neighbor each other, we must prevent them from being split by F in space three. Thus, the only place they will fit is in spaces one and two. A can be in space four or five. E can be in space five or six. B can be in four or six, but not five. The wording of this question is tricky, so be careful.
(A) It must be true that C is before B, so this could not be false.
(B) It must be true that F is before A, so this could not be false.
(C) * Yes, it could be false that B is before E. It could also be false that B is after E. Note how the other answer choices are "must be true" situations, but this answer choice is a "could be true" situation. "Could be true" is the same as "could be false."
(D) It must be true that A is after D, so this could not be false.
(E) It must be true that E is after F, so this could not be false.

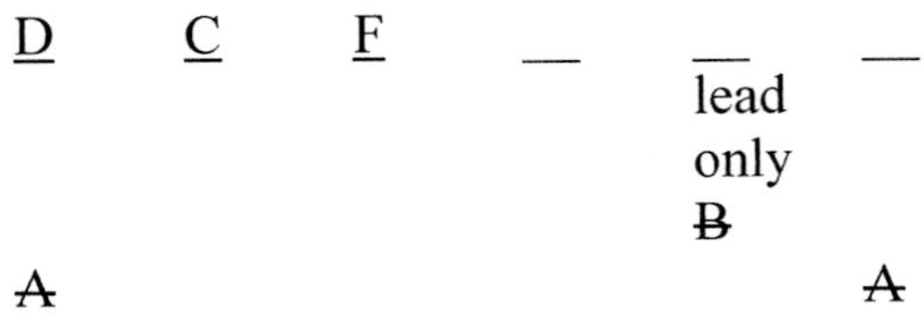

~~E~~ ~~E~~ ~~C~~ ~~C~~

Fig. 3

22. (A) – By placing D at the end, we can make two new conclusions about where the chain of C < A < E can fit. The important conclusion is that A cannot be in the fifth space. B and C also can't be in the fifth space. F is already in the third space. That means that only E is available to be in the fifth space. (Figure 4)
(A) * See the analysis, E must be fifth.
(B) A could be in the fourth space.
(C) A could be in the second space. B would be fourth.
(D) C could be in the second space. B would be first.
(E) B could be in the first space. C would be second.

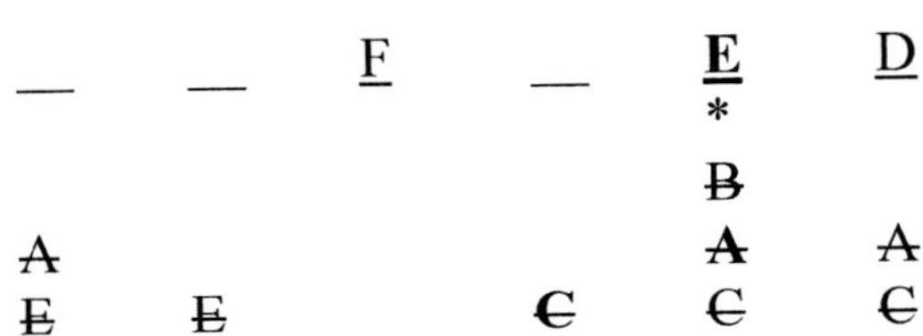

Fig. 4

23. (E) – A and E audition for both roles. Rule 2 is relevant, so we can conclude that neither A nor E is in space five. Looking at the diagram under space five, we see that neither B nor C can be there either. (Figure 5) Also, F cannot be fifth. This means that D is the only one left that can be in space five. We do not know exactly where the others are, so let's look at the answer choices.
(A) B could be in any of the open spaces.
(B) A could be second or fourth.
(C) C could be first or second.
(D) E could be fourth or fifth.
(E) * D must be fifth because no one else can be fifth.

__ __ F __ **D** __
*
~~B~~
~~A~~ ~~A~~ ~~A~~
~~E~~ ~~E~~ ~~C~~ ~~C~~
~~E~~

Fig. 5

Practice Test 14

Spend 35 minutes doing this practice test. When time is up, review the explanations to help you understand the questions that you did not answer correctly.

SECTION I

Time—35 minutes

22 Questions

Directions: Each group of questions in this section is based on a set of conditions. In answering some of the questions, it may b useful to draw a rough diagram. Choose the response that most accurately and completely answers each question and blacken th corresponding space on your answer sheet.

Questions 1–5

Seven printing projects, which are labeled A, B, G, R, S, T, and X, must be printed on a printing press. Each project must be completed before a new project can begin. The printing order is governed by the following restrictions:

Either A or G must be printed fourth.
Exactly two projects must separate R and S.
X is not printed immediately before or immediately after T.
A is printed before T is printed.

1. Which one of the following CANNOT be printed seventh?

(A) A
(B) B
(C) G
(D) T
(E) X

2. If A is printed fourth, then which one of the following CANNOT be true?

(A) B is printed first.
(B) G is printed second.
(C) R is printed second.
(D) S is printed sixth.
(E) X is printed sixth.

3. If T is printed immediately after G is printed, then which one of the following could be true?

(A) A is printed sixth.
(B) A is printed fourth.
(C) R is printed seventh.
(D) S is printed first.
(E) G is printed fifth.

4. If A is printed immediately before X is printed, then what is the earliest that T could be printed?

(A) third
(B) fourth
(C) fifth
(D) sixth
(E) seventh

5. If T is printed sixth, then which one of the following CANNOT be true?

(A) A is printed fourth.
(B) B is printed seventh.
(C) G is printed first.
(D) R is printed third.
(E) X is printed third.

GO ON TO THE NEXT PAG

Questions 6–10

A mechanic must service four cars—H, J, K, and M. The cars are serviced consecutively, each receiving one of the following four types of service: replace lights, recharge battery, rotate tires, or repair windshield. Each service is performed exactly once. The cars are serviced according to the following requirements:

The mechanic does not replace the lights of the first car.

If car J is serviced first, then the mechanic recharges the battery of car K.

If the mechanic rotates the tires of car M, then he repairs the windshield of car H.

The mechanic recharges the battery of the only car that is serviced between cars H and M.

6. Which one of the following could be an accurate matching of the cars and the type of serviced they received, in the order they are serviced, from first to last?

(A) J: rotate tires; M: recharge battery; K: replace lights; H: repair windshield
(B) K: rotate tires; H: recharge battery; J: repair windshield; M: replace lights
(C) M: rotate tires; J: recharge battery; H: repair windshield; K: replace lights
(D) J: replace lights; M: rotate tires; K: recharge battery; H: repair windshield
(E) J: rotate tires; H: replace lights; M: repair windshield; K: recharge battery

7. Each of the following could be true EXCEPT:

(A) J is serviced first and the tires are rotated.
(B) J is serviced first and the windshield is repaired.
(C) H is serviced fourth and the battery is recharged.
(D) K is serviced first and the tires are rotated.
(E) K is serviced third and the battery is recharged.

8. Which one of the following must be true?

(A) The battery of K is recharged.
(B) M is serviced second.
(C) Either M or H is serviced fourth.
(D) The car that receives a battery recharge is serviced third or fourth.
(E) Exactly one car separates K and J.

9. If the mechanic repairs the windshield of J, which one of the following must be true?

(A) J is serviced first.
(B) The lights of M are replaced.
(C) The tires of K are rotated.
(D) M is serviced third.
(E) J is serviced second.

10. If the lights of the third car are replaced, then which one of the following must be true?

(A) The battery of the second car is recharged.
(B) J is serviced fourth.
(C) M is serviced third.
(D) The windshield of H is repaired.
(E) H is serviced first.

GO ON TO THE NEXT PAGE.

Questions 11–16

A volunteer is making gift baskets. The four gift baskets—Amor, Bellagia, Dulcima, and Hampton—each contain up to five food types—chocolate, fruit, ham, juice, and scones. The volunteer must fill the baskets in accordance with the following limitations:

If a basket contains juice and scones, it cannot contain ham.
Bellagia contains at least three types of food.
Amor contains more types of food then Bellagia.
Dulcima and Hampton contain at least two of the same types of food.
Bellagia contains fruit.
Chocolate is in exactly two of the baskets.

11. Which one of the following could be true?

(A) Bellagia contains chocolate, fruit, juice, and scones.
(B) Dulcima does not contain chocolate or fruit, and Hampton does not contain juice or scones.
(C) Dulcima contains chocolates, fruit, ham, juice, and scones.
(D) Bellagia contains fruit, scones, and ham.
(E) Amor contains chocolate, fruit, and scones.

12. Which one of the following could be true?

(A) Bellagia is the only basket that does not contain chocolate.
(B) Bellagia and Dulcima are the only baskets that contain fruit.
(C) Amor and Dulcima contain the same foods.
(D) Dulcima contains only chocolate and ham.
(E) Hampton contains juice and scones and Dulcima does not.

13. If Amor is the only basket to contain ham and juice, then which one of the following must be true?

(A) Exactly three baskets contain scones.
(B) Exactly three baskets contain fruit.
(C) Dulcima and Amor have exactly two types of food in common.
(D) Hampton and Bellagia have exactly three types of food in common.
(E) Amor and Bellagia have at least three types of food in common.

14. Which one of the following must be true?

(A) Amor and Dulcima have at least two types of food in common.
(B) Bellagia and Hampton have at least one type of food in common.
(C) Amor and Bellagia have at least two types of food in common.
(D) Dulcima and Bellagia have at most one type of food in common.
(E) Amor and Hampton have at most one type of food in common.

15. If Bellagia is the only basket that contains ham and Dulcima does not contain fruit, then which one of the following must be true?

(A) Bellagia contains scones.
(B) Dulcima and Hampton contain exactly two of the same foods.
(C) Hampton contains fruit
(D) Dulcima contains chocolate.
(E) Dulcima and Amor contain exactly three of the same foods.

16. If only the baskets that contain chocolate also contain ham, each of the following could be true EXCEPT:

(A) Amor contains juice and scones.
(B) Dulcima contains fruit.
(C) Hampton contains juice.
(D) Bellagia contains chocolate.
(E) Dulcima contains juice and scones.

GO ON TO THE NEXT PAGE

Questions 17–22

During a two-day period, a professor will have five appointments with students. Each of the seven students will meet at least once with the professor. The students are seniors—Robert, Twalya, and Wilmer—and juniors—Anin, Dorin, Flores, and Mambo. The following requirements are the only ones used in scheduling the appointments:

Exactly one senior and one junior are scheduled for each appointment.

Anin and Flores cannot have appointments on the same day.

Mambo does not have an appointment on the same day as Robert.

Twalya does not share an appointment with Dorin.

17. Which one of the following could be an accurate listing of appointments held on the first day?

(A) Wilmer and Flores; Twalya and Mambo; Twalya and Dorin
(B) Robert and Anin; Wilmer and Dorin
(C) Robert and Anin; Twalya and Mambo; Wilmer and Dorin
(D) Twalya and Robert; Twalya and Flores
(E) Twalya and Anin; Wilmer and Mambo; Wilmer and Flores

18. Each of the following could be true EXCEPT:

(A) On the second day there are three appointments.
(B) On the second day Robert and Flores share an appointment.
(C) On the second day Robert and Anin share an appointment and Twalya and Mambo share an appointment.
(D) Mambo has an appointment on the same day as Dorin.
(E) On the first day Twalya has two appointments and Wilmer has one appointment.

19. If on the first day Robert has exactly two appointments with Anin, then which one of the following must be true?

(A) Wilmer has exactly two appointments.
(B) Twalya shares an appointment with Mambo.
(C) Twalya has an appointment on the first day.
(D) Wilmer shares an appointment with Dorin.
(E) Wilmer has exactly one appointment.

20. Which one of the following is a complete and accurate list of the students, any one of which could have exactly three appointments?

(A) Robert, Twalya
(B) Robert, Wilmer
(C) Twalya, Wilmer
(D) Robert, Twalya, Wilmer
(E) Anin, Flores, Robert, Twalya, Wilmer

21. If Robert and Dorin do not have an appointment on the same day, which one of the following must be true?

(A) Robert shares an appointment with Anin.
(B) There are exactly two appointments on the first day.
(C) Robert shares an appointment with Flores.
(D) Wilmer shares an appointment with Dorin.
(E) Wilmer shares an appointment with Mambo.

22. If Twalya and Wilmer each have exactly one appointment, which one of the following must be true?

(A) Robert shares an appointment with Anin.
(B) Robert shares an appointment with Dorin.
(C) Robert shares an appointment with Flores.
(D) Twalya shares an appointment with Mambo.
(E) Dorin shares an appointment with Wilmer.

S T O P

IF YOU FINISH BEFORE TIME IS CALLED, YOU MAY CHECK YOUR WORK ON THIS SECTION ONLY.
DO NOT WORK ON ANY OTHER SECTION IN THE TEST.

Answer key and explanations for Test 14

Answer Key

1. A
2. E
3. B
4. C
5. D
6. C
7. C
8. E
9. B
10. A
11. D
12. C
13. A
14. C
15. B
16. A
17. B
18. C
19. D
20. D
21. D
22. B

Printing order line

This easy game has seven slots, each to be filled by one member. Further simplifying your task, each member is used exactly once. This simple line game has some rules that are not commonly used. Rule 1 requires that either A or G be fourth. This is not a common rule, but fortunately it is easy to graph. (Figure 1) Rule 2 requires that two projects be placed between R and S. This also is not a common rule, and it often causes confusion for test takers. Be careful when interpreting rules that separate two members with either one or two spaces. If you are not sure whether the two members are separated by either one or two spaces, look to the questions and answer choices for clues. Normally, but not in this game, you can quickly clarify this kind of ambiguity by looking at the answer choices; especially answer choices that list all the members. Remember, the positions of S and R are interchangeable. (Figure 1) Moving on, consider what warranted conclusions you might make. You know that R _ _ S requires a total of four spaces. Because space four is already occupied, neither R nor S can be on space one or space seven. Note this on your diagram. Moving on, Rule 3 is a pretty common rule. X and T do not neighbor each other. Again, it doesn't matter if X is before or after T. Finally, Rule 4 says that A is before T. We can draw a warranted conclusion that T cannot be first, and A cannot be seventh. After quickly reviewing the rules, it does not appear that any additional warranted conclusions should be made at this time.

1	2	3	4	5	6	7
__	__	__	A/G	__	__	__
~~R~~						~~R~~
~~S~~						~~S~~
~~T~~						~~A~~

R _ _ S or S _ _ R

~~XT~~

A < T

Fig. 1

1. (A) – The initial analysis is adequate to answer this question.
   (A) * A cannot be seventh because A must be before T.
   (B) B could be seventh. Since B is a free agent, B can be just about anywhere.
   (C) G could be seventh, as long as A is fourth.
   (D) The only restriction on T is that it be after A.
   (E) As long as X and T are kept separate, X can be seventh.

2. (E) – A is fourth. What rules interact with A? Rule 4 dictates that A is before T. That means T must be fifth, sixth or seventh. What other rules interact with T? X and T cannot be next to each other. So X cannot be sixth.

(A) B is a free agent. A free agent is never the credited answer to a CANNOT be true question.
(B) G can be printed second. Either R or S would have to be third.
(C) R can be second. S would be fifth.
(D) S can be sixth. R would be third.
(E) * X cannot be sixth. If it were, it would conflict with T, which would be either fifth or seventh.

1	2	3	4	5	6	7
__	__	__	A	__	__	__
				T	T	T

Fig. 2

3. (B) – Adding the new information from this question, we can create the chain of A < G T. The quickest method is to do two graphs, placing A or G in the fourth space. (Figures 3a-b) When A is fourth, G T must be to the right of A. We also must fit in either R or S to the right of A. The only way to do so without splitting G T is to place G T on sixth and seventh, and either R or S on fifth. This pushes the other one to the second space. We don't know where B and X are. (Figure 3a) Now try a graph when G in the fourth space. T must be fifth. This forces R/S to be third and sixth. (Figure 3b) We don't know where the rest are.
(A) A is not sixth in either of the diagrams.
(B) * A can be fourth.
(C) R is not seventh in either of the diagrams. R is never seventh, as we learned in the initial analysis.
(D) Like R, S is never first.
(E) G is not fifth in either of the diagrams.

1	2	3	4	5	6	7
__	R/S	__	A	R/S	G	T

Fig. 3a

1	2	3	4	5	6	7
__	__	R/S	G	T	R/S	__

Fig. 3b

4. (C) – Again, the quickest way to find the correct answer is to first diagram it using A on the fourth space, and then diagram it with G fourth. When A is fourth, A X creates a block that R/S has to bookend. (Figure 4a) T must be after X, so T is seventh. Doing a new diagram, when G is fourth things are a

little more complex. A cannot be fifth, because X would then be sixth, and this block of G, A, X prevents R/S from being placed. Also, A cannot be sixth, because X would be seventh, and there would be nowhere for T to be placed. A cannot be second because this would cause problems for R/S. Thus, A must be first. Then R/S can be accommodated. (Figure 4b) The question asks for the earliest T can be. T can be fifth.
(A) See the analysis.
(B) See the analysis.
(C) * See the analysis.
(D) See the analysis.
(E) See the analysis.

1	2	3	4	5	6	7
__	__	R/S	A	X	R/S	T

Fig. 4a

1	2	3	4	5	6	7
A	X	R/S	G	__	R/S	__

Fig. 4b

5. (D) – If T is sixth, R/S is second and fifth. We also know that neither X nor A is printed seventh, so either G or B is seventh. Now look at the answer choices.
(A) A could be fourth without causing any problems.
(B) B could be seventh, see the analysis.
(C) G could be first. A would be fourth, X would be third, and B would be seventh.
(D) * No, R cannot be third, because this would conflict with T in sixth.
(E) See (C).

1	2	3	4	5	6	7
__	R/S	__	__	R/S	T	__

Fig. 5

Car services

This is a challenging game because Rule 4 is subtle. More on that in a moment. This puzzle requires a double line. The top line will be the car names, and the bottom line will be the type of service. Only Rule 1 is easy to diagram. Simply note a negative L under the first column. Rule 2 is a bit too complex to diagram, for now just use a J* to remind you to consult the rules. Rule 3 is also not conducive to placing on the diagram. Rule 4 is subtle. Does Rule 4 mean that there is exactly one car serviced between H and M? Yes, it does. If you weren't certain about this, question 6 would have made it clear. We can conclude that H/M will be either first and third, or second and fourth. This isn't the kind of conclusion we can diagram, but keep it in the back of your mind.

```
1     2     3     4

__    __    __    __     - car
J*

__    __    __    __     - service
L̶
```

If J is 1st → K=b
If M=t → H=r

```
H/M __ M/H
__  b  __
```

Fig. 1

6. (C) – Use each rule to eliminate the answer choice that violates that rule. The remaining answer choice is the correct answer.
   (A) This choice is wrong because it violates Rule 2. Since J is serviced first, K should get a battery recharge.
   (B) This choice is wrong because it violates Rule 4. The car serviced between H and M is supposed to get a battery recharge.
   (C) * This choice does not violate any of the rules.
   (D) This violates Rule 1. The first car cannot have the lights replaced.
   (E) This violates Rule 4 because H and M are not separated by one car.

7. (C) – This question did not add new information, so work through each of the answer choices to find the one that is not possible.
   (A) J can be first. When J is first, K must have the battery recharge. Since J is first, H/M are second and fourth. So K must be third. It works fine for Rule 4 that K is third and gets a battery recharge.
   (B) This analysis is similar to that of (A).
   (C) * The effect of Rule 4 is that neither H nor M ever has the battery recharge.

(D) K can be first. J would be third, and have a battery recharge. H and M would be second and fourth and split the lights and windshield work.
(E) There is no problem with K being third. J would be first.

8. (E) – Lacking any new information, consider the answer choices and do permutations if necessary.
(A) We can see in question 6(C) that K does not necessarily have the battery recharge.
(B) Once again, you can consult 6(C) to eliminate this choice. You could solve for this permutation, but why waste the time when you already have the correct answer (assuming that you answered question 6 correctly)?
(C) Once again, see question 6(C).
(D) The important thing to remember about the battery recharge is that it comes between H and M, so it can be second or third, but not first or fourth.
(E) * This is true. K and J are always separated by one car, either H or M.

9. (B) – If the mechanic replaces the windshield of J, then two things are true. First, he cannot rotate the tires of M (Rule 3). Second, and more importantly, J cannot be between H and M (Rule 4). So J is either first or fourth. Graph these two possibilities and see what emerges. (Figure 2) Since M cannot get the tires rotated (because J is getting the windshield repair), M must get the lights replaced and H must get the tires rotated.
(A) J can be first or fourth.
(B) * True, M must get the lights replaced.
(C) False, K must get the battery recharged.
(D) M can be first, second, third, or fourth.
(E) J must be first or fourth.

1	2	3	4
J	H/M	K	M/H
w	__	b	__

1	2	3	4
M/H	K	H/M	J
__	b	__	w

Fig. 2

10. (A) – When the lights of the third car are replaced, the third car does not get the battery recharge, which means that H and M are not on either side of the third car. So H and M are first and third, not second and fourth. Since H and M are first and third, the second car gets a battery recharge. Since either H or M gets the lights replaced, then it cannot be that M gets the tires rotated. We can't be certain about anything else.

(A) * True, the battery on the second car must be recharged.
(B) J or K could be fourth.
(C) M or H could be third.
(D) We do not know whether H gets the windshield repair or the tires rotated.
(E) M or H could be first.

1	2	3	4
M/H	__	H/M	__
__	b	t	__

Fig. 3

Gift basket contents

In recent years, LSAT games have been predominately line games, either simple lines or multiple lines. But once every two or three years they like to shake things up by using an unusual puzzle type. To solve the gift baskets game, you needed a matrix diagram. In the past, matrix diagrams were regularly tested, but they have become rare in recent years. The moral of the story is that if you want to ace the games, you must be an expert at all of the possible puzzle types, not just the lines. Even with a matrix diagram, this game is difficult because there are two warranted conclusions that are not immediately obvious, but are vital. More on that in a moment. First, create a matrix with the basket names on one side and the food types on the other. (Figure 1) Graph Rules 5 and 6 first, because they are easy to graph. Rule 1 requires that if a basket has juice *and* scones, it does not have ham. This requires a negative arrow from juice and scones to ham. Rule 2 means that basket B can have three, four, or five foods. Rule 3 states that A has more foods than B. That would mean that A has at least four types, and may have five. But if A has five types, then B cannot have five types. Wait, there is more. Consider the effect of Rule 2; if the basket has juice and scones, it does not have ham. This means that no basket can have all five types of food. Thus, A has four foods and consequently B has three foods. That was a tricky warranted conclusion. But wait, there is even more that can be done. Since A has four food types, A must have chocolate and fruit and two more food types. Moving on, D and H have two or more of the same food type. Note this underneath D and H. Looking at the chocolate row, we see that chocolate will never be one of the foods that D and H share, though one of them could have chocolate. Now move to the questions. Because matrix diagrams are large and complex, it is usually necessary to reuse your initial diagram, erasing information that pertains to specific questions once you finish that question.

Chocolate = 2	Yes			
Fruit	Yes	Yes		
Juice ↘				
Scones ┐				
Ham ← x				
	Amor	Bellagia	Dulcima	Hampton
	=4	=3	D and H share 2+	

Fig. 1

11. (D) – Use a combination of the warranted conclusions, the diagram, and the rules to eliminate four answer choices.
    (A) We concluded that B only has three foods because A can have no more than four.
    (B) This choice violates Rule 4. This choice would allow D and H to share only one type of food.
    (C) This choice violates Rule 1.
    (D) * This is a valid possibility.

(E) We concluded in the initial analysis that A must have exactly four foods.

12. (C) – Absent any new information, go directly to the answer choices.
(A) Rule 5 specifies that there are exactly two chocolates, not three. A, D, and H cannot all have chocolate at the same time.
(B) One of the warranted conclusions was that A must have fruit.
(C) * A and D can have all the same foods, including chocolate. This causes no problem with Rule 4.
(D) If D only has two foods, and one is chocolate (a limited commodity), then D and H will not be able to have two foods in common.
(E) If H has juice and scones and D does not, then they will not be able to have two foods in common.

13. (A) – The diagram makes it easy to keep track of this new information. A has juice and ham, and the others do not. (Figure 2) Thus, A cannot have scones as well. B must have three foods, so it must have the second chocolate and also the scones. The only two food types left for D and H are fruit and scones.
(A) * It must be true that B, D, and H all have scones.
(B) All four baskets have fruit.
(C) D and A have only one food in common, fruit.
(D) H and B have two types of food in common, fruit and scones.
(E) A and B have two types of food in common, fruit and chocolate.

Chocolate = 2	Yes			
Fruit	Yes	Yes		
Juice	Y	N	N	N
Scones	N			
Ham	Y	N	N	N
	Amor	Bellagia	Dulcima	Hampton
	=4	=3	D and H share 2+	

Fig. 2

14. (C) – Yet again, no new information means we have to weigh each of the answer choices.
(A) We saw in the previous question that A and D did not have two types of food in common.
(B) B must have three of five foods and H must have at least two of five foods. They can have entirely different foods.
(C) * A must have four of five foods and B must have three of five foods. There is no way they can avoid having at least two of the same foods.
(D) D can have up to four foods, so D and B can share more than one food type, as we saw in question 13.

(E) Similar to choice (D), H can have up to four foods.

15. (B) – Enter the new information about ham and B and fruit and D. B still needs one more food, but we don't know which. A must have four foods. D and H must have two foods in common. They can't have ham in common. They can't have fruit in common. They can't have chocolate in common. So they must have both juice and scones in common. Figure 3 contains everything we know for certain. Since this is a must be true question, that is all we will need.
(A) B may have scones, but it is not certain that it does.
(B) * Correct. D and H must have exactly two of the same foods, juice and scones.
(C) H may or may not have fruit.
(D) We don't know which basket contains the second chocolate.
(E) D may only have two types of food, so it is not true that D and A must have three types of food in common.

Chocolate = 2	Yes			
Fruit	Yes	Yes	N	
Juice	Y		Y	Y
Scones	Y		Y	Y
Ham	N	Y	N	N
	Amor	Bellagia	Dulcima	Hampton
	=4	=3	D and H share 2+	

Fig. 3

16. (A) – This question ends up being pretty easy. A has chocolate, so now A must also have ham. Thus, A cannot have both juice and scones, though it must have one of them. Since we cannot determine anything else with certainty, look to the answer choices.
(A) * A cannot have both juice and scones, since it now must have ham.
(B) D may have fruit.
(C) H may have juice.
(D) B can have chocolate. It would also have ham. D and H can have anything besides chocolate.
(E) D could have juice and scones, it would not be able to have ham, and by extension, chocolate.

Five appointments

This is a difficult double line puzzle. It requires a double line because each appointment has two people, a junior and a senior. It is difficult because we aren't told how many appointments are on each of the two days. Despite this ambiguity, there are some useful warranted conclusions to be made. Rule 2 dictates that A and F (both juniors) cannot have appointments on the same day. Therefore, one of them will be on the first day and the other will be on the second day. So we know that each day must have at least one appointment. Unfortunately, we cannot use this same trick with Rule 3, since M is a junior and R is a senior. Just keep Rule 3 in the back of your mind until you need it. Finally, Rule 4, T does not share the same appointment with D, is another rule we need to keep in mind. T and D do not share the same appointment; they can be on the same day if they have different appointments. Are we any closer to figuring out how many appointments must be on each day? No. It looks like there can be as few as one appointment on one of the days and four on the other, or two appointments on one day and three on the other. Oh well, you can't win them all. Go to the questions.

Day 1	Day 2
A/F|__	A/F|__

Fig. 1

17. (B) – With the "possible order" or "acceptable arrangement" question type, eliminate the four answer choices that violate the rules.
(A) T and D do not share an appointment, Rule 4.
(B) * This answer choice does not violate any rule.
(C) This answer choice violates Rule 3; R and M cannot be on the same day.
(D) This answer choice violates Rule 1; it has R and T in the same appointment, but they are both seniors.
(E) This violates Rule 2 because is has A on the same day as F.

18. (C) – Lacking any new information, go directly to the choices.
(A) There is no distinction to be made between the first day and second day. Either day can have three appointments.
(B) R and F can be together on one of the days. M and A would have to be on the other day.
(C) * This choice violates Rule 3 because M and R cannot have appointments on the same day.
(D) M and D can be on the same day along with either A or F. R would have to be the other day.
(E) T can have two appointments on the same day W has one. R would have to be on the other day so that M could be on the day with T and W.

19. (D) – If R has two appointments on the first day with A, then both F and M must be on the second day. Since F and M are both juniors, they will need to have separate appointments with either T or W. We don't know which day D will have his appointment.

(A) W must have one appointment, and may have two.
(B) T may or may not share an appointment with M.
(C) T could not have an appointment on the first day. Why? D is the only one left that needs an appointment. D can be on the first day, but Rule 4 prohibits D from being with T.
(D) * W must share an appointment with D, whether on the first or second day.
(E) W can have one or two appointments.

1	2
A|R	F|__
A|R	M|__

Fig. 2

20. (D) – Which of the students could have three appointments? There are a few ways you can approach this question. You can consider that R, T, and W each appear in four of the answer choices. That would indicate that all three of them are in the credited answer choice. You can consider that A and F are the only juniors listed. When you think about it you realize that no junior can be used three times, because there are four juniors to be used, and only five open appointments. You will need to check for R, T, and W to see if any of them cannot be used three times. Is it possible to have R three times in one day? Yes. D can be with R twice, and F can be with R once. A and M, the juniors that have conflicts, can be on the second day. A similar analysis shows that T and W can be on three days.

(A) See the analysis.
(B) See the analysis.
(C) See the analysis.
(D) * See the analysis.
(E) Neither A nor F can have three appointments, since this would prevent one junior from getting an appointment.

21. (D) – When R is on one day, M is on the other day. Thus, M and D are on the same day. Also, either A or F is on that day. The final thing we can conclude is that D must have an appointment with W, because D can't have an appointment with R or T.

(A) R may be with A or F.

(B) The fifth appointment could be on either day.
(C) See (A).
(D) * Yes, D must be with W.
(E) W may share an appointment with M, but it is not necessary that this be true.

1	2
A/F|R	A/F|__
	M|__
	D|W

Fig. 3

22. (B) – If T and W each have one appointment, then R has three appointments. Since R and M must be on different days, R must have three appointments on one day, and M must be on the other day. T and W must be on the same day as M, but we don't know which one is with M. D must be with R because there are no other open appointments for D.
(A) R may or may not be with A.
(B) * R must be with D.
(C) See (A). F and A share the same analysis.
(D) T or W may share the appointment with M.
(E) D will not share an appointment with W.

1	2
A/F|R	A/F|__
D|R	M|__
__|R	

Fig. 4

Official LSAT PrepTests & Explanations

Congratulations! You have done a great deal of practice and are ready to put the finishing touches on your LSAT skills. The following games are from the three most recent LSAT tests. Each test is followed by detailed explanations. Spend 35 minutes doing each practice test. Grade yourself, then turn to the explanations to help you determine why you missed the questions you missed. After you finish these games, you will be confident that you are ready for anything the LSAT might throw at you.

PrepTest 46

Spend 35 minutes doing this practice test. When time is up, review the explanations to help you understand the questions that you did not answer correctly.

SECTION I

Time—35 minutes

22 Questions

Directions: Each group of questions in this section is based on a set of conditions. In answering some of the questions, it may useful to draw a rough diagram. Choose the response that most accurately and completely answers each question and blacken t corresponding space on your answer sheet.

Questions 1–6

Exactly six guideposts, numbered 1 through 6, mark a mountain trail. Each guidepost pictures a different one of six animals—fox, grizzly, hare, lynx, moose, or porcupine. The following conditions must apply:

The grizzly is pictured on either guidepost 3 or guidepost 4.

The moose guidepost is numbered lower than the hare guidepost.

The lynx guidepost is numbered lower than the moose guidepost but higher than the fox guidepost.

1. Which one of the following could be an accurate list of the animals pictured on the guideposts, listed in order from guidepost 1 through guidepost 6?

(A) fox, lynx, grizzly, porcupine, moose, hare
(B) fox, lynx, moose, hare, grizzly, porcupine
(C) fox, moose, grizzly, lynx, hare, porcupine
(D) lynx, fox, moose, grizzly, hare, porcupine
(E) porcupine, fox, hare, grizzly, lynx, moose

2. Which one of the following animals CANNOT be the one pictured on guidepost 3?

(A) fox
(B) grizzly
(C) lynx
(D) moose
(E) porcupine

3. If the moose is pictured on guidepost 3, then which one of the following is the lowest numbered guidepost that could picture the porcupine?

(A) guidepost 1
(B) guidepost 2
(C) guidepost 4
(D) guidepost 5
(E) guidepost 6

4. If guidepost 5 does not picture the moose, then which one of the following must be true?

(A) The lynx is pictured on guidepost 2.
(B) The moose is pictured on guidepost 3.
(C) The grizzly is pictured on guidepost 4.
(D) The porcupine is pictured on guidepost 5.
(E) The hare is pictured on guidepost 6.

5. Which one of the following animals could be picture on any one of the six guideposts?

(A) fox
(B) hare
(C) lynx
(D) moose
(E) porcupine

6. If the moose guidepost is numbered exactly one high than the lynx guidepost, then which one of the following could be true?

(A) Guidepost 5 pictures the hare.
(B) Guidepost 4 pictures the moose.
(C) Guidepost 4 pictures the porcupine.
(D) Guidepost 3 pictures the lynx.
(E) Guidepost 3 pictures the porcupine.

GO ON TO THE NEXT PA(

Questions 7–11

Each side of four cassette tapes—Tapes 1 through 4—contains exactly one of the following four genres: folk, hip-hop, jazz, and rock. The following conditions must apply:

Each genre is found on exactly two of the eight sides.
Tape 1 has jazz on at least one side, but neither hip-hop nor rock.
Tape 2 has no jazz.
Folk is not on any tape numbered exactly one higher than a tape that has any rock on it.

7. Which one of the following could be an accurate matching of tapes with the musical genres found on them?

(A) Tape 1: folk and jazz; Tape 2: folk and jazz; Tape 3: hip-hop and rock; Tape 4: hip-hop and rock
(B) Tape 1: folk and jazz; Tape 2: folk and rock; Tape 3: hip-hop and jazz; Tape 4: hip-hop and rock
(C) Tape 1: folk and jazz; Tape 2: folk and rock; Tape 3: two sides of jazz; Tape 4: two sides of hip-hop
(D) Tape 1: hip-hop and jazz; Tape 2: folk and hip-hop; Tape 3: folk and jazz; Tape 4: two sides of rock
(E) Tape 1: two sides of jazz; Tape 2: folk and rock; Tape 3: hip-hop and rock; Tape 4: folk and hip-hop

8. Which one of the following must be true?

(A) If Tape 1 has two sides of jazz, Tape 4 has at least one side of rock.
(B) If Tape 2 has two sides of folk, Tape 3 has at least one side of hip-hop.
(C) If Tape 2 has two sides of rock, Tape 4 has at least one side of folk.
(D) If Tape 3 has two sides of folk, Tape 2 has at least one side of jazz.
(E) If Tape 4 has two sides of hip-hop, Tape 3 has at least one side of folk.

9. Which one of the following could be true?

(A) Tape 1 has jazz on both sides while Tape 4 has folk and hip-hop.
(B) Tape 2 has hip-hop on one side while tape 3 has hip-hop and jazz.
(C) Tape 3 has folk on both sides while Tape 4 has jazz and rock.
(D) Tape 3 has jazz on one side while Tape 4 has folk on both sides.
(E) Tapes 2 and 3 each have jazz on one side.

10. Which one of the following could be true?

(A) Tape 1 has two sides of folk.
(B) Tape 2 has both hip-hop and jazz.
(C) Tape 4 has both folk and rock.
(D) Tapes 1 and 4 each have a side of hip-hop.
(E) Tapes 3 and 4 each have a side folk.

11. Which one of the following CANNOT be true?

(A) Tape 2 has rock on both sides while Tape 3 has hip-hop on both sides.
(B) Tape 3 has rock on both sides while Tape 2 has hip-hop on both sides.
(C) Tape 3 has rock on both sides while Tape 4 has hip-hop on both sides.
(D) Tape 4 has rock on both sides while Tape 2 has hip-hop on both sides.
(E) Tape 4 has rock on both sides while Tape 3 has hip-hop on both sides.

GO ON TO THE NEXT PAGE.

Questions 12–16

One afternoon, a single thunderstorm passes over exactly five towns—Jackson, Lofton, Nordique, Oceana, and Plattesville—dropping some form of precipitation on each. The storm is the only source of precipitation in the towns that afternoon. On some towns, it drops both hail and rain; on the remaining towns, it drops only rain. It passes over each town exactly once and does not pass over any two towns at the same time. The following must obtain:

The third town the storm passes over is Plattesville.
The storm drops hail and rain on the second town it passes over.
The storm drops only rain on both Lofton and Oceana.
The storm passes over Jackson at some time after it passes over Lofton and at some time after it passes over Nordique.

12. Which one of the following could be the order, from first to fifth, in which the storm passes over the towns?

(A) Lofton, Nordique, Plattesville, Oceana, Jackson
(B) Lofton, Oceana, Plattesville, Nordique, Jackson
(C) Nordique, Jackson, Plattesville, Oceana, Lofton
(D) Nordique, Lofton, Plattesville, Jackson, Oceana
(E) Nordique, Plattesville, Lofton, Oceana, Jackson

13. If the storm passes over Oceana at some time before it passes over Jackson, then each of the following could be true EXCEPT:

(A) The first town the storm passes over is Oceana.
(B) The fourth town the storm passes over is Lofton.
(C) The fourth town the storm passes over receives hail and rain.
(D) The fifth town the storm passes over is Jackson.
(E) The fifth town the storm passes over receives only rain.

14. If the storm drops only rain on each town it passes over after passing over Lofton, then which one of the following could be false?

(A) The first town the storm passes over is Oceana.
(B) The fourth town the storm passes over receives only rain.
(C) The fifth town the storm passes over is Jackson.
(D) Jackson receives only rain.
(E) Plattesville receives only rain.

15. If the storm passes over Jackson at some time before it passes over Oceana, then which one of the following could be false?

(A) The storm passes over Lofton at some time before it passes over Jackson.
(B) The storm passes over Lofton at some time before it passes over Oceana.
(C) The storm passes over Nordique at some time before it passes over Oceana.
(D) The fourth town the storm passes over receives only rain.
(E) The fifth town the storm passes over receives only rain.

16. If the storm passes over Oceana at some time before it passes over Lofton, then which one of the following must be true?

(A) The third town the storm passes over receives only rain.
(B) The fourth town the storm passes over receives only rain.
(C) The fourth town the storm passes over receives hail and rain.
(D) The fifth town the storm passes over receives only rain.
(E) The fifth town the storm passes over receives hail and rain.

GO ON TO THE NEXT PAGE.

Questions 17–22

A reporter is trying to uncover the workings of a secret committee. The committee has six members—French, Ghauri, Hsia, Irving, Magnus, and Pinsky—each of whom serves on at least on subcommittee. There are three subcommittees, each having three members, about which the following is known:

One of the committee members serves on all three subcommittees.
French does not serve on any subcommittee with Ghauri.
Hsia does not serve on any subcommittee with Irving.

17. If French does not serve on any subcommittee with Magnus, which one of the following must be true?

(A) French serves on a subcommittee with Hsia.
(B) French serves on a subcommittee with Irving.
(C) Irving serves on a subcommittee with Pinsky.
(D) Magnus serves on a subcommittee with Ghauri.
(E) Magnus serves on a subcommittee with Irving.

18. If Pinsky serves on every subcommittee on which French serves and every subcommittee on which Ghauri serves, then which one of the following could be true?

(A) Magnus serves on every subcommittee on which French serves and every subcommittee on which Ghauri serves.
(B) Magnus serves on every subcommittee on which Hsia serves and every subcommittee on which Irving serves.
(C) Hsia serves on every subcommittee on which French serves and every subcommittee on which Ghauri serves.
(D) French serves on every subcommittee on which Pinsky serves.
(E) Hsia serves on every subcommittee on which Pinsky serves.

19. If Irving serves on every subcommittee on which Magnus serves, which one of the following could be true?

(A) Magnus serves on all of the subcommittees.
(B) Irving serves on more than one subcommittee.
(C) Irving serves on every subcommittee on which Pinsky serves.
(D) French serves on a subcommittee with Magnus.
(E) Ghauri serves on a subcommittee with Magnus.

20. Which one of the following could be true?

(A) French serves on all three subcommittees.
(B) Hsia serves on all three subcommittees.
(C) Ghauri serves on every subcommittee on which Magnus serves and every subcommittee on which Pinsky serves.
(D) Pinsky serves on every subcommittee on which Irving serves and every subcommittee on which Magnus serves.
(E) Magnus serves on every subcommittee on which Pinsky serves, and Pinsky serves on every subcommittee on which Magnus serves.

21. Which one of the following must be true?

(A) Ghauri serves on at least two subcommittees.
(B) Irving serves on only one subcommittee.
(C) French serves on a subcommittee with Hsia.
(D) Ghauri serves on a subcommittee with Irving.
(E) Magnus serves on a subcommittee with Pinsky.

22. Which one of the following must be true?

(A) Every subcommittee has either French or Ghauri as a member.
(B) Every subcommittee has either Hsia or Irving as a member.
(C) No subcommittee consists of French, Magnus, and Pinsky.
(D) Some committee member serves on exactly two subcommittees.
(E) Either Magnus or Pinsky serves on only one subcommittee.

S T O P

IF YOU FINISH BEFORE TIME IS CALLED, YOU MAY CHECK YOUR WORK ON THIS SECTION ONLY.
DO NOT WORK ON ANY OTHER SECTION IN THE TEST.

Answer key and explanations for PrepTest 46

Answer Key

1. A
2. A
3. D
4. A
5. E
6. A
7. B
8. C
9. B
10. C
11. B
12. A
13. C
14. E
15. D
16. B
17. C
18. C
19. B
20. D
21. E
22. D

Guidepost line

This game requires a simple-line diagram. There are exactly six members to be placed into six spaces. A simple line does not get any easier than this. Rule 1 tells us that G is either third or fourth. After diagramming this anchor rule, the next step is to combine the other rules. Rule 2 (M < H) can be combined with Rule 3 (F < L < M) to make the combination rule F < L < M < H. Apply this combination rule to the diagram. (Figure 1) It is important to determine where the members cannot be. Start at the left end, with H. Where can H not be? H must come after three other members, so H cannot be first, second, or third. Because of the location of G, it also turns out that H cannot be fourth. So H can be fifth or sixth. Next, where can M not be? M cannot be first or second. Also, M cannot be sixth, because H must come after M. Do the same analysis for L and F. Notice the symmetry in the diagram of H and F and of L and M. The only free agent is P. This is sufficient analysis to begin answering the questions.

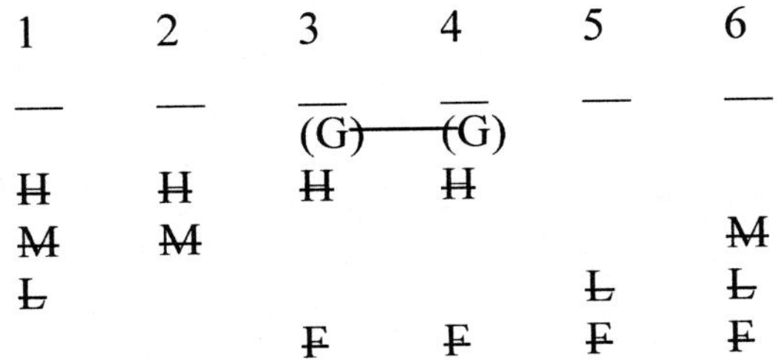

1	2	3	4	5	6
—	—	—	—	—	—
		(G) ——	(G)		
~~H~~	~~H~~	~~H~~	~~H~~		
~~M~~	~~M~~				~~M~~
~~L~~				~~L~~	~~L~~
		~~F~~	~~F~~	~~F~~	~~F~~

F < L < M < H

Fig. 1

1. (A) – It is best to answer this question by using rule-violation answer elimination. The advantage of using the rule violation technique is that it is hard to make a mistake. An additional benefit is that once you find the correct answer, you can refer to it when answering later questions.
(A)* This is a valid permutation.
(B) Rule 1 requires that G be third or fourth.
(C) Rule 3 requires that L be lower than M.
(D) Rule 3 requires that L be higher than F.
(E) Rule 2 requires that M be lower than H.

2. (A) – Since this question does not add any new information, you can simply use the information you learned from the initial analysis. What should you do if you did not do the initial analysis, or did not do it correctly? Certainly, you could work out the permutations, but that is a waste of time. One possible short cut would be to look at the correct answer choice for question 1. In it, you see that G is in space 3, so that eliminates choice (B). You then might want to shelve this question and return to it later, after doing some questions and gaining insight into the diagram. (As it happens, the next question also

deals with space 3, requiring M to be in space 3. So that would eliminate choice (D) in this question.)
(A)* See the initial analysis and figure 1. Neither H nor F can be in space 3.
(B) See the initial analysis.
(C) See the initial analysis.
(D) See the initial analysis.
(E) See the initial analysis.

3. (D) – Once you place M in space 3, F and L must then be placed in spaces 1 and 2, respectively. Also, since M is in space 3, the only space left for G is space 4. Finally, H and P must occupy the final two spaces. For P, the lowest possible space is space 5. (Figure 2)
(A) See the analysis.
(B) See the analysis.
(C) See the analysis.
(D)* See the analysis.
(E) See the analysis. The only restriction for H is that H must be higher than M.

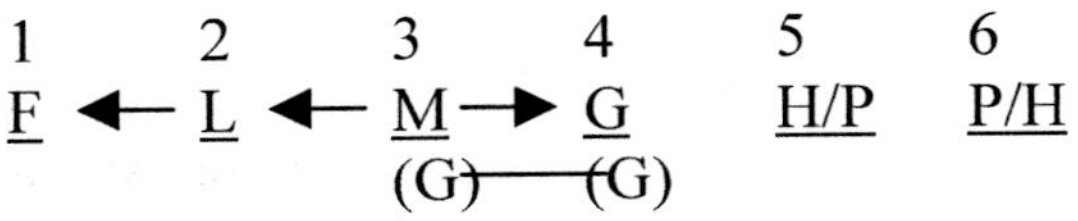

1	2	3	4	5	6
F ←	L ←	M →	G	H/P	P/H
		(G) —	— (G)		

F < L < M < H

Fig. 2

4. (A) – Since this question dictates where M cannot be, refer to the initial diagram and add the new information, M cannot be fifth. (Figure 3) The diagram now shows two options for M. M can be third or fourth. G must always be third or fourth. If M is fourth, then G is third. If M is third, then G is fourth. Their exact order has no effect on the rest of the members. Regardless of where M is, F and L will be first and second, respectively, and H and P will fifth and sixth, though not necessarily in that order.
(A)* Yes, L must be second.
(B) Figure 3 shows that the M and G are interchangeable in spaces 3 and 4.
(C) This choice has the same analysis as (B).
(D) P and H are interchangeable in spaces 5 and 6.
(E) This choice has the same analysis as (D).

1	2	3	4	5	6
F	L	M/G	G/M	H/P	P/H
		(G)	(G)		
~~H~~	~~H~~	~~H~~	~~H~~		
~~M~~	~~M~~			~~M~~	~~M~~
~~L~~				~~L~~	~~L~~
		~~F~~	~~F~~	~~F~~	~~F~~

F < L < M < H

Fig. 3

5. (E) – This is an easy question. The initial analysis partially limited the possible locations of G, H, M, L, and F. P is the only free agent.
(A) See the analysis.
(B) See the analysis.
(C) See the analysis.
(D) See the analysis.
(E) * See the analysis.

6. (A) – Now that M is exactly one number higher than L, this further limits the possible orders, since the block is now F < L M < H. What possible orders can be formed? If F is first, then L M are second and third, allowing G to be fourth. H and P will be fifth and sixth. If F is second, G has to be third and L M are fourth and fifth, with H sixth and P first. (Figure 4)
(A) * Correct. H can be fifth.
(B) Because of the L M limitation, M cannot be fourth.
(C) Either L or G must be fourth. P needs to fill the open space when all the other members are placed.
(D) Because of the L M limitation, L cannot be third. See (B).
(E) Either M or G must be third. P fills the open spaces. See (C).

1	2	3	4	5	6
F	L	M	G	H/P	P/H

1	2	3	4	5	6
P	F	G	L	M	H

F < L M < H

Fig. 4

Tape sides

The person that wrote this game assumed that people under the age of 25 know what a cassette tape is—a risky assumption. This puzzle requires a multiple-line diagram. Although this puzzle set is much more challenging than the previous puzzle, it is still only an average difficulty multiple line. Figure 1 shows a clean and easy diagram. You are told that there are four tapes (you have to know that there are two sides per tape, but even if you didn't know this, you should have figured that out, especially after reading Rule 1), and there are four types of music: F, H, J, and R. Rule 1 makes your life much easier by requiring that each of the four music types be used exactly two times. Rule 2 provides two useful pieces of information. At least one J is on Tape 1, and Tape 1 does not have H or R. (Figure 2) Therefore, Tape 1 has either JF or JJ. Rule 3 is simple to diagram, no J for Tape 2. The final rule (Rule 4) is not easily graphed, but it will prove to be important in several of the questions. The impact of Rule 4 is that if, for example, an R is on Tape 2, then no F can be on Tape 3. Note that F could be on Tape 2 *with* R. You may want to draw a circle around Rule 4 or put an asterisk next to it to remind yourself that it has not been diagrammed. You will do most of the work when you reach the questions, instead of at the initial analysis stage. Because there are many permutations, it is not worth your time to do them now. Besides, there is not enough room to write them all.

	1	2	3	4
Side A:	__	__	__	__
Side B:	__	__	__	__

Fig. 1

	1	2	3	4
Side A:	J	__	__	__
Side B:	J/F	__	__	__
	~~H,R~~	~~J~~		

2 each.

Fig. 2

7. (B) – You can use rule-violation answer elimination to quickly answer this question.
   (A) This violates Rule 3: J cannot be on Tape 2.
   (B) * This is a permissible permutation.
   (C) This violates Rule 1: it has three Js instead of two.
   (D) This violates Rule 2: H is not supposed to be on Tape 1.

(E) This violates Rule 4: R cannot be on the tape numbered exactly one lower than the tape F is on.

8. **(C) – Each of these answer choices contains an "if-then" statement.** This makes the answer choices time consuming. If-then answer choices require you to do new work to check each answer choice. Try to figure out the impact of the "if" statements in your head; diagram them only if necessary. When you find just one alternative valid permutation, you can eliminate the answer choice.

(A) If Tape 1 has two Js, then it is possible for Tape 2 to have two Rs, Tape 3 to have 2 Hs, and Tape 4 to have 2 Fs. This answer choice is not a "must be true" statement.

(B) If Tape 2 has two Fs, Tape 1 must have two Js. Tape 3 can have 2 Rs. It is not necessary that H be on Tape 3.

(C) * This must be true. If Tape 2 has two Rs, then F cannot be on Tape 3. So at least one F must be on Tape 4.

(D) This choice is invalid; J cannot be on Tape 2 (Rule 2).

(E) If Tape 4 has two Hs, it is possible to put two Rs on Tape 3.

9. (B) – Like the previous question, you need to invest work in each of these answer choices. Unlike the previous question, this is a "could be true" question; once you find a valid permutation, you have found the credited answer choice. This requires less time.

(A) If Tape 1 has two Js and Tape 4 has one H and one F, then the two Rs would have to be on Tape 2. But even doing this would not work, since the second F would have to be on Tape 3, so this order would violate Rule 4.

(B) * This could be true. Tape 3 has H and J. Tape 2 has H and would have to have one F. Tape 1 would have the other F as well as a J. Tape 4 would have two Rs.

(C) If Tape 3 has two Fs, then F cannot be on Tape 1. Thus, Tape 1 has to have two Js. There cannot be a third J.

(D) This looks promising but does not work. If Tape 3 has the second J, then Tape 1 has one F. This means that there are not two Fs available for Tape 4.

(E) This violates Rule 1. There are supposed to be exactly two Js.

10. (C) – Lacking new information, you can try to answer this using previous work, as well as eliminating the answer choices that violate the rules, and attempting to diagram any choice that looks possible.

(A) This cannot be true. Rule 2 reserves one space on Tape 1 for J.

(B) This cannot be true. Rule 3 prohibits J from being on Tape 2.

(C) * This looks like a possibility. Mark this and then try to eliminate the other answer choices.

(D) This cannot be true. Rule 2 prohibits H from being on Tape 1.

(E) A quick analysis using Rule 4 demonstrates that this cannot be true. If F is on Tapes 3 and 4, then at least one R must be on Tape 2 and/or Tape 3. Either way, this would violate Rule 4.

11. (B) – Yet again, you are forced to analyze each of the five answer choices. If you find that a permutation works, then you can eliminate the answer choice.

(A) This certainly is possible. J could be on Tape 1, R could be on Tape 2, H could be on Tape 3, and F could be on Tape 4.

(B) * This cannot be true. If Tape 2 has both Hs, and Tape 3 has both Rs, then Tape 4 must have one or two Fs. This violates Rule 4.

(C) This choice is similar to (A).

(D) Like (A) and (C), this choice properly keeps F from being immediately after R.

(E) See (D).

Weather and towns

This game is easier than average. In it, you must keep track of two things: the town names and the type of precipitation. A standard multiple-line with five spaces is perfect. (Figure 1) The set-up is quite clear, it describes how each of the five towns gets one type of precipitation and they get the storms in sequence. To make your life easier and avoid confusion, let's rename "hail and rain" as simply "hail". The first two rules are easy to diagram. Rule 1 allows you to fix P. Rule 2 specifies that hail falls on town 2. (Figure 2) Next, combine Rule 2 and Rule 3 to make a warranted conclusion. Rule 3 says that L and O get rain. Note this below the main diagram. Since town 2 gets hail, you know that neither L nor O is town 2. Graph this information on the main diagram. Finally, Rule 4 tells you that J is after both L and N. This is where the payoff comes. If J is after L and N, then J cannot be the first or second town. The earliest J could be is fourth. Now consider town 2. Since L, O, J, and P cannot be town 2, N must be town 2. After making this warranted conclusion, the questions will be much easier to answer. Should you do any permutations? You know that L or O must be town 1. You also know that L and O must get rain, so this allows you to make another warranted conclusion—Town 1 gets rain. Also, if O is town 1, where can L be? L cannot be fifth, since J must come after L. L would be fourth in this permutation. If, however, L is town 1, then O and J can be either town 4 or town 5.

	1	2	3	4	5
Town:	__	__	__	__	__
H_2O:	__	__	__	__	__

Fig. 1

	1	2	3	4	5
Town:	L/O	N	P	__	__
	~~J~~	~~L~~ ~~O~~ ~~J~~			
H_2O:	R	H	__	__	__

L=R
O=R

Fig. 2

12. (A) – Use the diagram and rule-violation answer elimination.
(A)* This is the only valid permutation.
(B) The second town gets hail, but O gets rain.

(C) This choice violates Rule 4; J must be after both L and N.
(D) The second town gets hail, but L gets rain.
(E) This choice violates Rule 1; town 3 is P.

13. (C) – If O is before J, then J is after N, L, O, and P; thus, J is fifth. Either L or O is first and the other is fourth. Both L and O get rain. (Figure 3) Look for a choice that contradicts the diagram.
(A) Either O or L is the first town.
(B) Either O or L is the fourth town.
(C) * The fourth town cannot get hail. The fourth town is either O or L. Either way, the fourth town must get rain.
(D) This must be true. J must be the fifth town.
(E) The analysis does not reveal whether J, the fifth town, gets rain or hail.

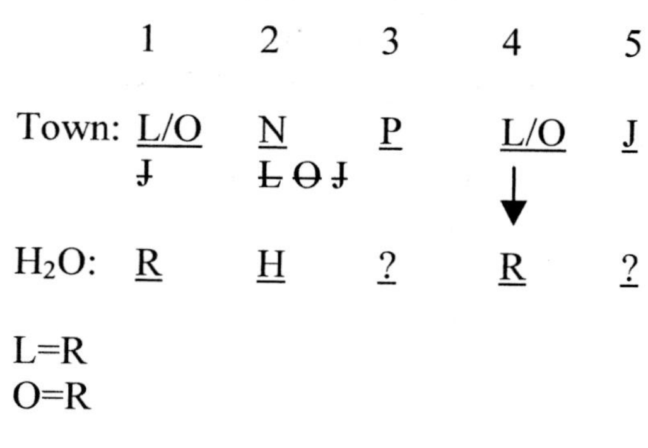

Fig. 3

14. (E) – Refer to figure 2. Notice that L can be either first, fourth, or fifth. If L were first, then the new information in the question would conflict with the fact that the second town gets hail, not rain. So, for this question, the only slots available to L are towns 4 and 5. But L must be before J. This means that L must be fourth. Since L is fourth, J is fifth. (Figure 4) You can now determine everything except the precipitation that town P gets.
(A) Could it be false that O is first? No, this cannot be false. It must be true that O is first.
(B) Could it be false that the fourth town gets rain? No, this cannot be false. It must be true that the fourth town gets rain.
(C) Could it be false that J is the fifth town? No, it cannot be false. J must be the fifth town.
(D) Could it be false that J gets rain? No, it cannot be false. J must get rain, because the question stated that each town after L gets rain.
(E) * See the diagram. P can get either rain or hail, so it could be false that P gets rain.

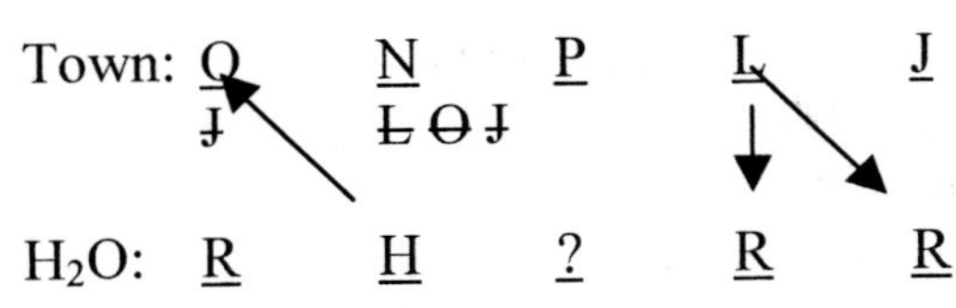

Fig. 4

15. (D) – Now, J is before O. This can happen only if J is fourth and O is fifth. (Figure 5) This means that L is first. You can now determine the type of precipitation for all of the towns, except P and J.

(A) Could it be false that the storm passes L before it passes J? No, it cannot be false; it must be true that L is before J. See figure 5; J is after L. Also, Rule 4 requires this.

(B) Since it must be true that L is before O, this cannot be false.

(C) Since it must be true that N is before O, this cannot be false.

(D)* It could be true or false that the fourth town, J, gets rain.

(E) It must be true that the fifth town, O, gets rain, so it cannot be false.

Town: L N P J O
J L O J

H_2O: R H ? ? R

Fig. 5

16. (B) – Once again, add the information and analyze. O is before L, and L is before J. N is also before J. Thus, J is fifth. The only open spaces are the first and fourth spaces, so O is first and L is fourth. This has almost the same analysis as question 14. Figure 6 shows what can be deduced.

(A) We do not know if the third town, P, gets rain or hail.

(B)* Yes, it must be true that the fourth town gets rain because the fourth town must be L, and L gets rain.

(C) This is false; the fourth town does not get hail.

(D) The fifth town, J, can get either kind of precipitation.

(E) See (D).

Town: O N P L J
J L O J

H_2O: R H ? R ?

Fig. 6

Committee groups

This puzzle is the most difficult of the section, but it is not overly difficult. Each member must be used at least once. That makes things easier. There are six members, and they must fill nine spaces in three groups. Clearly, some members are used more than once. Keep this in mind. The diagram is very basic. Use three rows of three dashes. (Figure 1) Now start on the rules. Rule 1 requires that one member be used three times. Okay, do the math, if one member is used three times, five other members must be used a total of six times. You can conclude that one other member is used exactly twice, and the remaining four members are used exactly once. Now move on to Rules 2 and 3. F and G are not together. H and I are not together. You can make a warranted conclusion by combining Rules 1, 2, and 3. Since F, G, H, and I each have a conflict with one other member, none of them can be the member that is used three times. Thus, either M or P is the triple member. Does this mean that the other one must be used twice? No. After considering the issue, it becomes clear that either F, G, H, or I could be the member that is used twice, as could M or P be the member that is used twice (whichever one is not the triple). There are far too many permutations, so don't waste your time doing them.

Group: 1 2 3

— — —

— — —

— — —

M or P = 3 times
F ≠ G
H ≠ I

Fig. 1

17. (C) – Rule-violation answer elimination does not work for this question. Instead, consider what it means when F is not with M. You know that F is used at least once. If F is not with M, then M cannot be the triple, thus, P is the triple. (Figure 2) Unfortunately, there are still many possible permutations. Maybe F is used twice and M and I are together in the third group. Maybe M is used twice. Maybe H or I is used twice. The list goes on. Rather than waste time doing permutations, see what the answer choices have to offer.

(A) The limited analysis we have done so far does not indicate that this must be true. Actually, the analysis does not indicate anything about this pairing.

(B) See (A). In this question, H and I have the same analysis.

(C) * Yes. This turned out to be easier than it first appeared. You learned that P must be the triple, and you know that I must be used at least once, so of course, P and I must be in the same group, at least once.
(D) There is no indication as to what M must do, because M is flexible.
(E) See (A).

Group:	1	2	3
	P	P	P
	—	—	—
	—	—	—

Fig. 2

18. (C) – This new information, that P is on every subcommittee with F and every subcommittee with G, means that P is either used twice or three times. Try doing a permutation using P twice and you find that it does not work. If P were used twice, M would have to be used three times, and the result would be MPG, MPF, MHI. But H and I cannot be together, Rule 3. Therefore, P, not M, must be used three times. The diagram is still sparse. (Figure 3) See what the answer choices have to offer.
(A) Can M (and P) be with both F and G? No, this would force H and I to be together in group 3, as discussed above.
(B) It is impossible for M to be with H and I. There is not enough room left in the groups once P is the triple. M cannot be the double in this situation.
(C) * Can H be the double? It looks like H could be the double member. Consulting figure 3, H could be with F and G. Then M and I could round-out group 3.
(D) Since P is the triple, it is impossible for F to be in every group that P is in. Also, F cannot be with G.
(E) Since P is the triple, it is impossible for H to be in every group that P is in. Also, H cannot be the triple because H and I cannot be together.

Group:	1	2	3
	P	P	P
	F	G	—
	—	—	—

Fig. 3

19. (B) – Now M and I are a couple. Can I be used once? Yes. Can I be used twice? This is tricky. The question says that I is used every time M is used. So there could be two Is and one M. But M cannot be the double member, because this would result in two Ms and two Is. Can I be used three times? No, there is only one triple member. This means that P is the triple member, again. (Figure 4) Since this is a "could be true" question, let's try a permutation. First, put I and M in group 3 to get them out of the way. Now consider F and G. Can the double member be F or G? No, because this would cause a conflict with the other one. So F and G are split between the two open subcommittees. Finally, H must be used at least once, but could be used twice in the two open subcommittees.

(A) M can only serve on one subcommittee.
(B) * I can serve on two subcommittees, or on one subcommittee.
(C) Since P serves on all three, I cannot be in every group P is in.
(D) As you can see in figure 3, F cannot be with M.
(E) F and G have the same analysis in this question. See (D).

Group: 1	2	3
P	P	P
H	H/I	I
F/G	G/F	M

Fig. 4

20. (D) – Once again, we have an open-ended "could be true" question. The initial analysis helps you eliminate a few of these answer choices.

(A) We know by now that only M or P can be the triple member.
(B) See (A).
(C) Since either M or P is the triple member, G cannot be in every group that either M or P is in.
(D) * Yes, if P is the triple member, then P can be in every group that both M and I are.
(E) Since either M or P is the triple member, they both cannot be in three groups.

21. (E) – Yet again, an open-ended question, though this one is a "must be true" question. Once again, if you did a good job at the initial analysis stage, you should be able to find the credited answer choice without doing additional work.

(A) There is no reason that G must be the double member.

(B) There is no reason that I must only be in one group.

(C) A quick analysis proves that F need not be in the same group as H. Also, if you thought about this one before doing the analysis, you would have realized that F and G share the same analysis in this question, so it is impossible that F must be with H, since it is just as likely that G is with H.

(D) This question has a similar analysis to (C); H and I are interchangeable. What is true for I must also be true for H.

(E) * Yes, since either M or P is the triple member, M must be with P at least once, but maybe twice.

22. (D) – Yet again, no new information. Yet again, a "must be true" question. Yet again, the initial analysis should be sufficient.

(A) No. The initial analysis proved that it is possible to have one F and one G, which means that one group would not have an F or G.

(B) See (A). Because there was no new limiting information, H and I have the same analysis for this question as F and G.

(C) Nothing we have done up to this point indicates that M, P, and F cannot be in the same subcommittee. You know that M and P must be together at least once (because one of them is the triple), and F does not have any special limitations vis-à-vis M and P that would prevent it from being in the same group as M and P.

(D) * Yes. The initial analysis was that one member is in exactly two committees.

(E) It is possible that M and P are the triple and double members. It is not necessary that one of them be used just once.

SECTION I

Time—35 minutes

22 Questions

Directions: Each group of questions in this section is based on a set of conditions. In answering some of the questions, it may useful to draw a rough diagram. Choose the response that most accurately and completely answers each question and blacken t corresponding space on your answer sheet.

Questions 1–6

Exactly seven products—P, Q, R, S, T, W, and X—are each to be advertised exactly once in a section of a catalog. The order in which they will be displayed is governed by the following conditions:

Q must be displayed in some position before W.
R must be displayed immediately before X.
T cannot be displayed immediately before or immediately after W.
S must be displayed either first of seventh.
Either Q or T must be displayed fourth.

1. Which one of the following CANNOT be the product that is displayed first?

(A) P
(B) Q
(C) R
(D) T
(E) X

2. If X is displayed immediately before Q, then which one of the following could be true?

(A) T is displayed first.
(B) R is displayed fifth.
(C) Q is displayed last.
(D) Q is displayed second.
(E) P is displayed second.

3. If P is displayed second, then which one of the follow could be displayed third?

(A) R
(B) S
(C) T
(D) W
(E) X

4. Which one of the following could be true?

(A) Q is displayed fifth.
(B) Q is displayed seventh.
(C) R is displayed third.
(D) W is displayed third.
(E) X is displayed fifth.

5. If R is displayed sixth, then which one of the followi must be displayed fifth?

(A) P
(B) Q
(C) T
(D) W
(E) X

GO ON TO THE NEXT PAC

Questions 12–17

In Crescentville there are exactly five record stores, whose names are abbreviated S, T, V, X, and Z. Each of the five stores carries at least one of four distinct types of music: folk, jazz, opera, and rock. None of the stores carries any other type of music. The following conditions must hold:

Exactly two of the five stores carry jazz.
T carries rock and opera but no other types of music.
S carries more types of music than T carries
X carries more types of music than any other store in Crescentville carries
Jazz is among the types of music S carries.
V does not carry any type of music that Z carries.

12. Which one of the following could be true?

(A) S carries folk and rock but neither jazz nor opera.
(B) T carries jazz but neither opera nor rock.
(C) V carries folk, rock, and opera, but not jazz.
(D) X carries folk, rock, and jazz, but not opera.
(E) Z carries folk and opera but neither rock nor jazz.

13. Which one of the following could be true?

(A) S, V, and Z all carry folk.
(B) S, X, and Z all carry jazz.
(C) Of the five stores, only S and V carry jazz.
(D) Of the five stores, only T and X carry rock.
(E) Of the five stores, only S, T, and V carry opera.

14. If exactly one of the stores carries folk, then which one of the following could be true?

(A) S and V carry exactly two types of music in common.
(B) T and S carry exactly two types of music in common.
(C) T and V carry exactly two types of music in common.
(D) V and X carry exactly two types of music in common.
(E) X and Z carry exactly two types of music in common.

15. Which one of the following must be true?

(A) T carries exactly the same number of types of music as V carries.
(B) V carries exactly the same number of types of music as Z carries.
(C) S carries at least one more type of music than Z carries.
(D) Z carries at least one more type of music than T carries.
(E) X carries exactly two more types of music than S carries.

16. If V is one of exactly three stores that carry rock, then which one of the following must be true?

(A) S and V carry no types of music in common.
(B) S and V carry at least one type of music in common.
(C) S and Z carry at least one type of music in common.
(D) T and Z carry at least one type of music in common.
(E) T and V carry at least two types of music in common.

17. If S and V both carry folk, then which one of the following could be true?

(A) S and T carry no types of music in common.
(B) S and Z carry no types of music in common.
(C) T and Z carry no types of music in common.
(D) S and Z carry two types of music in common.
(E) T and V carry two types of music in common.

GO ON TO THE NEXT PAG

Answer key and explanations for PrepTest 47

Answer Key

1. E
2. A
3. C
4. A
5. D
6. B
7. A
8. B
9. C
10. C
11. C
12. E
13. D
14. B
15. C
16. C
17. B
18. C
19. E
20. B
21. A
22. B

(E) * As you discovered during while making warranted conclusions, X cannot be first.

2. (A) – You are told that X is immediately before Q. Glancing at the diagram, you see that a few rules are relevant and should be combined. Once you combine them, there is a large block of members, which limits their possible locations. Combine Rules 1 (Q < W) and 2 (R X) to get R X Q < W. Now try to fit this big block of four members on the diagram. It quickly becomes clear that the only place R X Q will fit is on spaces 1 through 3 or spaces 2 through 4. If you try to place this block anywhere else, conflicts would arise. Before getting carried away and doing all of the permutations, check the answer choices to see what you can accomplish using just this information.

(A) * It appears possible to have T on space 1, followed by the block of these three members. W, P, and S can all then be placed without causing any problems. One possible order is: T, R, X, Q, W, P, S.

(B) Since R is at the beginning of the block of R X Q, R can only be on space 1 or space 2.

(C) This choice was easy to eliminate. Q can never be last, a result of Rule 1.

(D) Q can only be third or fourth in this situation.

(E) P cannot be second because either R or X must be second.

3. (C) – After you place P in space 2, you know that neither X nor R can be in space 3. This eliminates answer choice (E). Since P has no rules that directly affect it, look instead at the effect that filling space 2 has on the other rules. (Figure 2)

(A) The initial analysis determined that R can never be in space 3, for the simple reason that X can never be in space 4.

(B) Rule 4 stated that S is only first or seventh.

(C) * T seems like a candidate for space 3. Q would then be on space 4. R and X could occupy spaces 5 and 6, W could occupy 7, and S could occupy space 1. (Fig. 2)

(D) If W were to be in space 3, then Q would have to be in space 1, because of Rule 1. This would force T to be in space 4. But putting T next to W violates Rule 3.

(E) Because P is in space 2, X cannot be in space 3, because R must be immediately before X.

1	2	3	4	5	6	7
S	P	T	Q	R	X	W

Fig. 2

Control switches

This game was unusual for two reasons. First, it utilizes a unique rule. Second, this unique rule was not clearly written, causing many students to have trouble grasping what was happening. Although the LSAT is designed to be difficult, the difficulty normally results from the number of rules to keep track of, and the complexity of how those rules relate to one another. In this game, the difficulty results from a quirky rule and how it was phrased. Once you understand what this rule is saying, this puzzle set is not particularly difficult. The scenario is as follows: There are seven switches, which are turned on or off. Although it isn't immediately apparent, this requires a standard mono-group selection game diagram. Then the game introduces the concept of a "circuit load". If all seven of the switches are turned on, then the "circuit load" equals seven. If only one switch is on, then the "circuit load" is one. Now look at Rule 3. If all seven switches are on, and so the circuit load equals seven, then, by Rule 3, switch number 7 is required to be on. Alternatively, if exactly one switch is on, then the circuit load equals one, and, per Rule 3, switch number 1 is required to be on. So, what if, for example, four of the switches are on and three are off? In this case, the circuit load (the number of switches switched on) equals four, and thus, due to Rule 3, switch number 4 must be in the on position, along with three other switches. Is this a weird rule for a mono-group selection game? Yes, it is very weird. The LSAT has never before had this kind of rule, and may never have one again. But now that you understand how the setup and Rule 3 interact, the other two rules are straightforward. Rule 1 requires that if switch 1 is on, switches 3 and 5 be off. Rule 2 says that if switch 4 is on, switches 2 and 5 are off. Figure 1 shows a simple way to diagram this. Be careful though, figure 1 only shows the direct impact of the rules, it does not show the indirect impacts. What are the indirect impacts? For example, the indirect impact of Rule 1 is that if switch 3 or 5 is on, switch 1 is off. You could diagram the indirect impacts on figure 1, but it would get a little crowded. Before going to the questions, can we make any easy conclusions? Mono-group selection games often have a "maximum number" or "minimum number" question, so determine those. What is the maximum number of switches that can be on? If we turn on all the switches except switches 1 and 4, then five switches are on, and switch number five is on, so the maximum is five. There is no minimum number because none of the arrows go from the "off" column to the "on" column. Switches 6 and 7 are free agents. Try a permutation or two if you like to see if anything interesting crops up, then go to the questions.

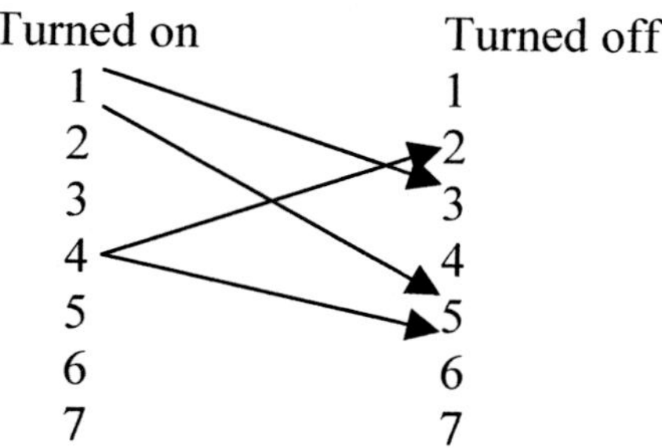

*The total number of switches turned on must equal the place number of a switch that is turned on.

Fig. 1

time. What about turning on switches 2, 5, 6, and 7? Again, we run into the problem of Rule 3.

8. (B) – If exactly two switches are on, then switch 2 must be turned on in order to satisfy Rule 3. What other switches have conflicts with switch 2? Because of Rule 2, switch 4 and switch 2 cannot both be turned on. This is the answer.
(A) See the analysis. Switch 3 can be on at the same time as switch 2.
(B) * Switch 4 must be off when switch 2 is on.
(C) Switch 5 can be on at the same time as switch 2.
(D) Switch 6 can be on at the same time as switch 2.
(E) In this situation, switch 7 has the same analysis as switch 6.

9. (C) – This time, switches 6 and 7 are off. This means that five switches are left. Of those five switches, either 1 and 4 can be on (but this fails Rule 3), or switches 2, 3, and 5 can be on. The maximum number that can be on at the same time is three switches. Since switch 3 is on, this satisfies Rule 3.
(A) See the analysis.
(B) See the analysis. Although switch 2 and switch 5 can both be on, and this satisfies all the rules, the question asked for the maximum circuit load (the maximum number of switches turned on.)
(C) * This matches the analysis.
(D) If switch 4 is turned on, it is not possible to turn on three other switches.
(E) It is not possible to have switches 1 through 5 all on at the same time because of Rules 1 and 2.

10. (C) – In this question, switches 5 and 6 are on. What other switch must be on? Well, in order to satisfy Rule 3, it will be necessary to have switch 3 on.
(A) This is definitely not possible. Switch 1 cannot be on if switch 5 is on (Rule 1).
(B) It is possible, but it is not necessary that switch 2 be on. If switch 2 is on, then it is necessary to have switches 3, 5, 6, and 7 on.
(C) * Yes, switch 3 must be on when 5 and 6 are on and there are exactly three switches turned on. Switch 3 must also be turned on in the permutation we did for answer choice (B).
(D) Switch 4 can never be on when switch 5 is on.
(E) As demonstrated in (C), switch 7 is not required.

11. (C) – This question asks for the maximum number of switches that can be turned on. If you did this analysis at the start, then you already know the answer. If you didn't, then solve it now. Because of rules 1 and 2, there cannot be a total of six or seven switches turned on. Can there be five switches turned on? Yes, as you saw in question 10, answer choice (B), we

Stores and music

This is an average difficulty puzzle. You must keep track of two things: the store names and the (one, two, three, or four) types of music each store carries. It takes a little experimenting to find the best diagram. As it turns out, a matrix diagram is the best diagram. The store names will be the horizontal axis, and the music types will be the vertical axis. Note how this matrix diagram looks similar to a multiple line diagram. (Figure 1) Sometimes the two types of games can look and function in much the same way. There are quite a few rules to organize. Start with the anchor rules. Rule 5 specifies that store S has jazz. (Figure 1) Now work through the rest of the rules. The first rule is easy; there are exactly two stores that have jazz. Mark this next to the jazz line using a "=2". (Figure 1) Rule 1 is even easier; store T has only rock and opera. Mark this in the T column. Rule 3 builds off the second rule. Since S has more types of music than T, we can conclude that S has either three or four types of music. Note this above the S column. Rule 4 builds off the third rule. X has more types of music than any other store. This allows us to make two conclusions. The first conclusion is that since X has more types of music than S, then X has four types of music. Also, we can conclude that S has exactly three types of music. (Figure 2) Review the rule again if this is not clear. Wait, there is even more we can do with this rule. Since X has four types of music, it must have the second jazz. Thus, neither V nor Z has jazz. This is a big conclusion. (Figure 2) Rule 6 says that V and Z have no types in common. It is difficult to graph this clearly, but a negative two-way arrow will serve as a reminder. You can conclude that V has either one or two types of music and that Z has one or two types. This is true because these two stores are mutually exclusive. This is a solid start on the diagram, so go directly to the questions. Because of the size and complexity of the diagram, it will be necessary to reuse the diagram, so do neat work.

	=3 or 4 S	T	X	V	Z
F	__	no	__	__	__
J=2	J	no	__	__	__
O	__	O	__	__	__
R	__	R	__	__	__

Fig. 1

of them must have opera, and the other has rock. Now eliminate the answer choices.

(A) V can only carry one type of music, not two. So S and V cannot have two types in common.

(B) * Yes. T and S must both carry opera and rock.

(C) Once again, V can only carry one type of music.

(D) Once again, V can only carry one type of music.

(E) Similar to V, X can only carry one type of music.

	=3 S	T	=4 X	=1,2 ~~V~~ x	=1,2 Z
F	**no**	no	F	**no**	**no**
J=2	J	no	J	no	no
O	**O**	O	O	__	__
R	**R**	R	R	__	__

Fig. 4

15. (C) – Lacking any new information, use the initial analysis as well as analysis for previous questions to eliminate the answer choices.

(A) T carries two types of music, while V carries either one or two types. As we saw in question 14, T carried two types of music while V carried one type.

(B) The initial analysis revealed that V can carry two types when Z carries one type, or vice versa.

(C) * True. The initial analysis revealed that S carries exactly three types of music, while Z carries one or two types.

(D) T carries two types of music, and Z carries either one or two types. So Z never carries more types of music than T.

(E) X carries four types of music. S carries three types of music. This is true because of the interaction of Rules 3 and 4.

16. (C) – Reuse the diagram. T and X already carry two rock, and now V carries a third rock. This means that S and Z do not carry rock. Turning to S, we see that S must now carry opera and folk. We do not know for certain what V and Z carry.

(A) S and Z could both carry either folk or opera. In fact, Z must carry folk and/or opera.

(B) It is not necessary for V to carry either folk or opera, so S and V may not have any types in common.

(C) * True. Z must carry folk and/or opera. S carries folk and opera.

Restaurant staffing

This game is difficult. The placement of members on the diagram is very flexible, and thus complex. There is a lot of information to keep track of. The basic diagram has five days with two people per day. A multiple line will work. (Figure 1) Since there must be at least one supervisor each day, it is clearer if we list the supervisors on the top line, and the three workers and the supervisors (since there can be two supervisors working on the same day) on the second line. Diagram the rules. Rule 2 specifies that O works at least Tuesday and Wednesday. (Figure 2) Rules 3-5 are not easy to diagram. Rule 3 says that N works on at least two consecutive days, and could work more than two days. Note this below the diagram. (Figure 2) As you review answer choices, you should eliminate any choice that does not show N working two days in a row. Rule 4 is not as confusing as it first appears. It says that S will not work before the first day that P works. S could work on the same day as the first day P works, but will not work before P does. So, when considering answer choices, eliminate any that show S working before the first day P works. Rule 5 is pretty confusing. What it means is that when K works, that is the first day that the other person works. A star or asterisk next to K serves as a reminder. Are there any conclusions that can be made? Count the number of times the people are used. N and O must each be used twice or more. This leaves up to six openings to use the other four people. Unfortunately, this is not much help, since there are still too many possibilities. Go to the questions, they will help you develop the diagram.

	M	T	W	H	F
Supers: J N P:	__	__	__	__	__
All:	__	__	__	__	__

Fig. 1

	M	T	W	H	F
Supers: J N P:	__	__	__	__	__
All:	__	O	O	__	__

N N + ?
S < P
*K

Fig. 2

18. (C) – Rule-violation answer elimination works well for this question.

Fig. 3

21. (A) – Which pair cannot work on Monday? Before jumping into the answer choices, consider the rules that might come into play. The most relevant is Rule 4, which says that S does not work before P's first day. The odds are good that S will feature in the credited answer.
(A) * Correct. S cannot work on Monday (unless P also works Monday.)
(B) K and P can both work Monday.
(C) P and S can both work Monday. See figure 3.
(D) This looks somewhat interesting at first, but it is possible to have N and O both work on Monday. This would still leave enough open spaces to accommodate the remaining workers.
(E) J has no issues at all. N has no issues that are especially relevant to Monday.

22. (B) – Yet again, there is no new information in the questions stem, but the five answer choices provide new facts to work with.
(A) No. Rule 3 clearly specified that N works on at least two consecutive days.
(B) * Once again, the solution comes down to understanding Rule 4. If S is on Monday, and P is on Tuesday, then P must also be on Monday to avoid violating Rule 4. (Figure 4). Now we must accommodate N and J. N can fill Wednesday and Thursday, while J fills Friday. K cannot be Thursday (because that is N's second day) so it must be Friday.
(C) K cannot work Wednesday, because that is O's second day.
(D) Again, K cannot work with N on N's second day.
(E) If K and O were both working on Tuesday, there would be no supervisor. It is interesting to note how Rule 1 ended up playing such a limited role in the questions.

	M	T	W	H	F
Supers: J N P:	P	P	N	N	J
All:	S	O	O	?	K

Fig. 4

SECTION I

Time—35 minutes

22 Questions

Directions: Each group of questions in this section is based on a set of conditions. In answering some of the questions, it may useful to draw a rough diagram. Choose the response that most accurately and completely answers each question and blacken t corresponding space on your answer sheet.

Questions 1–6

Henri has exactly five electrical appliances in his dormitory room: a hairdryer, a microwave oven, a razor, a television, and a vacuum. As a consequence of fire department regulations, Henri can use these appliances only in accordance with the following conditions:

Henri cannot use both the hairdryer and the razor simultaneously.

Henri cannot use both the hairdryer and the television simultaneously.

When Henri uses the vacuum, he cannot at the same time use any of the following: the hairdryer, the razor, and the television.

1. Which one of the following is a pair of appliances Henri could be using simultaneously?

(A) the hairdryer and the razor
(B) the hairdryer and the television
(C) the razor and the television
(D) the razor and the vacuum
(E) the television and the vacuum

2. Assume that Henri is using exactly two appliances and is not using the microwave oven. Which one of the following is a list of all the appliances, other than the microwave over, that Henri CANNOT be using?

(A) hairdryer
(B) razor
(C) vacuum
(D) hairdryer, razor
(E) hairdryer, vacuum

3. Which one of the following CANNOT be true?

(A) Henri uses the hairdryer while using the microwave oven.
(B) Henri uses the microwave oven while using the razor.
(C) Henri uses the microwave oven while using two other appliances.
(D) Henri uses the television oven while using two other appliances.
(E) Henri uses the vacuum oven while using two other appliances.

4. If Henri were to use exactly three appliances, then wh is the total number of different groups of three appliances any one of which could be the group of appliances he is using?

(A) one
(B) two
(C) three
(D) four
(E) five

5. Which one of the following statements, if true, guarantees that Henri is using no more than one of th following: the hairdryer, the razor, the television?

(A) Henri is using the hairdryer.
(B) Henri is using the television.
(C) Henri is not using the hairdryer.
(D) Henri is not using the microwave oven.
(E) Henri is not using the vacuum.

6. Which one of the following must be true?

(A) Henri uses at most three appliances simultaneously.
(B) Henri uses at most four appliances simultaneously.
(C) Henri uses at most one other appliance while using the microwave oven.
(D) Henri uses at most one other appliance while using the razor.
(E) Henri uses at least two other appliances while using the hairdryer.

GO ON TO THE NEXT PA(

Questions 13–17

In a repair facility there are exactly six technicians: Stacy, Urma, Wim, Xena, Yolanda, and Zane. Each technician repairs machines of at least one of the following three types—radios, televisions, and VCRs—and no other types. The following conditions apply:

Xena and exactly three other technicians repair radios.
Yolanda repairs both televisions and VCRs.
Stacy does not repair any type of machine that Yolanda repairs.
Zane repairs more types of machines than Yolanda repairs.
Wim does not repair any type of machine that Stacy repairs.
Urma repairs exactly two types of machines.

13. For exactly how many of the six technicians is it possible to determine exactly which of the three types of machines each repairs?

(A) one
(B) two
(C) three
(D) four
(E) five

14. Which one of the following must be true?

(A) Of the types of machines repaired by Stacy there is exactly one type that Urma also repairs.
(B) Of the types of machines repaired by Yolanda there is exactly one type that Xena also repairs.
(C) Of the types of machines repaired by Wim there is exactly one type that Xena also repairs.
(D) There is more than one type of machine that both Wim and Yolanda repair.
(E) There is more than one type of machine that both Urma and Wim repair.

15. Which one of the following must be false?

(A) Exactly one of the six technicians repairs exactly one type of machine.
(B) Exactly two of the six technicians repair exactly one type of machine each.
(C) Exactly three of the six technicians repair exactly one type of machine each.
(D) Exactly one of the six technicians repairs exactly two types of machine.
(E) Exactly three of the six technicians repair exactly two types of machine each.

16. Which one of the following pairs of technicians could repair all and only the same types of machines as each other?

(A) Stacy and Urma
(B) Urma and Yolanda
(C) Urma and Xena
(D) Wim and Xena
(E) Xena and Yolanda

17. Which one of the following must be true?

(A) There is exactly one type of machine that both Urma and Wim repair.
(B) There is exactly one type of machine that both Urma and Xena repair.
(C) There is exactly one type of machine that both Urma and Yolanda repair.
(D) There is exactly one type of machine that both Wim and Yolanda repair.
(E) There is exactly one type of machine that both Xena and Yolanda repair.

GO ON TO THE NEXT PAGE

Answer key and explanations for PrepTest 48

Answer Key

1. C
2. E
3. E
4. A
5. A
6. A
7. C
8. B
9. C
10. E
11. D
12. E
13. C
14. A
15. D
16. C
17. C
18. A
19. A
20. A
21. D
22. B

(D) A quick check of the diagram reveals that V and R are not permitted simultaneously.
(E) A quick check of the diagram reveals that TV and V are not permitted simultaneously.

2. (E) – Now you are told that the microwave is not being used, but two other appliances are being used. A quick check of the diagram reveals that the only two that can be used are R and TV. This question was phrased awkwardly in order to make it more difficult, but the answer is clear. Henri cannot use HD and V, in the situation where two appliances are used and MO is not used.
(A) See the analysis.
(B) See the analysis.
(C) See the analysis.
(D) See the analysis.
(E) * See the analysis.

3. (E) – Since this question does not add new information, go directly to the answer choices.
(A) MO is the free agent, the appliance that can be used with any other appliance. This makes MO a poor answer choice for a "CANNOT be true" question.
(B) See (A).
(C) MO can be used with R and with TV at the same time.
(D) See (C).
(E) * V can only be used with one other appliance, MO.

4. (A) – In the previous question we touched on the situation where three appliances are used. We learned that MO, R, and TV can be used at the same time. No other combination is possible, so there is only one possible group of three.
(A) * Correct. There can only be one group: MO, R, and TV.
(B) See the analysis.
(C) See the analysis.
(D) See the analysis.
(E) See the analysis.

5. (A) – Like question 2, this question uses awkward phrasing to make it difficult to understand. If this question were stated clearly, it would be too easy. The question stem says that the objective is to use no more than one of the following appliances: HD, R, or TV. Which of the five statements will ensure that it is only possible to use one of these appliances?

Harvest order

This game employs greater-than/less-than rules and a simple line. After diagramming the rules, figure 1 is the result. Although all the rules are diagrammed, there is still plenty of opportunity for error, especially if you have not practiced the "float," which is the whole reason the LSAT tests greater-than/less-than lines. For example, a quick glance at the diagram below might lead you to think that M must always be last, or second to last if J is last. But it is possible that J could be last and H second to last, with M third to last. This is why you must be careful of the float. Using this diagram, you could draw many warranted conclusions about where members can and cannot be, but it is more efficient to go to the questions now.

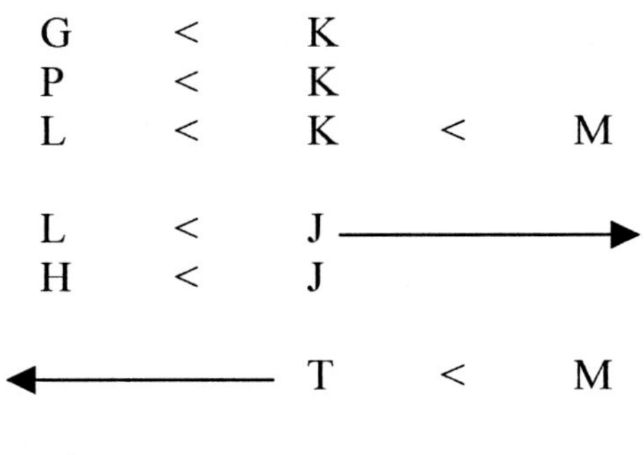

Fig. 1

7. (C) – Using the diagram and the rules, work through each answer choice.
(A) J cannot be first. At a minimum, both H and L must be before J.
(B) K cannot be second, because, at a minimum, L, P, and G must be before K.
(C) * M could be sixth, as long as H and J are harvested later.
(D) G cannot be seventh, because, at a minimum, K and M must be after G.
(E) T cannot be eighth, because, at a minimum, M must be after T.

8. (B) – If M is seventh, then J must be eighth. Which of the following cannot be fifth? We don't know anything definite about the others. Draw a quick diagram if you need to see the possibilities.
(A) H has no special limitations in this situation.
(B) * J cannot be fifth since J is now the only one available to fill the eighth space.
(C) K has not special limitations. K could be fourth or fifth.
(D) L has no special limitations.
(E) P has no special limitations.

9. (C) – Again, the focus is on the fifth space. Since the answer choices focus on different fields, the analysis from the previous question is of limited use,

(C) K must be after T.
(D) M must be after H in this situation.
(E) * M could be after J or before J.

__ __ __ __ L __ __ __

~~K~~ (under the 8th slot)

K & M & J (under the 6th and 7th slots)

Fig. 4

Fig. 2

13. (C) – Use the diagram. We know which machines Z and Y repair. We know which machine S repairs. We do not know all the machines that X, U, and W repair.
(A) See the analysis.
(B) See the analysis.
(C) * See the analysis.
(D) See the analysis.
(E) See the analysis.

14. (A) – Since this question does not add any new information, jump right into the answer choices and compare them to the diagram.
(A) * This must be true. Radio needed a fourth technician, and U was the only possible technician that could fill the fourth space. U repairs one other type of machine, but S does not.
(B) We don't know if this is true. X does not have much information, so it is difficult to say anything definite about X.
(C) See (B).
(D) If W were only to repair one type, then it would not be true that W and Y repair more than one of the same types.
(E) No, U repairs radios and one other machine. W does not repair radios. So U and W cannot have two machines in common.

15. (D) – "Must be false" questions are used to confuse you. Remember, four of the answer choices will be possible, and one will not.
(A) S is the only technician that is limited to one machine. W and X can repair one or more types. S, W, and X could all repair just one type.
(B) See (A).
(C) See (A).
(D) * Y must repair two types. U must repair two types. So it is false to say that exactly one technician must repair two types.
(E) Y and U are the only technicians that must repair two types. But X could also repair three types.

16. (C) – Lacking any new information, use the initial analysis. This question is asking, which of these pairs repair exactly the same machines?
(A) S repairs one type and U repairs two types, so they clearly don't repair all the same types.
(B) U must repair radios, and Y does not repair radios.
(C) * U must repair two types, one of which is radios. X is flexible, and can repair two types, one of which is radios. So this could be true.

Group stages

This puzzle incorporates a clever twist into a typical double-line game. Although this game is only slightly more difficult than an average puzzle, it was by far the most complex game of this section, because the other games were pretty easy. There are six music groups that will fill six spaces, and each will be used once. So far, we are off to an easy start. The quirk is that the north stage begins at 6 (AM or PM, it doesn't say) and the south stage begins at 8. Figure 1 shows how to diagram this. Move on to the rules. Rule 1 is a typical rule; p must be 6 or 12. (Figure 1) (Note - To make the diagram easier to read, capital letters are used for the folk groups, and lower-case letters are used for rock groups.) Rule 1 is similar to the kind of rule found in simple line games where the member must either be first or last in line. Rule 2 specifies that G performs sometime before H. (Figure 2) You can now make one quick warranted conclusion. G is not 12 and H is not 6. Rule 3 says that if a rock group performs at 10, no folk group does. This means that 10 has either two folk groups or two rock groups. This is difficult to diagram, so use an asterisk to remind you to refer to this rule. (Figure 2) Next, Rule 4 states that L and t perform on different stages. Use a mutually exclusive slash L/t to note this off to the side of the two stages. Finally, Rule 5, q (a rock group) performs immediately after a folk group, though not necessarily on the same stage. Note this below the diagram. (Figure 2) You can conclude that q cannot be at 6. Although we now have a lot of information on the diagram, there is still much we do not know. Are there any warranted conclusions that can be made? There are no obvious and useful conclusions to be made. Go to the questions, they will help you flesh out this basic diagram.

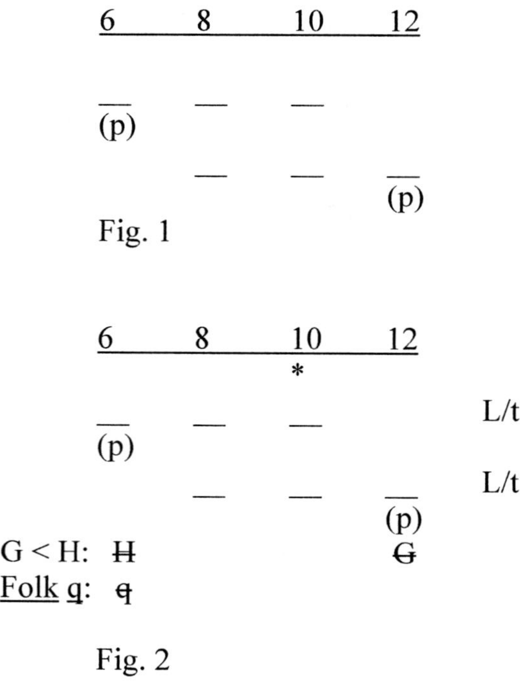

18. (A) – Rule-violation answer elimination works well for this question. Normally, the first question of every set is answerable using rule violation, but

(p)

Fig. 4

20. (A) – We are not provided any new information. The initial analysis, plus consulting previous questions, should eliminate some answer choices. Then, if necessary, you can resort to doing permutations. Question 18(A) shows that G can perform at 6. Since you know now that either G or p is at 6, you should add this to your initial diagram.

(A)* Simply use the work from question 18 to answer this question.

(B) In the initial analysis, we learned that H cannot be at 6. (Figure 2)

(C) Could L be at 6? No, it is not possible to make a valid permutation.

(D) In the initial analysis, we concluded that q cannot be at 6. (Figure 2)

(E) Could t be at 6? No, it is not possible to make a valid permutation when t is at 6.

21. (D) – If q is at 12, then p is at 6. This means that two folk groups are at 10. H must be one of those folk groups, and L must be the other. G must be at 8, along with t. Figure 5 shows this permutation. It is also possible to have H and L switch stages and to have G and t switch stages.

(A) This choice is easy to eliminate. It does not have p at 6, while the other four answer choices do.

(B) In both permutations, G and t must be on different stages. Also, the other three answer choices show t as the second group, so that means that t probably is, in fact, the second group.

(C) G and t must be on different stages.

(D)* This is possible. See figure 4.

(E) This violates Rule 4; t and L cannot be on the same stage.

6	8	10	12	
		*		
p	t	H		L/t
	G	L	q	L/t

Fig. 5

22. (B) – If a rock group performs at 10, then two rock groups perform at 10. The only two possible rock groups are q and t. The third rock group, p, must perform at 6 or 12. Let's check the answer choices to see if this is sufficient analysis to answer the question.

(A) No. Either p or a folk group performs at 6.

(B) * This is true. No rock groups are available to perform at 8, so folk groups must perform at 8.

Printed in the United States
68768LVS00001B/5-8